ADULTS

STRAIGHT FROM THE FORCE'S MOUTH

The Autobiography of Dave Prowse MBE

STRAIGHT FROM THE
FORCE'S MOUTH

The Autobiography of Dave Prowse MBE

DAVE PROWSE MBE

FOREWORD BY LOU FERRIGNO

APEX PUBLISHING LTD

First published in 2011, in hardback by
Apex Publishing Ltd
PO Box 7086, Clacton on Sea, Essex, CO15 5WN

www.apexpublishing.co.uk

Copyright © 20101 by Dave Prowse MBE
The author has asserted his moral rights

British Library Cataloguing-in-Publication Data
A catalogue record for this book
is available from the British Library

ISBN 1-907792-99-6
978-1-907792-99-1

Typeset in 10.5pt Baskerville Win95BT

Production Manager: Chris Cowlin

Cover Design: Siobhan Smith
Front cover photograph: Paul Crowther (Revolver Photo)
Back cover photograph: Michael "Hr" Nielsen

Printed and bound by
MPG Books Group in the UK

Contents

Preface

The year 2007 marked an auspicious anniversary - the thirtieth birthday of a film phenomenon, *Star Wars*, which appeared in May 1977. Little did I know then that Darth Vader, the role I played in an obscure, independent movie, would become the most infamous villain of all time, known worldwide.

My penning of this book has never been kept a secret; in fact, the whole sci-fi fan world has been aware of it and has been eagerly awaiting its publication. However, it is much more than a *Star Wars* book. The story, seven decades in the making, begins long before *Star Wars IV: A New Hope* emerged at Elstree Studios in England during 1976. I finally put pen to paper in the hope of sharing some of my most interesting experiences throughout a career spanning 50 years. Without wishing to sound either pompous or big-headed, I really have had a most extraordinary career encompassing fantastic 'highs', terrible 'lows' and happy 'in betweens'.

When I sat down to plan out the book I started by listing all the notable achievements that are relatively unknown to the public in general. For instance, did you know that I was registered as a 'crippled child' at the age of 13, yet eventually went on to become a Mr Universe contender and the British Heavyweight Weightlifting Champion? Or that it was me that introduced the most famous range of Australian swimwear - Speedo - to the UK sports trade? It was my photo, endorsement and advice that got the country 'Bullworking'. I featured in a TV commercial, directed by the now world famous Ridley Scott, as 'The Mighty Tonka', introducing Tonka Toys into Great Britain, and also appeared in a Max Factor commercial as Superman. I opened the very first private club in the then brand new National Sports Centre at Crystal Palace, where I was in charge of all the weight training from 1964 to 1969, before moving on to run three Health Studios in London.

Acting was never a career option for me. My only foray into the world of 'showbiz' was the part of 'Daddy Longlegs' in a church youth club production when I was 16, and here I am 60 years later with an acting résumé that encompasses many TV commercials, hundreds of TV appearances and over 20 films, including four of the most memorable of all time: *Star Wars IV, V* and *VI* and *A Clockwork Orange*. I was recently interviewed for an anthology of movie making entitled *The 100 Best Movies of All Time* and the director confided in me that I was one of only two actors who had four movies in the top 100 - the other being Charlton Heston!

For 10 years I served as President Reagan's Special Ambassador to The International Decade of the Disabled (1983-92). Also, for 14 years (1976-90), I was the figurehead of the Department of Transport's Child Pedestrian Road Safety Campaign - the Green Cross Code Man - which was the greatest and most fulfilling job I have ever had, helping to save over a quarter of a million children's lives. I would do it all again tomorrow if I were asked. The work of everybody involved in the campaign - the police, the road safety officers, the schoolteachers - was acknowledged when I was awarded an MBE in the Millennium Honours List and was presented with my 'gong' by Her Majesty The Queen at Buckingham Palace in June 2000.

Although never intended specifically as a *Star Wars* book, my role as Darth Vader has led to my spending the last 28 years travelling the world, appearing at conventions, doing in-store autograph signings and taking part in tours and publicity launches for the videos and DVDs. I consider myself as a goodwill ambassador for the *Star Wars* films as well as for 20th Century Fox and Lucasfilm and am happy to support their ventures. I was invited by 20th Century Fox in Belgium to meet the Belgian Press prior to the launch of the new DVD boxed sets. Also, I participated in the UK DVD launch for the Virgin Megastore in Bristol, where they had pre-sold over 3,000 copies prior to the official release in September 2004. I sat down for the signings at 10.30 a.m. and finished at 6 p.m. The queue was over three hours long and I was congratulated at the end of the day for my dogged perseverance.

I must point out, however, that I am not sponsored by either Fox or Lucasfilm or in the employ of anybody. I am an independent freelancer and all the work I get comes via my own efforts and through direct contact with convention organisers or store owners. As such I feel entitled to give my personal opinions on things as I see them or in terms of how they affect me, whether or not I occasionally cause offence. If I have done so in the past it has invariably been as a result of being misquoted in the press!

I hope this has whetted your appetite to read about 'a career most extraordinary'. I certainly think it has been and I sincerely hope you think so too.

And now for the Dedications!

When you get to my age (76) and you've been working on an autobiography that has taken something like six years to bring to fruition, it comes as a bit of a surprise to realise that a lot of the friends you have been writing about have now gone to that 'resting place' far, far away. So it is with great humility that I dedicate *Straight from the Force's Mouth* to the people who have had a great influence on my life and career.

My sincere thanks go first to my dear mother, Gladys Prowse, as well as to Don Lee, Alan Boyce, Eric Morecambe and Ernie Wise, Frankie Howerd, Kenneth Williams, John Grimek, Steve Reeves, Christopher Reeve, Bob Monkhouse, Peter Cushing, Sir Alec Guinness, Russ Meyer, Stanley Kubrick, Howard Keel, Bruce Boa, Russ Warner and George Lucas (who is still with us), and also to Lou Ferrigno for kindly agreeing to write the Foreword to this book.

I would also like to thank various photographers who have generously allowed me to use their work in my 'epic': Harry Myers, Joiner/Kurtz archive, Ian Blantern (who was my wedding photographer and took lots of the physique photos from my early days), Paul Moses Jnr, Derek Klemperer, Mervyn Rowles, Derek and Steve Rowe, Tony Lanza and Mark Ellis. If there is anybody I have not acknowledged, my sincere apologies.

Finally, a huge THANK YOU to my loving wife, Norma, who has steadfastly stood by me through 47 years of married life. Always happy to be in the background through my turbulent career, she has been a real rock and support.

Foreword

I've known Dave for many years and always had tremendous admiration and respect for the man. Dave and I go back to the days when I first competed in the NABBA Mr Universe contest and Dave had been the British Heavyweight Weightlifting Champion. Over the ensuing years our careers to some extent have followed similar lines: the promotion of physical culture as a way of life, films and TV, and supporting charities that are near and dear to us.

Dave has been a successful athlete-champion weightlifter for three years and competitor at the World Weightlifting Championships and Commonwealth Games. For many years Dave ran three successful gyms plus an exercise consultancy in the world's number one store - Harrods of London. His acting career started by playing the part of 'Death' on stage at the Mermaid Theatre and then moved on to numerous TV and film roles, which included working with Stanley Kubrick on A Clockwork Orange and George Lucas on the Star Wars trilogy, episodes 4, 5 and 6, playing the now iconic Darth Vader. The latter has brought him international fame and guest appearances at sci-fi and film conventions worldwide.

Dave actively supports the work of several charities. He is Vice President of the Physically Handicapped and Able Bodied Association (PHAB) and is involved with charity work for the Royal Marsden Hospital (where he was treated successfully for prostate cancer), the Urology Foundation and UNICEF. Dave is also associated with the Reeve-Irvine Institute, which is dedicated to stem cell research, through his friendship with the late Christopher Reeve, whom Dave personally trained for the part of Superman. Dave's autobiography is a roller-coaster ride through 50 years of amazing happenings, written with humour and lavishly illustrated with photos from his personal archive. Dave was awarded an MBE for his contribution to child pedestrian road safety and charity work.

What sets Dave apart is his ability to persevere and overcome adversity, and he continues to reap success from all his endeavours due to his unstinting commitment. I'm inspired by Dave's dedication to educating and influencing others in a positive way. It's an honour to call David Prowse my friend.

Best wishes
Lou Ferrigno

Chapter One
Stars in My Eyes

I've always believed that I am the living proof that life really can begin at 40. The year was 1976, Britain was sweltering in the longest, hottest heatwave in living memory and I was making a reasonable, if slightly erratic, living doing a succession of small film and TV roles.

I was extremely proud of the work I'd done for Hammer Films and working with the great Stanley Kubrick on *A Clockwork Orange* had been fantastic, of course. I'd had some rewarding TV jobs, too, including appearances with Benny Hill, Kenneth Williams, Morecambe and Wise and even The Beverly Hillbillies. As enjoyable as these roles were at the time, there was little of any substance in my portfolio. In fact, I suspected that most of my work was forgotten the day after it appeared. That's show business for you. Unknown to me, though, my career was soon to be moved light years ahead of anything I'd ever done.

My agent at the time was Penny Harrison and she called me with the news that 20th Century Fox were in London and casting for a big new film. The film's director was to be someone called George Lucas, whom I'd vaguely heard of thanks to his success as the director of *American Graffiti*, a box-office smash, in which a keen young actor by the name of Harrison Ford made something of a name for himself. I was told that George Lucas wanted to see me as soon as possible and an appointment was set up at short notice. Right on time, I turned up at the Fox offices at Soho Square in the centre of London, with no idea what George Lucas or his big new film were all about.

My first stop was the office of someone I did know, the Fox MD Peter Beale, with whom I'd already done some film work and whom I considered a family friend. Peter's wife had a passion for the colour red and employed every conceivable shade of it as a colour scheme throughout the house. Wall-to-ceiling crimson, pink, scarlet, cherry, carmine and rose pulsed from carpets and curtains, fixtures and fittings, roasting every visitor within seconds of entry. A fellow guest caught the impression perfectly one evening at dinner, when he remarked, "Bloody hell! It's like climbing back inside the womb!"

I chatted briefly with Peter, before he escorted me to my appointment with George Lucas. George looked like a keen young student, with all of the verve and enthusiasm of someone with unlimited ideas and something to prove. He explained that his latest venture was to be the first in a series of space fantasy films, entitled *Star Wars*. It was a project that George had been trying to get off the ground for some years and it was obviously of huge importance to him, both personally and as a director. After giving me a basic outline of his concept for the movie, George produced a pile of Ralph MacQuarrie drawings, depicting the main characters and film sets. While we pored over these superb pieces of artwork, George revealed that he'd seen most of my film work and that he'd been impressed by what I'd done for Stanley Kubrick in *A Clockwork Orange*. I had assumed that I had been called in to take part in an audition for whatever part I was being considered to play, but instead George spent the whole time asking me about what it was like to work with Stanley Kubrick. That suited me, as every aspect of my association with Stanley had been positive and rewarding, so whatever I said it could only be to my advantage.

During a lull in the conversation, George said, "There are two parts in this movie that I'd like you to consider." Having apparently passed my audition without really doing anything at all, I was slightly taken aback to be offered not one but two roles.

"Well ... er ... fine, George. What exactly are these parts then?"

"One's the part of a character called Chewbacca. He's a Wookiee and he goes through the film on the side of the good guys."

"What the hell's a Wookiee, George?" I asked, trying to recall if I'd seen such a creature portrayed in MacQuarrie's artwork.

"It's a sort of eight-foot, hairy gorilla."

Visions of myself spending three months zipped inside a gorilla costume throughout the heat of the summer made my mind's eye water. The sweat, the smell, the bodily deprivations ...

"What's the other part, George?" I asked, somewhat hastily.

"It's the film's main villain, a character by the name of Darth Vader."

"That's the part for me, George. I'll be Darth Vader."

"Okay," said George, "but tell me why you really want the part."

I could hardly cite the character's comparative lack of smell and sweat as my main motivations, so I offered a truism that had occurred to me very early on in my show business career.

"Well, George, if you think back over the films that contain heroes and villains as their main theme, it's always the baddie that's remembered.

Like in the James Bond movies, for instance. Everyone recalls Oddjob and Goldfinger, but who remembers if Sean Connery, Roger Moore or George Lazenby played opposite them?"

George considered my argument for a second, before replying, "I think you've made a very wise decision, Dave. I assure you, Darth Vader is one villain that no one will ever forget."

And that was that. After some idle chit-chat, George and I shook hands, his assistant told me that Bermans the theatrical costumiers would be in contact with me and I left. I was more than pleased with the day's events, but I've always wondered how I would have felt had I known that I'd just secured the role of the most memorable screen villain of all time. Yet how could I have known that this was more than just another film job? Who could have possibly imagined just how massive *Star Wars* was to become? I'll tell you who. A young director by the name of George Lucas. He knew.

I also did not know that Darth Vader was a masked character. I only found this out at my first consultation at Bermans with costume designer John Mollo. I soon realised that my gorilla suit avoidance scheme hadn't been quite as clever as I'd thought. Vader's costume, although a genuine masterpiece in quilted leather and fibreglass, consisted of 15 separate sections and weighed a full 40lb. Even the act of sitting perfectly still in this costume, well away from the heat of the studio lights, brought me out in the most uncomfortable sweat imaginable. I remember thinking to myself, add lights and action and I'm going to be worse off than the bloody Wookiee.

If the suit was a problem, then the Darth Vader mask, which became such a *Star Wars* trademark, was nothing short of a nightmare. Once it was fitted, I became virtually blind, and the heat generated by the suit obeyed the laws of physics and travelled upwards, straight into the mask. This immediately misted up the tinted eyepieces, which was inconvenient to say the least, but was not an insurmountable problem so long as I could look down through the triangular cut-out beneath the mask's nose moulding and use it as a spyhole. Through this I could see my designated place marks on the floor, so moving into the correct position wasn't too much of a problem. Then it was decided to darken my eyepieces and close up my nose hole. Now I really couldn't see.

These decisions were deemed essential because of fears that my eyes might be seen through the mask and that stray light entering via my breathing holes was likely to let the world see what was going on inside Darth Vader's head. Just to make certain that nothing was visible, it was also decided that my face should be blackened. Oh, the glamour of movie-making!

So there I was, supposedly the most awe-inspiring villain in the universe, sweating like a pig and as blind as a bat! But here is where my childhood experience of wearing a hideous leg splint for four years came into its own. Anyone who could survive that could easily stand around for a mere six hours at a time in a 40lb Darth Vader sauna-costume, under a battery of hot lights, doing as many retakes as the director required, whilst blinded by sweat and condensation and wearing a pantomime black face. I told myself this about 20 times every day, and by the time filming started I almost believed it.

Before any filming was scheduled, George Lucas telephoned me and asked if I would go to Elstree Studios to have lunch with him, the *Star Wars* producer Gary Kurtz and Sir Alec Guinness. Two days later, there we all were at a pleasant restaurant in Elstree, with Sir Alec as charming then as he would prove to be on every occasion thereafter.

The over-lunch conversation ebbed, flowed and meandered through various aspects of the filming we were all due to be involved in, until it settled on the big light sabre duel between my Darth Vader character and Sir Alec's Obi-Wan Kenobi. It's a mark of the effect that *Star Wars* has had on the consciousness of the nation that almost everyone now knows what a light sabre is. Back then, of course, the notion of fighting a duel with sticks of light was bizarre to say the least, but this was the movies, where anything and everything is possible.

When lunch was over, Sir Alec and I were taken to an empty studio on the Elstree lot, which was set aside to be our rehearsal room for the light sabre duel. Such stunts are meticulously choreographed, of course, and the man in charge of this particular number was Peter Diamond. I'd already worked with Peter on several of my movies and he'd impressed me as a master of his craft as well as a damn nice bloke, which is always helpful when you're working closely with someone over an extended period.

The duel scene was a major feature of the movie, and Sir Alec and I took every opportunity to rehearse our moves, either with each other or with Peter standing in. By the time we were due to go into the studio, every move in that epic confrontation between good and evil had been committed to memory, which was a good thing for me, considering that I wouldn't actually be able to see what the hell I was doing.

The scene for the duel was set in a long corridor and at one point in the proceedings Sir Alec and I were to clash at close quarters, light sabres crossed, in the time-honoured stand-off between hero and villain. With our sabres locked in mortal combat, Sir Alec tells me that I can never win, because evil cannot conquer good. At this point I give the great man a mighty shove with my forearm, just as we'd rehearsed time and time again. The problem was, in the heat of the battle we'd somehow lost our sense of position. So instead of Sir Alec being shoved a few feet across the width of the corridor and into the side wall, I propelled him along the full length of the set and he sailed on for several yards until he crash-landed in a most un-Jedi-like heap on the floor.

I was horrified. Here was one of the most distinguished actors in the business, a knight of the realm, a refined English gentleman, and I'd launched him like a paper dart. Everyone on set rushed to help Sir Alec, easing him to his feet and dusting him down, while at the same time apologising and enquiring as to his health. To his credit, he was far less bothered about his unscheduled flight than the rest of us and he regained his composure immediately. With me now mindful of the need to aim Sir Alec at the wall, we shot the scene perfectly on the retake.

That particular scene is often referred to by *Star Wars* fans when I appear at science fiction and space fantasy conventions. Usually I present a film and slide show, then do a talk about my experiences on *Star Wars* and finish with a question and answer session. It's during the questions and answers segment that I'm always asked how the light sabres worked.

The light sabres began life as something almost as spectacular and ingenious on set as they were to become in the film. Our special effects guys had surpassed themselves by taking what looked like a double-handed flashlight body and installing a battery-powered motor. Attached to this motor was the 'blade' of the light sabre, in reality a four-foot length of wooden dowel coated with reflective tape. When switched on, the motor caused the dowel to rotate at high speed, reflecting light from all angles and giving the impression that the devices really were glowing and pulsating with light energy. As Vader himself might have remarked, the whole effect was 'impressive - most impressive'.

Unfortunately, the sabres weren't nearly as impressive when we began to use them in fight scenes on set. They were so fragile that, as soon as my sabre hit Obi-Wan's, pieces would fly off all over the place and we would have to stop filming while the technicians scrabbled about on the studio floor picking up the bits. It wasn't quite what was required of such an awesome piece of space weaponry, so after a series of rethinks and modifications the special effects crew issued us with solid, non-revolving light sabres, which didn't hum, flash, extend or retract, and, most importantly of all, they didn't disintegrate when good and evil were bashing the hell out of each other.

What appeared on film was a triumph of after-shoot wizardry. Literally hundreds of hours were spent by film laboratory artists, who meticulously painted in the light-blades of the sabres, by hand, frame by frame. These days, of course, that work would all be done by computers, but that first time around it was pure artistic dedication that got the job done, and at a conversion rate of 24 frames' worth of painting for every second's worth of on-screen action. Now that's what I call impressive!

Working on *Star Wars* turned out to be a major reunion for me. Apart from Peter Diamond, the stunt arranger, I found to my delight that I would be working with the great Peter Cushing, whose company I had so enjoyed during the making of Hammer's *Frankenstein and the Monster from Hell*. I had already met Carrie Fisher as a result of appearing in *The Debbie Reynolds Show* at the London Palladium. Kenny Baker was an old friend of mine, too, from my distant past in Bristol, and I knew many of the technicians and extras from previous productions. All in all, it was a delight to be working with everyone again. Peter Cushing was a particular delight to be on set with and he would always do his utmost to make less experienced actors feel like part of the 'family'. He had helped me on our first movie together, and he did the same for Carrie Fisher during *Star Wars*.

People tend to forget that *Star Wars* was Carrie's film debut, but Peter didn't overlook it for a minute. I remember him teaching her the tricks of the trade that he'd mastered so ably, explaining how lighting works on set and the importance of make-up, and his unfailing patience when going over Carrie's lines with her. I lost count of the times I saw Peter, dressed as Moff Tarkin except for wearing carpet slippers and white gloves, rehearsing with Carrie. Incidentally, Peter wore those gloves to prevent his fingers becoming stained with nicotine from his heavy smoking habit. This wasn't vanity; it was purely out of consideration for the make-up lady, who would otherwise have had the hassle of covering the stains before each scene was filmed. I only wish that Peter had shown as much consideration for himself and given up smoking altogether.

The carpet slippers were no affectation either. Peter found that the boots made for him as part of the Moff Tarkin uniform were acutely uncomfortable. In his usual polite manner, he informed George Lucas that the boots were causing him serious pain and asked if it would be possible to film Tarkin from the waist up, or to have him sitting at various desks and consoles with his comfortably slippered feet tucked away out of shot. George readily agreed, and Peter's feet were only booted when strictly necessary. Peter Cushing and I remained friends right up to his death in August 1994 and I was delighted to be included among the special guests when *This Is Your Life* finally honoured him.

Carrie Fisher and I didn't really say much to each other after our introduction during my stint on *The Debbie Reynolds Show*, but then she was barely 16 and I, in my 30s, must have seemed like an old man to her. After I'd completed my stage strongman routine, I would always make a point of making my way to the wings in time to hear Carrie sing her big number. The song chosen for her was vocally demanding to say the least, with a glass-shattering high note as its finale. Carrie's voice hadn't had time to be polished to perfection, and several times - in fact most times - she would struggle to hit that last note, but that never stopped her trying. Night after night that little girl would be out there on one of the most famous stages in show business, giving her all for her audience. She was well worth the price of a ticket, and I've always thought that casting her as Princess Leia in *Star Wars* was a demonstration of perfect foresight.

I met up with Carrie a few years ago, when she, Billy Dee Williams and I launched the special boxed sets of *Star Wars* videos at Alexandra Palace in London. She was delightful company, as ever, and the three of us enjoyed the occasion enormously, and in the manner of friends meeting up we promised to keep in touch. I actually managed to keep my part of the bargain, when I called Carrie in 1998, but I have to admit that I had an ulterior motive. I was organising a big sci-fi convention in the UK, called Multicon '98, and I was trying to get Carrie over as its main guest star. Carrie was glad to hear from me but explained that conventions weren't really her scene. I tried to persuade her that this one would be, but she countered my argument with the fact that she was busy writing and raising her daughter, and in the end Carrie won and I lost. Screen daughters - what can you do with them, eh?

Kenny Baker and I have been friends since our youth. We met in a Bristol bowling alley over 40 years ago, where I had the job of throwing out drunks and miscreants, while Kenny was starring in a production of *Snow White and the Seven Dwarfs*. Kenny and his fellow dwarfs, along with Snow White, were posing for some publicity photos and I was being used as the stooge, due to the amusing contrast between my proportions and theirs. One of the most prized photos in my extensive collection shows me holding a bowling ball in one hand and Kenny in the other. That photo stunt couldn't be reproduced today, though, and it's nothing to do with the passage of time reducing my lifting power. Kenny has simply put on too much weight!

Ken and I were constant companions on the set of *Star Wars*, often going to his home during our lunch breaks to be fed by Kenny's lovely wife, Eileen. During these excellent lunches, Kenny would regale me with tales of the adventures he'd had as part of a very successful double act called The Mini Tones, with his partner Jack Purvis. Just before Kenny was offered the role of R2-D2, Jack and Kenny were doing well as a cabaret duo and were lined up for an appearance on the hit UK talent show, *Opportunity Knocks*. This was a great break for any act and Kenny was immediately thrown into a panic about accepting the *Star Wars* offer. Concerns about what Jack would do to make a living while Kenny was away filming, and how the *Opportunity Knocks* appearance could be juggled to fit in with the *Star Wars* schedule, all tumbled around in his mind, until Lucasfilm provided a solution by offering Jack a part in *Star Wars*, too. The Mini Tones made a successful debut on *Opportunity Knocks* and topped the voting until the next act displaced them, leaving Kenny and Jack able to continue their even more successful partnership in Terry Gilliam's *Time Bandits*.

Kenny and Jack were very talented performers. Their musicianship was first-class and few could deliver a joke like The Mini Tones. Tragically, Jack died following a car accident a few years ago and he is greatly missed, but Kenny is still with us, as funny and as talented as ever and a welcome sight at *Star Wars* conventions all over the world.

Just after we'd completed *Star Wars*, during what was obviously an extremely slow news week, a national newspaper contacted me to get some photos of my participation in a new craze that was (they said) sweeping the nation. What was the nature of this leisure time phenomenon? Welly-throwing. Yes, the hurling of a rubber gumboot had apparently gripped the population of the UK in a frenzy of sporting endeavour. Up and down the land, no garden party or school fête was complete without its welly-throwing tournament, and glory-hungry warriors would devise throwing techniques designed to turn a size ten Dunlop into an all-weather projectile.

Like all pointless pastimes, welly-throwing soon died the death of a thousand yawns, and other, more exciting objects found themselves being chucked around in the name of sport. I remember tyres were tried out, then bales of straw, and even cow pats enjoyed a brief fling for a while. The craze of throwing things for fun finally peaked (most would say 'troughed') when dwarfs became the missile of choice. Most 'persons of restricted growth' understandably took great exception to this latest piece of nonsense and the resulting fuss even became the subject of TV debates and documentaries.

As a means of showing the dwarfs getting their own back on the big folks, the newspaper that had carried the original welly-throwing piece wanted to show Jack and Kenny throwing me into a swimming pool. Great idea; shame about reality. I weighed a prime 20st (around 280lb) and the odds of The Mini Tones even lifting me were shorter than they were. We tried, with Kenny and Jack recruiting their wives to help with the task, but simple physics dictated that they were never going to do it. Instead, we settled for some shots of Kenny and company dragging me along the ground, which lightened the news in the national press the next day.

Meanwhile, back at the *Star Wars* set, I'd been given a copy of the script and I studied it like a student at a crammer. I wanted to decipher and absorb every facet of Vader and portray him as the script demanded. Vader came across as the personification of pure evil and, if it was at all possible, that was exactly how I wanted to play him.

The only way of presenting Darth Vader as the ultimate baddie was to show virtually everyone else either terrified or completely awestruck whenever he was around. The ludicrous prospect of actors such as Peter Cushing and Alec Guinness becoming awestruck in my presence gave me a most un-Vader-like attack of nerves. Such thoughts would need to be banished if I was to do justice to my character's Dark Side, however. Besides, it was Vader that everyone would find awesome, not me. For my part in the 'awesomisation' of Darth Vader, I had to begin with the basics. If Vader was to be regarded as a super-villain, he had to walk like a super-villain. Obviously, he'd need to talk like a super-villain, too, but I thought that wouldn't cause too many problems. Funny how things turn out sometimes, isn't it?

I've listened, enthralled, while the great and good of the acting profession have discussed the finer points of characterisation, and I'd always wondered why these renowned performers placed so much emphasis on getting the character's walk just right. I'd even been told that once the walk is established the rest would fall into place. Vader's walk required total authority. A Dark Lord would never hesitate in his stride or falter in his direction. Vader's cape must flow and his minions must trail in his wake, almost running to keep up with their master.

Backing up my awesome walk would be something known as 'body acting', which is exactly what it sounds like. With Vader encased in black leather and his face totally obscured by a mask, his body language was his only means of non-verbal expression. I was left with head posture, stance and arm movements to convey Vader's demeanour - and de-meaner I could make him de-better.

Body acting and bodybuilding are more closely related than most people would imagine, and all that posing I'd done to impress the judges in my early years now began to pay dividends. From within the black leather suit, I treated Vader's every gesture as a bodybuilding pose, refining here and exaggerating there, until my character 'spoke' with every tilt of his head or movement of his arms. When I watch those *Star Wars* movies (which I still do, from time to time) I'm quietly pleased at the amount of expression that Vader manages to convey without a facial expression to his name, save for the fixed menace of that mask.

The mask itself was still causing all sorts of problems. I'd been dressed by the costume department and I was sitting around, at the start of *Empire*, awaiting the delivery of the revamped Vader helmet and mask. After the latest round of hassles attaching the mask to the helmet, a simple Velcro fastening was now being tried. The eventual solution proved to be a completely new 'male and female' fixing system, which slotted the mask into the helmet to form a totally stable unit. This system couldn't be shifted under any circumstances and held firm even when I stood in front of an aeroplane propeller during the famous gantry scene in *Empire*, where I reveal to Luke that I am his father. That scene and a proper fitting for Vader's mask were both a long way off - three years, in fact - as I sat on set waiting for the crowning glory of my costume.

Eventually, Lord Vader's headgear arrived and with it came instruc-tions that George Lucas, producer Gary Kurtz and lighting cameraman Gil Taylor all wanted to see how the Dark Lord handled his redesigned headgear. With the helmet and mask somehow wedged on my head, the Dark Lord looked pretty damn awesome, but inside the suit I was having problems.

"Move your head from left to right, Dave, so we can see how the mask moves," said George, so I did a controlled swivel of my neck to give George what he'd asked for. Unfortunately, while my head turned obediently, the mask remained facing straight ahead. After all the effort, planning and expertise that had gone into it, the mask was still miles too big. It looked as though it was back to the drawing board for a remould. However, George had other ideas. He wanted Vader's headgear to stay exactly as it was, so there had to be an alternative solution. Now I really knew that I was in trouble.

"Have the inside of the helmet padded out with foam, so that Dave has to practically squeeze his head into it," ordered George, as I contemplated what it was going to feel like with my head stuffed inside a foam-filled box, under the studio lights, during the hottest summer the UK had ever known. I didn't have too long to contemplate anything, because within a couple of hours the helmet was back, lined with foam and fitting perfectly. It moved exactly as George had wanted and everyone gave it their hearty approval. Except for me. In the few minutes it took to gain the approval of all who saw it, the eyepieces of the mask had misted up completely and I was blind.

From the many conversations I've had with *Star Wars* fans over the years, it seems that there is a popular belief that I had an air-conditioning system installed inside the helmet, or even in the whole Vader outfit, as in spacesuit technology. After all, we were the state of the movie-making art. In that sweltering summer of '76 a cold flannel would've been a godsend, let alone in-suit air conditioning. As it was, I had neither, and I roasted. There was nothing else for it; I just had to have the mask and helmet removed and mopped out after every take. It was awkward and uncomfortable and the sweat stung my eyes, but I knew there were plenty of ordinary, safe and thoroughly tedious jobs out there in the real world, so I just made the best of it.

Uncomfortable as I was, there were others that were worse off. Tony Daniels had to be bolted into his C-3PO suit and, if a particular scene required excessive time to get it right, Tony stayed bolted in until it was finished. I've seen Tony Daniels extracted from his newly unscrewed suit looking like a poached lobster. Tony wasn't the best-loved member of the *Star Wars* cast and he frequently fell victim to a handful of practical jokers who lurked among the on-set technicians. These cruel sods would slope off at lunchtimes, leaving Tony completely trapped in his C-3PO suit until they returned and rectified their 'error'.

Kenny Baker has always claimed that working inside the R2-D2 costume was like living in a dustbin with the lid on. Kenny's 'dustbin' was incredibly awkward to control, too, and because he could only move his feet a few inches at a time he found it impossible to keep up with the action. Now, here's where technology actually did make a difference. The production boffins overcame Kenny's inability to keep pace with the action by making a radio-controlled R2-D2 unit that could be used for all the wide shots. The only problem was, to get the new unit literally up to speed it needed an extra leg. Avid *Star Wars* watchers can now tell when

Kenny is on screen, because his R2 unit has only two legs, while the radio-controlled one has three!

To return to the Vader portrayal, my first opportunity to use my much-practised walk came in a scene where I walk along a corridor, accompanied by one of the captains. A track was built parallel to the corridor, on which a camera dolly ran. This would allow the cameraman to follow the action in one smooth shot, and it is a common filming technique. On George's call of "Action!" I unleashed my awesome walk. I must have overdone the speed on my first time out, because the poor captain could hardly keep up with me, let alone deliver his dialogue. By the time we reached the end of what is a very long corridor, the actor playing the captain and the bloke pushing the camera dolly were both panting like dogs. George then called "Cut!" and came over to give me a little friendly direction.

"Dave," said George, "you've just got to slow down! The captain's having to run and speak at the same time, and the camera can't track fast enough. Slow it down, huh?" And so ended my first, and last, piece of critical direction from George Lucas. I slowed down my Vader walk, with no loss of menace at all, and George must have approved because he never had me change my depiction of his arch-villain again. Vader's physicality really was awesome, even if I do say so myself.

On major movies the director has his first, second and third assistants, who spend their entire working lives hustling things along in an unceasing quest to save time. In the movie business time is costed out by the minute, and I imagine that the only place where time is deemed a more precious commodity is on Death Row. Once the studio clock begins to tick, the production people see dollar signs fly away with every passing second and so the relentless chase for time is on. Producers load up their schedules and fire them at directors, and they in turn deflect the flak towards the first assistant, who ducks most of it and lets it hit the second assistant, who tries as hard as possible to ensure that the third assistant feels the impact. The ricochet effect of all this is an attempt to propel the artistes into general speed-up mode, often in areas where no more velocity is possible. On *Star Wars* the first assistant director was Dave Tomlin, one of the best in the business. He did his job extremely well and without making unrealistic demands on anyone, proving that efficiency and courtesy really can go hand-in-hand.

From an artistic perspective, the person whose job is almost as crucial to the success of the movie is the lighting cameraman. The director calls the shots, but it's the lighting cameraman who sets them up and decides on vital factors, such as exposure settings for the cameras and the lighting set-up for each scene. Gil Taylor had that responsibility on the first *Star Wars* and, although the manual of film-making tells us that every lighting cameraman should work very closely with his director, Gil and George didn't seem to be that close whenever I saw them. In fact, they seemed to spend most of their time arguing with each other. George was continually demanding more light on each scene, and Gil was equally adamant that he already had more light than he knew what to do with. These key figures in the *Star Wars* filming equation really didn't get on with each other at all. Both men knew their jobs and they also knew what they wanted to happen on set, so there was only one way that this situation was ever going to be resolved. George offloaded Gil as soon as filming on *Star Wars* was completed, replacing him with Peter Sujitsky on *Empire*, who did a superb job in my opinion. Peter even managed to avoid rowing with George, so their ideas on lighting must have been fairly similar. Or perhaps George had decided that it was time be a little more flexible and allow the lighting cameraman to get on with his job. No, it was the similar ideas thing - no doubt about it!

Once George had decided which scene we would be shooting, the set erupted, as everyone leapt into action at once. We'd have riggers, scene shifters, lighting technicians, camera operators, actors and dressers running about all over the place, accompanied by the second and first assistant directors, who were still trying to get more action for the production company's time and money. It was total madness at times and it didn't take me too long to work out that there was no merit whatsoever in my getting in costume, only to stand around for ages while the set was prepared for filming. There was an incredible amount of preparation involved in most scenes, too. In addition to the lighting and cameras, props had to be in place, including the handing out of the various space weapons, then the special effects had to be planned to the split second, camera tracks had to be laid and a dozen other vital tasks had to be performed, before the actors could run through a full rehearsal or go for a take.

My dresser and I learned to judge the scene preparation process time to the minute, so that Darth Vader would be ready to go, costume immaculate and helmet sparkling (it was polished for every take), at the required time, rather than three hours beforehand. Poor Tony Daniels never seemed to achieve the same sense of timing with his dresser, so he would be screwed into his C-3PO gear and broiling away long before he needed to be. That suit was hellish uncomfortable, as were the ones worn by the stormtroopers. The actors inside the stormtrooper outfits wore black jumpsuits, over which was fixed white plastic 'armour'. These plastic sections cut into the wearer's skin and pinched like crazy whenever the actors were required to move, and those stormtroopers were on the move practically all of the time, as any fan will know.

Meanwhile, Peter Mayhew was producing his share of heavy perspiration inside Chewbacca's hairy bodysuit, with only Carrie, Mark and Harrison enjoying any degree of comfort. I must say that the three American stars were most sympathetic towards the rest of us, although I suspect that never a scene went by without them praising the gods of casting that they had been spared a costumed part.

In total, I worked on the first *Star Wars* movie for five months, which is the longest period of work I ever did on any film, and at times the excitement was incredible. Occasionally, frustration set in and the job became tedious, and once or twice it even lapsed into flat-out boredom. When members of the cast were together, though, boredom was never a possibility. Anyone who could entertain boredom while in the company of people like Sir Alec Guinness, George Lucas and Peter Cushing really shouldn't be in the film business. I loved the hours I spent chatting to Peter or Sir Alec, as we sat in our 'named' movie chairs within the studio's quiet area. Anyone who wasn't required to work for any period of time would drift over to this area, just to gossip, learn lines or exchange banter. With so many wonderful stars involved, such encounters were an enjoyable bonus of working in the movie industry.

Chapter Two
The *Star Wars* Chronicles

On Tuesday 2 January 1979 I began to keep a daily diary. At that time I was about to begin work on the second film in the *Star Wars* trilogy, *The Empire Strikes Back*, and by now I'd realised that I was involved with something very special indeed. With the success of the first *Star Wars* movie changing my life and work almost on a daily basis, I wanted to keep a written record of what went on from day to day. The following chapter is reproduced, word for word, from the pages of my diary. It's a unique record of what, rightly or wrongly, I felt about what took place during the filming of *The Empire Strikes Back* and *Return of the Jedi*. I believe that readers would prefer an unedited version of these chronicles and that's why this chapter is presented as it happened, warts and all.

2 January 1979

It's 10.30 am and I'm at the EMI studios, Elstree, just north of London. I am waiting with Peter Mayhew, who is reprising his role of Chewbacca the wookiee and we are due to meet up with Robert Watts, the assistant producer and Peter Diamond, the stunt arranger for The Empire Strikes Back. Peter Mayhew is lined up for mime lessons and I'm here for kendo and fencing coaching.

I've just learned that the final fifteen minutes of Empire features a light sabre duel between Mark Hamill's Luke Skywalker and myself as Darth Vader. Mark is already having bodybuilding, karate and fencing coaching in Los Angeles.

Still no sign of any script, although my action pages have been promised for tomorrow. I am astounded at the degree of secrecy surrounding this script. It's being treated like some sort of super-secret document that could threaten national security!

After I'd finished at Elstree, I had an appointment at Bermans the costumiers, where I bumped into John Barry who was about to start work on Saturn 3.

Back to the gym in the evening. The place is like the inside of an iceberg, with all of the water pipes frozen solid and three-inches of snow in the toilets and shower room. I have to fix these problems myself, before I go to bed. I can't imagine Harrison Ford or Mark Hamill having to work into the night playing janitor after a day on the set. I eventually get to bed at 2 am, very tired and grumpy.

3 January

My first fencing rehearsal with Peter Diamond at a Sports Centre about five miles further north of the studio. Did approximately one and a half hours after which my knees and thighs were aching like mad. We started off with basic moves and positions; luckily I remembered a lot of the work we did for the Obi-Wan Kenobi fight sequence in Star Wars with Sir Alec Guinness.

Went for lunch at the studio with the production people and Bob Simmons, the stunt arranger for the Superman film. He seems amazed that people should actually be standing in lines to see the Superman film and even more amazed when I told him I enjoyed the film very much. By all accounts they already have about 60 per cent of Superman 2 completed. Went to visit Andrew Mitchell - the head of the Studio - and his secretary Wendy, during the afternoon. He must be really kicking himself, as the news is out that George Lucas offered the EMI studio group a share of the profits, in lieu of paying the studio rental. EMI opted for the rental and Star Wars looks set to become one of the biggest if not THE biggest grossing movies of all time. Who knows the untold wealth the percentage deal would have brought to the studio had they gone the other way? I was welcomed with open arms by Andrew who is now really friendly towards me. Even got asked to sign the studio VIP book and was then presented with the Parker pen - to think, it's taken me twelve years of working at Elstree to get this sort of acclaim.

Spent Thursday Friday and Saturday in Harrods in my capacity as their Fitness Consultant. On Friday the 5th I knocked a dog down on my way to the Store and had to go to the police station later in the evening to give them my version of the accident.

The sergeant at the station didn't seem all that concerned and did nothing else but make comments about the dog not knowing his Green Cross Code. Idiot.

Had a telephone call from a TV commercial company who want me to do a Star Wars type commercial for South America. Have told them to contact the stunt arranger and arranged to meet up with them next Tuesday.

Did a photo session with my family for the front cover of my book Fitness Is Fun. It really is hell working with my three kids. None of them enjoy having their photos taken and take part only under terrible sufferance. To be honest I really think it embarrasses them that their father is becoming famous and they seem to do all they can to distance themselves from my professional life. All the Stars Wars toys and merchandise that is sent to me by the various manufacturers is all given away, either to kids in the street, hospitals or charities because my lot don't seem to be the slightest bit interested. They really enjoyed Stars Wars but that's about the only piece of work in my entire film and TV career that they've shown any interest in. I guess to them my job is just like any other dad's job. It's probably a good thing, really.

8 January

Into Harrods for the day after doing my morning fight rehearsal. Had a visit from film producer Elliot Kastner who came in with his kids to purchase some tennis equipment. He says that Irving Kershner (our director on Empire) is a great buddy of his and he owes Elliot a favour so if there's anything I want, just ask. I said I'd like my name above the film title!!!!

9 January

Went to see the TV commercial company about the job I was offered last week but it is so close to Star Wars that I am certain I wouldn't be allowed to do it without special clearance from George Lucas. The commercial is set for filming in Venezuela.

10 January

A quite unbelievable amount of interest being shown in me by the National Enquirer and the TV Guide. All hell broke out thereafter with the British national press getting wind that the National Enquirer were to do a feature on me. Darth Vader has a huge cult following worldwide and the US media are about to delve into the actor behind the mask.

11 January

Tony Frost of the National Enquirer turned up in Harrods and we did the interview in the Upper Circle restaurant. US magazine also came into the store to take photos but I managed to steer them to the gym where we did the photo session.

12 January

National Enquirer spent over an hour taking pics of my wife and myself exercising. Brian Moody, a well known British photographer, wants to take photos of us both on the 21st for one of the British tabloid newspapers.

18 January

Had a call from the BBC wanting me to take part in one of the most popular shows on TV - Noel Edmonds' Multi Coloured Swap Shop. It's primarily a kids' programme which also has a huge teenage and adult following and goes out on Saturday mornings. They want to film on the 27th and have offered me three spots on the show and I'm appearing alongside Donnie and Marie Osmond.

22 January

Took my son James along to the fencing rehearsals at the Hartsmere Leisure Centre. Whilst I was there, I received a hand delivered letter from Lucasfilm detailing just what I was and was not allowed to do, which is practically nothing.

24 January
Another fencing rehearsal at Hartsmere. Whilst there we got the message through that there had been a big fire at the Elstree Studio. Stage 3, where Stanley Kubrick is in filming The Shining with Jack Nicholson and Shelley Duval, has gone up in smoke but fortunately no one has been injured. Rumours are already rife that the film allegedly was way over budget and that the fire was deliberate in order to recoup some money from the film's insurance people.

27 January
Multi Coloured Swap Shop filming at the BBC. Tried to take my son James on the studio floor but they wouldn't allow it, so he had to watch the show from the producer's box. Noel was very amiable and my three stints on the show were very well presented and received. One of the features on the show involved a phone-in alongside the Osmonds and I was congratulated afterwards, as there were more phone calls for me than there were for them. Wanted to have a chat to them after the taping of the show was over but they were whisked out of the studio to avoid all the fans that were hanging around.

Took my family to see Jesus Christ, Superstar in the evening which we all enjoyed.

29 January
Went for another fencing rehearsal in the morning. Peter Diamond, the stunt arranger for the film, had a copy of the Empire script, the first one I've seen. Managed to have a quick scan through and discovered that you do get to see a bit of Darth Vader or Dave Prowse in this movie - the back of his bald, scar-covered head. Had a call from the greatest bodybuilder of all time - John Grimek of York, Pennsylvania, who is now managing editor of the world's most prestigious body-building magazine - Muscular Development, who wants to do a major feature in the mag about myself and specifically about the training programme that I put Chris Reeve through when getting him in shape for the part of Superman.

30/31 January
Took the train up to Birmingham so that I can be there in preparation for the filming of the Tiswas television show. I am to appear, playing the role of Tarzan, but they also have a 'cod' (spoof) Tarzan in the shape of well known Carry On comedian – Charles Hawtrey!

Did a radio interview first thing in the morning and then went onto Manchester to film the programme at the famous Granada Studios.

Started the day off with a publicity feature for the Daily Mail who had arranged for me to have my pics taken with some chimpanzees they had brought in from Stockport Zoo. I'd worked with chimps before on Bruce Forsythe's Generation Game so I was prepared for the worst. The actual show was complete chaos with the chimps not doing a thing they were supposed to do and Charles Hawtrey cocking everything up from beginning to end. However both the audience and the production people enjoyed it and was asked if I would be interested in doing an exercise spot for kids in a new Saturday morning show that is going to be filmed on a ferry boat plying across the Mersey at Liverpool. It's going to be called The Mersey Pirate.

Before leaving the Granada studios I got a message to say that The Three Degrees vocal group had been rehearsing in another studio and had wanted to see me. This had proved impossible because of their schedule so they'd left a request for some autographed Dave Prowse/Darth Vader photos.

1 February

Had to be at Bermans the costumiers for a fitting for the Darth Vader suit. My business manager came on the phone, regarding a promotional vehicle that we have been offered by a major Ford dealer in Wheaton Ill, just outside Chicago. By all accounts, he had met a guy in a hotel in Los Angeles who turned out to be the sales manager for the main Ford agents. Over a few drinks we were offered a recreational vehicle for our promo tour in the States. They are going to arrange for the vehicle to be customised and it will be delivered to wherever we want it in the US.

Mike Francis from the Department of Transport and Bernard Potten from the Central Office of Information called regarding my Green Cross Code Child Accident Prevention Campaign. They are going to use the old commercials for the March, April and May showings and then shoot new ones in September. Mike is trying to put together a nationwide tour for me and has left me with a load of dates to try to fix in to my already hectic calendar. Everything is hanging in the air at the moment as I am still awaiting my contractual dates for Empire Strikes Back.

Had a call from Graeme Garden's wife (Graeme of The Goodies fame) wanting me to do a personal appearance for her at her children's school. By all accounts the BBC who produce the Goodies TV programme had wanted me for their Montreaux Festival entry but I wasn't available.

5 February

Went to rehearse the sword duel again this morning - Peter Diamond now has a much better idea as to how the duel is going to be planned.

Drove on to Elstree studios to meet up with friends on the production teams of

Empire and The Shining. Lunch at the local Chinese restaurant in Boreham Wood High Street where I bumped into Gary Kurtz and Irving Kershner, our producer and director - and got the impression that I wasn't very welcome. They probably had highly secretive things to talk about which they obviously didn't want me listening in on.

7 February
Fencing rehearsals again all morning. Managed to continue reading the remainder of the script.

11 February-3 March
A big publicity tour of Los Angeles, Sacramento, San Francisco and Chicago. Whilst in LA I did things like appearing on the Steve Edwards Show. Greg Hunters Brown Derby radio show is actually taped at the famous Brown Derby restaurant. Had a birthday dinner with famed film producer/director - Russ Meyer, did Jim Brown's show for BBC and press interview for the Hawaii newspaper.

Was in Sacramento for two and a half days, during which time I managed to fit in three television shows, three radio shows, one press interview, one visit to a school to give the kids there a road safety talk and personal appearance at a SCI-FI store. Over 5,000 people turned up to see me and I signed autographs from noon to 6 pm non-stop.

Spent the next four days as guest of Marin County. My first appearance there was an absolute disaster. I was scheduled to do three talks in an 800 seater theatre - we had a hundred people in for the first show, about the same for the second and only thirty in for the last. Flew out to Chicago that evening. Picked up at 9.30 am to go to Packey Webb's Showroom (the big Ford agent in Wheaton). They had advertised that I was going to be there so we had loads of kids and their parents coming and going all day. The van looks great, silver with red lettering, blue and plaid interior - really the last word in customised vans. Had loads of press photos taken and did radio and TV interviews too, during the course of the day. Went to dinner with my business manager and the sales manager and his wife to a very swish Chicago restaurant called Arnies and then onto an even swisher disco. Finished up the evening going to Roger Ebert's place for drinks. (This was at time when Roger was doing more writing and had only just started doing his film critiquing for which he is now world famous.) *I knew him through film director Russ Meyer with whom he had collaborated to produce the script for Black Snake, which was eventually released under the title of Slaves. Whilst we were in the house he called Russ and we had a chat on the phone about the success of Star Wars and the interest my portrayal of Darth Vader was creating.*

We agreed to have dinner together during my forthcoming visit to Los Angeles.

Spent the whole of the following week holidaying in New York seeing lots of theatre such as Chorus Line, Dancing, On The 20th Century and Dracula where I had the pleasure of going backstage to meet Dracula himself, Raul Julia. Ate at all the best restaurants, including The Russian Tea Rooms and Sardi's and was invited by famous New York columnist Earl Wilson to be his guest at Studio 54 in the evening. He must have put it out to the press that I was going to be there as the photographers turned out in force.

Arrived back in London 7.30 am, where I was met at the airport by Norma and the kids.

6 March

Had a visit from Tony Daniels (C-3PO) in Harrods. He was moaning like mad about the treatment he'd been receiving from 20th Century Fox and Lucasfilm and had heard about the terrific publicity success that I was having. He almost turned green when I recounted the publicity experiences of the last three weeks. He wants to be involved in my publicity tours so I'll have to have a word with my business manager to see if he can join the team. We have a lunch appointment arranged for Friday the 9th.

12 March

Lunch at the film studios, where I met up with both Ridley Scott and Bob Kellett (who is doing the 'UP' series of films). Had a 2.30 appointment with Stuart Freeborn to have my complete head cast moulded. Met George Lucas wandering round the studio, but as usual he had precious little to say.

23 March

Big Day! Got my call for my first day's work on Empire Strikes Back. Have to be at the studio on Monday at 10 am.

26 March - Day One

Took the kids to school and arrived at the studio at 10 am. Apart from a fencing rehearsal with Peter Diamond, I did nothing all day. Put the Vader suit on in the afternoon but the helmet is not sitting straight so alterations have to be made. There's a documentary unit here to film the film being made and they're waiting to get film of Mark and me sword fighting. Mark is due to be at the studios tomorrow.

27 March

A short rehearsal with Mark and the stunt arranger, but other than that nothing else happened that affected me. Learned today that my old friend Bruce Boa is

21

going to play one of the major running characters.

Also heard today that actor Jeremy Bulloch, who used to train with me at my gym in South London, is also going to be working in the film as a bounty hunter called Boba Fett.

28 March

Did one shot today of me storming through the wreckage of the control centre. Had the mask and the helmet on for the second time, the first time to actually work in it. It's still awful. The mask doesn't sit right on the face and the helmet angle is all wrong, exposing the back of my neck, added to which I cannot see out of the eyepieces so I don't know where I'm going on set.

29 March

Did nothing today except a short fencing rehearsal.

30 March

All of the Random House Book people are on set today. They have the rights to the Star Wars books and to date have already sold over 4.5 million copies. They are very interested in my Fitness Is Fun book, which is due out soon. I must get my literary agent in New York to contact them.

Was in Harrods all day on the Saturday and then had to do a personal appearance for the Green Cross Code campaign on the Sunday. I wonder if there are any other actors who have to hold down two major jobs whilst trying to film in a major epic!

2 April

10 am call at the studio but I did nothing all day except an interview for the film's publicity department. They are in the middle of a very complicated scene involving the Wampa, in which they've put stuntman Terry Richards (who in the past has done various bits of stunt work for me). They spent nearly all day getting the technicalities of the scene right, forgetting that Terry was cooped up inside this ten-foot high Wampa suit for over three hours. First, the robots wouldn't function properly, then the new camera (which is all computer controlled) wouldn't function at all and finally the plasterers had built the breakaway wall too strongly and Terry just couldn't get through it. They eventually released Terry from his Wampa suit at 5.30 pm, when he was on the verge of collapse and suffering stomach cramps.

All of the General Mills Toy people from the US and their English counterparts like Dennis Fisher Toys, Palitoys etc were on set watching filming during the afternoon.

3 April

Once again called into the studio for 10 am and did nothing all day, not even a fencing practice. They are still struggling with the Wampa shot which so far has not been successful. They've now brought in another stuntman to take over from Terry Richards who must be very relieved to be out of it. How many days behind schedule they are I can't imagine but everybody seems happy and they are all excited about the rushes they are getting. Had lunch at the studio with the two technicians from Marin who have brought over the special computer camera (which is still not working).

4 April

10 am standby at the studio again. Once again did nothing all day although I did come close to actually working at around 5 pm. Did a little fencing rehearsal with Peter Diamond and then invoiced the company for all my rehearsal time spent at the Hartsmere Leisure Centre. Had loads of portrait pics done by the publicity dept - by all accounts the company want plenty of pics of me OUT of the mask.

Had dinner in the evening with the head of 20th Century Fox publicity at The Grange in King St. My wife, Norma, accompanied me, as did my business manager and his wife. Bob Dingilian kept dropping little bits of information about my publicity involvement with the film's promotion, the most surprising of which was the fact that Empire Strikes Back is having its premier both in London and Washington and that they are chartering Concorde to fly us to and fro. They're also hoping that President Carter will be attending, so it is all looking well, publicity wise, for this year and next.

5 April

8.30 am call at the studio. I'm required for the second shot. Shot entailed blowing out the side of the ice cave and for Darth Vader to make his dramatic entrance as per the one I made in Star Wars. I am to be preceded by stuntmen dressed up in stormtroopers gear and I am followed by more stormtroopers coming out into the corridor, with us all marching past camera. All was well during rehearsals, but on the 'take' the special effects men had overdone things with the explosive charges, and there was debris everywhere.

The stormtroopers were falling over like ninepins, because of the smoke and the clouds of polystyrene. I couldn't see where the stormtroopers had gone down, and then to cap it all, one stood on my cape and wrenched it off. Fortunately the take was OK up until then, so we'll complete it as a pick-up shot tomorrow.

6 April

Gary Kurtz is directing the 2nd unit to do my pick-up shot. We shot my walk up the corridor followed by the stormtroopers and fortunately there were no cock-ups today. Eric Idle of the Monty Python team was in today with his small son watching the filming. Had lunch at the Studio with the girls from the accounts department.

9 April
Had to be at the house of a personal training client - Charles St George, the well known racehorse owner, at 8 am. Bob Chesne the famous LA heart specialist was in London on his way to a symposium in Switzerland. Heard the bad news this morning that our friend Carol Rosenbloom, owner of the Los Angeles Rams football team, had been drowned whilst swimming in Florida. By all accounts he had got caught in a rip tide and carried out to sea. Charles is leaving straight away to go to LA for the memorial service. I had only met Carol once when I had been invited to watch the Rams play whilst I was on a US tour. Viewed the game from the plush surrounds of the owner's box, together with Rod Steiger's wife Sherri, Ricardo Montalbam, Tippi Hedren of Alfred Hitchcock's Birds fame and Candice Bergen and her mother, the ever lovely Ingrid.
   No calls at all this week for the film.

16 April
Apart from a call on Tuesday for wardrobe and make-up tests (for the unmasking of the top of Vader's head) and laser sword rehearsals with Mark Hamill, Peter Diamond and my stuntman - the British fencing coach - Bob Anderson, precious little else happened. The stills man took some interesting pics of Mark and myself rehearsing during the afternoon. Clearly, he had been briefed on the father/son confrontation at the end of Empire and the studio wanted to be prepared with photos of the two of us for future publicity opportunities.

24 April
Call came through late last night calling me into the studio for 8 am. No scene numbers or no idea given as to what I was going to be expected to do so I went into the studio completely unprepared and unrehearsed. Had the worst day's filming ever, all over one stupid line in scene 280 which I just couldn't remember. We actually shot until Take 14 before I got it right and everybody was happy. We are doing all my scenes in the Star Destroyer. Caught them today rehearsing my unmasking scene, with my stuntman made up for the part of Vader. Let the production people know in no uncertain terms that it was me that was going to be used for the unmasking, not any stunt double.

25 April

Much better day today, although filming is painfully slow. Kersh is a meticulous man and the sets and set-up seem to be very complicated. Started on scene 316 with all the Bounty Hunters. They've given my stand-in - Moray Bush - a part as one of the Bounty Hunters so I've been given a new stand-in, Roy Everson. Filming went into overtime and we finished around 7 pm. I was supposed to be in Bristol (about 150 miles away) in the evening for the West Country launch of my book Fitness Is Fun, but obviously was unable to make it, much to the publisher's annoyance.

26 April

Continued filming scene 316. In fact, we spent nearly the whole of the day on it. Seem to be getting loads of requests for autographed photos; even our lighting cameraman - Peter Sujitski - has requested three for his kids. Film producer Sandy Lieberson and his son came in to see me and stayed for lunch.

30 April

9.15 am call at the studio. Another long day which was spent in lots of preparation but not much shooting. Still doing the walk-throughs for scenes 55, 59 and 429. Worked right through till 6.30 pm.

1 May

Another slow day at the studio. Kersh seems reluctant to shoot film!! Had a call from the press officer at the Department of Transport wanting to make certain that I was going to be OK to go up to Newark (Nottinghamshire) on Friday night for a weekend Green Cross Code appearance. I told him that filming was going very slowly and I would probably only be able to drive up on the Friday evening, getting there late.

2 May

8 am call. Continuation of Darth Vader's Star Destroyer scenes. Quiet day again, long and boring with precious little personal involvement. Had a call from a female nut case from New York, who keeps ringing me to tell me that she wants me to star in an epic she is making. The part I'm being offered is that of the big hero, but I think it's all pie in the sky and she's just fantasising.

One of our national daily newspapers, The Daily Mail, called, wanting me to do a photo shoot for their ladies section - Femail. Don't know at this stage whether I can fit it in.

3 May

At long last we've got to the Vader chamber scenes. Had to have my hair cut very short in preparation for going into the bald cap. In the make-up chair for one and three-quarter hours. Eventually went to set just before lunch for a line-up and to let everybody see what it looked like but the cap started to ride up which meant I had to go back to Stuart Freeborn's department and spend the whole of the lunch hour in the make-up chair having it re-fitted. Everybody was happy with the final result. Did some 2nd unit work with Gary Kurtz and I have more chamber work (with the Emperor) tomorrow.

4 May

Still in Vader's chamber. Got to the scene where I'm confronted by the Emperor. It's been a hectic two weeks with most of the filming involving me but we are scheduled to finish all the chamber shots by next Tuesday. Kersh paid me a nice compliment today - said that I was solid, dependable, strong, always ready and never complained!

Finished at the studio at 6.30 pm and then had to drive about 150 miles up to Grantham in preparation for the Newark and Nottinghamshire Agricultural Show on the Saturday where I'm appearing in my guise of The Green Cross Code Man.

7 May

Today is a public holiday in the UK so Gary and his wife Meredith have decided to throw a big kids' party at their stately home in honour of Mark and his wife Marilu. My daughter Rachel, who is 8 going on 9, was thrilled to bits meeting them both.

8 May

8 am call. Finished off all my scenes in the pod. George Lucas has arrived for a week's work on the special effects. At the end of the day's shooting Kersh asked if he could have his photo taken with me in the pod and George came up and asked likewise.

10 May

Called into the studio for 10.30 am but purely for fencing rehearsals. Haven't fenced for so long that I've forgotten most of the sequences. However, they all started to come back after a little practice. Went over to the stills department to put in an order for all the pics of George, Kersh and myself, but there's a whisper going round to the effect that Gary Kurtz is putting a block on print orders. Hope not. The Mersey Pirate people from Granada TV have been in contact and all looks set for a fourteen week TV series, starting 2 June.

11 May
Started on the dining room shots, with Han Solo trying to shoot me. Have had explosive charges attached to my gloves, which by all accounts look quite effective when they go off.

14 May
Spent the day finishing off the dining room scenes. Worked till quite late in the evening.

15 May
2.30 call to reshoot the Emperor scene with new dialogue and viewed from behind me on the matt backing. Got to the studio for 2.30, sunbathed till 3.30 and actually started filming at 8 pm in the evening. Finished by 8.45 pm. The boots that Darth Vader wears in the film are actually ones that I'd had made for myself a few years ago. Since my early teens, getting shoes to fit has always been a problem. I have large, very wide feet and made to measure footwear is the only answer. The boots are a relic from my motorcycling days. The studio have asked if they can buy them from me.

16 May
Into the studios for 2.30 pm again and we finished the day at 7.30 pm. Kersh and Gary Kurtz have both asked if I would pose for photos with them and two of the Bounty Hunters. I've said 'yes' of course. If I can ever get my hands on them, the pics should be great for my publicity folder.

18 May
10.30 am call at the studio. The morning was spent doing more rehearsals for the light sabre duel. In the afternoon they started on the scenes where Han Solo is in prison before he goes into Carbon Freeze, but unfortunately Harrison has sustained a kick in the face, his nose is bleeding badly and what is worse, his face is marked. Called to rehearse scene 371 at 4.30 pm with the possibility of starting it if Harrison's nose proves difficult to film on. All eventually OK and we start filming scene 371 on Monday morning.

21 May
Started the week off with the scenes where Han is being tortured in the cell. Worked right through till 7 pm (from 8.30 am) and we still have one 'over the shoulder' shot to do to complete the scene.

Did virtually nothing during weeks 10 and 11 but restarted work in earnest with week 12 (week commencing 11 June).

18 June

Did scene 376 today but had loads of trouble with it. It's the Carbon Freezer scene and we shot it thirteen times before Kersh was satisfied with it. The studio broke at 1.30 pm because quite a few of the production personnel wanted to go to John Barry's funeral. I spent the whole afternoon having press photographs taken and doing an interview for The Daily Star.

19 June

Another day like yesterday with no actual shooting before noon. We're doing scenes 376/9 - the Carbon Freezer scenes - and it's baking hot on set with all the lights and the steam. Things are becoming fraught between Kersh and Harrison. Had two phone calls in the evening, the first from Albert Finney wanting me to supply him with some exercise equipment, the second from my brother Bob telling me that Prince Khalid bin Sultan bin Abdul Azziz, Crown prince of Saudi Arabia, had cancelled our training contract in view of the fact that he was about to go to 'War College' in the United States. I'd been looking after Prince Khalid's physical welfare for about three years, with my brother acting as his personal trainer and European aide. I was sorry to see the contract end as I very much enjoyed the prince's company as well as my visits to Riyadh and Jeddah.

20 June

Long, slow morning. Work didn't start before 9.45 because of a conflab between Kersh, Kurtz, Harrison and Carrie. Just used for lines off and eye lines. Had lunch at the local Chinese restaurant with R2-D2's wife, Eileen Baker.

21 June

More Carbon Freezer scenes. The set is just like a Turkish bath with all the heat and steam. It must be about 120 degrees up there and I have to have my helmet and mask removed after every take or rehearsal as the eyepieces mist up very quickly and I cannot see where I am walking. After the end of each scene I've walked from one side of the Carbon Freezer to the other and I then have to wait for one of the Ugnauts to lead me back to my start position where my dresser has the job of getting the helmet and mask off, wiping the eyepieces out and mopping me down.

The studio manager Andrew Mitchell has asked me for a copy of my book - Fitness Is Fun - which is just hot off the press.

22 June

Misjudged my timing for the drive to the studio and arrived there dead on time (instead of half-hour early) to find the production people were in a state of panic, thinking that I wasn't going to turn up. We were trying to complete the filming of the Carbon Freezer scenes with Milton, Jeremy Bulloch and Billy Dee Williams. Finished the day still with work left to be done.

25 June

On Monday we finished off the Carbon Freezer scenes and then started preparation for the light sabre duel with Luke Skywalker. There was still work left to be completed on the Tuesday but we then ran into problems on the set. We hung about all morning waiting for a start, but at noon we were all dismissed for the day.

By all accounts there are problems with Mark Hamill over a promised day off (his wife Marilu had their first baby, Nathan, yesterday) and that plus a thumb injury he's sustained stopped production for the day.

27 June

Still problems with Mark. I changed and got ready for 8 am, only to be told at 10 am that shooting had been cancelled for the day and would probably be off tomorrow, too. Mark's thumb was still no better on the Thursday or the Friday, so the studio decided to cancel filming for those two days and give Mark the weekend to get better.

Knowing the film business as I do there was probably very little wrong with Mark's thumb, but it was a great excuse for him to have a couple of days with Marilu after the birth of Nathan. No doubt an insurance claim went in for Mark's injury.

2 July

Spent all day at the studio doing precious little. The master shot of the Darth Vader/Luke Skywalker light sabre duel was shot using our two stuntmen - Bob Anderson for me and Colin Skeaping for Mark. Called into the studio every day but did very little work of any consequence, mainly pick-up scenes for the Carbon Freezer, pick-up shots on the Cloud City set and watching Bob, Mark and Colin getting the master of the light sabre duel shot right.

9 July

Only one day at the studio this week, and that was to have a stills session. The remainder of the week was spent chasing around the country for the Green Cross Code campaign and getting ready for the first day of Harrods' July Sale.

I was still managing to put appearances in at Harrods but of course, although my original contract was to put in three days a week, Harrods now had to fit in with my filming schedule. I'd already agreed to reduce my commitment there to one and a half days a week (one of which had to be a Saturday) but the writing was on the wall that with my film, TV and publicity commitments taking over, it wasn't going to be long before I was going to have to bow out of Harrods altogether. The Sales Director - Rex Cannon - had already offered me a testimonial, but I enjoyed so many things about my stints in the store: all the famous people I met whilst working there, all my friends coming into the store to meet up, the store's 'ambience' and, of course, the sizable discounts on purchases that my buyer's rank entitled me to.

It was amazing the friends one collected as soon as they knew you could get quite hefty discounts. Friends whom I know to be extremely wealthy would come in wanting me to buy them shoes because they knew that I could get them at practically half price. Film producers, famous name actors and acquaintances I hardly knew would all come in asking me to buy them goods with my buyer's card. Although it was strictly against the rules of the store to use a buyer's card to purchase goods for other people, I used to oblige wherever I could and you developed a group of buyer friends around or throughout the store who would do you favours and for whom you would do likewise. However all this was not to last much longer.

16 July

About ten days ago Billy Dee Williams had come into the studio dining room with a very attractive lady who was obviously doing a press interview with him over lunch. I had no idea who the lady was, but to my surprise sat opposite her in the Borehamwood Chinese restaurant whilst having lunch today. She informed me that she was with the local newspaper, had already interviewed Billy Dee and would love to do an interview with me, both for her own paper and for one of the nationals. Thinking that all was kosher I invited her to the studios on the Tuesday.

On the Tuesday morning we just did one shot of my feet jumping into shot and then it was lunch with my business manager and prospective US agent who between them were trying to arrange a US personal appearance and lecture tour for me. The lady from the press - Jan Collie - arrived after lunch and was seen walking around the studio lot looking for me by somebody from the publicity staff. Little did I know it but Miss Collie had been declared persona non grata by Lucasfilm and was eventually caught up with by Robert Watts, the associate producer, who had her removed from the studio lot in no uncertain manner.

Subsequently studio security and producer Gary Kurtz were brought in on it. I was given a rap over the knuckles, told that I was a naughty boy and told not to do anything like that in the future. I never did find out why Miss Collie wasn't welcome, or what she had done to incur the wrath of the production office. It was obviously something quite serious about which I knew nothing. I even had to appear before the studio security people the following day and by all accounts Gary Kurtz was absolutely furious.

Had a party at the studio in the evening to celebrate Carrie's finishing on the film. Most of the work this week at the studio has concerned the laser duel with Mark, Bob and Colin doing most of the work with the second unit. Much of Friday was spent preparing for the scene where Darth and Luke are fighting and Darth causes all sorts of objects to be hurled at Luke. They have these terrific wind machines on set which are actually full-size aeroplane propellers and every available person had to stand on set obviously behind camera and behind the wind machines, and hurl polystyrene blocks into the gale the wind machines were creating. All the items thrown went through the sugar window behind Luke, and eventually his stuntman went through too. We shot the scene around 3 o'clock in the afternoon and it looked sensational.

24 July

Complained today about the continual use of my stuntman. It must have sunk in as Kersh has actually started using me again - on both sets. I think they are getting so concerned about being so far behind schedule that they are using both my stuntman and myself in an attempt to catch up.

25 July

8.30 am call. They are using my stuntman again which really pisses me off. The day continued with the stuntman doing all the work and me doing nothing until I was eventually released at 4 o'clock. By all accounts Gary Kurtz has issued a directive that I am to be used for everything but the fighting scenes but it doesn't look as though the production people are taking much notice of it. Have been given the 'excuse' that the laser sword scenes are quite dangerous and they cannot afford to have me, as one of the principals of the film, injured, and therefore it is sound filming sense to use a stuntman who is more expendable. Add to this the fact that my stuntman - Bob Anderson - is the British Fencing Coach and obviously much better at fencing than myself and that enhances the part of Vader.

Whilst I appreciate the 'excuse' I do feel that both the fans and myself are being cheated. I have trained for months to do this fight scene and my duelling is the equal at the very least of Mark's. If it hadn't been for the fact that Mark's face is seen most of the way through the duelling scene, they would have had no compunction in using his stuntman more than they have. The fans don't go to see the film to see two stuntmen performing - they want to see Mark and myself battling it out together. Once again I am complaining bitterly, firstly to Peter Diamond who says it's nothing to do with him, then to Kersh who refers me to Robert Watts in the production office. Robert is only the Lucasfilm minion or yes-man, and it is obvious the directive has come from director and producer George Lucas and Gary Kurtz.

26 July

8 am call at the studio. Same procedure as before. More fight scenes being done by my stuntman. New dialogue has arrived for scene 400. Actually started work at 5 pm and finished around 6.45 pm. After struggling all day to learn my lines, by the time we get up on the gantry to deliver them to Mark, they have the big wind machines going which make such a racket that he can't hear a word I'm saying and I can't hear one word of his dialogue.

Little did I know at this stage that they had deliberately given me false dialogue so that I wouldn't know the crucial twist to the plot that was about to unfold. The final part of my dialogue on the gantry has me with my arm outstretched beckoning to Luke, saying, "Come, come and join me, together we will rule the Empire for ever," but as we all know now that line of dialogue was over-dubbed by James Earl Jones saying, "But Luke, I am your father!" Mark was privy to the real plot, but for some obscure reason it was decided that I shouldn't know the real dialogue and I didn't discover that I was Luke's father until I went to see the film premiere a long time afterwards.

I'll always remember sitting in the film theatre and thinking when this particular scene came on, well that's news to me. At the time I wasn't disgruntled or annoyed in any way. I'd enjoyed the film so much that I thought it was just a clever and novel twist to the storyline. Mark has since written that he was scared to death of me sitting in the cinema with everyone, as he thought that when I got to know the real dialogue I was going to jump over two rows of seats to thump him for not putting me in the picture.

In his biography Harrison Ford dismisses my seven-year involvement with the *Star Wars* saga in a couple of lines specifically referring to this incident in the film. I quote: "When the sequence was shot, David Prowse, the bodybuilder who played Vader, was speaking entirely different dialogue; the confession was dubbed in later during post production by James Earl Jones. At the London premiere Prowse was sitting directly behind Kershner. When the scene revealed itself the strongman leaned over and thumped the director on the back. 'Why didn't you tell me?' he implored".

I cannot remember wanting to thump Mark, and I cannot remember 'thumping' Kersh. The things I do remember about the premiere were (a) what a wonderful job Kersh had made of *Empire* and (b) what a novel situation we now had, with Darth being Luke's father. I think the complete lack of trust by the company dawned on me later, but at the time I was just thrilled to be part of the *Star Wars* team and to be in two of the biggest grossing films of all time.

Referring back to Harrison Ford's biography, it really does annoy me that I was thought of only as a bodybuilder. Sir Laurence Olivier used to train regularly at a very well known gymnasium in London, Albert Finney trained with me at my Health Studio, Christopher Reeve trained with me for the part of Superman, but you never read of Sir Laurence Olivier being referred to as a bodybuilder or fitness freak. I came into the acting business after a long career in bodybuilding, weightlifting and Highland Games, but in 1965 I embarked upon an acting career, albeit capitalising on the physique and strength that I'd developed over the previous 15 years.

To me those 15 years were like an apprenticeship that then enabled me to cope with all the things that were thrown at me in an acting career that spanned 25 years. By the time I went into *Stars Wars* in 1976, I had already been in something like ten movies (Harrison had done seven, Carrie none and Mark one) and I'd appeared in over one hundred television shows, covering everything from comedy, through Shakespeare to drama series. When we did *Star Wars*, with the exception of Sir Alec Guinness and Peter Cushing, I was the most experienced actor on set and had already appeared in one of the most controversial films of all time - Stanley Kubrick's *A Clockwork Orange*.

27 July

Took my son Steven into the studio, as he is very interested in art and modelling and wanted to meet the special effects crew. Continued working on the gantry scenes in the afternoon. Stuart Freeborn, the head of the make-up department, came to see me later in the evening with a model that my son had made whilst he was in their department. He said that Steve, who was thirteen at the time, had great talent for modelling and design and should definitely think about it as a full-time career on leaving school. At the end of the day we were all invited to a special screening of George's latest effort - More American Graffiti. Quite enjoyed it and it was interesting to see Harrison playing his cameo role as the traffic cop (totally unrecognisable).

30 July

On standby at home and eventually got the call at 2.30 pm. I thought this was a bit stupid as there was no way that I could get to the studio before 4.30 pm, London traffic being what it is, but they still insisted that I be there. Arrived at 4 pm and was told to get into the Darth Vader suit straight away as Gary Kurtz was hovering around on set and it would look good in his eyes to be seen ready and waiting even if there was no hope of using me. Ah, the politics of the film business!

Got changed, walked on set and was then told to go home as there was no way that they were going to get to me. That's showbiz for you.

31 July

At the studio for 8 am. One of the buyers from the meat department of Harrods came to the studio today at my invitation, with his family. It was a real boring day however as all we were doing was pick-up shots on the gantry and I think by the end of the day they were totally disillusioned with the glamour of showbiz.

1 August

8 am call for more pick-up shots. Filming today against the blue backgrounds (so that eventually they can matt in the scenes of unending space and all the space paraphernalia which they won't have to build). Broke at noon and went over to the Italian restaurant, Baffi's, for lunch. Sat on the next table to Liza Minnelli who is filming at the ATV television studios on The Muppet Show.

Did some dialogue work in the afternoon, then had to re-shoot one of the gantry scenes, the film of which had got ruined in the development tank. Am flapping around at this juncture as I am supposed to be going on a major publicity tour for 20th Century Fox and I don't yet know whether all my filming is going to be completed by Friday. Robert Watts has been to see me and Friday looks quite hopeful for my release from the film.

2 August

Took my sons Steven and James for a final tour of the sets before it all gets dismantled. Not much happening for myself other than more backing and insert shots. Steve spent most of his day back in the SFX shop.

3 August

My final day on the film. Took my daughter Rachel and her friend Hazel to meet up with Mark. He was very pleasant and friendly to them and seemed to spend ages with them laughing and joking. They had hoped to have some photos taken with Mark, and had brought along a cheap kids camera to record their meeting, but somebody from production saw them with it and it was taken away from them with the lame excuse that they didn't want them selling their pictures to the press. Whoever thought that two eight-year-old girls would be into selling their snapshots to the press I just do not know, but that shows you how paranoid the production people here have become about publicity leaks.

Lee's the electrics people who supply all the lighting for the film threw a big party in the evening to which everybody was invited. Stuart Freeborn presented me with the model that my son, Steve, had made on his last visit and was still waxing lyrical over it and saying what a great career he would have in the SFX business if he wanted it on leaving school.

Everything is fixed for my departure tomorrow. Leave Heathrow London at 11 am and arrive New York at 1.35 pm. It's going to be a very hectic two weeks with something like twelve cities to visit in just fourteen days.

4-24 August

I had never done a publicity tour on behalf of a film company before and little did I know that the next three weeks were going to be three of the busiest weeks of my life. Tony Daniels (C-3PO) accompanied me on the trip.

Left London at 11.30 am on the Saturday morning and arrived in New York at 2.20 pm. Met by driver with huge stretch limo and taken to the Sherri Netherlands Hotel which is right on Central Park. Went to a strangely named restaurant - One If By Land, Two If By Sea - for dinner, after which I went out for a stroll before returning to the hotel. On the Saturday we left New York en route for New Orleans, where we arrived at 2 pm. Met by business manager who has managed to inveigle his way onto the tour at Fox's expense. By all accounts he is now looking after Tony Daniels too. New Orleans very hot and humid. Did a tour of the French Quarter with the 20th Century Fox rep Pat Dwyer and did a press interview over dinner at our hotel, the Royal Orleans.

6 August

Tony Daniels and I arrived at Houston at 5.15 and checked into the Houston Oaks Hotel. Dinner was at the Brownstone's restaurant which included the now customary interview, this time with Eric Graber of the Houston Post. The restaurant was interesting, done out just like an antiques shop with all the items on display for sale. Tony Daniels left as soon as the interview was through, as he had a date with one of the National Airlines stewardesses whom he'd met on the plane. Good luck, Tony!

7 August

Tony and I have split up for the interviews. It turned out to be a good idea as we both got much longer and better interviews. Schedule was incredibly punishing, though - hardly a minute between sessions. This is more tiring than training with heavy weights.

8 August

Somehow, we've moved on to Dallas but although it's a new city the routine's the same and there's another hectic schedule lying in wait.

Five more interviews later, I managed to squeeze in a sunbathe and a swim in the hotel pool whilst I was waiting to be collected to fly to our next stop which was St. Louis. Met a hairdresser from Champagne Illinois, who was in Dallas looking for a job. The temperature today was 97°F so I dived into the pool to accompany her on a few lengths. I hadn't swum more than about 20 yards when I suddenly realised that I had three thousand dollars' worth of Cartier watch on (a present from Prince Khalid of Saudi Arabia) and the watch wasn't waterproof. I beat a hasty exit out of the pool and got the hotel concierge to get my watch to a repairer so that it could be cleaned out before the innards went rusty. I was later informed that I had only just made it in time. Another few seconds in the pool and my precious Cartier would have ticked its last.

9 August

Went straight to a shop in St. Louis and bought myself a new waterproof watch! Interviews started at 8 am in the breakfast restaurant. Schedule as mad as ever. With another half-dozen interviews completed, we left St. Louis at 5.30 and arrived in Cincinnati at 7.30 pm.

Met up with the Fox publicists - Gary Goldstein and Larry Dieckhaus. We had dinner in the hotel - The Terrace Hilton - where we did an interview with Dale Stevens of the Cincinnati Post which went on till nearly one am. I can't believe how tiring this 'glamorous' life is.

10 August

Today, I think we are in Cincinnati, although I could be wrong. This tour is beginning to remind me of the old film about Americans on European tours - 'If it's Wednesday it must be Paris'. So far we've hit six major US cities and I've seen practically nothing of any of them. Once again it's an 8.30 am start, followed by flat-out interviews before being whisked off to the airport - Chicago next stop. Or at least I think it is.

11 August

Staying at the Ritz Carlton Hotel but I didn't sleep very well, bed too hard, pillow too soft. Woke up early and went to the hotel Health Club where I had a workout and a steam bath.

Went to WGN Radio and TV where I did interviews with Roy Leonard. 2.30 interview on Radio WLS with Jeff Davis and then on to the Chicagofest to sign autographs for two hours. Went out in the evening with Larry (the Fox publicist) and his family to a place called Moretons, where I had the biggest T-Bone Steak I've ever eaten. It always amazes me, the American capacity for food and drink. At Moretons I really had to struggle to get through my steak, but Larry's wife, a petite little thing, wolfed hers down, was finished about 10 minutes before me and I swear would have eaten another if it had been offered. Wow. I'm glad Norma's not American - I don't think I could afford to feed her.

12 August

At last, a day of rest. Spent the morning at the poolside in the sunlounger and the whirlpool. Then had to vacate our rooms as the schedule has been changed and we are catching the 6 am morning flight to Minneapolis. Lunched at the hotel, then spent the afternoon wandering along the North Shore front. In the evening Larry and his family took me to a 'concert in the Park'. It was a lovely evening, the weather was beautiful, the classical music great and we feasted on buckets of Kentucky Fried Chicken, washed down with wine. Pure class!

13 August

The second week of the tour and if I thought last week was busy I was in for a big surprise. Up at 5 am to leave for Minneapolis and at 8 am we are met at the airport and ushered to our hotel. Here we go again - this time with the schedule in full overdrive.

Interviews are now being stacked so tightly that those conducting them are bumping into each other. I've explained the answers (in enthusiastic detail) to the same set of questions so many times that I'm beginning to lose track of who's asking what about which subject. C'mon Prowse - stay on track.

Can't recall how many radio and TV slots we did today. It could all have been one long interview for all I know. The only thing I'm certain of is that we jumped an early flight to Chicago and arrived back at the Ritz Carlton at 8 pm. Was then taken to Whitesox park for a media party by Larry and Roger Ebert.

When talking or writing about Roger I'm always pleased that I knew and met him before he became famous. In 1979 he was an unknown writer and, if I remember correctly, when we were together in Chicago he was really struggling to make ends meet. Now, of course, the Gene Siskel/Roger Ebert film critic team are internationally famous and I've just heard that there is even a Siskel-Ebert street in Chicago named after them - that's fame for you.

14 August

Full day of interviews ahead but fortunately quite a few of them are going to be conducted in the hotel. Usual day - long blitz of questions and answers, punctuated by a very nice lunch, with a mad dash to catch the 9 pm flight to Los Angeles as a full stop. We thought Larry had done such a great job, publicity-wise, over the last couple of days that we decided to give him a present as a token of our appreciation. We went out and got him a travel clock!

15 August

Chaos at the airport. First, there was no sign of the limo driver. Plane took off an hour late and our driver had parked in the car park and, would you believe, didn't have any money on him to get the limo out of the park! When we eventually caught up with him and gave him some money, he couldn't get the car to start. To cap everything he also couldn't get the trunk open. We eventually got to the hotel to find that there were no reservations for us, but they eventually found us 'put up' beds at 2 am. What a crap day.

Fortunately today is going to be a quiet day with only one appearance - judging a Star Wars Fancy Dress competition at a cinema. The competition was covered by three TV stations, two radio stations and loads of press, after which we went to have lunch in the executive restaurant of 20th Century Fox.

Had the pleasure of being entertained at the table by Mel Brooks who was very funny. Met Herb Ross and the two new chiefs at Fox, Ashley Boone and Dennis Stanfill. Everybody is very excited about the fantastic amount of publicity we have been getting on the tour and even more excited about the news coming out as to how good Empire Strikes Back is looking.

All the Lucasfilm people came over for drinks in the early evening and then we retired to a Japanese restaurant for dinner.

16 August

At last, a day with no interviews!

The limo picked us up at 10 am to go to the airport - next stop Toronto. Left via Air Canada at 1 pm, arrived in Toronto at 7.55 in the evening. Dianne Schwalm of Fox met us at the airport, and for some reason we had trouble at the passport control on entering Canada but it all got sorted out quickly. I have two cousins in Toronto, both of whom I tried to contact. Just my luck, one is away on holiday with his family in Niagara and the other is going to come to the hotel for dinner tomorrow evening.

17 August

Here we go with the schedule, again. Wall-to-wall interviews, culminating at 8.30 pm at the York Theatre for a showing of Star Wars. The Toronto Sci Fi Club put on a horrendous mock Darth Vader/Luke Skywalker battle - two performances that had to be seen to be believed!

18 August

Up at 6.45 am. Left the hotel at 7.30 to get the 9.05 am flight to San Francisco. Arrived at one o'clock and it being a beautiful day went on an afternoon's sightseeing. Went to the Olema restaurant for dinner and later got in touch with my old friend, radio personality Jim Eason. I've known Jim for quite a few years and whenever I am in San Francisco I have an open invitation to guest on his very popular radio show.

19 August

Had a tour around the Golden Gate Park area and visited the Aquarium. In the afternoon went to visit Jim Eason at his home and was amazed to find the place surrounded by mist. By all accounts it's a naturally occurring phenomenon in the Bay area. Jim arranged for us to go and see his old buddy - Mel Tormé - who is appearing at the Fairmont Hotel in the evening. And what an evening it turned out to be.

Dinner first at an Austrian restaurant right on the waterfront, followed by a first class show with Mel in superb voice. Ever since I was a youth when I purchased my first Mel Tormé record - Mountain Greenery - I have been a huge fan, so you can imagine my excitement when he introduced me to the packed audience and then, even better, I went up to his hotel suite for drinks and a chat after the show.

We chatted about loads of things, singing, jazz, George Shearing and, of course, films, at which point I said something like "Of course you were married to an English actress - Janet Scott and had a very famous English actress - Thora Hird - as your mother-in-law" at which point Mel launched into a whole diatribe of vindictive against his ex mother-in-law - the air practically turned blue and I began to wonder whether I should have ever brought up the subject. He calmed down eventually, but it was painfully obvious that he blamed his mother-in-law for everything that went wrong in the marriage.

I met Janet at a horror convention just recently; a very pleasant, attractive lady who was totally nonplussed over the fact that the horror fans are retaking an interest in her horror film appearances. She didn't have a lot to say about her former husband, but, from the little she did, I got the impression that she still remembers Mel with affection. Of course, I also came across (Dame) Thora at various charity functions in the UK, but I was very careful not to mention the name Mel Tormé!

20-23 August

Most of the official business of the tour is now over and I am actually leaving the US for home on Friday 24 August. 20th Century Fox have agreed to let me travel home via Concorde (it'll be my first ever trip on the plane) and I'm really looking forward to it. Spent the Monday and Tuesday in LA having all sorts of meetings with various people who are interested in furthering my career, people like publicists, agents, literary agents and a few personal friends. Russ Meyer called me whilst I was doing a radio phone-in show and arranged to take me out to dinner on the Tuesday evening.

Had a very nice lunch at Ma Maison at which Jack Lemmon was also dining. On the way there, we'd stopped at a gas station and I was totally gobsmacked when Lauren Bacall drove up to the next petrol pump and started filling up her car! These things just don't happen when you're living in London.

Wednesday and Thursday were spent in New York where I visited the headquarters of the Starlog Group who produce the two biggest sci fi and horror magazines in the world - Starlog and Fangoria. Starlog magazine, or more precisely its owner, Norman Jacobs, has been more instrumental in getting me publicity in the States than any other journal or group of journals. As a result Norman and his family and the staff of Starlog have become great friends and I always do my utmost to include a visit to the Starlog offices whenever I get into New York.

Had the pleasure of meeting up with Susan Sackett - Gene Rodenbury's secretary on Star Trek, whom I had photos taken with. Went out to lunch with a film producer called Ed Sumner who is trying to interest me in the part of Conan in a forthcoming series of films featuring this big, muscular warrior. This is the second time the subject of Conan has cropped up. A few years back, I was approached by a film producer in Britain - Milton Subotsky of AIP - who asked me to go away and read some of the Conan stories and to let him know if I was interested in playing Conan. As it transpired, Milton never did anything with the rights to the stories on which he had the option and they were eventually relinquished. They were then taken up by an American company and the rest is now history, with Arnold Schwarzenegger getting the Conan role and subsequently going on to become the enormous star he now is.

Arnold has been a friend of mine for years. I met him when he was a young lad coming over to London from Munich to compete in the Mr Universe contest at the age of 18 or 19. Years later I had the pleasure of being one of the judges at the last Mr Universe contest he entered. We met up again at the premiere of *Empire Strikes Back* when he was there with the Kennedy family (more about this later) and I usually try to make contact with him whenever I'm in LA if his work schedule permits.

I was in LA in 1994, just before *True Lies* premiered, and he invited me over to his restaurant, Shatzi's on Main, for lunch. He was a really gracious host and made time to sit with me and a business colleague at our table. It's strange that when he was a young competing bodybuilder I really used to think that he was an arrogant, self-centred sort of man. Over the years, success, wealth and a very happy marriage have mellowed Arnold and turned him into a very likeable, feeling person who puts his family life before everything. Whenever I meet him these days I always come away with the impression that I've been with somebody who is very 'special' and that he has a certain regard for me, too.

24 August

The rain is pouring down; I've never seen a downpour like it. All the roads to the airport were flooded and I only just made it in time for my Concorde flight. Apart from the timesaving aspect I did feel a bit let down by the trip. There was more room that I expected, the service was terrific - cocktails when you got on, followed by a five-course meal, by the end of which you'd arrived in London. The thing which disappointed me most was the fact that you didn't get any conception of the speed at which you were travelling apart from a dial on the wall which read MACH 1.2 up to MACH 2.1 which meant you were travelling at twice the speed of sound, or about 14 to 15 hundred miles per hour. The observation windows are very small, too, and the sky is much bluer when you travel at 60,000 feet.

The journey to London took just over three hours, a saving of 3 to 4 hours on the normal flying time. Thinking back on it, though, unless I was fabulously wealthy or in a job where time was of the essence, I don't know whether I would want to pay the astronomic cost just to save a couple of hours. It's nice to tell people that you've travelled on Concorde (I've done it three times now), but to be perfectly honest I think I would rather save the money and travel First or Business.

From the end of August 1979 onwards my life just seemed to get busier and busier. Not only did I have the health studio to run but also I was trying to hold down my part-time position as keep-fit equipment buyer and exercise consultant to Harrods. The Road Safety tours and allied promotion work were increasing and I was getting more and more requests to do promotional tours of the US in connection with my Star Wars work. In addition to all this I had a wife and young family to look after, and it has always been one of my major regrets in life that my career was snowballing at such a pace that I just seemed to be spending less and less time at home with my wife, Norma, and the three kids,

Steven, James and Rachel. The fact that they have grown up into three fine adults is down 90 per cent to Norma's influence and upbringing and about 10 per cent to me being the provider.

The period from August to the middle of November was spent doing primarily Green Cross Child Pedestrian Road Safety tours, and all sorts of commercial concerns were trying to get in on the success of the campaign. Range Rover and Portacabin offered us vehicles for a travelling road safety exhibition to accompany me wherever I was appearing, Volvo gave us a vehicle for a tour, a major pharmaceutical company got involved with a children's soap product and had me appearing at their branches all over the country, a clothing company wanted to market children's wear under the Green Cross banner and numerous publishers were hounding me to write children's road safety books.

I eventually did a book on Child Pedestrian Road Safety and took it to a publisher in London who had shown a lot of interest. They thought that the book would have a greater appeal if we covered all aspects of safety - safety whilst travelling, skateboard safety, safety whilst out fishing, safety whilst swimming or boating, and then decided to give the book a 'personality' image and contacted lots of British TV and film celebrities to see if they would 'front' the various features. Agreements were reached all round and the book eventually came out under the title *Play Safe with the Stars* and was a huge success.

I also made a single for the Green Cross Code called, appropriately, 'The Green Cross Code Song' or 'Stop, Look and Listen', which turned out to be very popular with the kids. Flushed with success, I went on to record an LP of me singing children's songs, the words of which had been changed slightly so that we could incorporate the road safety message. I had great fun recording all the well-known kids' songs, such as 'On Top of Old Smokey' - which became 'On Top of Spaghetti', 'The Grand Old Duke of York', 'Old MacDonald's Farm', 'Ten Green Bottles' and many more. It never ceases to amaze me just how popular the Green Cross campaign really was, and even now, years after the campaign ended, no matter where I do my personal appearances somebody always comes up to me either wanting to tell me what an influence on their lives I'd been as the Green Cross Code Man or wanting to buy the book and the records.

Did a big Star Trek Convention in Denver the first week of September and then came straight home to start touring the UK visiting the schools (three a day) to do my road safety show for the kids. Back to the States again for another two-week tour, this time to Chicago, Champagne Illinois, Houston, Los Angeles, San Diego and Denver. This tour was different from the previous ones, in as much as I was combining sci fi conventions, talks around the colleges and personal promotion. I was able to do things like visit the Shead Aquarium in Chicago, have Thanksgiving dinner in Houston with Carlotta Barnes and her family, a fantastic visit to the Houston NASA Control Center for a VIP guided tour, which included sitting in the Shuttle Control module and finishing up in the actual centre that we all see on TV, when all the technicians are congratulating each other. My old friend Jimmy Doohan - Scottie of Star Trek fame - was touring the Centre the same day as myself and the assembled press and photographers had great difficulty trying to decide which of us to follow around.

Over the years Jimmy and I have become good friends. We are forever meeting up at various conventions in America, and at one time we were trying to plan a temporary house swap so that we could both work in each other's countries. I was quite keen to see if I could get my career off the ground in the USA and Jimmy was raring to come back to the UK to, as he put it, get back into the real theatre again. Unfortunately it never came to fruition.

My first college lecture was at the famous USC, a huge Los Angeles campus with thousands of students and I was a bit worried about attendance, as they'd scheduled my show for 12.30 am, which meant that the students would be getting up and going either to lunch or to the various lectures they had to attend. I needn't have worried, however, as the auditorium was jam-packed with over 1,000 students who received my talk very enthusiastically, staying right through to the end and then standing in line for hours to get my autograph.

Did another talk at the Whitter College which, although we had a smaller audience of about four hundred, was equally well received. Next stop on the tour was Reno, where I was to give a lecture at the Susanville College auditorium. Booked into the MGM Grand Hotel, which is unlike any hotel I'd ever been into. I'd never been to a gambling town and I was amazed by the acres of slot machines. There was also a real, live lion at the photographers and fantastic cabaret artistes performing to nonexistent audiences who were only interested in the sound of the coins going through the slot machines.

I was given a beautiful suite of rooms, all the walls were papered in a silver-foil type covering, and I had a huge circular bed with curtains all the way round, plus a completely mirrored ceiling and a Jacuzzi in the bathroom. Susanville, which has a population of about seven thousand, hosted my appearance and I was knocked out when a fifth of the population turned up for my lecture. It was the biggest crowd they'd ever had, with all the parents bringing in loads of kids to see me. I signed autographs until about two in the morning. Went on to Denver, where I did a TV interview with yet another Star Trek personality - Persis Khambatta, a lovely lady who'd grown her hair since the film and now had a really luxuriant growth. Finished the tour by going on to New York, then Chicago, to get my flight back to London, arriving home at 9 o'clock in the morning.

1980

Life proceeded at its normal hectic pace for the first four months of the year, but there was a lull in the *Star Wars* activity as everything was being geared up for the premiere of *Empire Strikes Back* in the middle of May.

I was still involved in all my Green Cross Code activities, was acting as personal trainer to one of Britain's foremost racehorse owners - Lloyds insurance broker, Chas St George, working hard trying to get my own Fitness Is Fun Gym Mat manufactured and into the major stores, completing my book - *Play Safe with the Stars*, still putting in my stints at Harrods, running the gymnasium and fitting in the odd television show here and there.

I was very fortunate to be offered a second appearance in *The Morecambe and Wise Show*, which was a higher accolade in the UK than being asked to appear on the *Royal Variety Show*. Eric Morecambe and Ernie Wise were the most successful comedy duo ever to have come out of the UK and their shows commanded some of the biggest viewing audiences ever achieved on British television. On one particular Christmas their *Xmas Spectacular* had over half the population of Great Britain watching - something like 25 million viewers - and all the great names of film and television were lining up to do even the most menial of parts in the shows. No matter who it was, they all entered into the fun of the show and were used quite blatantly as the butt of the duo's humour.

Unfortunately Eric died in 1984, and Ernie without Eric was like bread without butter. However, the great trouper that he was, he soldiered on, doing the rounds of TV chat shows, personal appearances and pantomimes, and he was a much-loved character both in and out of showbiz, right up to his death in 1999.

I did another famous British kids TV show, *Tiswas*, for ATV in Birmingham and took my daughter with me to watch the filming. She was about eight at the time and had never stayed in a hotel before and was thrilled to bits that she'd been given a room all to herself. We went to the hotel restaurant for dinner, during which my favourite comedian - Les Dawson - came in and sat on the other side of the restaurant.

The next thing that happened was that the restaurant manager was sent over to our table and we were asked if we would like to join Les at his table. Over we went and it turned out that Les, who went on to become one of Britain's' most famous funny men, was a great *Star Wars* fan and spent most of his dinner time plying me with questions about the film. He also found out that Rachel was having piano lessons and invited her to go and play the piano with him.

Now anybody who has ever heard Les play the piano will know just what to expect. Les has an uncanny knack of playing tunes off-key or just inserting wrong notes every so often. He's a great pianist, but his comedy antics at the piano have overshadowed his real playing, so rarely did you ever hear Les play properly. However, on this night Rachel and Les sat and played duets together for hours and had the entire restaurant convulsed with laughter. We both got invited to a party with Les's manager and singer Don Estelle, which apparently went on until 4 am. Rachel was out on her feet by 2 am, at which time I decided it was time we got back to the hotel and bed. The *Tiswas* show on Saturday was great fun, with me appearing alongside Britain's most famous wrestler - Big Daddy, strongman Tony Brutus, and two famous comedians - Frank Carson and Bernard Manning.

I presented the awards at the World Cup Powerlifting Championships in London, where I met up with lots of my old weightlifting colleagues, including the former World's Strongest Man - Larry Pacifico, who was there commentating for NBC.

A couple of days before the meet I'd been for an audition for a new film - to play the part of a prehistoric man. I didn't want to do it, as I considered it a retrograde step after doing the two *Star Wars* films, but my agent obviously wanted to keep me working and lured me there with the promise that I would be meeting a very talented French director who, even if I didn't do this film, might well want to use me in the future.

Anyway, I turned up at a church hall in Chelsea, only to be confronted by about 50 other people vying for the parts of the Neanderthal man, most of whom I knew as stuntmen, bodybuilders, wrestlers and dancers. I think it was probably the most degrading audition I have ever attended, as we were all made to parade around the hall in front of the French director and the casting agent, trying to walk and look like orang-utans!

Trying to mimic a monkey's gait played havoc with my knees and nobody could have been happier than me when I didn't get the job. Unfortunately, as a consequence of the audition, within two days one of my knees was swollen up like a balloon, and it got progressively worse as the days went on.

I did the weightlifting championships on a walking stick and the following day had to fly out to Los Angeles and Seattle, where I was giving one of my presentations at the Everett Centre. Seattle was to be just a short trip, i.e. leaving London on the Wednesday and returning home Saturday lunchtime.

16 April

Was up at 6 am to pack and get everything ready so that I could be at London airport for 11.30 am. Norma is surprised and annoyed that I am not taking the boys (Steve and James) with me on the trip - when will I get her to understand that this trip, or indeed any of my US tours, is not a holiday and to travel halfway around the world for a one day appearance is not my idea of a family outing?

My knee is still very swollen and painful and I am having to use a walking stick to get around. I really shouldn't be doing this trip with my knee in the state that it is. Arrived in LA after an uneventful trip and found no one there to meet me. Have to make my own way by taxi to the hotel that I normally stay at - The Beverly Hillcrest. Got to the hotel to find it fully booked and was sent down the road to the Ramada. Opposite was the LA Accident and Emergency Hospital, which I practically had to crawl into, to try to get someone to look at my knee and ease the pain.

Was eventually there for four hours, although they wanted to keep me in for two days and practically refused to let me out - especially to go to Seattle. They aspirated my knee, removing two whole cups of fluid, put a tight splint on it, told me to rest or better still get back to London as soon as possible, and then put me on crutches. Was not allowed to leave the hospital until I'd signed pictures for all the staff in the Emergency department. Will have to see how the knee feels tomorrow and decide if I'm well enough to go up to Seattle. Travel agent unable to get me back to London so will go north if all is well.

17 April

Am hobbling around on crutches, knee still swollen and stiff, but I might as well go up to Seattle as stay around LA doing nothing. Driven to the airport by a representative of my Lecture Agency and got wheelchair assistance onto the plane.

Met in Seattle by the reps from the Everett Centre, who are very relieved to see me. Went first to a radio station to do an interview, then on to the centre to meet the winners of a drawing competition. Hobbled on stage at 7.30 pm on my crutches and completed the show around 9.15 pm. Then, of course, I had to deal with the autograph line which went on for hours, by which time I was really feeling rotten and all I wanted to do was get back to the hotel so that I could rest my knee.

It's been announced that the US premiere of Empire Strikes Back will be in Washington on 17 May, followed by the London premiere three days later. We are all to travel out on Concorde, returning to London on 18 May so that we can all attend the press showing on the 19th and the Royal Premiere on the following day.

Came back from the US still suffering with my swollen knee, which doesn't seem to have gone down at all since last week. The publicity is certainly beginning to build up for the launch of Empire. The national newspaper, the Daily Mirror, wants me to do the prestigious Jean Rook interview, Photoplay have been in touch and I have to do an interview for Screen International. This week, before the premiere, also saw me auditioning for one of the best acting roles I have ever come across in my career, the part of Stanley in a three-part thriller for the BBC called The Rose Medallion. Stanley is the slightly backward cousin of a run down private detective and over three episodes they get involved in the search for a missing treasure in Sardinia, murder and a chase by the Mafia. Peter Ellis is directing and they plan to shoot the whole thing in and around the Cheddar area down in the West Country - no chance of getting to Sardinia on the BBC budget!

Got to see one of the country's top knee specialists who was absolutely horrified at the state my knees were in and says that I must stop all heavy squatting in my training, put my leg in a tight brace and REST! Managed to do two out of the three, but resting at this point in my career is almost impossible.

2 May
Travelled down to Dorking for a charity preview of Empire. Was supposed to be making a big entrance, and it had been arranged that a chauffeur-driven limo would be picking me up, but when the time came, I was picked up by a mini cab driver who turned up very late in a beaten-up old Renault. On the Saturday, the day of the Empire showing, I was taken to the cinema in an old estate car. Spent ages signing autographs after the show, but felt very despondent about my treatment at the hands of the organisers of the preview.

4 May
The press preview. Syd Gannis is over from the States for the previews, since he's looking after the publicity for Lucasfilm and 20th Century Fox. Everybody is coming up to me and talking about the sensational twist in the plot where Darth Vader reveals to Luke Skywalker that they are, in fact, father and son. I honestly have to say that up until the time of the press previews, I didn't have an inkling of the plot direction. They had obviously given me false dialogue whilst we were filming so that I wouldn't know what was going on. I remember the scene vividly:

standing on the gantry with the wind machines making so much noise that you couldn't even hear yourself speak and me delivering the line 'Come, come and join me, and we will rule the Empire together'. On finding out the real dialogue I can't remember being upset at all, although I think by the time we got to the Royal Premiere in London I had seen the film a few times and I was beginning to get annoyed at the press stories that Fox and Lucasfilm had been putting out, implying that they had considered me a security risk.

I think at this time the rot was beginning to set in, and everybody from the production office backwards seemed to be ultra careful about what was being said in my presence.

When one works on a movie of this magnitude, everybody is paranoid about information leaking out which might possibly be used, for instance, by another film company - who in turn just might get 'stolen' ideas onto film before the original company. Neither 20th Century Fox nor Lucasfilm ever bargained for the success of Vader, and over the years they had done precious little to publicise my efforts in helping create a character who is now regarded as the ultimate screen villain.

After *Star Wars* there was a concentrated effort to deny me any publicity. No stills of myself were ever released, they over-dubbed my voice with that of James Earl Jones without telling me (even though George Lucas and myself had frequently discussed the fact that Darth Vader lines would be re-recorded in the Elstree sound studio) and I was denied the right to do Darth Vader personal appearances. Fox felt that using me would be far too expensive. It was cheaper to use the suit with any large guy inside it and hopefully nobody would know the difference.

In all the years I've been working with the *Star Wars* movies, I have only ever agreed to do four personal appearances - and each of those were here in the UK. I feel furious when I recall the number of times that I have had to explain to fans who turn up to see me all over the world that the 'Darth Vader' character that they met and bought some scrawled, autographed photo from, was not me. Worse still is the fact that the various licensees actively promote the idea that the fan is actually meeting Dave Prowse inside the Vader suit, but because of contractual problems 'Vader' is not allowed to speak or sign 'Dave Prowse' on the photos they sell.

For example, I once did an autograph-signing session in a big newsagents in Glasgow, but because I couldn't wear the Darth Vader suit they dressed up the office manageress - all 5 foot 2 inches of her - and proceeded to parade her round the store looking, to my mind, utterly ludicrous. Another time Lucasfilm refused one of the major British TV companies permission to do a take-off of *Star Wars*. The TV people wanted me to play Vader, but when permission wasn't forthcoming they changed everything around and I played Han Solo and the Dark Lord was played by a tiny little girl who, at the end of the show, zapped us all with her light sabre and turned the entire cast into Shirley Temple lookalikes! (I've still got my pink gingham Shirley Temple dress in my wardrobe. I occasionally get it out and wear it to fancy dress parties, which causes quite a stir).

On another occasion, I went to Harrods (this was after *Return of the Jedi* when I was no longer working there) to do some shopping and happened to walk into the toy department to find it jam-packed with people who had turned up to see an exhibition of the *Jedi* characters. As soon as I walked into the department I was recognised and surrounded by autograph hunters. All of a sudden there was tap on my shoulder. It was the buyer of the department and she wanted me to accompany her to her office. When I extricated myself from the hordes of fans, I got to her office only to be told – "Mr Prowse, you are an embarrassment to the department. We are holding an exhibition of the *Jedi* characters and we are about to parade Darth Vader. Everybody in the store knows that you are the real Vader, so how can we parade our Darth Vader with you standing in the audience? We would therefore be obliged if you would leave the store." Once again it was a case of the licensee fobbing off the public with a fake Darth Vader and trying to give them the impression that they were seeing me. I left the store as requested, but it left a very bad taste in the mouth.

Another exhibition of the figures was put on at the Horticultural Halls in Westminster, London, as part of the Sports and Toy Exhibition. The Lucasfilm representative saw me in the audience and once again I was asked to leave or make my presence scarce whilst they paraded their own 'dress-up' character.

Star Wars won the Oscar for best costume, and the powers that be decided that they should have a Darth Vader on stage whilst John Mollo collected the award. If ever there was a personal appearance that I should have done, it was this one, but did they ask me to appear? Hell, no. Another of the myriad of dress-up characters was paraded. Even after all these years I still get people coming up to me thinking they saw me at the Oscar presentation ceremony.

Another honour that was awarded to *Star Wars* was the famous foot-printing ceremony outside Mann's Chinese Theatre in Los Angeles.

Lucasfilm flew in Tony Daniels to get into the C-3P0 outfit, they had the empty R2-D2 unit there, but they dressed up some other character as Darth Vader rather than get me in to receive the honour on behalf of the company. Although most of the world think that it was me in the suit doing the footprinting ceremony, quite a few people who know me well have been to look at the footprints and can tell instantly that they're not mine!

The only really good thing that happened to me whilst I was being denied all the publicity and public appearances was that I was approached by John Hagner of the Hollywood Stuntmen's Hall of Fame, who told me that they would consider it an honour to induct me into their organisation the next time I was in California. This was duly done, so I finally had my own personal footprinting ceremony. To this day I am immensely proud of the personalised Hall of Fame t-shirt that was presented to me.

I don't know why, but even some of the major publicity photos that the licensees put out are not pictures of me in the Darth Vader suit. The licensees, or Lucasfilm, or 20th Century Fox, might not think that it makes any difference and that it could be any Tom, Dick or Harry inside the suit, but it means an awful lot to the fans who specifically want pictures of Darth Vader with ME inside the suit. The stand-up figures and the Darth Vader posters are not me, but I have given up telling the fans because of the disappointment I have seen registered on their faces. I now sign everything and don't say a word.

9 May

Up at 6 am to get packed to go to New York and Washington for the US press junket and the premiere in Washington. Was late arriving at the airport, Gary Kurtz was flapping like mad, and am surprised to find that we are all flying out on Concorde. It's interesting with supersonic flight: we leave London at 11.15 in the morning and, after a three and a half hour flight, arrive in New York 35 minutes before take-off time, i.e. 10.40 am. Thirteen of us are in the party, which includes Kersh, Gary Kurtz, Syd Gannis, Harrison, Carrie, Mark and family et al. Didn't go to the New York press screening - would you believe there were no tickets for the cast?

10 May

Up at 7.30 am for the start of the press junket at the Essex Hotel at 9 am. It all started off with the general press conference, then we split up and sat at ten different tables, spending about ten to fifteen minutes at each answering the press's questions. Lunch at the hotel then back to the grind of the TV interviews.

Once again we all split up into pairs - I was paired off with Mark Hamill - and we worked through till 6.30 in the evening doing a televised interview every ten minutes. All invited out to a big dinner at a Japanese restaurant on 58th Street, which didn't finish till around three in the morning. Staggered back to the hotel, but couldn't sleep and was up at 7.15 am rarin' to go for the next series of interviews.

11-13 May

On the Sunday, we did twenty-eight different TV interviews, finishing around 6 pm. I went back to my room and lay down for a while as I was feeling extremely tired after a long, hard day, plus of course I hadn't slept much the previous night. Fell asleep almost straight away and the next thing I knew it was 6 am.

Our flight out of New York for Los Angeles didn't leave until 6.20 pm, so I had all day in New York to myself. It poured with rain for most of the day and, as I can't think of anything worse than sightseeing in New York in the rain, I decided to stay in the hotel and catch up on my phone calls. Phil Stearns, the famous Penthouse photographer and a great friend, called me, as did Peter Ellis, the BBC television director who is after me for his Rose Medallion.

Today we all heard the news that Darth Vader has made the front cover of Time magazine, which I suppose is in some way a back-handed compliment to myself, although nobody from either Fox or Lucasfilm has come up to congratulate me on the fact that the character that I portrayed in the movie has just achieved one of the biggest publicity coups ever. Flight to LA long and boring. Even the film - The Coalminer's Daughter - didn't help much. Arrived in LA minus one of my bags and was taken straight to the Academy for a screening of Empire. The following day, Tuesday, started for me at 8.20 am with a TV interview with Steve Edwards.

9.30 to 10.30 am was taken up with a general press conference and the rest of the morning had us doing the 'round the table' interviews. Lunch was at the 20th Century Fox Executive diner after which Mark and I spent the whole afternoon doing TV interviews together.

14 May

Spoke with Russ Meyer first thing in the morning. He wants to see me for dinner tomorrow night and by all accounts it's my turn to pay. We see each other every time I come into LA and we usually alternate as to who picks up the tab.

Did my first interview at 8.20 am in the hotel's Presidential Suite and then from 9.30 to 1 pm attended a press conference at the Fox Studios where we entertained the newspaper, TV and the feature writers on Stage 21.

Did the Regis Philbin interview during our lunch and then it was back to Stage

21 to work till 6 pm doing all the interviews with the out of town press.

15 May
Have almost lost my voice - have done over eighty TV, radio and press interviews over the last four days. Thankfully, today is a rest day so I decided to take the limo out to do some sightseeing and shopping. Bought a load of presents for the kids and went to both the Golds and World Gyms. Russ came to see me in the evening with his long-time girlfriend - Kitten - who has the most outrageous figure and flaunts her huge breasts to everybody. We all went in my limo to a very nice Italian restaurant for dinner - I don't think the waiters will ever get over Kitten!

16 May
Today we will fly to Washington and we've just heard that we are staying in the notorious Watergate Hotel.

Left LA at 10.15 am and arrived Washington at 6.30 in the evening. I have never been on a flight where there have been so many different personalities. Not only did we have the entire Empire cast aboard, along with several production execs, but Art Garfunkel was also on board, as well as my all-time jazz singing idol - Ella Fitzgerald, who was sitting about two rows in front of me.

We were all up in first class and I was sitting next to a young man who very quickly engaged me in conversation. When the flight took off I had no idea as to who else was on the plane, but my fellow passenger started up a conversation by saying 'Wouldn't it be terrible if this plane was to crash, the world would lose so many celebrities'. I thought that this was an odd way to begin a conversation and, thinking primarily of myself, said 'Yes, it would'. But then thought, well just who else is on the plane besides the Star Wars crowd? My newfound friend promptly started pointing out quite a few American name personalities whom I must confess I 'd never heard of but who obviously meant a lot to him. He finished up the list by pointing out Ella Fitzgerald, at which point I went into raptures as I'd been a collector of all her records for over forty years.

'Would you like me to introduce you?' he asked.

'Too true,' said I. 'Do you know her?'

'No,' he said, 'but that doesn't matter.'

And with that he got up and went to sit in the empty seat next to Ella. After about five minutes he came back to say that she had said that she'd love to meet me but could it wait for a hour, as she was tired and wanted to have a sleep. About an hour or so later we saw that she was wide awake so the pair of us trotted over. He made the introductions and then left me in the company of my jazz idol.

For the next half hour I was in heaven, just sitting talking and listening to Ella and at the end of the conversation I produced my autograph book and asked her to sign it for me. I shall never forget her reply - 'Me sign for you? You're the famous one. You should be signing for me. Can I have a couple of autographed photos for my grandchildren?' And so we exchanged signatures and photos and I left her to try and get some more sleep, returning to my seat feeling both very humble and proud about the things she had said to me.

On arriving I learnt that Tony Daniels (C-3PO) was taken ill whilst in LA. He has a foot infection which has spread and he is now in hospital in Washington. Had dinner in the evening with my business manager and his wife at the hotel, one of the worst meals that I have ever had in my life! Charlie Webber of Lucasfilm hosted a reception in his hotel suite later in the evening that we all attended.

17 May

'EMPIRE STRIKES BACK' Premiere Day - Washington.

Picked up at 10.30 am to go to the Kennedy Centre for an 11 to 12 noon press call. Met up with Eunice Kennedy and was invited to have lunch with her and her daughter. At the lunch Eunice is very keen to hear about my charity work in the UK, especially my road safety work, and she wants to know if I would be interested in getting involved with her charity work in the US. The Special Olympics movement is her major charity push and she wanted to introduce me to her friends at the National Organisation on Disability - Alan Reich and Bernie Posner.

I eventually met up with Alan Reich and this led to me being asked if I would MC the annual general conference of the Presidents' Committee on Employment of the Handicapped. This I did for three years running, during which time I met some wonderful people from all over the Americas. The National Organisation on Disability also contacted me as a result of this lunch meeting with Eunice and asked me if I would like to tour the States, publicising the activities of the NOD. I did several tours on their behalf, until the money ran out and they could no longer afford to fund the tour expenses.

It was quite interesting how we attracted publicity to the campaign. Obviously the fact that I was Darth Vader caught the media's interest, but their major interest centred around the fact that I was the figurehead of the British government's Child Pedestrian Road Safety Campaign, and the media used to turn up in droves when they knew that Darth Vader, in the guise of the Green Cross Code Man, was going around the American schools, giving talks to American kids about how to be safe on the roads.

Back at home I am still very much involved with charity work. I am a member of the Stars Organisation for Spastics (who recently changed its name to SCOPE) and The Variety Club of Great Britain, I am a patron of a home for handicapped kids and I am closely associated with Arthritis Care and the Arthritis and Rheumatism Council. I am also a vice president of PHAB (the Physically Handicapped and Able Bodied Association) and have had great pleasure working with our Presidents, Rolf Harris and Ed Stewart.

The Washington premiere was organised specifically for the Special Olympics movement and the audience was full of kids with learning difficulties and their helpers. To say the film was well received would be the understatement of the year - they loved every minute of it. In the early part of the evening it was dinner at a very 'swish' restaurant, F Scotts, after which we all went to the Schrivers' house for a big party.

The Schrivers have a lovely home with spacious grounds which includes its own lake. Teddy Kennedy had been invited to the party and he was still reeling from the terrible press he was getting over the Chappaquiddick affair where Mary Jo Kopechne, one of the senate secretaries, drowned in the back of his car when it careered off a bridge and sank. All of the eligible females at the party were being jokingly warned that if Teddy wants you to go down to the lake - DON'T GO!!

At this very same party I made one of the biggest gaffes I have ever made, when I was introduced to Eunice's husband, Sergeant. I never realised that Sergeant was his Christian name and, when we met, almost the first thing that I blurted out was, 'How come you've been a sergeant for so long, how come you've never been promoted?' He looked at me askance, said something to the effect that 'Sergeant' was his Christian name and then politely excused himself. There's never a chasm handy when you need to leap into one, is there?

Arnold Schwarzenegger came to the premiere with Maria Schriver, whom he hadn't been going out with for very long, and whenever we meet he is always most complimentary about my work.

18 May
Went sightseeing in the limo around all the famous Washington monuments, then out to Dulles Airport to get the 1 pm Concorde flight back to London. Art Garfunkel came back to the UK with us.

19 May
British Premiere Week.

They have done it again. Would you believe it that Fox and Lucasfilm have just issued the press packs for the Empire Strikes Back without one jot of information about myself. Everybody else in the movie, from Harrison to R2-D2, have got potted biographies and photos in the kits - but there's absolutely nothing about myself. Complained all round about the omission and Syd Gannis, the head of PR, has promised to do something about it.

Of course, it's all very well to say you're sorry and that you'll rectify the situation, but the damage has been done by the omission. I know full well that the distributors are not going to put out new kits, or do a special release about myself a.k.a. Darth Vader. Wish I knew what was behind it all, so that at least I could make some attempt to rectify the problem that Lucasfilm has with me. I suspect that Lucasfilm are still trying to exert complete control over the Darth Vader character and are probably nonplussed by the fact that he has become the trilogy's cult figure.

All the way through both Star Wars and Empire, I have made it clear that I would be only too pleased to work with them in any capacity required. I want the movies to be as huge a success as possible. I honestly don't think they can stomach the idea that Darth Vader has become a cult figure of the series, usurping by far the interest shown in any of the three main characters who have the full backing of both the Fox and Lucasfilm publicity machines behind them.

Have been requested by George Lucas not to sign my Dave Prowse / Darth Vader autograph cards - Dave Prowse IS Darth Vader - 'Please leave the IS out,' I've been requested. My reply was that it is my name that is up on the credits of the film and that I am perfectly entitled to sign my pictures that way. They came back with the lame excuse that Darth Vader was an amalgam of three things, me playing the role, James Earl Jones over-dubbing my voice, and my stuntman Bob Anderson doing some of the light sabre work. To get all this in perspective, I am up on the screen credits as playing Darth Vader. When we did Star Wars, the fact is that I learned, and delivered, every word of Vader's dialogue. George Lucas continually assured me that although all the dialogue coming through the mask was not good enough from an audible quality point of view, we would be going into the recording studios to rerecord all the dialogue. Then, the dialogue would have the special effects added, such as dropping it a tone and adding the heavy breathing (which was, in fact, underwater breathing apparatus).

When filming work in the UK was completed, everybody chased back to the States to put the film together and to add all the special effects that weren't available outside the US.

It was at this point that James Earl Jones became the voice of Vader - and what a marvellous job he made of it - yet he specifically asked for no credit on the first film. Whilst I would have liked to have had the opportunity of recording all the Vader dialogue, I realise now, knowing the political and financial ramifications, that it would never have been possible but had it been so, I know I would have done an equally good job. Don't believe me? Next time you see me at a convention - ask me to 'do' my Vader voice. It's impressive - very impressive!

With the advent of Star Wars, I started appearing at sci fi conventions throughout the US and no matter where I was appearing there would always be some black guy in the audience shouting out – "Why aren't there any of our black brothers in *Star Wars*?" At the time I didn't know what the real answer was, so I used to fob them off with non-committal answers like, "Don't ask me ... ask Fox or Lucasfilm."

As far as the stuntman was concerned, when you have one of the principal parts in a movie - and especially if the part involves dangerous action - it is common practice to employ the services of a stunt performer. For the light sabre duels both Mark and I had our own stuntmen. As a principal in the movie (more so in Mark's case than mine, because he is seen facially) the film company cannot afford to have you injured. As you remember, Mark's injury to his thumb held up production for almost a week, and this involved a big insurance claim. The duelling sequence in Empire was going to involve working on high gantries and various stunt work, so it was decided that I should have a stunt double. Luckily for me, the film company employed the services of Bob Anderson, the British Fencing Coach, who, although being tall and slim, could double for me well at a distance, and because of his prowess as a swordsman his participation would only enhance the part of Vader.

What was unusual, however, about both *Empire* and *Return of the Jedi*, was that the stuntman started to get screen credits. Normally on a film all the stunt performers are lumped together, usually under the direction of a stunt co-ordinator, but now I am being told that Bob Anderson is to get special credit as Darth Vader's stunt double. Can you think of any other film where the stunt double is listed alongside that of the major artist? I certainly can't.

Bob Simmons, who co-ordinated all the stunts for the Bond movies, was only ever listed as stunt co-ordinator, although time and again he must have performed on behalf of Sean Connery or Roger Moore. I just saw the dubbing of my dialogue by James Earl Jones and the stuntman saga as just additional nails in the Dave Prowse/Darth Vader coffin. I still don't know what I've done (other than contribute) to incur their wrath, but situations like the ones I've already mentioned were to continue right through to the end of *Return of the Jedi* - without doubt the worst filming experience I've had, in a career spanning 25 years and over 20 movies.

Anyway, back to 20 May 1980 and the London Royal premiere of *Empire Strikes Back*.

After much sweating and many phone calls, my dress suit was ready. Made in Savile Row, it had navy blue trousers and a powder blue jacket with contrasting navy lapels - it really stood out amongst all the men's suits at the premiere. As to the ladies, Carrie Fisher turned up in a sheer, see-through top, which looked quite discreet until the photographers started flashing their cameras, when it became very revealing indeed!

We all had to be at the theatre for 7 pm and Princess Margaret turned up at 8 pm, at which point we were all lined up and introduced. This was my second meeting with the princess - the first time was when I was running the Harrods Keep Fit department, and she came in with her son Viscount Linley to look at bicycles. We'd chatted very briefly then, but I doubt very much if she would have put two and two together when I was introduced to her as 'Dave Prowse, Ma'am, he's Darth Vader - the evil villain of the film.'

After the film it was dinner and dancing at the famous Dorchester Hotel and the wonderful evening ended around 2.30 am. During the rest of the week I did lots of national press interviews, had a photo session at home with my wife, Norma, for People Magazine in the States and was then whisked off to do an autograph signing session at the Forbidden Planet Bookshop with Mark Hamill. Was supposed to be doing this one with Tony Daniels, but the infection he caught whilst in Washington has still not cleared up so Mark deputised, much to the fans' delight. The line was miles long and unfortunately we both had to leave before we'd even got halfway through.

Appeared on the Blue Peter children's' TV show and also had another wardrobe fitting for my part in The Rose Medallion. Rehearsals start next week and then we are all off to Cheddar, down in the West Country, the following week, to start filming. Had another photo session for the New York Star, who wanted pictures of me sniffing the roses in the local park - I think they're trying to show the tender side of Dave Prowse, who is not the evil character that he portrays on the screen.

1982 started off in the usual hectic way. I was already under contract for *Return of the Jedi* (which was originally called *Revenge of the Jedi*, but the powers that be decided that Jedi knights didn't resort to revenge, and thousands of dollars' worth of pre-film publicity material had to be scrapped) from mid-February. In the six weeks prior to that I did a whole variety of different promotional things.

I did the popular kids' television show *Tiswas*, and had a photo session in Hyde Park with Sebastian Coe, the former British world 1500-metres record holder, for the Special Olympics movement. I attended a charity function for underprivileged kids organised by the Taxi Drivers' Association, visited hospitals and did radio broadcasts - I was even having discussions with world-famous press agent Max Clifford, who at the time was very interested in handling my publicity affairs. However, at £500 a week I just could not afford him. Years later Max never seems to be out of the news, handling the press affairs of 'notorious celebrities', who hit the headlines for nefarious reasons and then go to the press to sell their stories. Government ministers, mistresses, sneaky royal photographers - anybody who has an interesting story to sell eventually ends up with Max. Max and I are still friends and I speak to him frequently when I need help with my arthritis charity publicity. He has a daughter who is an arthritis sufferer, so the charity is very close to his heart.

In January I was inducted into the Variety Club of Great Britain and even managed to fit in a weekend visit to Miami for a big sci fi convention before work started for me on *Return of the Jedi*, on Monday 8 February. The convention was held at The Holiday Inn, Fort Lauderdale, where I got a terrific reception and stayed up signing autographs on the Friday evening until 2.30 am. Met lots of old friends there, including Jeremy Bulloch (Boba Fett) who was guesting at the convention with his wife.

Friday 5 February was also a memorable day in aviation history, as Laker Airways - the cut-price British airline - went bust. On the Saturday when I left Miami I only just managed to get the last seat on the plane back to London, as the airport was crowded with British tourists who'd been left stranded in Miami by the Laker collapse. Whilst in Florida, I also paid a visit to the Space Museum, who urged me on enthusiastically when I went through the astronaut tests - I did 60 press-ups, 50 sit-ups and 8 chins and passed with flying colours!

Chapter Three
Return of the Jedi

Prior to the movie starting, we had a very enjoyable and relaxed get-together for all the cast and crew at the Elstree Studios restaurant, and we were all introduced to our new director, Richard Marquand. A nice social evening was had by everyone present, including George Lucas and Gary Kurtz, as well as most of the cast and crew.

Secrecy about what we were doing was the watchword. Only a few actual scripts were produced and these only went to key personnel - and that didn't include me, even though I had one of the major parts in the film. The rest of us had to put up with just our day-to-day pages, so we had no idea where the bits we were filming fitted into the overall story. I was kept completely in the dark, although I did realise that there were to be some characters in the film called Ewoks. I only discovered this because the first assistant director, Dave Tomblin, wanted to do a promo film for the lad who was playing the main Ewok, named Wicket, and had brought him - Warwick Davis - to my gym to have some gimmicky shots taken. The main photo was one where I am seen to be lifting a barbell, with Warwick hanging on one end instead of the barbell discs.

8 February
First day on the set of Return of the Jedi. Filmed right through to 6.15 in the evening, but only got through four lines of dialogue. It looks as though I'm only going to get individual pages again, i.e. no complete script.

Met up with the old crew and technicians who are virtually the same unit as before. George, Gary and Howard Kazanjian are all very much in evidence. Richard Marquand is very pleasant and has talked to me about wanting Vader's dialogue to be delivered in a very slow and deliberate way. Stunt co-ordinator Peter Diamond is on set and my stuntman - Bob Anderson - arrives from Canada tomorrow. Went back to the gym in the evening and had a good training session, bench pressing 420lbs and only just failing on 440lbs.

9 February
Rail strike on today, so the journey to Elstree took me nearly three hours. All that's

scheduled for today is a photo session with Mark Hamill. Photographer very slow. The session started at 10.30 am and we didn't finish until 4 pm. Mark brought his wife Marilu and the baby (who's now two and a half) with him and they all had their pictures taken with me in the full Darth Vader get-up.

Didn't work again until Friday the 19th when we did the scene of me coming out of the lift with Jerjearod on the big stage (No.6). It looks as though I'm going to be working most of next week.

22 February
Filmed on the big set with over 250 extras. Lots of walking to and from the spaceship. The ramps played havoc with my knees, as did all the kneeling before the Emperor.

23 February
8 am call at the studio. Took my daughter Rachel and her friend Michelle to the set so they could meet up with some of the stars. They thoroughly enjoyed themselves, especially after meeting Mark, Carrie and little Warwick.

24 February
Called in for 11 am but only to do an interview with the Star Wars fan magazine Bantha Tracks which took till lunchtime. Back to the studio at 2 pm for another photo session, this time with the stormtroopers and the black R2's, which took all afternoon. Eventually called on set to work at 5.45 pm to do more walking, this time with Mark, up and down the ramps and across the studio. Finished around 7 pm.

25 February
Worked all day in the Emperor's Chamber, a fantastic set on Stage 4. Got back to the gym for 7 pm to find a letter from Eunice Kennedy, requesting that I be her representative at a big Special Olympics dinner. Spoke with Tyne Tees TV, who are very interested in my ideas for a children's TV show.

26 February
Into the studio for 8 am to continue and complete yesterday's shots. Lots of walking to and from the lift. Bob Anderson got into his Darth Vader suit to do some work at the end of the day but they just didn't have the time.

28 February
The Department of Transport arranged for me to do a personal appearance at the Holiday on Ice Spectacular at Wembley. Appeared in my Green Cross Code outfit

and was very well received by a sell-out audience. Met up with the star of the show - former world ice skating champ, Robin Cousins, who is also a Bristol boy same as me, so we had plenty to chat about.

1 March

Pick-up shots on the VistaVision Camera. The set on Stage 4 (the Emperor's throne room) is huge and we have five or six scenes to be shot. These include the laser duel with Colin doubling for Mark and Bob for myself. Had lunch today at the local Chinese restaurant with Dave Tomblin, the first assistant director.

2 March

Have caught a terrible cold from somewhere - must be all the sweating in the Vader suit. Met up with Richard Marquand's mother, who was introduced to me on set.

3 March

Spent all day doing pick-up shots again. I think by now Richard must have covered the scene every possible way.

4 March

At the studio all day from 8.30 am but did absolutely nothing. My accountants came to see me at the studio (just an excuse for them to get onto the set and be introduced to all the personalities) and stayed for lunch. They left soon after, saying they didn't realise film work involved so much hanging around doing nothing and was so boring. When even accountants think your work is boring - you know there's something wrong!

5 March

At the studio for 8 am but didn't start work until 4.30 pm on scene 118. Released after three quarters of an hour with loads left to be done. By all accounts they are working with Yoda (Frank Oz) on Monday and Tuesday and Sir Alec Guinness (Obi-Wan) on Wednesday and Thursday, so it doesn't look as though I'll be back working until next Thursday at the earliest.

9 March

Have now been working on the set for several weeks and I am still no wiser as to what the film is all about, or where the bits I have filmed so far fit into the overall production.

Received a telephone call from someone called Paul Donovan, a journalist with the Daily Mail, one of the major British daily newspapers. He wants to come into the gym to do an interview. After some polite conversation, he asks me whether he could come and interview me for the newspaper about my film, TV and road safety career, to which I replied that I was interested in doing the interview, but warned him not to ask me any questions about Return of the Jedi because I didn't know anything. He replied to the effect that he wasn't interested in the film, it was the rest of my career and my Green Cross Code work that he wanted to know about, and he duly turned up that evening at my gym to do the interview.

After some chit-chat and some personal questions about my home life and family he came out with the dramatic statement - 'Of course, you're going to be killed off in this latest movie, aren't you?' You could have knocked me down with the proverbial feather. This was the first I'd heard of it, and I am certain if this was actually the case then I would have heard the news from George Lucas himself, or from Gary Kurtz the producer, or at the very least from the director Richard Marquand.

'You must be joking,' I said. 'They wouldn't kill off Darth Vader, he's become the major figure of the movies.'

'Oh yes they are, and not only that but they've already got another actor playing the dying Darth Vader, and they are already filming in another part of the studio so that you don't know what is going on.'

'I'm sorry but I cannot confirm or deny,' was all I could think of saying, but I was very shaken and upset by what I had just heard.

The reporter just continued – 'When you go into the Studio tomorrow check on the daily work sheets and you'll see that underneath your name is the name of an actor called Sebastian Shaw. He's playing the dying Darth Vader but on the call sheet he's listed as Annakin Skywalker.'

I thought the studio, or at least the producers and directors of the Star Wars saga, had been very underhanded with me on previous occasions (for instance when they overdubbed my voice without consulting or telling me, and again in Empire Strikes Back when I discovered that I was Luke Skywalker's father only when I went to see the film for the first time - there was nothing in my pages to this effect.) If they were now pulling a stunt like substituting another actor for me in what should have been the climax of an outstanding role, and which would have given me recognition for the last six years' work on the saga, then I would definitely have it out with George, Gary and Richard when next I worked.

After the reporter had left, I checked on the call sheets and sure enough there was Sebastian Shaw playing Annakin Skywalker working in another studio, whilst I was doing my Darth Vader bit elsewhere. To say that I was upset by what I had just been told would be the understatement of this book. I couldn't sleep that night for thinking about it; it played on my mind all the following day and I seethed throughout the entire hour and a half's drive up to the studio on the Thursday morning.

When I arrived, I was immediately told to report to George Lucas's office and I was confronted by George, who had that morning's copy of the *Daily Mail* in his hands. There on page 3, in bold headlines, it stated - DARTH VADER TO BE KILLED OFF IN THE NEXT STAR WARS MOVIE and a sub-heading which stated - IN AN EXCLUSIVE INTERVIEW WITH DAVE PROWSE. The story went on to tell the Annakin Skywalker story exactly as told to me by the reporter, but the article was written in such a way that it looked as though all the information had come from me.

No matter what I said, George wouldn't believe me. If he had only thought about the situation, he would have soon realised that it wasn't me who was giving information (or more likely selling it) to the press. I hadn't been working on the film all that long and had only received a few scraps of paper with my dialogue on for the scenes that we were going to do that day. So how could they possibly think that I had access to this privileged information?

In addition, we were forever getting lectures about not giving any news out about the films to the press and being warned of the consequences both to ourselves and to the film if other film-makers got wind of what we were doing, so there was no way that I would risk destroying the confidence that Lucasfilm had in me.

However, somebody, somewhere on the production, had access to this confidential information and was obviously selling it to the press and I unfortunately got saddled with the blame. No matter how much I denied their allegations, there was the evidence in the *Daily Mail* in black and white.

The result was that I was virtually ostracised from the film and the producer and director seemed to go out of their way not to use me. Of course, I was still under contract for the role of Darth Vader and for the next few weeks I endured one of the most humiliating film experiences I have ever had. To be honest, I eventually couldn't wait for it all to end. I used to sit around all day and watch them dress up my stuntman to do work that I should have been doing, and although I still got on well with the rest of the cast, my contact with the production people was practically nil. The director - Richard Marquand - was part of the ostracising group and never spoke to me again for the entire production.

I have had virtually no contact with George Lucas either since the end of *Jedi*, although I did try to see him once when I was touring America and was in San Raphael, the home of George's studio complex and his special effects company - Industrial Light and Magic. I went there with a friend, who was looking for a studio to do various film work for her and we were offered a conducted tour. At the first studio we were taken to, what were they doing? Why, none other than a TV commercial using the *Star Wars* characters. They had flown in both Tony Daniels and Peter Mayhew to reprise the C-3P0 and Chewbacca roles. They didn't need anybody for R2-D2 but dressed up an American extra to play my character - Darth Vader. It must have been a very embarrassing situation for George and he wouldn't leave the production suite to come down and meet me.

12 March
My chat yesterday with Howard Kazanjian has cleared the air a lot but I am still very concerned about the production team's attitude towards me.

Worked a little in the morning and got permission from Robert Watts the assistant producer to bring some guests onto the set. Took a friend and his two children on a conducted tour of the studio, eventually finishing up on Stage 4 where we did the bit where Vader gets his arm chopped off. Watts turned up and told me off for having guests on set! Then, to cap everything off, I was collared by Howard who told me the Daily Mail article had been picked up by the 'powers that be' in the States, and that everybody over there was unhappy regarding the publicity situation. On top of all this, Richard Marquand had a real go at me over my moves in the final scene - not a good day!!!

15-19 May
In some small way I am about to get the opportunity to redress my situation.

I am called into the studio early on the Monday morning and as usual I am hanging about the set only half into the Darth Vader costume, waiting to be called to do something, when all of a sudden I see them dressing my stuntman once again and also getting the Emperor's stuntman ready. I asked what was happening and was told that this scene didn't concern me, as it was where Darth Vader throws the Emperor to his death over the gantry or balcony.

I thought, this is going to be fun, as my stuntman, although a great swordsman, was neither the most athletic of people nor was he all that strong. Then, they bring in the guy who is going to stunt for Ian McDiarmid (the Emperor) and start attaching wires to his waist. The idea is for one very large, strong man to haul on the wire and the stuntman is supposed to go up in the air and land on my stuntman's outstretched arms. That was the theory, but in practice it just didn't work. The Emperor landed up everywhere but on top of Darth Vader, and after two days of trying they just gave up.

The following day, Wednesday, the stuntmen bring in what is known as a 'teeter board' which is nothing more that a seesaw. Now, the theory is that the Emperor's stuntman stands on the bottom of the seesaw whilst somebody heavier jumps from a height onto the top end. As a result the man at the bottom end is catapulted skywards, and in all good circus and variety acts lands on top of his partner's hands, which are held aloft, waiting. Again, there is a big difference between theory and practice and after another two days of the two stuntmen falling all over the place, the teeter board had to be dispensed with, too.

This scenario had now gone on for over four and a half days, had cost the production a small fortune and they were still no nearer getting it completed. I then went over to the first assistant director and said that all that it needed was for me to be given the Emperor across my chest, holding him as I would a barbell. As he wasn't very heavy, on the given cue, I would press him to arm's length, then walk with him towards the balcony and toss him over.

"Do you think you could do that?" they asked.

"Of course I can, or I wouldn't have suggested it," says I.

"Right, first thing Monday morning we shoot the scene."

Over the weekend of 20-21 May I did something to my right knee, which caused it to swell up like a balloon, and became very painful. I went to the London Clinic for Sports Injuries, where they aspirated the knee joint, strapped it up and put me on crutches. It was even more painful on the Sunday and I got a note from my doctor to go to the casualty department of Guys Hospital where they aspirated it again, taking off loads of fluid. I then had to get down to my gym to do some filming with Warwick Davis for the promotional film Dave Tomblin is making. We finished around 7 pm.

Was still in a lot of pain with my knee on the Monday morning when I had to turn up at the studio, but there was no way that anything was going to stop me doing the stunt I'd promised to do. I was still on crutches, my knee was killing me just with the pressure of walking, but I got to my dressing room, put on the first half of the Vader suit (trousers, t-shirt, boots and shin guards) and then hobbled onto the set. The scene was all set, the stuntmen had their boxes and mattresses in position, the lighting cameraman had done his stuff, so all I had to do was to get my dresser to get me into the rest of the suit. Then I had to shut out the pain for long enough to do the throw.

Of course, by this time it was painfully obvious to everybody that I was having great difficulty walking, let alone doing any stunt work, and the first assistant, Dave Tomblin, said I could call it off if I wanted to. There was no way that I was going to call off the stunt, but I did say that I would like to do it with only one step towards the balcony, before making the throw. This was fine with everybody and on the "action" call the Emperor was lifted up across my chest. I slowly pressed him out to arm's length, took one step towards the balcony rail and then tossed the stuntman over.

We had just done in one take what they had been trying to do for a solid week. If they'd involved me in the first place, instead of shutting me out, I would have saved them hundreds of thousands of pounds.

I felt very proud of myself that day but it didn't make any difference, as neither Lucas nor Marquand ever spoke to me again.

23 May
Am at the studio for 10 am but they are shooting the scene where Vader does a backflip down the stairs, which will be done by another stunt artist. We move to Stage 3 in the afternoon.

24 May
Spent all day at the studio working through from 8 am to 7 pm. Did the shot of Vader coming out of the lift in the redwood forest. Richard delivered the Vader dialogue. Knee getting better, and I managed to get some anti-inflammatory drugs from the studio doctor. George Lucas goes home tomorrow and brought in a going-away cake. I presented him with copies of my book and road safety record for his kids.

Chapter Four
Star Wars - Questions and Answers

Having travelled the world appearing at sci fi conventions for the last 25 years, here is a list of the most frequently asked questions, which I answer to the best of my knowledge.

Q. (The most frequently asked question) *How hot was it in the suit?*
A. Baking. The basis of the suit was quilted leather and added on were the two capes, fibreglass breastplate and epaulettes, leather gloves, plastic shin guards, a leather boxer's protector plus all the electrical gadgets. On top of this you have the helmet and mask and knee-high leather boots. We filmed Star Wars during one of the hottest summers Britain has ever experienced (1976) and I used to sweat buckets.

Q. *How well could you see out of the mask?*
A. Originally the mask had grey lenses in the eyepieces, which made vision quite good but, as the film progressed, the cameraman kept saying that he could see my eyes flickering inside the mask. Amber lenses replaced the grey ones, but one could still see eye movements. A darker amber lens (which actually made seeing very difficult) was eventually inserted and this cured the problem.

Q. *What was breathing like inside the mask?*
A. To start with, it was okay, but as the films went on the cameraman started picking up movements of my mouth when I was delivering Darth's dialogue through the two triangular vents at the front of the mask. The first thing they did was to black the whole of my face up, as they thought black against the black inside of the mask wouldn't show, but that still didn't do the trick, so they covered the two triangular vents with black gauze. This didn't affect my breathing too much, but I used the lower of the two vents to find my way exactly to my camera-focusing marks. With this lower vision vent now covered, I had to count the number of steps that it was going to take me to get to my mark, and try to remember my lines and deliver them in the right place - no mean feat.

Q. How heavy was Darth Vader's outfit?
A. It comprised 15 different pieces and weighed a total of about 30lb (15kg).

Q. What did you wear under the suit?
A. Just swimming trunks and a t-shirt to soak up all the sweat.

Q. Could you go to the bathroom okay?
A. I had to remove the codpiece and there was a fly in the trousers, so I could go for a pee anytime. If it was anything more 'serious', I had to time my visits to the toilet when I was only wearing part of the suit, i.e. when I was waiting around for filming to start on my next scene.

Q. How long did it take you to get in or out of the suit?
A. Usually about 15 minutes. I had a dresser who used to look after me all the time and not only did he help me with the dressing and undressing, he also used to keep the helmet and costume pristine.

Q. How tall was Darth Vader?
A. When I did Vader I was 6ft 7in (2m) tall and weighed in at about 270-280lb (around 125kg). Wearing the boots, helmet and mask took my height to about 7ft.

Q. What was the writing on Darth's chest controls?
A. Upside-down Hebrew (I've no idea what it read).

Q. Did you really lift that guard up with one hand before choking him?
A. No. The scene consisted of three shots. In the first we stood the guard on a chair and got him to come down in height by bending his knees. I then put my hand around his throat and made to lift him and all he did was to straighten his legs. This shot was filmed from the waist upwards. In the second shot I lifted the guard bodily off the ground, and the scene was shot from the waist down so that you could see his feet dangling in the air. In the third shot we substituted a stuntman for the guard and stood him on a low table, and all I did was throw him off the table into the wall. Simply done but very impressive.

Q. Did all the principal actors have their own stuntmen?
A. Yes. We had a stunt arranger for the trilogy - Peter Diamond - and it was his job to arrange all the necessary stunt work and employ stunt

doubles for everyone who needed one. Lots of actors are proud of the fact that they do their own stunts, but as far as the film company is concerned they're far happier when stunt doubles are being used - they're expendable; your main actors don't get injured, thus holding the production up, plus they make the actor look that much better. In the trilogy Bob Anderson, the former British fencing coach, did some of the light sabre duels for me. Mark had his stuntman, as did Ian McDiarmid who played the Emperor Palpatine (it was the stuntman I threw off the gantry - they couldn't get a stuntman for me for that scene, but it was an easy one for me anyway).

Q. How was Obi-Wan Kenobi made to disappear?
A. The miraculous disappearance of Obi-Wan Kenobi relied little on painstaking attention to artistic detail and even less on state-of-the-art special effects. In fact, it was all down to a few feet of sewing thread.
First, with Obi-Wan in full costume, he was filmed in his final position at the moment my light sabre was about to strike the fatal blow. Then, with Sir Alec safely out of the way and his Obi-Wan costume suspended by the vital length of thread, filming resumed and the mortal blow was duly delivered, snapping the thread and sending the empty costume to the floor. No trapdoors, no mirrors and no fancy effects, just a simple trick and a great result.

Q. What were all the other characters working on the three movies like, and what were they like to work with?
A. The best way to answer this question is to give you 'thumbnail' portraits of how they came over to me at the time. Here goes:

Mark Hamill
A very likeable, all-American boy, full of enthusiasm and, in my opinion, a great actor and a superb voice-over artist.

Harrison Ford
A likeable rogue. At the time I wouldn't have put him in the same class as Mark, although I liked what he did on screen. The Han Solo role was almost typecasting and, if I'd been 20 years younger, a part I would love to have played myself.

Carrie Fisher
This was my second time working with Carrie. She came to the UK in

1974 with her mother, Debbie Reynolds, who was starring at the London Palladium. At the time she was a very vulnerable 15 year old who had just one song to sing in the show. *Star Wars* was her first major film break and she was a very nervous actress working alongside the 'greats' like Sir Alec Guinness and Peter Cushing. Peter took her under his protective wing and his encouragement was part of the reason for the high standard of Carrie's performance as Princess Leia. I really enjoyed working with her the second time around.

George Lucas

Whilst I'm the first one to admire George's work on the *Star Wars* trilogy, the biggest compliment that I can give him is that working with him is similar to working with Stanley Kubrick - one is working with a cinematic genius. He employs the very best of technicians and actors - people he knows can give him what he wants. As with Stanley, I got the impression that the end product was the all-important thing, and that everything - from costumes to make-up to special effects to sound to lighting to the actors acting their hearts out - were all integral parts that he, as the director, brought together.

He employed you to do your job and, provided he was happy with what you did, there was absolutely no interference. We used to talk occasionally on a social level, but not once did he ever question the way I was playing Vader, which to some extent I appreciated. I did, however, get the impression that he was a quiet, shy, introverted individual whom you would love to have seen come out of his shell occasionally. George and his *Star Wars* saga have achieved their rightful place in cinematic history, and I feel very proud to be one small part of it and to be able to say that I've actually worked with George.

Irving Kershner

Irving directed *The Empire Strikes Back*, and the difference between the two directors' styles was immense. At the very outset he said to me that *Empire* was going to be the "thinking man's Vader" and that my role was going to be a lot more thought provoking. He would sit down with me, go over the script and explain everything in detail - where I was coming from, what I should be thinking about, my motivation for my action and just about everything he could think of to prepare me for the coming scene.

Another of Kersh's quirks on *Empire* was that Darth always had to be pristine, with the helmet glistening and the cape well brushed. He never seemed to be worried about the constrictions of time and would shoot and shoot a scene till he got exactly what he wanted, and in the end he produced what to me was the best of the first three *Star Wars* movies.

Maybe it didn't have the excitement and brashness of *Star Wars*, and of course the film ended with the audience clamouring for more, knowing full well that they were going to have to wait three years to see Han Solo's predicament resolved. Perhaps it didn't take as much money at the box office as *Star Wars*, but to me it will always be one of my favourite work experiences in the film business.

Billy Dee Williams

Another likeable rogue. I didn't have a lot to do with him on the set, but I was able to give both him and Harrison training advice when they had a barbell set delivered to the studio. I met up with him again a few years ago when he, Carrie and myself launched the new *Star Wars* videos in London. We met briefly on stage and exchanged pleasantries, but he left the launch early before we could say very much. I see him now occasionally on TV commercials for the Psychic Channel here in the States.

Gary Kurtz

Gary was George's co-producer on *Star Wars* and was a very quiet, sombre figure when he came on the set. He was married with a young family and rented a big house with plenty of grounds near Pinewood Studios, where we all used to get invited to the occasional 'family' party. I never really got to know him socially all that well, but he was always very pleasant to deal with or work with, on the odd occasions that he used to handle second unit direction.

He came to see me some time after *Star Wars* came out, when I was in Hollywood visiting the 20th Century Fox studios. We were having breakfast together and I said to him, "Just why didn't you use my voice for the voice of Vader?" to which he replied that they'd decided that they just couldn't play Darth with my English accent. (I had already heard otherwise from the publicity office of 20th Century Fox.) I know I have a colloquial accent from Bristol, and even Harrison used to nickname me 'Darth Farmer', but I've heard snippets of myself delivering the Vader dialogue and I can sound very much like James Earl Jones when I want to.

James Earl Jones

We've never met, but I'd love to organise a meeting either at a convention or on a TV programme where we can just natter together. He's always very complimentary of my acting role of Darth, just as I am of the voice-over job he did. But I still think that, given the opportunity, I could have delivered an acceptable Darth Vader voice.

R2-D2 - Kenny Baker

Just the opposite of his screen counterpart C-3PO, Kenny is one of the nicest guys you could wish to meet and, by his own admission, "one of the luckiest dwarfs in the world". He's a great comedian, first-class musician (playing harmonica and vibes) and one of the world's great vodka tonic drinkers. To do shows with Kenny is always a pleasure and he certainly knows how to keep us all amused. Besides working together on the convention circuit we also see each other regularly socially.

Chewbacca - Peter Mayhew

I always say that Peter ought to be eternally grateful that I've been around, as the two major jobs he's had in the 'business' have both been indirectly through me. Peter is a 7ft 4in giant of a man, gregarious for most of the time but with a quick and active wit when the mood takes him. He can also be the most cantankerous of people and sometimes embarrasses the hell out of me when he gets in one of his moods. He doesn't suffer fools easily, and although we get on well together I always feel that I'm treading on a minefield when I want to discuss anything with him - you never know what kind of reaction you're going to get. I think Peter made a tremendous job of Chewbacca, and as the Wookiee he is one of the most popular characters on the convention scene. We get on well and all the *Star Wars* gang were thrilled for him when he was awarded a lifetime achievement award by MTV.

The two jobs that Peter got through me were *Sinbad and the Eye of the Tiger* and, of course, the *Star Wars* trilogy. I was cast to play the minotaur in the *Sinbad* film and, although I'd met up with special effects genius Ray Harryhausen and been to see the costumiers, my agent was still haggling over the money and I was refusing to go out to Spain until a satisfactory deal had been reached. After meeting up with Ray at his house several weeks went by and I contacted my agent to see what was happening. She told me that the production company had left for Spain and because I was being adamant about wanting more money they had found one of the tallest men in Great Britain - Peter - and gone off to Spain with him.

Peter was at the time a hospital porter and an article appeared in the national press to the effect that Peter was the tallest hospital porter in Great Britain. The producer of the movie - Andy Donnelli - read the article and got in touch with Peter, who promptly became an ex hospital porter, and the rest is history.

When *Star Wars* came up, George Lucas asked me to consider one of two roles in the film - Chewbacca or Darth Vader. I turned Chewie down, as I'd made a decision that I didn't want to do any more 'creature' type roles, and accepted the role of Darth. Peter was contacted, and as soon as they saw this 7ft 4in gangling giant of a man they realised they had the perfect Chewbacca.

Boba Fett - Jeremy Bulloch

Jeremy and I go back many years. He used to be part of a group of actors who used to train at my gymnasium, which in Jeremy's case was a vain attempt to get fit. Jeremy is steeped in the acting profession, having been to stage school as a youngster, and has been doing primarily stage and TV work all his life. He is a fine actor with a great sense of humour, and he's a pleasure to work with. He finds it ironic that after over 40 years of acting he has suddenly found fame and fortune playing Boba Fett, a character who was only in three movies for a total of four minutes, had only four lines of dialogue, and all those were over-dubbed by a voice-over specialist. That's show business, folks!

Sir Alec Guinness

Sir Alec was always very pleasant, most polite and fitted in with whatever was asked of him. After *Star Wars* finished in 1976/77 we did not come across each other again for over 20 years, when I went to see him give a talk at the National Theatre, where he was launching one book and relaunching another.

He did a question and answer session during the talk and I was most surprised that he wouldn't answer any questions at all about *Star Wars*, dismissing the whole subject with a statement to the effect that the film was a director's medium and as an actor one didn't have any control over one's contribution to the film - the director could do absolutely anything he wanted with your performance!

After his talk he did an autograph-signing session and the audience was told that he would only sign his own books and that all one would get would be the signature 'Alec Guinness'. I'd brought with me a photo of the two of us taken during the *Star Wars* shooting, which showed me standing beside him looking very happy and friendly, and I thought it would be nice if he would dedicate it to me. When I got to the autograph line, it was miles long and stretched all around the auditorium and down the stairs to the ground floor, so I went with my photo and stood directly behind where Sir Alec was signing, accompanied by a lady assistant from the publishing company.

Without disturbing Sir Alec I showed my photo to the lady and said that Sir Alec and I had worked together on *Star Wars* and that I'd very much like to say hello and get my photo signed. She promptly took the photo from me and placed it face downwards on the table. After about ten minutes of waiting behind the table Sir Alec eventually looked up and fortunately recognised me. "How are you, dear boy? Working?" I replied that I was very busy and asked if he was going to have any involvement in the new movies. "No," he said. "They rang me the other day and wanted to know the colour of my eyes! I told them they had enough footage of my eyes from 1976 and put the receiver down on them." With that, he turned back around and continued autographing his books. I thought, I'm obviously not going to get my picture signed this way, so I got the photo back and proceeded to wait at the end of the line, which was about two hours long. When I finally got to Sir Alec I said, "Would you do me a great favour and sign the photo 'To Darth, Best Wishes, Alec Guinness'." He took the photo off me and signed it in red ink with his fountain pen "Alec Guinness". Then, just as I was about to take the photo from him, he pulled it back and added "Best Wishes" and promptly returned the photo to me before being ushered out of the building. So I gave up on the idea of getting "To Darth" on the photo.

An autograph dealer friend has for years been asking me to supply copies of this Alec Guinness/Dave Prowse photo. I normally sign it "Dave Prowse is Darth Vader", whereupon it gets sent to Alec's home in Hampshire and he signs it, with a fountain pen and usually in red ink, with his customary "Alec Guinness". Not long before Alec died, my friend asked me to sign yet another batch of photos, but this time he asked if I would inscribe the photos with an apt line from the movie. Phrases like "May the force be with You", "The force is strong in you" and "Beware the power of the dark side" all sprang to mind, but then I remembered the line I spoke during the light sabre battle in Star Wars, just before I killed him off (or whatever you do to Jedi knights!) So, with this flash of inspiration, I signed several photos with the words "Your powers are weak, old man", along with my customary signature "Darth Vader - Dave Prowse". The balance of the photos, probably about another half dozen, were signed, "Dave Prowse is Darth Vader".

I don't know whether we caught Alec at a bad time or what. All the photos were returned duly signed, but on the ones where I'd signed "Dave Prowse is Darth Vader" he'd written, "Alec Guinness is Alec Guinness", and on the others he'd written "Why don't you take that stupid black mask off and show us who you really are?"

I sincerely hope that when the photos were sent to him his real powers weren't diminishing and that he realised that I wasn't alluding to anything personal, just quoting a line from the film. The autographed photos are now real collectors' pieces.

Peter Cushing

No matter whom you talk to within show business, the person who all other actors hold in the highest esteem is Peter. I've had the pleasure of working with him twice - on *Frankenstein and the Monster from Hell* and then on *Star Wars*. I also took part in the *This Is Your Life* tribute to him, and finally did one of the last interviews with him just before he died. He was the consummate 'gentleman actor', considerate to a fault and a pleasure to work with. I went to his funeral and the dedication service that was held in his honour at the actors' church, St Paul's in the centre of London's West End.

I'll always remember working with him on *Monster from Hell*. We did a great stunt shot together, which involved Peter taking a flying leap to land across my shoulders - a stunt for which everybody on the set stopped work and applauded. When we were working on *Star Wars* I watched him take young Carrie Fisher under his professional wing, to give her a crash course in how to hold your own on set. He was the ultimate pro, loved by all, a credit to the profession, and somebody I'm very proud to have been associated with.

Chapter Five
Outfoxed at the Premiere

Although nobody ever advised me officially, it had become general knowledge that George Lucas had decided to relaunch the trilogy in an enhanced version. The film negative had been cleaned up, the sound system improved, plus new footage (some which had been shot and not used when the films were first made all those years ago) had been specially shot using available Lucasfilm personnel. New special effects were also added, all of which gave George the satisfaction of producing what he regarded as the 'finished and complete version' of *Star Wars*.

I had been asked if I would attend a charity premiere at a provincial London cinema in aid of the Marie Curie Cancer Appeal (which I unfortunately couldn't attend, due to my convention commitments in the States), so, with no other official information to hand, I continued accepting bookings to do personal appearances and sci fi conventions all across America.

Two of my contractual agreements were to appear at conventions in Baltimore on 15 and 16 March and Detroit the following weekend. You can imagine my consternation when a couple of days prior to the Baltimore event I received an 'official' letter from 20th Century Fox stating that "Mr George Lucas and Mr Rick McCallum request the pleasure of your company at the premiere in London on the evening of the 20th March, which is being organised on behalf of the Prince's Trust.

HRH Prince Charles will be attending and has expressed a desire to meet the members of the *Star Wars* cast."

I hadn't seen or had any contact with George over the preceding 15 years and I'd never met Rick McCallum, so I was both pleased and excited by their kind invitation. I'd met Prince Charles years previously, when I was doing my road safety work with the kids. However, charming man though he is, the prospect of glad-handing the Prince wasn't as much of a turn-on as meeting up with George and Rick.

Pulling out of either of the conventions I was contracted to would have meant letting down friends and business colleagues by the score, not to mention the fans, many of whom travel hundreds, sometimes thousands of miles to attend these functions. However, with the premiere falling on the Thursday night, right between the two conventions, it was theoretically possible for me to keep everyone happy. I now had the logistical problem of organising a whistle-stop visit to London.

In fact, I did have a return ticket to Heathrow, which I could use to get me to the premiere, but when I tried to make arrangements to get back to Detroit on the Friday every airline I called told me their flights were full. I had heard that 20th Century Fox were flying Mark Hamill and his wife over from Los Angeles, likewise Carrie Fisher - which was going to cost the company approximately £5,000 per ticket - so I thought, why not get the publicity people from Fox to use their influence to get me a one-way economy ticket back to Detroit on the Friday? I didn't want or ask them to pay for the ticket, since I was quite prepared to do this for myself. All I wanted was for them to arrange a one-way flight so that I could attend the premiere with my wife Norma, and then honour my contract with the Detroit convention organisers who had invested considerably in my appearance.

I called the publicity office of 20th Century Fox in London well in advance of the premiere, only to be told, "Arranging a ticket for you is not within our budget". Needless to say, I was extremely disappointed that they wouldn't do anything, not even make a phone call on my behalf. In the end, honouring a contract or commitment was much more important to me than attending a Royal Premiere or publicity function, no matter whose names were on the invite, so consequently I stayed on in America. Thus, on the Thursday night, when I would have liked to have been in London with all my *Star Wars* colleagues, and Prince Charles of course, I was actually flying into Detroit to perform at one of the best and busiest appearances I've ever been involved in.

As a sequel to all this, I decided to call Lucasfilm in California to apologise to George and Rick for not appearing, only to be told by some receptionist that she'd never heard of Rick McCallum - and he's only No. 2 in the world's most famous film production company!

From what I can gather, the premiere in London was a huge success, with Mark Hamill, Kenny Baker (R2-D2) Peter Mayhew (Chewbacca) and Tony Daniels (C-3PO) all attending. Carrie Fisher didn't show up, which no doubt pleased 20th Century Fox, as without having to fork out for her ticket to London their budget was that much healthier.

And Finally ...
Back in October 1996 a friend of mine from San Rafael, California, got

in touch with me to ask if I'd heard that George Lucas was having problems with the Marin County officials over an application that he was making to have 3,000 acres of designated agricultural land converted to industrial use, so that he could expand his film-making activities and bring all his facilities under one roof. The new complex would obviously attract film talent from all over the world, bring employment into the already prosperous Marin County and establish Marin as one of the world's finest film capitals.

In 1978 I had been made an Honorary Citizen of Marin County by the board of supervisors, and it was thought that if I made an appeal on George's behalf this might possibly influence the legislature into granting George the permissions he required.

The following is the text of the letter I sent to George, offering my help:

7 November, 1996

Hello George,

It's been a long time since we've been in contact with each other (since 1983 in fact), but I heard recently that some moral support might possibly help you in your desire to expand your Lucasfilm enterprise and below is my letter to the Marin County Legislature, which unfortunately did not get read out at the recent hearing. If you like the gist of the text I would be quite happy to send it both to the Legislature and the Marin County and the San Francisco Press if you think it would help your cause:

Over eighteen years ago I stood in the Marin Board of Supervisors Chambers as Supervisor Barbara Boxer handed me a very special document. The document was signed by each of the Marin Board of Supervisors and bestowed on me the privilege of an honorary citizenship of your great County in respect of my work as Darth Vader in the Star Wars trilogy and my International Charity involvements. I have known George Lucas for over 20 years and I am constantly in awe of his creativity and his genius. Am I opposed to the expansion or a proponent? I am neither. I am for the highest good of all and I have great confidence in all of you to find that place.

I am indeed honoured to be counted a citizen amongst you,

With sincere regards,

Dave Prowse.

It was sent with a covering letter to Jane Bey, George's personal secretary, which stated:

Enclosed please find a letter which I would like you to forward on to George. It is self-explanatory. As an Honorary Citizen of Marin County I just wanted to lend my support to his expansion plans. Please advise if I can be of any further help. My regards to you all at 'The Ranch'. Am looking forward to a great involvement with you all in the forthcoming Star Wars years.
Sincerely,
Dave.

I never even received an acknowledgement from either George, Jane or anybody at Lucasfilm, but soon afterwards George received the planning permissions he required from the Marin County State Legislature.

Chapter Six
The Beginning

I was born in 1935, a 10lb bouncing boy and a new brother for my three-year-old sister, Jeanne. Brother Bob followed in September 1938.

My family lived in a private house in Southmead, in an area abutting an established council estate, and the City of Bristol was in the process of developing a huge new estate of council houses adjacent to the old one. Our living accommodation was a three-bedroomed 'modern' (for the late '30s and early '40s) terraced house on one of the main roads leading out of Bristol towards the Bristol Aeroplane Company (BAC) and onwards to the wilds of Gloucester.

The area had plenty of fields and farmland, and a major local farmer - Captain Bethel - owned many riding horses that roamed and grazed there. Nearby was the Filton Golf Course, where I would later work as a caddy, and it had one of the finest newting ponds to be found for miles. In addition, not far away was the BAC's sports ground, where one could watch football and cricket almost at leisure. Although it was tied to the company and, I suppose, only really for the use of the employees, the public must have had some form of access as all and sundry used the place to walk their dogs. The local Sea Scouts troop occupied one corner next to the tennis courts and it was also the favourite haunt of model aeroplane flyers.

When I was about three years old, just before my brother Bob was born, my parents had moved to Southmead from an older part of Bristol - Easton - where they had run a drapery shop in Bannerman Road. Mum (Gladys) and Dad (Charlie) were a happy-go-lucky couple. Neither of them was business minded and what little money came in got frittered away on day-to-day living, plus ample supplies of whisky, Dad's favourite tipple. The drapery business eventually failed and they sold up and decided to move. The Southmead house purchase was financed by a mortgage, for the then substantial sum of £500, but my father, not being the greatest financial wizard, neglected to invest in life assurance cover.

Dad was a tinsmith (sheet metal worker) at the BAC, building the fighters for which the BAC became world famous - including the

Beaufighter, which featured so prominently in the Second World War. Employment at the BAC was regarded as highly prestigious among the working classes, very much like working on the docks, where whole families would labour together - fathers, sons, brothers, cousins and wives - with a sense of accomplishment. I don't remember much about my dad, other than that I used to wait outside the house at the age of three or four, watching for him to come cycling home either for lunch or after work in the evening, and as soon as I saw him coming I would run up the road to greet him and get a lift back to the house on the crossbar of his bike. He was also a keen sportsman and played football for the works team, and I do remember going to watch him train and play when I was about five years old.

My mum and dad were extremely happy together. However, when Bob was barely a toddler, Jeanne was at the local junior school and I was about to start in the infants, disaster struck.

In 1940 my dad's whisky-drinking habit caught up with him and he developed a duodenal ulcer. It was causing him a lot of pain and discomfort, so it was arranged for him to be admitted to Southmead Hospital to have the ulcer removed. It was supposed to be a routine operation - two weeks in hospital and then back home to convalesce. He seemed happy and cheerful and I received regular letters from him telling me that I had to be a good boy and look after mum, Jeanne and Bobby. My mum wasn't informed of any complications and my dad was due to come home a couple of days after the stitches had been removed. I was never told exactly what happened, except that the stitches had burst and my dad had died within hours, presumably due to a huge loss of blood.

My mother was devastated by my dad's death. Not only had she lost the love of her life, but also she had been left with three young children, aged eight, five, and two, and with no means of support. Worse still, no insurance policy was in place to cover his death and settle the mortgage repayments. My dad had some great friends at work, many of whom rallied round to help and organise collections. One friend in particular, Harry Mortimer, took it upon himself to help my mother in any way he could. Appreciated as it was, however, their assistance was nowhere near enough to extricate my mum from the financial hole in which she now found herself. Full-time work couldn't be considered with three young kids to look after, so she cashed in on the only asset she had - the house - and decided to take in lodgers or boarders to ease our plight. My mum arranged for notices to be placed in the BAC's apprentices club, The

Aces, and very soon our house seemed to be permanently occupied by a succession of apprentices, all in need of a home away from home. They were mostly teenagers, who had come from all over the country looking for employment and a career qualification with the BAC. Three or four apprentices stayed in the house at any one time, so sleeping arrangements were very tight and, of course, my mother had to do everything for the boarders, including cooking their meals, washing and ironing. Teenagers were just as dependent back then as they are today. Mum worked really hard to make the lads feel at home, and it was testimony to her success that they never seemed to want to leave and kept in touch for years after their apprenticeships had been completed.

At the time I was born, life was good, but it would change radically within a few years when Hitler declared war in 1939 and the whole of Europe got sucked in. The BAC was turned over completely to the war effort and Bristol, in particular the Filton area, became the regular target of German bombers. Consequently, many of the kids in the area were evacuated out into the rural countryside away from the danger, and we were no exception. Although Jeanne went quite happily, I screamed like mad at the time of separation from my mum and dad, so it was decided that I could continue living in close proximity to the BAC with my mum, dad and baby Bob, who was born the very month the war started.

Every home had an air-raid shelter, which was either a brick-built outhouse complete with a blast wall in front of the entrance, or an Anderson shelter, which provided more underground cover. Bristol took a heavy pounding from the German bombers and the entire centre of town was reduced to rubble. Strangely, the bombers never managed to obliterate their main target, the BAC. Only one stray bomb landed on an air-raid shelter within the factory and the loss of life was restricted to just one poor soul. Although the houses where we lived never received a direct hit from the bombing, various incendiary bombs did land in the allotments at the back of the house, causing great excitement for the local kids, who went searching for souvenirs of bomb case remnants and shrapnel.

Apart from rationing, I can't recall being unduly affected by the war. All food was rationed and the allowances for essentials such as butter, milk, cheese, tea, etc., were small. For me the worst part was that sweets were rationed and I was only able to have a couple of quarter-pound bags of sweets each month. Gas masks were also issued to everybody just in case there was a gas attack, but the only time I wore it was to give my young brother a fright!

At school I had no academic ambitions whatsoever, given my physical orientation, and my educational journey was unremarkable from the local infants school to the secondary modern school, both on Fonthill Road, in a less than salubrious area of Southmead in Bristol.

When I eventually progressed from infant to junior school I started attracting attention as a schoolboy athlete, my forte being sprinting. I was a big kid, tall and rangy, but I could run like the wind and was easily the fastest boy in the school. At the age of 12 I joined the Westbury Harriers Athletic Club, where I was able to compete and train with more mature athletes. On several occasions I had the pleasure of training with Mary Bignal, who eventually became Mary Rand, our 1964 Olympic Gold Medallist. I was winning all sorts of local events - 100 yards, 220 yards, long jump, high jump and hurdles - and athletics very quickly became an all-consuming passion. Fortunately, the junior school was very supportive, as all the wins I achieved gained good publicity for the school.

My rapid growth and training needed fuelling and I was the bane of my mother's life, as I was always hungry and would eat anything and everything I could lay my hands on. It was not unusual for me to come home from school and eat a whole loaf of bread with marmalade. Afterwards, I would be eagerly awaiting the evening meal and would wolf that down, polishing off anything that was left by the family or the lodgers. I would then head off to my mate's house and clean up any leftovers there. Despite all the eating, however, I never became fat; I simply extended in the other direction and before my thirteenth birthday had reached the grand height of 5ft 9in.

At this time, besides athletics, I had a passion for racehorses. I used to think (and still do) that they were the most beautiful animals in all the world and I kept scrapbooks full of racehorse pictures that I'd cut out of magazines and newspapers. I dreamed that, at some stage in my life, I'd be able to work with horses. I was a great follower of the famous jockeys of the day, like Gordon Richards, Ken Gethin, Charlie Smirke and the Smith brothers.

To my surprise, I was deemed one of the brighter kids in the school and was appointed as head boy. I took the 11+ scholarship examination but failed, much to my teachers' disappointment, although I was apparently borderline. As a result, I was asked to go for a selection interview, which I attended accompanied by my mother. I was dressed to kill in a brand new grey flannel suit with long trousers, and at 5ft 9in tall and weighing over 10 stone I was bigger and heavier than most of the adjudication panel. It all seemed to be going well until I was asked what I'd like do as a career, and I replied that I'd love to become a jockey. Needless to say, in view of my vital statistics, the interview ended in an uproar of laughter and I didn't pass.

I did, however, move up to senior school and, as well as having great success in the interschool athletic competitions, I was top of the class. Consequently, I was offered another shot at the scholarship. This time, with a further year's tuition under my belt, I sailed through and, better still, I was offered a place at the prestigious Bristol Grammar School (BGS). Going from Fonthill Road Secondary Modern to the BGS was a major transition, and it soon became very clear that the academic standards between the two schools were worlds apart. I descended from 'A' stream to 'X' stream and even then found it hard to keep up. I was introduced to Latin and French, neither of which I had a clue about. Luckily for me we had a very intelligent lodger, John Leach, who helped me with the conjugation of Latin verbs and also coached me on my French pronunciation, but they still remained a terrible struggle, and I was only just coping with subjects like Geography, History, Maths and English. However, I did excel at Art, Gym, Woodwork and, of course, Sport.

I foolishly thought that my athletic prowess would help me, as the BGS prided itself on its rugby and athletics reputation among the Bristol schools, but nobody showed the slightest bit of interest in me until I played in my first game of rugby. I had never played rugby prior to going to the grammar school, so I was totally ignorant about the rules of the game. I just thought that when you got the ball you simply ran like hell to get it over the other team's line. Things such as passing, kicking, line-outs, scrums, etc., I thought, were for those who couldn't run fast enough!

At this time I was 12 going on 13 and was regarded as one of the fastest schoolboy sprinters in the country. Because of my size, I was selected to represent my class and my house in rugby, even before anyone had seen me play. I was so fast that nobody could catch me and, being bigger than all the other kids on the pitch, I could swat away my opponents like flies and was able to score try after try. My speed (and obvious lack of rugby knowledge) very soon brought me to the attention of the housemaster, Mr Morris, so I was singled out for special coaching to teach me the rudiments of the game and hone my skills and was then immediately put into the school's under-13 house team, which was quite an honour for a new boy. Initially, because of my speed, I was cast as a wing three-quarter, but as such I was dependent on the other three-quarters and if they weren't up to scratch I would be lucky to get my hands on the ball during a match. My size and desire for more action meant that I quickly changed from wing three-quarter to second-row or lock forward, and with my height advantage and speed I was soon getting the ball either from line-outs or scrums and scoring regular tries. I was also a prodigious kicker and could get the ball through the posts from all angles and from a great distance, so I would often get the job of converting tries into goals. I was very soon representing the school all over the Bristol area in inter-school matches with other grammar schools, such as Queen Elizabeth's Hospital (QEH) - a great school with an admirable academic tradition, Cotham Grammar, Fairfield Grammar and many more. I only had a couple of seasons playing school rugby, but I was the highest try scorer the BGS ever had.

School sports were rugby and hockey in the winter, and cricket (which I hated and still do) and athletics in the summer, plus a court game called 'fives' - similar to squash and played on a small court, but using a gloved hand instead of a racquet. I was more than happy to play rugby where and whenever I was asked, but I would do anything possible to get out of cricket or fives. Fortunately, because of my athletic ability and the fact that I was in the school athletic team, I was always able to substitute one for the other and do athletics training during the summer months. I competed in the 100 yards, 220 sprint, long jump, high jump, hurdles, javelin and shot-put, and very soon I'd broken all the athletic records at the school for my age group in the sprint and jumping events. I even held the school record for throwing a cricket ball, despite my hate for the game. I had three training sessions a week with the school and a further two with the athletic clubs.

Academically, I was improving slowly and had progressed from 3X to 4Y, where French was dropped (disappointingly) as well as Latin (thank God), and I was top of the class in my new form. My form tutor, Mr Carter, taught Geography and Mr Strachan was the Maths master, who had a great teaching method. He cut the double Maths period into two sections, the first half for all things mathematical and the second half for asking questions about anything we liked - how a radio works or the principles of the jet engine, for instance. He was a most knowledgeable teacher. My Woodwork teacher was Mr Tapp, but I can't remember making very much other than a cigarette box for my mum.

Although I was beginning to enjoy some of the schoolwork more, to get into the A or B streams was well beyond my capabilities. To be perfectly honest, I hated the grammar school, probably because I realised I was out of my depth and I would have been much happier back at the top of the secondary modern school. Schoolwork never came easy and homework was always a struggle. I also became tired of all the cheating that went on in the class. You could spend hours doing homework in the evening and then on arrival at school in the morning it would be 'borrowed' by the kids who hadn't done theirs. Sometimes they were caught out by the form masters, as the same mistakes appeared in all the work, and their punishment took the form of one-hour detentions after school or, for the more serious offences, being sent for the 'whack' in the headmaster's office. Our headmaster was a Mr John Garrett, a noted Shakespearean scholar, whom I absolutely detested. He never did the whacking, however; it was administered by the school 'sergeant', the school's major domo, who was a lovely man and had the respect of all the pupils. He kept a special rod especially for the occasion. On entry to the head's office, the offence would be read out to you before being asked to bend over the head's desk, your face resting on a cushion, and then the sergeant would apply the number of strokes deemed appropriate by Mr Garrett. Fortunately, in all my five years at the grammar school I wasn't awarded a single detention and neither did I ever get the whack. I wasn't a 'goody two shoes', I just knew how to avoid trouble; also, they possibly wanted to 'keep me sweet' due to my sporting abilities.

By the age of 13 I'd moved up to the second year, and in the first half-term exams I somehow managed to come top of the class. My rugby and athletics were both going well and I was gaining respect from fellow pupils and various form and house masters. However, life was about to take a dramatic turn.

Chapter Seven
TB or Not TB ...

It was 1948. I was a normal adolescent, gifted with an exceptional sprinting ability, seemingly fit and healthy, growing like mad, and eating like the proverbial horse. If I wasn't out training on the school's playing fields I was training at home or even free-range in the fields. I was running for my life - almost like a 'Forrest Gump' of the late '40s. I was always trying to knock a few more seconds off my times in the running events and jump that little bit higher or further.

Then everything started to go wrong. The first thing I noticed was that my left knee was slightly swollen and I was having difficulty straightening or bending it fully. Then I found that due to the swelling I wasn't able to achieve my usual speed and performance. I wasn't in any pain and didn't have any symptoms of illness, just a swollen left knee, so I started working even harder. Not once did I consider slowing down or taking it easy; training was everything to me.

Several weeks later, with no sign of the swelling subsiding, my mum thought that perhaps I ought to see our GP, Dr Fells. She didn't seem all that concerned; in fact, she was so sure it was nothing serious that she didn't attend the appointment with me. After prodding around my knee area for a while and assessing my range of movement, the doctor decided that I should see an orthopaedic specialist at the Bristol Royal Infirmary. An appointment was duly made and this time my mum decided to come with me. I only ever knew the surgeon as 'Mr Jones', although I think his first name was David. In those days surgeons had an aura of majesty about them, and as a mere boy I wouldn't have dreamed of using his Christian name. The most famous orthopaedic surgeon working out of Bristol at the time was the former British shot-put champion and our 1936 Olympic Games representative, Mr Ken Pridie. On ward rounds he was always addressed as 'MISTER Pridie' and was treated by everybody from matron down to nursing assistant with godlike reverence.

I can't remember much about my initial consultation with Mr Jones, other than the word 'tuberculosis' cropping up every so often. Within a week my mum was asked to take me to the Winford Orthopaedic Hospital, which sat on the side of a hill overlooking the little village of Winford, about 15 miles from Bristol. I was supposed to be going in for tests to determine what was happening to my knee, but when I got to the hospital I discovered that it was primarily a TB (tuberculosis) sanatorium. I'd always thought that TB was a serious chest complaint and had no idea that it also attacked the joints. I was put on a ward of predominantly pre-teens and teenagers, and the boys there had either rheumatic fever (heart trouble) or TB spines, hips and knees. The recommended treatment in those days verged from the sublime - plenty of fresh air, milk and bed rest, to the radical - new drugs and, as a last resort, fusion of the joints.

I could envisage both my athletic career and any possibility of playing rugby for England rapidly going down the toilet. Still, I thought, I was only there for tests. What I didn't know was that Mr Jones and his cohorts strongly suspected that I had TB of the left knee and the tests had been arranged to prove their theories. I hadn't been there very long before Mr Jones decided to do an exploratory operation on my knee, but nothing untoward was found. Unfortunately, the wound became infected and took ages to heal. Mr Jones later took a sample from a gland in my groin, but again nothing concrete was discovered. The fact that every test came back as a resounding negative didn't deter the medical team, however, so they prescribed fresh air, milk and bed rest - and they really did mean rest. I wasn't even allowed to get up to go to the toilet. Bedpans were the order of the day, together with blanket baths administered by the nurses to keep me clean and smelling reasonably sweet while hospitalised. At the tender age of 13 I wasn't lusting after these delightful nurses, but I was certainly soon lusting for a good wallow in a hot bath and a proper sit-down toilet!

Bed rest for me lasted the best part of a year, and my dear old mum, with all her problems - looking after Jeanne, Bob, a houseful of apprentice BAC lodgers who came home for lunch and expected a cooked dinner in the evenings, and her invalid mother - made the trek out to Winford by bus twice a week at least, and although she was going through a terrible time financially she always managed to bring me some sort of treat every time she visited, such as home-cooked food, or sweets and chocolates.

Back at home the four young apprentices occupied the two double bedrooms, I had been allocated the single bedroom, and Bob, Jeanne and my mum slept downstairs. Mum was the second youngest daughter of a family of six: one brother, Clifford, and four sisters, Elsie, Ivy, Hilda and Lena. The sisters all lived in the Bristol area and her brother, who was a policeman, lived in Chard, Somerset, with his wife Beattie and daughter Joy. My grandfather had died in my early childhood and grandma Burt lived on her own for years. However, when she became frailer and none of the rest of the family wanted the burden of looking after her, my mum took her in and another bed was installed in her downstairs bedroom to accommodate my grandma. Mum patiently nursed her for many years, even when she became totally bedridden, until she died. As if that wasn't bad enough, my mum's sister Hilda lost her home and she too descended on us, meaning that I was forced to give up my bedroom and sleep downstairs on the settee. How my mum coped with it all I'll never know, but she did and, with the exception of grandma, everyone mucked in and got along well. Things eased after a couple of years when Hilda found a man friend who lived nearby and she moved out. I then got my small bedroom back, but I had to share the bed with brother Bob.

Life in bed in hospital at the age of 13 was very strange, to say the least. It began with the application of a 'Thomas Splint' - a device rather like a medieval leg iron, one end of which fitted snugly into my groin, at the top of the thigh, and extending right down to about six inches past the foot. Rods ran down both sides of my leg, the back of my knee rested on a leather pad and a leather cover wrapped around the leg, with flaps secured by buckles to secure the knee, rendering the entire leg stiff, straight and unbendable. Prior to being strapped into the splint, the whole of the leg from groin to ankle was encased in sticking plaster, which itches like mad and plays havoc with your skin and the hairs of your leg whenever it has to be removed. The bottom end was the 'horror' bit, as the whole contraption was finished off by being tied to a 'T' piece fixed to the end of the bed, thus maintaining the leg in an elevated position and rendering you completely immobile. The nurses regularly tightened up the tourniquet that was attached to the splint to ensure that the knee joint was relieved fully from any pressure, and sometimes additional weights were added to the carrier that dangled from the end of the splint that projected over the 'T' piece.

However, although I thought I was having a bad time of it, others on the ward were going through far worse. The boys who had TB spines were confined in a full-body plaster cast and spent alternate months lying on either their back or front. The eldest boy on the ward was 15-year-old Brian Buckland, who became my bedside companion. When I arrived on the ward he had already been in the cast for months, and he was still there when I left the hospital ten months later.

The prescription of fresh air was fulfilled in equally dramatic fashion. The TB wards of the hospital were on the side of a hill, and whatever the weather, except for heavy rain, we would all be wheeled out onto the veranda to bask in ten hours of fresh air and whatever else the elements decided to chuck at us.

I soon adapted to hospital life: regular mealtimes, veranda outings and looking forward to visits from friends and relatives. I ate like a horse, drank gallons of milk, learned the joys of masturbation and shot up like a beanpole. One positive outcome of being in hospital was that I was away from the grammar school, but I couldn't escape schooling altogether. The hospital had its very own school run by two able teachers, headmaster Mr Harry Morgan and his assistant Miss Harding, both of whom were lovely. Mr Morgan was quite excited about having a BGS boy under his tutelage and did his very best to give me the extra work that he felt my educational status merited. He tried, unsuccessfully, to teach me colloquial French and, despite the fact that I'd moved into a school stream that learned neither Latin nor French, he persisted during the many months of my incarceration. The teaching at hospital was generally pretty fundamental, and when I finally returned to the grammar school I found I'd fallen miles behind. Even to this day I regret not having learned about logarithms, calculus and various aspects of history and geography. And I'd also missed a whole year of being top dog on the rugby and athletic fields.

So there I was - an orthopaedic mess at the age of 13. I'd gone to see my doctor about a swollen knee and had ended up in a TB sanatorium, post-surgically scarred and infected, and tied to a bed in a medieval torture device invented by the maniacal Mr Thomas. My school athletic career was in ruins, I'd had two pointless operations, one of which had left my left knee disfigured for life, I was still no further along the road to finding out what was actually wrong with me, and there seemed to be no imminent sign of release. Mr Jones was not going to give up on me that easily.

Penicillin, the wonder drug that had recently come on the scene and was regarded as a cure-all for most diseases, was the next step. It was decided to put me on a three-week course of eight shots a day, i.e., injections every three hours both day and night. My backside eventually resembled a pin cushion! It didn't appear that this treatment had any appreciable effect on my condition; no further TB tests were carried out to confirm this either way, and I was still kept tied to the bed. It was then determined that I should be put on a three-week course of another new, and very costly, drug called Streptomycin. Compared with my Penicillin treatment this was more like a holiday, as I only had to be injected twice daily. This didn't appear to have any benefit either, however.

So, after about ten months of restrictive, invasive and prescriptive torture, it was decided that, as not the slightest trace of TB had been found in me whatsoever, I could at long last get up and start learning to walk again.

When the splint was removed, my left leg had practically withered away from prolonged inactivity, so I embarked on a course of physiotherapy. The doctors, of course, were still convinced that something was seriously wrong with my knee, so a condition of my release from the sanatorium was that I must wear a leg calliper - a sort of mobile version of the Thomas Splint. Once again, it extended from my groin right down to my ankle, and it was anchored in the heel of my shoe, with the knee strapped in and buckled down. Although I was now up and about, I had to wear the calliper all the time, even in bed.

When I got the all-clear to get out of bed, the first thing I did was to spend a 'happy hour' in the bath and toilet - ah, bliss! I then got straight in touch with my mum to ask her to bring in my clothes as soon as possible. I got quite a surprise when I tried to get into my trousers! When I'd been admitted to hospital ten months earlier I was 5ft 9in tall. Now, when I stood up straight, after almost a year in the splint, I had stretched to 6ft 3in - the fresh air and milk had obviously worked wonders! As you can imagine, the trouser bottoms were halfway up my calves, so my mum had to go out and buy a complete set of new clothes for me, using Provident vouchers (a form of hire purchase, whereby you can buy now and then pay it off in weekly instalments). I continued to grow at a tremendous rate, so needing to buy longer-legged trousers became a regular occurrence.

Just as it had taken time to become accustomed to living in bed, it was now a case of getting used to walking around with a permanently stiff leg. Not being able to bend my knee resulted in all sorts of problems. If I went to the cinema I could only sit in the right-hand aisle seat so that my leg could rest in the aisle; I couldn't run for a bus, and when I got on one usually I would have to ask the conductor for permission to stand on the platform in front of the luggage compartment, as it was impossible for me to sit in the normal seats. In every instance, I had to be very careful where I sat and very conscious of where I placed my stiff leg, as it was so easy for someone to trip over it.

I wore the calliper for nearly two years after leaving hospital, feeling like a freak as well as a cripple as my 14th and 15th birthdays passed by. Finally, at the age of 15½ and another two inches taller at 6ft 5in, I was given the all-clear to get rid of my portable hospital and was allowed the freedom to start doing some exercises to strengthen the leg and knee joint. Swimming was suggested as an effective therapy for increasing my mobility. I liked doing remedial exercises in the pool at Bristol North Baths on the Gloucester Road, but I wasn't a great swimmer and, try as I might, ploughing up and down the pool doing endless lengths just bored the trunks off me. It didn't really have any effect on my knee either.

Incidentally, my son Steve is a great swimmer and when he was in his teens he was like greased lightning in the water. He was approached by trainers and coaches, who thought he had an international swimming career in front of him, but he felt the same about swimming as I did: he couldn't stand the thought of all the hours of training and never-ending laps up and down the pool just to be able to swim 100 metres really fast. I've been a personal trainer for over 30 years now, and I've never been able to fathom out why training takes as much as three sessions a day and hours and hours in the pool doing countless lengths just to be able to exert yourself fully for what is now a record time of just under 50 seconds. To me it's the overload principle gone wrong and I would personally like to see the whole training system overhauled and rethought.

As a point of interest, only a few years ago, after giving a lecture on a Saga cruise liner in which I spoke about my knee troubles in my early teens, a passenger approached me and said, "You know, what you were suffering from when you were having the knee trouble was 'Osgood Schlatter Disease'. Of course, nobody knew about it back then. All you needed to do was lay off all the running and training and just rest it"! In fact, my granddaughter Hannah - a great athlete, runner, swimmer, diver and gymnast - started to have similar knee troubles and was indeed diagnosed with OS Disease and was advised to rest until the knee pains went away - and they did!

However, returning to the 1950s, back at school I was in for a rude awakening on both the academic and sporting fronts. I was in a class named 'remove H', which was the least academically blessed of all the classes for my age group (15-16 year olds). We had a pleasant form master, Mr Lucas, and we were all supposed to be working like mad for the end-of-term exams and School Certificate, which was replaced by the General Certificate of Education (GCE) the year I sat my final exams. Most of the subjects were compulsory: Maths, English, History, Geography, Chemistry/Physics and Art. For Art, an assessment was made of samples of paintings and drawings done over the year, with an additional written appreciation of art in general. Most of the lads in the class were terrible at this subject (or couldn't care less about it!) However, I was not only quite good at it, but also fast - in a 45/50-minute Art lesson I could dash off a few paintings quite easily. With a business eye, and to quell my ravenous appetite, I sold my paintings to fellow pupils in exchange for sandwiches. Practically every boy in the class submitted a portfolio of three paintings brush-stroked by me! Nobody ever found out and everyone passed the Art exam with flying colours! The results of my final exams in other subjects were not so impressive, however, and I failed miserably in most, apart from Maths, General Science and, of course, Art.

I did my best to get back into sports and attempted to play rugby again, but the years in the splint and the calliper had left me with a knee that would only bend about 90 degrees. This had a severe impact on my running ability, and from being the fastest boy on the rugby field I had now become the slowest. This, together with my tall, gangly physique, meant that playing rugby was no longer fun. In my final game I was tackled under the posts and hit the upright post so hard that the crossbar dislodged and came crashing down on my prostrate body - landing, of all places, on my bad knee. End of rugby career!

Life at home at that time was even more chaotic, with a household filled with lodgers, my mother's sister Hilda, my old and infirm grandmother, and now also my sister Jeanne and her new husband. How everybody fitted into that house I do not know!

I was rapidly approaching the end of my school days and I had absolutely no idea what I wanted to do in terms of work or a career. Apart from the apprentice lodgers that came and went at home, I had no male or 'fatherly' figure to influence or guide me in this respect. In previous years I'd been keen to work with horses, particularly racehorses, and I'd considered agricultural college, but my year out of school had scuppered my chances of obtaining decent exam passes.

However, while returning home from a trip to the baths one day, something happened that changed my entire life.

Chapter Eight
Inspiration for My Destination

It was a cold January day in 1951, and after a swimming session I opted to walk home rather than take a bus. Little did I know at the time, but that seemingly random decision was to set me on the path to where I am today.

Within a few hundred yards of the Bristol North Baths was Pigsty Hill, where there was a small newsagents. In the shop window I happened to notice a copy of the bodybuilding magazine, *Health & Strength*, a fortnightly publication founded in the early 1900s and devoted to attaining the 'body beautiful'. The cover of the 25 January issue featured a French bodybuilder named Robert Duranton, and I stared in awe and wonder at his fantastic physique. He looked like a Greek god as he stood on the top of a mountain somewhere in the south of France. I was eventually to learn that he had adopted what is termed a 'lat spread pose', with hands tucked into the waist, in order to make his tanned chest look as big as possible. All I knew at that moment was that I wanted to be just like him, with a great physique and two good legs!

I bought the magazine for the princely sum of sixpence (about 2½p in today's money), and it turned out to be the greatest purchase of my life. From that momentous day onwards, I became hooked on the concept of the 'body beautiful'. My whole life became dedicated to health, fitness, strength and physique, and my body eventually became my passport to fame and a wonderful career.

I read the magazine avidly from cover to cover many times over, marvelling at the physiques pictured inside. I couldn't wait to get my hands on the next issue, which would feature one of the all-time greats of the physical world, the legendary Steve Reeves, who had just won the 1950 Mr Universe title. Robert Duranton now had a very serious rival for my admiration! I discovered that England also had one of the great physiques of the world - a bodybuilder from Leeds called Reg Park, who came very close to beating Steve for the Universe title.

More important, however, in terms of my own course in life, was information contained in the magazine about the Health & Strength

League. One of the articles mentioned that an area organiser for the League, John Irwin, lived in Bristol, on Herkomer Close on the new Lockleaze Estate. I immediately jumped on my bike to visit him and discovered that he instructed aspiring young bodybuilders in weight training in his house and garden. There I saw my first sets of barbells, dumb-bells, benches and squat racks - all the paraphernalia that body-builders needed in order to develop their physiques - and I soon began my training with him, taking to it like a duck to water and setting aside three evenings a week for it.

The boys at the grammar school were watching my progress with great interest, as I was an 'easy gainer', although I felt that, at 6ft 5in, progress was too slow and not too noticeable. My mother was watching my progress, too, but with a certain degree of trepidation. When I think back, she probably had every reason to be concerned about my sudden fanatical interest in my new hobby. After all, I was 15½ years old, and because of my hospital incarceration I'd had very little exposure to life as a teenager and all that it involved. I didn't associate with any girls, apart from a little cracker named Sonia who lived across the road, and I had two rather strange mates, one of whom ended up in charge of the mortuary at Southmead Hospital; the other, Dennis Cosh (always referred to as Coshdog), always used to walk around with a long overcoat thrown around his shoulders. I don't think I ever saw him with his arms in the sleeves, and to top it off he wore a long white silk scarf, which dangled way down past his hips. I heard recently that he is somewhere in the Australian outback running an English tea room! And here I was, now bringing home magazines that primarily featured semi-naked men in the briefest of trunks and displaying their hugely muscled torsos!

Women did play a small part in the magazines, but they always seemed to be very much an afterthought and most looked as though they'd entered the Miss Hideous competition. Men definitely ruled the roost in the physical culture magazines of the time. Bikinis hadn't yet arrived on the scene and the one-piece regulation swimsuits weren't exactly flattering.

I bought all the bodybuilding magazines I could get hold of, which meant regular trips to the newsagent/bookshop in the Christmas Steps at the top of Colston Street. *Health & Strength* was the only British magazine, but the newsagent stocked four major US publications: *Muscle Power* and *Your Physique* (both published by The Weider Company, based in New York and Los Angeles), *Strength & Health* (published by Bob

Hoffman of the York Barbell Company in Pennsylvania) and, the best and most respected of all, *Ironman* (published by husband and wife team, Peary and Mabel Rader, from Alliance, Nebraska). Some of the foremost authorities on all aspects of the sport wrote for *Ironman*, and it dealt with bodybuilding and weightlifting equally, diet and historical strength athletes, and was always the first with all the major competition results. The York Barbell Company's foundry supplied most of the weight training and Olympic weightlifting sets in the USA, and Hoffman also sponsored and controlled the US weightlifting team, who at that time were the world's best. Bodybuilding was a much more popular sport over in the USA at that time.

In the late 1940s and early '50s bodybuilders seemed to be able to get their hands on the necessary food, especially the steak and protein supplements needed to turn beanpoles into musclemen. I don't remember whether the USA was more liberal in those days, but it was obvious from the photos in the magazines that neither the bodybuilders nor their photographers were averse to nudity. Not that you ever saw any genitalia; the photos were taken with foliage, ornaments, furniture or the bodybuilder's own hands strategically placed over the offending parts. If all else failed, the photo retoucher would be called in to paint a posing pouch (about the size of the thongs that the girls wear these days that are laughingly called bikinis) on the photos. This often led to comical results, as some of the pouches went halfway down the model's legs - they were a well-blessed lot in those days! Obviously, the photos in these physical culture magazines pandered to the then 'underground' homosexual market.

Mum obviously thought that I was going that way and, when I informed her of my intention of cycling up to see John Irwin, warning bells began to clang and red lights started flashing. Although she didn't make any attempt to stop me, she did stipulate that I had to take my younger brother Bob with me as some sort of protection. That was a joke if ever there was one, as I was well over 6ft tall while Bob, aged about 13 at that time, was around 5ft 6in - great protection! My friendship with one of the well-known bodybuilders of the time, Reub Martin, also fuelled Mum's worries. He was a great character and one of the top physiques in the country. He had been placed third in the 1950 Mr Universe contest, behind two of the greatest physiques in the world, Steve Reeves from the USA and Reg Park from Leeds. He ran a gym in Holcombe Road, Tottenham, wrote for the *Health & Strength* magazine and was the bottom man of the world-famous hand-balancing act, Les

Trios de Mille. For years this act was one of the highlights of the notorious show, *Folies Bergère*, featuring lots of lovely nude ladies - the first time this had ever been done (discounting the stationary nudes of the Windmill Theatre productions after the war). Reub's column for *Health & Strength* covered the interesting people and bodybuilders he'd met while performing at the various variety halls around the UK and included an open invitation to meet the trio backstage, so when they scheduled a show at the Bristol Hippodrome I decided to go and see them. You can imagine my mum's thoughts: her teenage son, going to a nude show to meet up with three guys who were probably gay, too! In reality, nothing could be further from the truth. The act consisted of Reub as the bottom man - 215lb of strength and muscle, Len Talbot as the middle man, and Rusty Sellars - one of the greatest hand balancers in the world - as the top man. Once again, I was only allowed to go to the show if my brother came along, too. We met Reub at the stage door and he invited us to their dressing room for a chat. It was like a dream come true. Reub showed a lot of interest in me and thought that, as a big-boned lad of 6ft 5in, I had a lot of potential and could go far in the bodybuilding world. From that evening on, we became great friends and I was mentioned regularly in his column, 'Ramblin' with Reub', so the bodybuilding world got to know the name of Dave Prowse at a very early stage.

In the end, I managed to persuade my mum that her worries were unfounded and that I was interested purely in meeting three physical culturists at the top of their profession. John Irwin turned out to be a real physical culturist and as straight as could be, too. He had an attractive wife and young children and had a genuine interest in promoting the Health & Strength way of life and encouraging people to exercise on a regular basis, and his house became a mecca for every aspiring weight trainer for miles around. 'Sacred thy body even as thy soul' was the motto of the Health & Strength League, which basically meant looking after yourself through sensible eating and regular training. One of John's duties was organising the annual Mr and Miss West Britain contests at the YMCA hall in the centre of Bristol, as well as area shows that incorporated bodybuilding, keep fit for men and women, hand balancing, wrestling, boxing, gymnastics weightlifting, chest expander work (strand-pulling) and an art called muscle control, which really came into prominence years later when a famous muscle controller, Tony Holland, ran away with the top award as the 'musical muscleman' on Hughie Green's TV show, *Opportunity Knocks*. Who will ever forget Tony's act to the music of 'Wheels Cha Cha Cha'?!

I had started my exercise career with a Charles Atlas course, which I shared with my brother-in-law - 'u too can have a body like mine' (if you're not careful!) However, my introduction to weight training was a complete eye-opener. Remember, I was still getting over my knee troubles, so any form of squatting was out of the question for a while. But, if my memory serves me right, I did manage to get about 70lb above my head in the two-hands-press movement and 80lb in the bench press, with all the other lifts being equally mediocre. Just to show you what can be achieved through training, I eventually ended up with a standing press of 330lb and a bench press of 500lb! I was never a really strong squatter and being so tall was a distinct disadvantage, but I still managed a 500lb squat at my gym and that was with a dodgy left leg.

While I was with John I was always dead keen on my training and was fully committed to my three sessions a week. I liked to think that I complemented the team of dedicated enthusiasts who turned his back garden and kitchen into exercise yards. He encouraged me to enter my first contest, the Junior Mr West Britain. It was an interesting experience, not only because it enabled me to meet up with all the local young bodybuilders in my area, but also because it brought me into contact with the man who would eventually become one of the most important people in world bodybuilding, Oscar Heidenstam. At the time he was employed by the *Health & Strength* magazine and organised their national competitions, and he was the number one physique judge in the UK. My training with John Irwin was cut short, however, when John's wife said that my attitude was too flippant and that I told too many jokes, while the other guys were giving their all. So I was told, none too politely, never to darken their training establishment again. Fortunately, by this time I'd met up with other Bristol bodybuilding enthusiasts, so I didn't have any lack of either training partners or locations.

Initially, I seemed to be hampered by lack of money to buy all the food and supplements that were needed to take me from ordinary to extraordinary. On leaving school I began working in the accounts department of the Bristol Aeroplane Company in a glorified pen-pusher's job and was earning the princely sum of £1 18s 6d per week (£1.93 in today's money). I gave my mum £1 10s as my contribution to the household costs, which didn't leave much for all my special needs, even though I had very few outgoings - I cycled to work, took sandwiches, etc. Fortunately, however, as I progressed with my new job I was able to work more overtime, which on a good week could increase my earnings to just under £4. So with full overtime I was in clover and could spend all the extra money on food.

To get anywhere in any sport, training and nutrition are the two main ingredients for success, but a bodybuilding diet and food intake are vital. I was still buying all the bodybuilding magazines, which detailed the dietary secrets of all the top physiques, and it was obvious that a progression to the top of the bodybuilding ladder was very much dependent on how much money one had to spend on food and just how much protein could be stuffed down. Meat in those days was disproportionately expensive, so I was always looking for cheaper high-protein alternatives, the two most readily available being soya flour and baked beans. Of course, they were both vegetable proteins and therefore incomplete as far as the spectrum of essential amino acids was concerned, but that didn't worry me in my quest for the body beautiful.

Gaylord Hauser was the big health and nature cure authority of the day and I used to read all his work avidly. He maintained that the four wonder foods, which he termed 'nature foods', that should be included in a healthy diet were wheatgerm, honey, blackstrap molasses and soya flour, so I became a regular at the health food shop in Henleaze so that I could stock up on these God-given nutrients. I used to mix the soya flour with milk and then add the molasses and honey. When heated up the resulting mixture, although it looked pretty foul, didn't taste too bad, as I have a sweet tooth - it was a bit like drinking warm, sweet mud! I would drink pints of this goo on a daily basis and it seemed to do the trick, helping me to increase my body weight and develop some semblance of a physique.

I doubt whether Mr H. J. Heinz ever realised just how much effect his product would have on the budding Darth Vader, but I ate literally saucepans full of his wonderful baked beans in tomato sauce, heated up and combined with loads of raw onions. My stomach now churns at the thought of this concoction, but I don't think it churns quite so much as all the stomachs of the people who had to live and train with me. Word went around about the effects of this mixture on me and nobody ever dared to stand behind me when I was training, for fear of the pungent gas that escaped at very frequent intervals! *Blazing Saddles* had nothing on me; I could've supplied the sound effects for the famous bean-eating scene all on my own!

By now I'd purchased my own set of weights, moved with my mother to a council house on Southmead's new estate in Ambleside Avenue and converted a coal shed into a makeshift gym. When the weather was good

99

I trained in the back garden, and I found myself two training partners, both of whom were a great influence on my bodybuilding career and on my life in general.

One training partner, Don Lee, was an insurance agent for the Prudential, but in his spare time he used to train regularly. He was also the bottom man of a very good hand-balancing act called the Boston Trio. He was a good balancer himself, but because he was the strongest and best built of the three he always got the job of the bottom/support man. Don had a loving wife Muriel and two children, Barbara and Vic. Barbara was the light of her dad's eyes - very attractive, great figure and keen on training, and she eventually went on to win the Junior Miss West Britain and Junior Miss Britain titles. His son Vic showed only minimal interest in the weights and was passionate about cars, motorbikes and girls - not necessarily in that order - much to his father's despair. Don had a gym in his back garden, which consisted of a bar, assorted barbell discs, a few dumb-bells and a bench. To the enthusiast this was heaven, so every Tuesday and Thursday evening and Sunday morning we would congregate in Don's back garden and go through our routines, which involved around two hours of heavy training.

I don't think Don ever trained indoors in his life. If it rained we would shelter in the shed and then run out into the pouring rain to lift when our turn came round. Snow and ice were no deterrent either, and I've even trained when we've had to chip weights out of the ice. I trained with Don and the rest of the team for many years and, although Don was intensely proud of me, no matter how much I improved, how many titles I won or how many records I broke I never received any praise or compliments. When I was weightlifting, for instance, and breaking all sorts of Western County and British records I always had to duplicate the feat on his equipment in his back yard before he would accept the achievement. If we heard of some weightlifter breaking a record, the comment would always be, "I'll bet he couldn't do that round here in our gym!"

My other training partner, Bob Osborne, was a self-employed house renovator and second-hand car dealer. He didn't seem to do much work during the day, but attended evening car auctions held in and around Bristol, and he seemed to make a reasonable living buying and selling old bangers. I eventually found myself a job that only entailed working evenings, so we could both train at my house or at Don's at any time during the day. Years before training with Bob, when I first started and worked at the Bristol Aeroplane Company, I used to see this enormous guy ambling up Filton Hill going to work and people would say with some sort of awe, "That's that Bob Osborne, the strongman," but in those days I never got to meet him.

I trained with Bob and Don from my early bodybuilding days in the late '50s through to the time I left Bristol to go and work in Croydon in 1963. Ever since I've lived 'up in the smoke', as London and its environs are often referred to, I've still made excuses to get back to Bristol for the odd weekend, and on the Sunday morning we'd all be back in Don's garden pumping iron.

Before I left Bristol I bequeathed my old dead-lifting bar to Don and the rest of the gang. The piece was just a 7ft long bar with a thickish sleeve made out of gas piping. It only had two weights on it, but they were both cut from 2in steel plate and weighed 2cwt (100kg) apiece. Therefore, the bar was always loaded to a minimum of 500lb (230kg). You had to be strong and hardy to train at Don's. Many lifters came to his training sessions to try to lift this barbell, but in most cases the thickness of the sleeve put them off and very few ever got it off the floor. Don eventually decided to paint a 'Scroll of Honour' on the inside of one of the plates and my name topped it with a lift of 660lb (300kg). Both Don and Muriel died a few years ago and they are sadly missed. However, Bob is still ploughing on regardless, I'm pleased to say.

Living in Bristol, I was part of the West Britain area as far as body-building championships were concerned, as each area held its own annual competition and area winners went on to the final - the Mr Britain contest, held in London and organised by The Health and Strength League through the *Health & Strength* magazine. The winner of Mr Britain went on to compete in the annual Mr Universe contest, also held in London. This was organised by the National Amateur Bodybuilders Association (NABBA), whose official journal or organ was the *Health & Strength* magazine, and it attracted the greatest physiques from all over the world. The 'Britain' contests comprised three categories - Mr and Miss (aged over 18 and less than 40), Junior Mr and Miss (under 18) and Senior Mr (for over-40s).

I never had much success in bodybuilding competitions. My good progress never seemed to show as much, compared with the other guys who were about 12 inches shorter than me. My bodybuilding career also seemed to be blighted by Bristol bodybuilders who were proportionately much better than me. Graham Price was the first in my junior days, rapidly followed by John Pegler and Ron Thomas in the senior competition. I was never placed above them and I only ever won one competition, Mr North Bristol (probably because John Pegler and Ron Thomas had decided that the North Bristol show was beneath their standards!) The contest was judged by one of the greatest bodybuilders of the day, Leo Robert of Canada, who was on a tour of the UK giving posing exhibitions. Leo was very encouraging and we corresponded for many years after that first meeting. However, I was becoming despondent about entering physique contests, even though my obsession with bodybuilding and weight training continued undeterred in pursuit of the body beautiful.

Little did I think, back in the 1950s, that I would eventually compete against the York Weightlifting Team in the 1962 World Championships; be a guest at the York Barbell Club; become a personal friend of the world's greatest bodybuilder, John Grimek, and his lovely wife Angela; and become European sales manager for the Weider organisation, introducing their products to major UK retail outlets such as Harrods and Lilywhites.

Chapter Nine
Funding My Obsession

Work had always been a sore point with me. I appreciated that I had to earn a living, but other than my training nothing ever interested me sufficiently to want to make a career out of it. I think if my father had been around I probably would have been apprenticed to something or other at the Bristol Aeroplane Company after which I could have chosen the direction I wanted to go. As it was I just drifted from one job to another, packing them up if they interfered with my training programme.

I never had much difficulty getting work, even if I wasn't really interested in it except for the remuneration to help with my training goals. My Bristol Grammar School education and GCE passes worked wonders in terms of clinching jobs, but in many cases they also had reverse effects. I would apply for manual types of work to help with my bodybuilding and I would get turned down because I was over-qualified.

Work in the accounts department at the Bristol Aeroplane Company continued on for a couple of years, but it wasn't exactly the sort of fulfilling job I was looking for. However, one of the interesting tasks that came with the job was doing the pay round. On a Friday I would take boxes filled with workers' pay packets round the factory, escorted by one of the BAC's police force. The BAC had installed one of the UK's first computer-based wages systems and the computer, housed in the basement of Filton house underneath the first-floor accounts office, was enormous, taking up most of the basement space. It was a far cry from modern-day computers; even the smallest laptop today has more power and capabilities than that whole basement of equipment ever possessed - that's progress!

A couple of years at the BAC on minimal wages was enough for me, so I started looking for a better job and found one at Smith's of Bristol that paid the princely sum of £6 per week. The only trouble was that it was in Knowle, at the top of Broadwalk, which was on the other side of Bristol to my home in Southmead. So I cycled to Smith's and back every day for my new job in export sales. My office was above the ironmongers, C. G. Smith of Bristol, and my boss was the son of the owner. I was the assistant to his secretary, whom he eventually married.

The firm employed a sales rep, Arthur Wild, in West Africa, who sold ironmongery wares (steel barns) to Nigeria, the Gold Coast and Sierra Leone. The barns were prefabricated in the factory at the back of the shop and shipped out with an instruction sheet compiled by me - someone who couldn't even nail two planks together! In truth, the instruction sheet was a pro forma leaflet containing blank spaces that needed to be filled in according to the size of the barn being shipped. I'm not sure what use I was there, as the young Mr Smith checked all my work in detail and might just as well have done it all himself! The other major products that went to South Africa were the gaily printed rolls of cloth that the African women make into all sorts of personal apparel. Arthur Wild loved West Africa and on his return to the UK every six months he used to regale me with stories of his adventures in far-flung places such as Accra and Freetown and many more. Hearing about all his exotic travels made me quite envious and only too aware that £6 a week wasn't going to take me very far.

I very quickly became tired of cycling to Knowle in all weathers. I had met another aspiring young bodybuilder, who worked for one of the meat wholesalers in Bristol. He told me that he could get plenty of cheap or even free meat through his firm and so, always on the lookout for more protein to aid my bodybuilding efforts, I decided to leave Smith's and get a job in the meat business. I also thought that all the meat 'humping' (carrying hinds of beef, halves of pigs and whole lambs to the waiting butchers' vans) would toughen me up and make me stronger.

My first venture into the meat industry was being taken to an abattoir in the Hotwells Basin of Bristol. It was a real eye-opener to come face to face with the slaughter of pigs and cattle - how anyone could kill animals every day as a living is beyond me. I know I eat meat and always have, and I know that animals have to be slaughtered to provide it, but the inhumanity of it all appalled and disgusted me, and spending just a couple of hours there turned my insides over. Slaughterhouse work was definitely not for me.

My friend then introduced me to a company in the Old Market district called Sansininas, a meat wholesaler that supplied all the Bristol butchers. On introduction to the manager, I told him that I was looking for a job as a meat humper, but when he found out about my grammar school education he said that I was overqualified for that job. Consequently, he offered me a position as a check-weighman, which involved checking and weighing all the carcasses that came into the depot from the cold stores at the docks at 5 a.m. and then checking it all out when the butchers came in to buy meat for retail. The wage was about £10 per week, considerably more than I was on at Smith's, so I accepted the job.

I left home on my motorbike at 4.30 a.m. to be at work for 5 a.m., and then from 5 till 11 a.m. I checked meat in and out of the depot. I didn't enjoy the work. There was no humping or lifting involved and there was no free meat on offer as they were whole carcasses, although I did get a small discount from a nearby butcher's shop that the company supplied. Needless to say, that job didn't last very long, and after an unfortunate confrontation with the manager, who accused me of stealing three pig's kidneys, I handed in my notice and left. In truth, I'd actually found the kidneys on the floor, covered in sawdust, and was going to take them home for the dog.

Two more jobs followed in quick succession. The first was working in an accountants' office. On the first morning the senior partner gave me a ledger and asked me to total up the columns of figures. I completed the additions, page by page, but every time I rechecked them I came up with a different figure. I decided it would be best to use an adding machine, but when I enquired where it was I was told, "Nature gave you the greatest adding machine in the world - your brain - so get back out there and use it!" I went out for lunch and never returned.

Next came some navvy work on a church that was being built in the Henleaze area, but I hated sitting in a shed on the site drinking tea out of tin cans and decided that there must be something better that I could do.

A chance meeting with an old boss from the BAC's accounts department, Fred Yeo, got me back into the company, this time as a progress chaser. I was attached to the electrics section in the Britannia Hangar and my job was to make sure that all the components that the electricians needed in order to operate were actually in the electrical store, so that the engineers weren't wasting time hanging around waiting for missing parts. The components were made in different workshops all over the BAC site, which covered hundreds of acres, so I had to travel around the factory buildings on foot, chasing the workers for the parts needed for the electrical store. The boss, Mr Helliker, was a nice man and I shared the storeroom with storekeeper Arthur Ponsford, who was also an amiable fellow. He lived in the St Paul's district, very close to my long-time friend Den Welch, who at that time had recently opened a gym, The Empire Weightlifting Club, in the basement of an old church, where top bodybuilders and competitive weightlifters used to train on a regular basis. Sadly, Den is no longer with us, but the EWC has grown and is now the most successful gym in the West Country.

Although I was enjoying my work as a progress chaser, once again it was not helping me to achieve my goal of becoming a top-class bodybuilder, although all the walking around must have made my legs stronger. The Britannia Hangar where I worked was a huge structure and was originally known as the Brabazon Hangar, as it used to house the Bristol Brabazon, the biggest aeroplane of its time. The Bristol Brabazon turned out to be a complete disaster, costing millions of pounds to develop and eventually being sold to a scrap metal merchant for £10,000! The aircraft's inaugural flight took place when I was 13 and ensconced in Winford Hospital, so I only managed to catch a glimpse of it as it passed over.

The hangar's name was changed when a new passenger airliner, the Britannia, was developed at the BAC for the El Al airline. I was fortunate - or unfortunate - to be asked by a good friend at the hangar, John Luton, if I would like to go on a test flight, and as I'd never flown before I jumped at the chance. So, at 8 p.m. the aircraft, filled with volunteer passengers, took off for a flight around the Bay of Biscay. The interior was sumptuous and package meals were served all round, but what my good friend John hadn't told anyone was the actual purpose of the flight - stall tests! When we landed back at Filton in the early hours of the morning the plane stank of vomit, as most of the passengers were violently sick! Never again did I accept any of John's offers, but we've stayed in touch over the last 40 years.

Chapter Ten
Bouncing High

I was always a regular for Sunday morning training but didn't do much evening training as I'd landed myself a job as a ballroom supervisor, a posh name for a bouncer, at Mecca Dancing, also known as The Glen/Locarno. Apart from my passion for training, my social life consisted of weekend visits to the Mecca ballroom, and that's how the job came about. I wasn't a great dancer, although I'd had a few ballroom lessons when I was much younger. The object of going to the dances was to meet people other than bodybuilders - girls in particular. I can't say I had much luck on that front, though. I think I was a daunting prospect at 6ft 7in and could almost read girls' minds: 'How do I get myself out of any trouble with a guy his size?' However, I did enjoy my visits there. Because of my weightlifting prowess I was becoming a known character and there was never a shortage of people to talk to, mostly lads. I was getting a fair amount of publicity at that time in the three Bristol newspapers - *The Evening Post*, *The World* and *The Western Daily Press*. I also got on well with the staff: manager Alan Boyce, his assistant Dave Adams, the bandleader Johnny Allan and the leader of the trio Tommy Allen.

The Glen was situated in an old quarry that was originally a play area for children. Cowardines, the Bristol Tea Merchants, then built a tea room and ballroom there and the place became a popular spot for families during the day, with a full dance band playing at weekends from 7 p.m. to 11 p.m. Gradually, however, the playground and café were used less and less and the dances faced competition from hotels such as the Grand Spa and jazz clubs like the Avon Cities Jazz Club and the Chinese Jazz Club at the Bristol Corn Exchange. As a result, Cowardines sold out to the major company in the dance business, Mecca Ballrooms, which built Bristol's first commercial dance hall, The Locarno, at the bottom of the quarry. The old dance hall and tea rooms were converted into a licensed club and renamed Tiffany's. The box office was at the bottom of a steep flight of steps off the main road opposite the car park. Once the entry fee had been paid there was a long walk down to the dance hall to be greeted by the staff. In my early dance days I used to travel to The Glen on a tandem bicycle, and if I met a girl I liked I would offer her a lift home. Little did she realise that she would be pedalling on the back half of my tandem! Needless to say, 'relationships' didn't last very long.

One evening Alan Boyce asked me to come to his office. He told me that he'd been watching my career as well as my conduct as a patron of The Glen for a while and was impressed by the fact that I seemed to be a popular person who commanded respect. "How would you like to come and work for me as supervisor on the three rock 'n' roll sessions?" he asked. I quickly considered whether they would clash with my training, realised they wouldn't and so accepted his offer to join the ranks of Mecca Dancing for a remuneration of £2 per session.

At The Glen it was rock 'n' roll on Mondays, Thursdays and Saturday afternoons, and on other nights, Sundays included, it was general dancing. The three rock 'n' roll sessions attracted youngsters from miles around and it seemed that no session was complete without a fight breaking out, often erupting into a free-for-all involving around 50 boys and girls. Most of the fights comprised a bit of punching, headbutting and maybe a kick or two, but the lads never seemed to be 'tooled up' like they are today. The girls were by far the worst, as at the first sign of trouble off came the stiletto-heeled shoes, which were absolutely lethal and capable of inflicting some nasty injuries. Consequently, the ballroom was starting to get a bad reputation. Saturday afternoons were for those aged 14 to 17 and these sessions seemed to attract more bad behaviour than any of the others; Mondays and Thursdays tended to attract 16-18 year olds. This was the Teddy Boy era, with its own distinctive fashions: DA haircuts, skintight trousers, velvet jackets that reached down to the knees, bootlace ties and suede shoes with 2in crêpe soles, known as 'brothel creepers', for the boys; and skirts with layers of frilly petticoats and really high stilettos for the girls.

I was still working at the BAC during the day, but for three sessions a week I would don a black suit, white shirt and bow tie and become a ballroom supervisor, in charge of three or four other part-time supervisors. Between us (Alan, Dave Adams, Dennis Dawson and myself) we set about making the rock 'n' roll session fight-free and a place where any parent would be happy for their kids to go, as many parents were keeping their children away for fear of their becoming involved in the trouble, intentionally or otherwise.

Our first plan was to institute a dress code that must be adhered to by all patrons of the ballroom, irrespective of which nights they attended, so out went the trappings of the Teddy Boys as well as the stiletto shoes, which apart from being used as weapons also played havoc with the ballroom floor. Everyone was expected to dress smartly, with no casual clothing. When I wasn't patrolling the ballroom I played the unofficial role of box office manager, protecting cashier Mrs Flowers and also vetting everyone as they came in, turning away all the undesirables, the known troublemakers and those who didn't conform to the Mecca dress code. This form of supervision was received in good spirits, as anyone barred on Monday would be back on Thursday or Saturday and now conforming to our dress code requirements. The Glen was the place to be for Mods or Teddy Boys and to be banned was the last thing they wanted.

I very quickly worked out a way of dealing with any trouble effectively and I got rid of the supervisors that didn't help when fights erupted (grown men had been known to dash off to the toilets and hide out of the way when trouble broke out!) At the first sign of trouble we would wade in and remove the lad who was getting a beating and throw him out, frogmarching him all the way up the slope away from the dance hall, which was quite a distance. Then at our leisure, when everything had quietened down, we would get the perpetrator and throw him out, too. Supervisors came in all ages, shapes and sizes, but with my height, weight and strongman reputation I tended to command the most respect, and my strategy was to be friendly with everyone and spend time chatting with the various groups of patrons to gain their confidence. We soon had these rock 'n' roll sessions well under control and the parents' confidence restored. To this day I still get approached by people who remember me from my Glen days. In fact, it has become something of a boast to have been thrown out of The Glen by David Prowse!

I could see how popular the rock 'n' roll sessions were becoming, particularly now that all the trouble had ceased. So, with the help of a friend, Eddie Smith, I decided to have a go myself. We hired the hall of the local St Stephen's Church on the Southmead New Estate, hired a DJ with all his own equipment, and touted 'The White Church Rock Nights'. Our Saturday night sessions soon attracted rockers from all over Bristol and it became the 'in' place to go. Eddie's mum and my mum took care of the catering side - tea, coffee, cakes and biscuits - and trouble was very rare.

My manager at The Glen, Alan Boyce, heard that I was running the rock nights and decided to make me an offer I couldn't refuse. He suggested that, although the rest of the dance sessions at The Glen were relatively trouble free, I should supervise all of them, pointing out that the additional pay would enable me to give up my day job and devote more time to my training. This was everything I was looking for and presented a perfect solution for me, as I was finding it difficult juggling two jobs and fitting in time to train. The job, working from 7 to 11 p.m., was nice and easy; the ballroom was trouble free, all the staff were pleasant, and I was going to be surrounded by girls! My summers would be great, as I'd be able to get up when I wanted, train as the whim took me and spend my free time at the Fishponds Lido, perfecting my tan and chatting up even more girls.

My new earnings of £12 per week were enough to pay my way at home and buy petrol for my motorbike and provided enough to live on generally. I also managed to top up my wage by taking on an additional job at The Glen, as a relief nightwatchman on a Tuesday night, which helped to pay for the all-important food and bodybuilding supplements I needed for working towards my goal of entering the Mr Universe contest. The nightwatchman's job was pretty much a doddle. The dance floor had to be pristine, as several professional dancers used to come in and practise during the early part of the 7-8 a.m. session, so I had to sweep the ballroom, clear up the evening's mess and spend a couple of hours scraping the chewing gum off the ballroom floor and carpet, which could be quite a task sometimes but was made less onerous due to the fact that I could listen to the latest records on the ballroom's hifi system while I worked. Although spending the night in an empty dance hall at the bottom of a disused quarry sounds a little bizarre, I was never short of company. The local police dropped by for cups of tea and coffee to while away their night shift, and girls from the home for unmarried mothers located nearby often sneaked out at night to spend time with me - all quite innocent, I must add, but I was more than happy to have people to talk to in the middle of the night.

It was actually at the bottom of the box office steps, while working at The Glen, that I met the future Mrs Prowse, a gorgeous girl named Norma, who was proof that the notice stretching over the ballroom doorway was true: 'Through these doors walk some of the most beautiful girls in the world'. She came in regularly on a Sunday night with a boyfriend of similar height to hers, and I'll always remember the orange coat she used to wear. I would often beckon her out of the line on the pretext of 'inspecting' her and usually ended our brief conversation with the line, "When are you going to stop coming in with that little fellow and let me take you home?" Norma's response would be to turn up her nose and walk back to her boyfriend in the queue. This went on for several weeks, until one weekend she appeared with a couple of girlfriends rather than her boyfriend. Once again I pulled her out of the line. "Where's that funny little fellow you normally come in with?" I asked. She replied that she wasn't seeing him anymore. "Then I'm taking you home tonight," I said. She declined, explaining that she had to be in by 11 p.m., before my shift ended, and would be in serious trouble if she was late. Using all my persuasive powers, I told her that I'd got my motorbike and could have her home by 11.10 p.m., and luckily she was waiting for me at the end of the evening. I raced the three-mile journey to her house in Filton but it was about 11.20 p.m. by the time we'd said goodnight and she landed on the doorstep. Much to my dismay, Norma's mother was waiting in the doorway and, before I could apologise or explain, she grabbed her daughter and thrust her inside, slamming the door behind her.

Fortunately, before dropping Norma off I'd arranged to take her out for a ride on my motorbike the following day, after my Sunday morning training session with Don and Bob. So, after a good workout and still wearing my old weightlifting gear, I turned up at Norma's house to meet the family. My tracksuit bottoms were old and worn; in fact, they were in shreds, revealing plenty of thigh! I don't think I made a very good impression and overheard her mother saying, "You're not going out with him dressed like that, are you?" However, my dishevelled state didn't worry Norma and we had a very pleasant afternoon together at Severn Beach. Thereafter, our courtship continued and eventually, after three years, we were married.

The summers of this period of my life were great. I had my evening job at The Glen, I spent my mornings weight training with Bob, and my afternoons were spent at the open-air lido in Fishponds, sunbathing, swimming and diving, as well as meeting up with friends from The Glen and the Grand Spa Hotel.

The lido was actually another quarry that, unlike The Glen, had been filled with water. Obviously the place was only open over the summer months (from the beginning of May to the end of September), and the owners used the 'down' period to refurbish it and restock it with fish, as fishing was a popular pastime there, too.

One year, right at the start of the season, the sun worshippers' peace was broken when half a dozen policemen arrived and dashed around to the far side of the lido. A fisherman had hooked a dead body. The police launched the lido boat, rowed across the lake to get the body out of the weeds and dragged it back through the water to an accessible point, where colleagues were waiting with a makeshift coffin. A city councillor had committed suicide during the winter months by stuffing his pockets with stones before leaping into the water. His body had remained undiscovered for almost four months, by which time the fish had had a good feed and he stank to high heaven. The police managed to get the decaying body out of the water and into the coffin, but carrying it up from the water to the top of the slope, where a large crowd had gathered, was proving a struggle. As I looked strong and able I was asked to lend a hand, so I volunteered to take one end. Giving me the lower end of the coffin proved to be a wise decision from the police's point of view, for as we proceeded up the slope, supporting the coffin on our shoulders, putrid water ran to the bottom end of the box and started leaking out, pouring all over me. Once the coffin was lowered to the ground at the top and the police had taken it away, I raced off to the nearest shower and spent ages soaping and rinsing myself to get rid of the terrible stench. Then it was back to perfecting my tan!

My Glen days came to an end after Alan Boyce was promoted within the ranks of Mecca and was offered another management position in Bradford. He made me various offers to go to Bradford with him, but I didn't fancy a move to the north. Everything I wanted was in Bristol: my mum, my home, my training partners and Norma. Also, Mecca were using Alan as a troubleshooter and I wasn't keen on the idea of 'cleaning up' another Mecca ballroom. A new manager, Mike Lyons, took over at The Glen and there was an instant dislike and incompatibility between us. Working there was no longer fun for me and I cut back on the time I was putting in, before eventually leaving to find pastures new.

Apart from my last few weeks at The Glen under the new manager, I remember my days there with affection, especially my association with Alan Boyce. Without him I wouldn't be where I am today. He was a great boss, and an even greater friend.

Chapter Eleven
Mr Universe: Pounds and Feet

Apart from my training partner Don's back garden gym and my own place at home, I hadn't had much in the way of gymnasium training before I went on to work in Croydon. The little I did have was at my friend Den Welch's Empire Weightlifting Club (EWC). The club wasn't all that big, and although it was called a weightlifting club it didn't have an official weightlifting set, e.g., an Olympic barbell, just ordinary weight-training equipment, barbells, dumb-bells, benches and squat stands. Den, obviously wanting publicity for the EWC, invited me to train there, as I was then preparing for the 1960 Mr Universe contest and competing in local and national strength set competitions and breaking British weightlifting records into the bargain.

I owe a great debt of gratitude to Alan Boyce for his interest in my training and also for his help with the development of the EWC during the time I was working for him. As the EWC wasn't making much money and an Olympic set cost around £400 in the early 1960s, Den asked me to have a chat with Alan to see if there was any chance of organising a charity night at the ballroom to raise funds so that the club could purchase its first Olympic barbell. This would mean that the club would then be able to organise local and area championships under the banner of the official weightlifting organisation - The British Amateur Weightlifters Association (BAWLA). Alan readily agreed and on one memorable night we raised sufficient money to buy the set. What Alan didn't tell either Den or myself was that he had already bought the set in anticipation of raising the cash, and you can imagine our surprise and delight when they rolled the set out onto the ballroom floor and Alan made the presentation to Den.

In those days there was a major move to get bodybuilders to compete in contests that featured their favourite lifts: the two-hands curl (a biceps-developing exercise), the bench press (to develop the large pectoral chest muscles) and the squat (which develops the thighs). The three lifts became known as the 'strength set'. Proper weightlifters, i.e. the guys who trained for strength rather than just pure muscular development, competed on the three recognised weightlifting movements: the two-hands press, the two-hands snatch and the two-hands clean and jerk - the lifts that are, or were, competed for in World and Olympic championships and were known as the 'Three Olympics'.

While I was still bodybuilding seriously, it was as a strength set lifter that I competed. Besides being the Western Counties champion, I was also the British record holder on the two-hands curl at 197lb (90kg). I held the Western County record at 5lb heavier (i.e., 202lb), but the rules of the Weightlifting Association state that three qualified referees must be present at a British record attempt and on the day that I did 202lb there were only two, so the 202lb lift never went into the record books. I also held the British record on a couple of odd lifts - the straight-arm pullover (160½lb) and eventually the two-hands dead lift (678¾lb - just under 320 kilos), which earned me the title of Strongest Man Wales and the West. I was presented with a magnificent trophy by Danny Blanchflower, the former Irish football international and Tottenham Hotspur captain, who was at that time fronting a sports programme for Television Wales and the West (TWW, as it was then known).

The 1960 Mr Universe contest was held at the London Palladium, with judging the day before in the Royal Hotel in Russell Square. The amateur contest is divided into three classes: class 1 - 5ft 9in and over; class 2 - 5ft 6in to 5ft 8¾in; and Class 3 - under 5ft 6in. Mr Universe has a professional contest, too, comprising two classes: under and over 5ft 9in. I was competing in class 1, and at 6ft 7in and weighing in at 17st 3lb I was the tallest competitor ever to compete. However, in the Universe contest size is not everything and judging is based on a whole variety of criteria, such as proportion, size, muscularity, skin, definition and posing ability. Each of the 10 to 15 judges has his own idea of what the perfect physique should look like - and in 1960 I wasn't it!

To be perfectly honest, although I'd been invited to enter and was regarded as one of the top 20 physiques in the country, I really wasn't ready for it and could have done with a couple more years training to attain the maximum muscle size that my 6ft 7in form could have held. I had a 50in chest that expanded to 54in, a 36in waist and 18in biceps, but on a frame of my height it didn't look anything out of the ordinary. The press turned out in force to cover the contest and very quickly I became the centre of their attention due to my tall stature - I was one of the largest the competition had ever seen (Arnold and Lou Ferrigno were bigger than me, but they came later). The smallest guy in the contest was a 5ft 1in bodybuilder from Hove in Sussex, George Cox, and the press totally ignored the two winners, Henry Downs and Paul Wynter, in order to get photos of George and myself posing together. We even made the front cover of the *Health & Strength* magazine.

I realised that I just wasn't good enough, but an even bigger disappointment was on the horizon when I was taken aside by the chief judge, Oscar Heidenstam, who told me that I would never win a major physique award because I had ugly feet and the judging panel would take this into consideration when choosing a winner; my feet would detract from the overall look and I would always be marked down. I replied to the effect that there was nothing I could do about the problem, i.e., one cannot train one's feet to become more shapely as one can with other body parts. Oscar then suggested that I should have a word with the association's medical advisor, a famous orthopaedic surgeon named Ian MacQueen, who by strange coincidence practised in my hometown of Bristol. I spoke with Ian about the problem, who was undoubtedly quite amused by the prospect of working on my feet but said he would have a word with one of the foremost orthopaedic surgeons in the country, our old friend Ken Pridie.

I returned to Bristol thoroughly disconsolate about the whole sorry Mr Universe weekend, but soon received a phone call from Ian telling me that he had made an appointment for me to have a consultation with Mr Pridie. So it was back to Winford Hospital, where both Ian and Mr Pridie were consultants, which brought back memories of my stay at the hospital 11 years earlier. Mr Pridie took one look at my feet, complete with hammer toes and abnormally big toe joints that looked like bunions, and uttered, "Yes, I can see what they mean - they are ugly."

Then followed a series of questions.

"Can you walk on them?"

"Yes."

"Can you run okay?"

"Yes."

"Can you train okay?"

"Yes."

"Do they hurt you at all?"

"No."

"Then in that case I'm not going to touch them. Having feet operated on purely for cosmetic reasons is not acceptable. Feet are the worst part of the body to muck about with and although I could operate on them and they might look slightly better you could be in pain for the rest of your life if anything went wrong. As long as you're in no pain the answer is no operation. When they start to hurt, come back and see me."

Forty years later I've still got ugly feet, but they've never hurt and dear Mr Pridie has long gone.

These circumstances effectively ended my bodybuilding career, with my boyhood hopes of being crowned Mr Universe completely dashed. However, all was not lost.

As I mentioned earlier, I was becoming quite strong and was winning local contests and titles, and it was at one of these contests - the Western Counties Strength Set Championships - that fate delivered a double whammy. The contest was held in the church hall, part of the now expanding EWC, and the whammies came in the shape of two personalities who were at the event. The first was Dennis Hillman, who was going to referee the event, and the second was former American bodybuilder, Lud Shusterich, patron of the club and newly appointed managing director of the recently established UK arm of the Weider empire, Weider Barbell Company (WBC). Den was hoping that WBC would become official sponsors and inject some much-needed finances into the club's coffers.

Dennis Hillman is one of the nicest fellows you could ever wish to meet. At that time he was a regular soldier based in Reading and weighed in at 21st (around 135kg), and he was the British Heavyweight Olympic Champion to boot. I know that Dennis won't mind my next observation: he wasn't exactly God's gift to weightlifting technique and whenever he lifted in a competition it was always debatable whether he was going to do a good lift or end up flat on his arse, and it was invariably the latter. He was, and still is, a very strong giant of a man. He refereed my class, which I duly won, and to my surprise he suggested that we give the audience a bit of additional excitement by having a pressing contest, with him doing the two-hands press (his favourite lift, in which he'd done 340lb in training), and me doing the press behind neck, which is a bodybuilders' exercise and much more difficult. I knew there was no way in which I was going to beat him, but I reckoned I could still give him a good run for his money. In the event, he only beat me by 30lb, achieving a 300lb press as against my 270lb one.

When it was all over Dennis said to me, "Dave, I don't know why you bother with all this strength set lifting. It doesn't have international recognition and you're strong enough and athletic enough to have a go at Olympic lifting. Why don't you give it a try?" I told him I'd think about it and left it at that. At that time I was becoming despondent about strength set competitions, as one of the three lifts was the squat and tall men are invariably bad squatters, plus of course my left leg was always under par. I was at that stage where I already had the curl record under my belt and was only 2lb short of the 432lb British record on the bench press. But I was woefully down on the squat, struggling around the 400-430lb mark, whereas the shorter, stockier lifters were achieving in excess of 600lb. As a result, I could go into the final squat phase of the competition 70-80lb ahead of my rivals and have that lead completely wiped out and overtaken, pushing me into second or third place. Whilst I enjoyed competing, I also enjoyed winning. Once again, as with my Mr Universe aspirations, the writing was firmly on the wall.

A few years later the governing body of the weightlifting association re-evaluated the strength set and decided to drop the curl, as it was subject to so much controversy from a refereeing point of view. The two-hands dead lift took its place, and strength set lifters all of a sudden became power lifters.

Lud Shusterich, of Yugoslav descent, was the holder of the title of America's Most Muscular Man in the early '50s. He was an engineer by profession and had somehow persuaded brothers Joe and Ben Weider of the mighty Weider bodybuilding equipment and magazine publishing empire to let him open a UK offshoot of the company, so Lud had set up in business in a disused garage in the centre of Croydon. He was doing everything he could to ingratiate both himself and the Weider company into anything official that would give them credibility in the much broader spectrum of international weightlifting and bodybuilding.

Right from the start Lud was up against brick walls. All the bodybuilding in the UK was controlled by Oscar Heidenstam and his organisation, The National Amateur Bodybuilding Association (NABBA), and all weightlifting was controlled by a rival association, The British Amateur Weightlifters Association (BAWLA), run by a committee but effectively controlled by one man, Oscar State. To make matters worse, Joe Weider in the USA and his brother Ben in Canada had formed their own association, The International Federation of Bodybuilders (IFBB), and they too were trying to establish their federation as an officially recognised national body.

What they were all looking for was international recognition and hopefully eventually getting bodybuilding accepted into the Olympic Games as an official Olympic sport. Out of BAWLA, NABBA and the IFBB, the only association that had official recognition from the Olympic Association was BAWLA, which Oscar State controlled with an iron fist. There was the ridiculous situation of Shusterich courting Oscar State of

BAWLA in the hope that Oscar could influence the Olympic Association and BAWLA to come together and admit the IFBB into the Olympic brotherhood. BAWLA decided they wanted to run the bodybuilding in the country. Oscar Heidenstam controlled his NABBA and stuck two fingers up at everybody, as his Mr Universe contest was the biggest event in the bodybuilding calendar and nobody was going to take it away. Also, the Weider brothers actually employed Oscar State to write weightlifting reviews in the Weider bodybuilding magazine, so while he was on the payroll the Weiders had the ear of someone indirectly connected with that glittering prize at the end of the rainbow - Olympic recognition.

So it was that Lud, as patron of the EWC, came to Bristol for the Western Counties Championships to present the awards, and I got the dubious pleasure of looking after him whilst he was in Bristol. I had obviously made some sort of impression, as when I came to escort him to his train to go back to London he asked me if I might be interested in a position in the Weider organisation should one ever arise, to which I replied that I would so long as my amateur status wasn't prejudiced. He said he would keep in touch and returned to London, and I thought that would be the last I'd hear about it.

Chapter Twelve
Dipping My Toes in New Waters

So I was out of work again, had no money, and was in the embarrassing situation of living off my mum. The summer season was over, so the lido was closing and, worse still, I was persona non grata at The Glen because of the feud with the new manager. Training was going well, but that was the only bright light on the horizon.

However, news that I was no longer working at The Glen got around Bristol fairly quickly and I received an offer of the job of 'supervisor' at the new Kingswood Bowling Alley. Once again, it was an evening job, so I would still have plenty of time to continue my daily weight training schedule. It turned out that there wasn't much supervising to do, the place being mainly trouble free, so instead of just endlessly patrolling round I decided to teach myself the basic rudiments of ten-pin bowling and ended up spending most evenings instructing the clientele. My services as a 'supervisor' were plainly not needed, so to pre-empt the inevitable I started to look for another job.

I discovered that the prestigious Henleaze Lake Swimming Club, one of the oldest swimming clubs in Bristol, was looking for a lifeguard/superintendent/groundsman, so I decided to apply.

Henleaze Lake stretched a quarter of a mile from Henleaze (the posh area) to the Southmead Estate (the rough area). A committee controlled the affairs of the club and it had an elite membership of swimmers and divers, who used the lake during the summer months. Unfortunately, inebriated lads from the Southmead end were causing trouble by insisting on climbing over the fence for a late-night swim, having had their fill of scrumpy at the nearby pubs of Westbury-on-Trym. So the committee thought that my presence there as a superintendent might help stop this dangerous and unsociable behaviour. The idea was also that I could take weight training equipment to the lake and train the swimmers in order to maximise their fitness and strength, thereby improving the club's competitiveness.

By the time I heard about the job the summer season was all but over, but there were other jobs that needed to be done over the closed winter season, such as attending to the garden beds, painting the changing room, re-concreting the paths, patrolling the lake by boat and clearing up the mess left by frequent flooding of the lake in winter. The lake was also renowned for trout fishing and had a very exclusive membership of only 12 fishermen, who would take up their spots once the swimming club had closed for the evening, so another job was keeping poachers out.

I brought my mum in to run the tea shop, a position she thoroughly enjoyed, while I did mundane tasks such as keeping the dressing rooms and toilets clean, mowing the grass, checking memberships and keeping an eye on the younger element of the club to ensure that they weren't causing any offence or annoyance to the older, more staid members. I had two very happy seasons there. When the weather was good, it was idyllic; when it was bad, I sat in the tea room and waited for the sun to shine again. During the winter the water level in the lake rose by six to ten feet, so the surrounding lawns, car park and flower beds were flooded almost to the tea room, where I now tethered the rowing boat. Although very little happened in the off-season period, there were two events that gained the attention of the local press.

The first incident was when, on a routine inspection of the lake in my rowing boat, I discovered piles of waste paper floating in the water. I called the police and it turned out that it related to a robbery at a post office not far from the lake. The burglars had thrown all the unwanted documents over the fence into the Southmead end of the lake, thinking that it would disintegrate over the winter and disappear without trace. They hadn't bargained for hawkeye Dave Prowse! The local *Evening Post* got hold of the story and it made the front page of the newspaper, together with a photograph of me in my rowing boat, surrounded by sodden documents, which I helped the police to scoop out of the lake. I don't know whether the police ever caught the burglars, but I do know that I never got a thank you from the Post Office for helping to recover their property.

The next incident was more traumatic. The police arrived on a Sunday morning with the news that a Southmead lad was missing. He'd been out drinking scrumpy on the Saturday night with his mates and on his way home he'd decided to climb the fence and cool off in the lake. What he'd forgotten was that the lake was a disused quarry and, although the swimming club end was perfectly safe, the Southmead end was full of submerged rocks. He had dived in while under the influence of alcohol and had smashed his head on the rocks, killing him outright. I rowed the police down to the Southmead end, where we found the body, and it was dragged behind the boat back to the club so that it could be removed from the water and taken away.

My training at the lake was going really well and I'm certain that, although I went on to become the British Heavyweight Weightlifting Champion, I was never as basically strong as I was during my 'lake' period. To give you an example, whilst I was training at the lake I didn't have any squat stands (where the bar is placed on the stand at shoulder height and you stand with your shoulders under the bar, lift the bar off the stand and do squats or deep knee bends, then stand up straight and replace the bar on the stand). Without stands, I was limited as to how much I could squat and by how much I could lift up to my shoulders. At this time I used to pull 370lb from the floor to my chest, heave it over the back of my neck so that the bar was comfortably across the back of my shoulders, do my ten repetitions of the squat, then jerk it over my head to the front of my chest and place it back on the floor - and I used to think nothing of it. Years later, when I was the British Champion, the greatest weight I ever put above my head was 370lb and that was after years of technical coaching. I might have become a better technical lifter, but I was not as powerful.

Whilst we were training at the lake I got it into my brain that, although we were getting stronger, we really could do with some additional fitness training, so Bob and I decided it would be a good idea if we put on some heavy work boots to run round the outside perimeter of the lake, a distance of one mile. Neither of us had ever run any distance before and all the training we did with weights was of the stop-start variety, i.e., exertion for the short time of lifting and then resting to recuperate for a couple of minutes. A lot of Henleaze Lake members came to try and train with us, but we were lulled into the false impression that, as well as being strong and looking good, we were reasonably fit, too.

I had plenty of free time to train and Derek Jenkins (affectionately known as 'Postie', as he was the local postman) sometimes joined us. Although Postie did the odd bit of weightlifting, he was definitely out of our league. When Bob and I were discussing our new fitness routine Postie turned up and said he would like to join us. Bob and I looked at each other, wondering how this little overweight character would be able to keep up with us on our laps of the lake, but he obviously wanted to come so we decided to humour him.

Bob and I got into our tracksuits and running boots, while Postie simply took off his jacket. The three of us trotted slowly up the slope and out of the gate, and that was the last we saw of Postie as he sprinted off into the distance. Bob and I still felt a sense of achievement on completing that one-mile course, even though we sweltered and staggered round it, had to stop for a rest five or six times and arrived back absolutely shattered. While we were struggling, Postie had breezed round the course, got back, showered and made the tea! And there he was, waiting for the two supermen to appear, with his biscuits and tea in hand. Needless to say, that was the end of our new fitness regime and Postie from then on was always referred to as "that fat little fit bastard"!

All during my time at the lake my training was improving and, in order to hone my technique on the three Olympic lifts, I'd enrolled in various weightlifting courses which in those days were held either at Bisham Abbey or Lilleshall. I had the pleasure of being coached by the then national weightlifting coach Al Murray and his assistant Ernie Peppiatt, who eventually became my coach and manager when I was selected for the Empire and Commonwealth Games in Perth, Australia, in 1962. Also on the course was one of the world's great mid-heavyweights, Louis Martin from Jamaica, now living in Derby, and his coach Bill Miller, an oil company executive. I thought it would do my lifting good to train with Louis as often as possible, so I used to motorcycle from Bristol to Derby to stay at the Miller home and get some training sessions in with Louis. These did me the world of good, especially the coaching I got from Bill. Although Al was the tops as a technical coach, Bill was a motivator who just seemed to inspire. Bill and Louis were a great team, and I couldn't help but wish I had somebody like Bill to look after me.

On the very first Bisham Abbey course I attended I had the pleasure of training with John Lear, a schoolteacher from Boreham Wood, who ran a small weightlifting club just across the road from the film studio, and we became great friends. The major difference between us was that I wanted to become a champion weightlifter and he, although a good club lifter, wanted to progress through the ranks of instructor/senior instructor/coach/staff coach and eventually become a national coach. All credit to him that on Al Murray's retirement John got what he was after - the national coach's job.

In the early '60s success had started to come. I'd been invited to enter the Mr Universe competition, although after Oscar Heidenstam's comments about my feet it had been a big anticlimax. Apart from unadvisable surgical intervention, there was nothing I could do about my big toe joints and hammer toes and, as I was breaking all sorts of weightlifting and strength records, my ambitions had changed focus from the 'body beautiful' to the 'strongest'. I'd won the Western Counties Olympic Weightlifting Championship and was subsequently placed third in the British Championships, which were held in the Shoreditch school hall. My old soldier friend, Dennis Hillman, had clinched first place, but only with about 30lb in excess of mine.

Nobody outside the Bristol area had seen much of my lifting, so it was amazing to me how much interest I attracted. The various officials from the association were looking on me as the next 'white hope' and I was getting all sorts of offers to train at various weightlifting clubs around the country. The best offer I received was from a well-known German coach, Wolfgang Peter, who was working in Newport, South Wales, and he offered to come to Bristol every Saturday just to give me technical coaching. Besides lacking in technique, I didn't have a weightlifting belt that all lifters wear as a back support, and, worse still, I used to lift in a pair of gardening boots!

I will always remember the then secretary of the association, Wally Holland, coming to see me and falling about with laughter at the sight of my boots, which were huge. Wally said he hoped I was a squat lifter (where foot movement is minimal), and when I replied that I was a fore and aft splitter he stood there scratching his head wondering how I was ever going to get my feet off the floor!

Another innovation I brought to both bodybuilding and weightlifting was that of always wearing my spectacles when competing. I didn't really need them, but ever since my early days of training I had always come up against the stigma attached to bodybuilders and weightlifters by the general public, i.e., that we were all as thick as proverbial pig shit. So I had these rather large horn-rimmed spectacles made to make me look intelligent and I would wear them in competitions. Admittedly, they would fall off occasionally, but that all added to the fun.

During the time of the 1961 Championships I'd started to have a rethink about my life and the direction in which it was going, and to be perfectly frank, apart from enjoying myself, it wasn't going anywhere. I was still courting the lovely Norma but I had nothing in the way of security and I didn't want a regular pensionable job. I had absolutely no money, I was still living at home and sponging off my mother, I was 26 years old, and I think the writing was on the wall - if I was really going to make it big in the bodybuilding and weightlifting world something major, like huge financial sponsorship, would be needed, or I would have to go over to California to train with the 'greats' out there. With none of this in my foreseeable future, I decided to get myself a decent job.

In Bristol there were quite a few major firms that offered good employment with executive positions and prospects, so I decided to write to all of these respected companies and, depending on their replies, choose which one of them I would honour with my services. I managed to get quite a few responses, but the fact that I only had three GCEs and for the past ten years had been doing things like lifeguarding and dancehall bouncing didn't impress prospective employers too much.

However, in the public eye at this time was a 'shilling a week' football lottery run by a young company called Regional Pool Promotions Ltd (RPP), and their reply was quite encouraging. The company was based in the Stokes Croft area of Bristol and had been set up by two men, Doug Arter and Mr VanNeste, together with three or four co-director friends, as a means of raising funds for the Spastics Appeal. In the lottery, each participant paid a shilling and was allocated four numbers relating to teams in the English Football League, and every Saturday the numbers were checked against the football results. If the numbers corresponded with the teams that scored the highest number of goals, the lucky winners could win a jackpot prize of several thousand pounds.

RPP employed a whole network of full- and part-time agents all over the UK, with about 600 permanent staff based at Stokes Croft who had the unenviable task of keeping around four million membership cards in some semblance of order. Supervisors, controlling small territories and employing sub-agents to collect money, worked on a commissions basis. The thought of working in a company where the staff consisted of about 50 males and 550 nubile young females held great appeal for me, so I accepted a position as a Pools Claims Clerk. My task was to investigate claims from members who thought they had struck it rich. Hopeful gamblers would either write or phone to enquire why they hadn't received the winnings from their matching lucky numbers. I then had to locate the section that covered their part of the country and the name of the collecting agent, study the list of the numbers he/she serviced, and then find the counterfoil for the member's four-number registration. I would often have to dash the enquirer's hopes, as in 99% of cases they were mistaken and weren't prize winners at all.

RPP was a good firm to work for, I got on really well with all my colleagues and initially promotion through the ranks was rapid. When my progress up the ladder started to wane and others were being offered positions that I felt should have gone to me I decided to seek some answers. Taking the bull by the horns, I went to see my favourite director, Mr Don Long, and asked him what was going on. He told me that they were more than happy with my work but felt that I wouldn't be with them for very long, expecting that sooner or later somebody within my sport would make me an offer I couldn't refuse and I would leave. My immediate reaction was that he was talking nonsense. I hadn't received even an inkling that anybody was interested in me and, besides, I was enjoying my job at RPP and was saving to get married and settle down, so a secure job in Bristol was exactly what I wanted.

As it happened, however, the company's suspicions proved right and a long-forgotten conversation about work opportunities would lure me away from RPP after a couple of years there.

Chapter Thirteen
The Weight of the World

In 1962 I became the British Heavyweight Weightlifting Champion, beating my old rival Dennis Hillman, and I will always remember sitting in the dressing room after the show in a complete daze that I was now deemed the strongest man in the country. Various officials kept coming in to offer their congratulations, as well as the national coach, Al Murray, my old pal John Lear, at whose house I'd stayed the night before, and then Wally Holland, who gave me a few little words of advice: "Don't think that just because you're the British Champion that's the end of it. For you it's just the beginning. There's the World Championships in Budapest in September to prepare for and possibly the Empire Games in Perth in November. So get back to Bristol and train like you've never trained before."

So, with the silver cup in one hand (which had to be given back at the end of the year) and a tiny, cheap, plastic plaque inscribed 'British Heavyweight Champion' that didn't even have my name on it in the other, I made my way back to Bristol more determined than ever that I was going to train even harder and make something of myself in the weightlifting world.

It was back to the EWC and also to RPP, where everything continued apace. Then one day a letter arrived from the BAWLA Secretary, Wally Holland, informing me that I'd been selected to make up the British team for the World Weightlifting Championships in Budapest. However, the letter contained a sting in the tail, in that if I accepted the invitation I would have to pay all my own travelling expenses. I took the letter to Don Long at RPP and he told me not to worry and that the firm would have a whip-round to help me out, and they raised an amazing £80 (a lot of money back in those days).

The British team comprised me as the heavyweight, Louis Martin from Jamaica as mid-heavyweight, Sylvanus Blackman lifting as light heavyweight and George Newton as the featherweight both from the West Indies, and Mike Pearman from Balham, who was coming out as a guest and not selected, plus team coach Al Murray and team manager

Wally Holland.

After a long train journey across Europe we arrived in Budapest, the capital of Hungary, a very austere place with walls still peppered with bullet holes from the 1956 uprising. We were accommodated in what was called the Teachers Hostel, where the sole source of nourishment was Wiener Schnitzel, served in huge amounts at breakfast, dinner, tea and supper, and nobody spoke any English. However, I had arrived at the weightlifting mecca and I was rubbing shoulders with the greats: men such as the World Heavyweight Champion Yuri Vlasov, who could probably beat me with one hand tied behind his back; Norbert Schemansky, the American former World Heavyweight Champion, who had bulked up from 12½ stone to over 20 stone (175lb to 280lb); and Gary Gubner, new on the scene but already the World Shot-put Champion. Then there were the Hungarian World Champions Veres and Foldi, and from Poland Baszanowski and Zelinski. I was in a state of awe and wonder at all these famous champions and overheard Wally Holland discussing me with the other team coaches: "This man of ours, a totally unknown powerhouse, he'll start when all your men have finished." I thought to myself, what a load of crap! They're all going to be sorely disappointed when I'm the first lifter to go on and they see the sort of poundages I'm struggling with. To give you some idea of the situation, on my big night I pressed 287lb and Vlasov did 412lb; I failed to get a jerk in and Vlasov set a new world record of 446lb.

When it came to selecting training times, I suggested that it would be beneficial if we all trained in the evening, the time of day that the competition would be held, but I was immediately shouted down. The coach and manager obviously wanted to keep the evenings free for socialising in the bars of Budapest and so they persuaded the others that training at 10 a.m. would be the best time. Being one voice amongst seven, I accepted the 'joint' decision but let everyone know that I wasn't happy with it.

We were also told that the main focus must be on Louis Martin. As he was the only team member that stood any chance of winning, everything was to be sacrificed for him. Whilst I agreed to some extent, in the forefront of my mind were all my RPP colleagues, who had pooled their hard-earned money to give me a chance. How was I going to face them on my return? Would they appreciate it if I were sacrificed so that another team member, totally unknown to them, could get a medal?

On the first training session I pulled my trapezius muscle and ended up with a stiff neck to end all stiff necks. To my mind, this was a direct result of heavy training so early in the day. I let my feelings be known, but the team manager and coach seemed totally unconcerned and their response was to suggest that perhaps it might be better if I trained on my own in the evening, as I was having an upsetting effect on the rest of the team. So there I was, out in Budapest, miles away from home, suffering an injured neck that nobody seemed the slightest bit interested in (I wasn't even offered a massage), I couldn't speak the language, I hated the food, and yet I was preparing to perform in the biggest weightlifting event of my career. I wandered round the training hall feeling heartily sorry for myself and stopped to watch Tony Assaro, a lifter from South Africa, who was in Budapest on his own and had found an Austrian weightlifting coach to help him with his training. We got talking and I told him of my problems, whereupon he suggested that I train with him and his coach, and I was very thankful for the offer.

I trained lightly to start with and the neck pain slowly eased off, but in the ensuing ten days I saw very little of my teammates, coach or manager. If anyone wanted to contact me (which was very seldom), a note was left on my bedroom door. 'Ostracism' was the word that rapidly came to mind. I was being ostracised by the members of the team, who all seemed to think that I was colour-prejudiced, and my palling up with a lifter from South Africa, where strong apartheid policies existed, didn't do my cause any good. Although Tony and I were training together, I really couldn't conjure up the necessary intensity. I hadn't recovered from the neck strain, I wasn't eating well, and it bothered me that the rest of my team were not even speaking to me.

When training was over I would wander aimlessly around the streets that encompassed the hostel. One evening I decided to send postcards home and went to a little kiosk to get stamps, but I couldn't make myself understood as the lady behind the counter didn't speak a word of English. I was becoming increasingly frustrated when out of the blue a lady behind me piped up, "Is there anything I can do to be of help?" I turned to see this little lady of about 50 years old and blurted out something like, "My God, somebody who speaks English!" She then explained that she had lived for many years in the Marble Arch area of Edgware Road but had come home to Budapest to be with the rest of her family. The stamps were bought and I was invited to her flat, located opposite the hostel, for a good cup of English tea. Her flat was stocked with English produce, most of which had been sent out from big stores such as Harrods and Selfridges on a weekly basis. This lovely lady then looked after me for the remainder of my stay in Hungary.

A couple of days before I was due to compete, I was out sightseeing and came across a fruit seller who had the biggest and juiciest grapes I'd ever seen, so I promptly bought myself a kilo and tucked in. I never even considered that they needed to be washed, and the result of this indulgence was the worst case of dysentery known to man or beast. Lifting became impossible (try it yourself next time you have dysentery) and all I could do was hope and pray that I would be over the worst before the competition.

My lady friend had arranged a big surprise for me: a trip to the classiest place in Budapest, the famous Hotel Geliert, accompanied by her daughter and two male cousins. I was to be at her flat at 8 p.m. to meet the teenage boys and her daughter Agnes. Agnes, a trainee physiotherapist, was a real beauty - blonde, pretty, lovely figure - but she didn't speak one word of English. If only the team could have seen me walking out with Agnes on my arm, although it was probably better that they didn't, as they might've put two and two together and come up with the wrong answer. We had a great night at the hotel and, being the good, conscientious lifter that I was, I escorted them all back to the flat before leaving for the depressing atmosphere of the hostel.

Finally the competition day dawned for the heavyweights. It was normally a day to relax, as all the training had been done, and so I spent a pleasant day with Agnes walking in the parks. Because of the great interest in the heavyweight lifters, the organisers decided to change the venue from the indoor hall to the outside stadium in order to accommodate the expected crowds. I turned up at the stadium with Agnes on my arm, only to be met by the most forbidding of looks from Al and Wally. In their minds it would seem that I was now not only colour-prejudiced but also a fornicator! Agnes made her way into the stands to watch the contest while I went down to the dressing room to warm up. However, it was soon quite obvious that I was not over the ravages of dysentery and every warm-up weight I handled felt like half a ton! I decided to take 286lb for my first lift and only just got it, failing on the next two. I took 231lb for my first and only snatch and then had to face the ignominy of not being able to jerk 330lb on my first attempt. I'd managed to get the weight up to my shoulders okay, but every time I dipped to squat and drive the bar up it felt as if my entire insides were about to be dumped on the floor. In the end I failed all three attempts and therefore didn't make a total. I slunk away from the stadium feeling as if my whole world had crashed around me.

The following day we left Budapest for home and the first thing I noticed was that none of the black guys in the team wanted to sit in the same compartment as me, and all across Europe the atmosphere was strained. At Dover we got off the train to stretch our legs and buy a newspaper. Imagine my surprise when I saw across the back sports page the heading: 'Dave Prowse selected as heavyweight representative for the Empire and Commonwealth Games in Perth, Australia, in November'. I could feel the tension between myself and the rest of the team growing. I knew they thought I was racially prejudiced by going off on my own in Budapest and palling up with the South African, but the strange thing was that in reality they were actually prejudiced against me. I was the only non-black person in the Budapest team, and the team that was selected for Perth once again consisted of four West Indians plus me. Louis Martin, who had just won the World Mid-heavyweight world title had to be physically restrained by the others to stop him throwing a punch at me. Al (coach) and Wally (manager) both said that if it had been up to them I would never have been selected for Perth, and so we travelled back to London with me in one coach and the rest of the team in the next coach. It wasn't exactly the most auspicious start to my international weightlifting career.

The Empire Games were only about two months away. The authorities had studied the weather patterns over the previous 50 years and had decided that early November, at the start of the Australian summer, would be the most equitable time to run the event. In the two-month build-up to Perth I was back into hard training, Al Murray had been appointed team coach and an old weightlifting stalwart, Ernie Peppiatt, was to be the team manager. I had received a somewhat apologetic letter from the Weightlifting Association (Wally Holland), telling me to put the Budapest experience behind me and to concentrate on getting myself into the best possible condition, as there was a realistic chance that I might get into the medals, even though it was unlikely to be more than a bronze.

The British team consisted of Louis Martin at mid-heavy, George Manners at light heavy, Carl Goring at lightweight, George Newton at featherweight and me at heavyweight. All was friendly when we met up in London for the flight out to Perth and we had a very pleasant trip, stopping off in Rome, Tehran, Bombay and Singapore. When we got to Perth we were all bussed out to the Empire Games Village, a new one-storey house complex built about a mile inland from a very nice beach called City Beach. Our apartment had three bedrooms, one with three beds and the other two with two beds in each, and Al and Ernie chose the best of the two-bed rooms for themselves. The next thing I saw was one of my teammates moving one of the beds out of the other small bedroom in order to make the larger room a four-bed room, leaving the remaining room with just a single bed. When I asked what was going on I was effectively told that they all thought I'd like to be on my own (shades of Budapest all over again), to which I replied, no way, we all stick together, we train together, we eat together, we sleep together. So the lone bed was moved into the main bedroom, making it now a very cramped five-bed bedroom. This gesture on my part really struck a chord with the other guys and I was welcomed back into the fold just like one of the brothers.

Our training headquarters was the police gymnasium just two miles away in Scarborough. The walls and roof were constructed of corrugated iron sheets and in the summer heat it was worse than working-out in a sauna bath. Despite this, it was here that I did some of the best training of my life, with World Champion Louis Martin as my training partner. Mention of the weather reminds me that we had the most dramatic changes of climate while we were there, so those studies of the last 50 years' weather conditions proved absolutely useless. Just before we arrived, there had been the most torrential rain ever experienced on the west coast of Australia and everything was flooded; then, when the sun shone it did so with a vengeance and Perth sweltered in 100 degree-plus temperatures. It was so hot that walking barefoot blistered my feet.

Socially, Perth was most enjoyable. The residents had been told to go out of their way to make the competitors as welcome as possible and there were always queues of cars at the entrance to the village waiting to take out any competitor wearing an Empire Games blazer.

My company back in the UK, RPP, who raised funds for the spastics charity, had arranged for me to meet the head of the spastics organisation in Australia, Joe Michell. The first thing that Joe did was to invite me to a special Sunday morning brunch. I don't know whether it happens now, but each year the spastics organisation held the Miss Australia Quest, a beauty contest in which the girls were not only beautiful but also had to raise funds for the charity. The title holder in 1962 was a lovely lady from Adelaide by the name of Tricia Reschke, who was a dead ringer for Ava Gardner, and Joe had the idea that it would be great publicity for the charity if I could meet up with Tricia and act as her escort during her visit to Perth. Just to show the team that everything was above board, I took Al and Ernie to the brunch with me and a great morning was spent with about 30-40 other guests. Tricia was every bit as attractive and charming as I'd been told and I had the pleasure of escorting her to various functions whenever training allowed. When the games finished Joe made me an offer of work in Australia, helping to organise the Miss Australia Quest contest, which I reluctantly turned down.

The England weightlifting team attracted an enormous amount of attention, primarily because we had World Champion Louis Martin, but also because there had been a minor revolution in weightlifting that the entire British team were incorporating, and the rest of the Commonwealth wanted to see what was going on. In the Three Olympics, as the competition used to be known, the contestants competed on three lifts: the two-hands clean and press, the two-hands snatch and the two-hands clean and jerk. The first of the three lifts was the most controversial in terms of refereeing. It involved lifting the bar from the floor to the shoulder and then, on the referee's signal, pressing the barbell overhead to arm's length using only the power of the arms and shoulders. In a perfect lift there would be little or no back bending and the bar wasn't supposed to stop at all on the way up. It was the little or no back bend element that was causing trouble, as each referee had his own idea as to what was passable and what was excessive.

Over the years, the referees' interpretation of limited back bend had become more and more lax, until reaching the situation where lifters were bending back so much that their shoulders practically touched their backsides. In 1960 a Russian light heavyweight named Rudi Pluckfelder arrived on the scene with a totally new way of performing the press lift and he actually won the world title. Rudi was very quick and agile; in fact, he looked more like a large gymnast. The referees had never seen anything like his revolutionary pressing style before, and although they knew that something wasn't quite right they couldn't pinpoint exactly what it was during the competition and all his lifts were getting passed.

All the world's top coaches went home from the World Championships armed with loads of cine film of Rudi doing his thing. In the comfort of their own viewing rooms they analysed the footage in slow motion, discovering that Rudi was cheating like mad. However, rather than discipline Rudi for his infringement of the rules, the coaches thought that if this was what Rudi was getting away with then this was the method of lifting that now ought to be taught. Without getting too technical, Rudi's technique was that once he'd cleaned (hoisted the weight to the shoulders) he put his body into a bow-like position with what was termed a soft knee lock. The bow position was the first infringement and the soft knee lock the second. At the referee's signal to press, it was just as though the string of a longbow had been cut. Rudi snapped his knees straight, which began the upward propulsion of the weight. He then sank into a back bend position just as his arms were almost straight and then came very quickly out of that position, pressing or pushing the weight out into the arms locked position (straight up) to complete the lift. Rudi was a very athletic lifter and from the referee's signal to the completion of the lift only a second or two elapsed. Therefore, the referee had to make a very quick decision. To the naked eye, Rudi hadn't bent his knees, whereas in reality he had done so, but it was so quick that the referee was unable to register it. He was in and out of the back bend position so fast that it was impossible for a referee to determine just how far he'd bent back, and in addition the bar hadn't stopped at all in its upward travel to the press out position. So Rudi was crowned as the new World Champion and record holder using a new style of lift that broke most of the rules in the book.

So the coaches in different countries started coaching the new technique. At the same time, the referees analysed their films and decided that the new style of press was an infringement and ought to be stamped out. Worse still, for me personally, was the fact that most of the Commonwealth countries never lifted in the World Championships so they had never seen the lift in the first place.

Back home I'd been training like mad with my German coach, Wolfgang Peter, and with this new technique I'd pressed 330lb in training, which was very close to a new British record. I'd also snatched 270lb and clean and jerked 370lb, so all I had to do was get all three maximums on the night of the competition and I'd be in for the bronze medal. The gold and silver medals were going to be decided between the Australian and New Zealand lifters, Arthur Shannos and Don Oliver, and I was confident that I could get the bronze ahead of the Jamaican lifter Brandon Bailey. The one thing we'd completely discounted about the new press was that Rudi was a very athletic 5ft 9in light-heavy, weighing around 175lb, while I was a 6ft 7in, 19 stone (260lb) lumbering giant, and any moves that I did would be a lot more obvious to the referees.

I went into the competition in the best condition of my life and opted to take 295lb for my first attempt. The weight came up to my chest as though it was nothing, I got into the bow position, and on the referee's signal I rammed the weight aloft. I got the signal that the lift was completed and started to leave the platform to fantastic applause, only for the applause to turn into boos and hisses. I'd been given red lights - the sign of a no-lift. Al and Ernie got me off the platform and both of them seemed as much in a quandary as I was. I wanted to know what was wrong but neither of them could tell me. The speculation was that perhaps I had twisted slightly as the weight went up and Al suggested that I take the same weight for my second attempt, which I performed with ease. Again, I got the red lights and now I was in real trouble, as if my third lift wasn't accepted I would be disqualified from the competition. Again I asked Al what was wrong and he'd reached the conclusion that my soft knee lock was too obvious, so the same weight was called for my third and final attempt and I went out onto the platform with the instruction to go back to the old style of pressing and to get the weight overhead with no knee movement and minimum back bend. Once again, the weight sailed from the floor to my shoulders, I braced my knees straight, and then I pushed for all I was worth, making sure that the weight was securely aloft.

As I was putting the weight back down on the platform, boos started ringing out again. I turned round and saw more red lights. I was out of the competition. Al complained to the jury of appeal, only to be told that the lift had been failed as it had stopped on the way up! I slunk back to the warm-up area and all but broke down. I'd failed to make a total in Budapest and now I'd failed to make a total in Perth - I felt a complete failure. Both Al and Ernie were very sorry about what had happened and told me to put it all behind me and just set my mind on training for the Olympic Games, which were due to be held in Tokyo in two years' time, adding that I'd been a first-class member of the team and a credit to the Games.

And so, after an exciting but non-productive few weeks in Australia, I returned to the UK - back to training at home and at the EWC, and back to work for the Spastics Football Pool firm.

Chapter Fourteen
Local Boy Makes Good!

The date of the 1963 British Championships - July, in Shoreditch - had been announced and Norma and I had set our wedding date for 5 October (much to her mother's relief!) Club matches, which I won, came and went, as did internationals against Denmark and Sweden, which I also won.

To my surprise, however, only a few weeks later one of my co-workers at RPP rushed in to tell me that there was a phone call for me - from Paris. It was Lud Shusterich calling to offer me a business opportunity in Croydon. His plan was to open a three-floor premises on the high street there. On the top floor would be a gym, to be run by my old mentor Reub Martin; the basement would be converted into a sauna/massage parlour, to be run by another physical culturist friend, Ted Durante; and the ground floor would become a sports shop, which he wanted me to run. The shop would sell all the Weider products - weights, magazines, supplements, etc. - and I would be able to stock it with whatever I wanted in the way of clothing, trainers, swimwear, etc. I told Lud that I needed time to think it over and discuss it with Norma. In view of the fact that it was June and we were only four months away from our planned wedding date and the start of our new life together, we came to the conclusion that it was a great opportunity and an offer I couldn't refuse. I would have my own retail business and would be able to make a decent living on which I could support my wife and future family. Although I enjoyed working for RPP, the job wasn't really going anywhere either, so I therefore accepted the offer and agreed with Lud that I would start working for the Weider Organisation on the Monday following the British Weightlifting Championships at the end of July 1963.

The British Championships heavyweight class was a really interesting mix and included two new characters, Bob Niles from the West Indies and Terry Perdue from Swansea, South Wales. Bob was a stylish lifter, with a good personality and great physique, but he wasn't quite ready to take the title from me (he took it in 1965 when I'd retired). Terry was an enormous bull of a man, a scrap dealer, and he didn't have a clue about the technique of the lifts. He was like an unleashed tiger on the platform and was difficult to coach and control. It was all brute force and ignorance in those early days, and nine times out of ten his technique was so bad and his behaviour so erratic that he failed to register a total, so it was quite easy for me to beat him. However, I could see the writing on the wall. He was stuffing himself with all the performance-enhancing drugs that he could get his hands on and subsequently became one of the strongest men in the world. If only he'd paid more attention to the technique of the three lifts instead of relying on sheer brute force he could have become a great lifter. As it was, his appearances on the platform were always a bit of a joke and brought great hilarity to what was normally quite a serious occasion. Sometimes he lifted enormous weights and at other times he'd fall flat on his arse with them. We never knew what he was going to do, but it certainly made for interesting competitions.

I had previously met Terry in a dead lift competition organised by TWW (Television Wales and the West). The show went out as a sports programme every Friday night and Danny Blanchflower, the former Spurs and Ireland football captain, was compèring the show. The dead lift is probably one of the simplest of lifts in terms of both competing and refereeing, as all the lifter has to do is pick up as heavy a barbell as he can manage and stand up straight with it. In those days, the bar could stop on the way up, resting on the thighs, to allow time to readjust the grip. Practically anything was accepted, apart from the bar starting to go back down when it was supposed to be moving upwards.

The show contained a dead lift strength contest and a phone-in challenge. The contest had started with smaller guys lifting around the 300-400lb mark, progressing over the weeks to Terry doing a lift of 525lb. I was doing a lot of training on the dead lift at home and was way up over the 600lb mark, so I phoned in with a challenge and found myself on the show dead-lifting against Terry. We started at 525lb, moving up to 550lb, then 600lb, and we both ended the show for that week with a lift of 625lb. Not one person phoned in to challenge us, so we were back on the following Friday for the big showdown. We both took 625lb, which Terry only just managed. I then went on to 650lb, which I did easily, and I eventually called for the new British record poundage of 675lb. I won the competition and when the bar was officially weighed it was 678¾lb, a record that stood for many years. I was presented with a wonderful silver cup for my efforts, which I treasure to this day. Just after the competition had finished and all the congratulations were over, I was asked if I'd like to attempt 700lb, and although all the impetus of the competition had gone I still had a go and actually got the bar up as far as my knees before regretfully conceding, but I was happy with the new British record.

Only two years later, I was doing a tour of Scotland with the legendary US bodybuilder George Eiferman, giving weightlifting and bodybuilding exhibitions. The tour was organised by the famous Scots physical culturist and World Highland Games authority, Dave Webster, who asked me if I would like to have a go at lifting the infamous Dinnie Stones at the Bridge of Petrarch while I was up in Scotland. Legend has it that Donald Dinnie, a Scottish athlete of the late 1800s, was helping his father point the bridge when their horses started to stray down to the river. "Bring the steens," (stones) the father shouted to Donald, who was up on the riverbank about 18 yards from the bridge. The steens were used for tethering the horses and were nothing more than granite boulders, each of which had an iron hook embedded into it. At his father's command, Donald climbed up the riverbank, picked up the stones by the hooks and, taking one in each hand, walked the 18 yards back to the river. He put down the stones and then went to retrieve the horses and tethered them to the hooks. Donald had been good Highland Games athlete, competing in all the events, but he wasn't renowned for being super-strong. News of the feat soon got around and the stones were eventually weighed, revealing that they were a staggering 784lb in total!

Over the years, whenever a visiting strongman has visited Scotland, Dave Webster has invariably collared him and invited him to go to Petrarch to see if he can duplicate Donald's feat. My turn came in September 1963, the week before I was married. Dave took both George and myself to Petrarch by way of Inver, where I carried the Inver Manhood Stone, an egg-shaped granite boulder weighing 268lb. It sits on the village green and anyone who can pick it up and carry it into the local pub is rewarded with a glass of the publican's best ale. When we eventually arrived in Petrarch, reporters from the press, radio and TV had already gathered, plus a crowd of curious onlookers. The steens - the lighter one triangular and the other rectangular - were chained to a rail outside a public house for fear that visiting rugby clubs would steal them. To be honest, they didn't look all that formidable. Once unlocked, Dave suggested that I warm up by lifting the stones singly. At this stage I'd better point out that in all the years since Donald Dinnie nobody had ever lifted the two stones together, let alone walked with them, and some of the world's strongest men had tried.

So I started with the three hundredweight boulder, picking it up and putting it down a few times just to get the feel of it. Then I did the same with the heavier one. Neither of them seemed to be a problem. I then placed them side by side, about 18 inches apart, and made ready to have a go at lifting the two together. At that point Dave broke off from his interviews with the reporters and hurried over, advising me not to try to lift the stones side by side. He explained that back in the 1800s it was common to wear long leather boots as leg protectors from the heather and bracken, whereas I was only wearing tracksuit bottoms, so he was concerned that I would take all the skin off the sides of my legs as I hauled the stones up if they were in that position. He advised me to use a fore and aft straddle instead, i.e., one stone placed in front and one behind, with my legs wide apart. This is not the best mechanical way of lifting heavy weights, and with only a week to go to my honeymoon I didn't want anything to go wrong! Dave then alerted the press that I was ready and the two stones, all 7cwt of them, came up quite easily. So there I was, legs wide apart with 7cwt of boulders dangling, and Dave shouted, "Right, now walk the 18 yards down to the river." Walk, with that huge weight lengthening my arms by the second?!

The most I could do was to shuffle my feet a few inches, and after around six shuffles I'd only moved about two feet. I put down the stones and everyone raced over to congratulate me. "What do you think of Donald Dinnie now?" asked one of the reporters, to which I replied, "I think he was a bloody liar!" I reckon that he actually took the stones over one at a time and that the story has snowballed with the telling. I am in the record book as being the first person ever to lift the Dinnie Stones together, and I'd also kept my manhood intact, so I would be okay for my wedding.

Anyway, back to my move to Croydon. I left Bristol in a blaze of publicity - 'Local weightlifter wins British Heavyweight title and takes up position in London running his speciality sports shop'. My firm had arranged for me to go into lodgings with one of their agents in the Shirley district of Croydon, and Lud had already signed the lease for the property on the high street, so, having won the British Championships for a second time, I was now on my way to fame and fortune up the Smoke, as London was affectionately called.

Formerly a garage, the Weider office was a short lease premises in the centre of Croydon. The staff consisted of Lud as MD, together with business manager and mail order/direct mail specialist Ed Casson, Lud's loyal secretary Mrs Mutter, and mad Hungarian barbell packer Steve Hubay. Although this was the headquarters of the firm, I was more interested in viewing the shop so that I could start stocking it and getting it ready for opening.

Introductions over, I was ushered into Lud's office. He was sitting in a huge leather chair behind a huge wooden desk, and above his head was a huge picture of him and President Kennedy. Then he dropped a bombshell. He told me that he'd offered the shop to someone else -a former agent of Weider who ran a retail outlet in Greek Street, Soho. I was flabbergasted! I had left a good job in Bristol, left home, left Norma and had been promised the earth by Weider, and now in one sentence all my hopes for the future had been dashed. To return to Bristol, after leaving in a blaze of glory, would be humiliating to say the least.

Ed Casson took me to one side and asked me if I would like to become his assistant, helping him with the running of the business, with the aim of establishing Weider as a major force in the British physical culture field, and getting involved in the production and promotion of the European editions of the two Weider muscle magazines, *Muscle Power* and *Your Physique*.

As disappointed as I was, I decided to give it a go and accepted Ed's offer. Thus began an association with the company that would eventually see me become European sales manager, opening accounts with all the leading sports and department stores and culminating in my being given my own Keep Trim department in Harrods, running weight training at the National Sports Centre at Crystal Palace and going into show business.

Ironically, the shop was never opened, the sauna attracted limited business, and the gym found itself facing competition from another health club that set up nearby, so Lud eventually surrendered the lease. So maybe, although I didn't know at the time, fate was playing a hand.

Chapter Fifteen
Climbing the Weider Ladder

One attraction of being up in London was that I would be able to visit the major weightlifting clubs and train with other champions and their coaches, but finding my feet within the Weider company was proving difficult. I was on the same pay as I'd been earning in Bristol - £15 per week - and my living expenses were so much more down in Croydon that I was only just making ends meet, with no chance of saving anything for my forthcoming wedding. Consequently, I decided to hand in my notice.

Lud, who worshipped the Weider brothers, couldn't believe that I didn't want to work for the organisation and promptly tore up my notice. He then put one of his long arms around my shoulder, said that he'd been thinking about my future and had decided to appoint me as the European sales manager. That sounded very grand, but Weider had no sales staff either in the UK or in Europe, their products had never been sold to the retail trade, magazines sold on the continent in very small numbers, and any mail-order business went direct to the USA. Lud wanted to open up the retail trade business, but there was a lot of opposition from store owners and buyers to companies that were trying to cash in on both markets - the retail trade and the mail-order trade. It seemed one did either one or the other, not both.

Lud thought that my status as a champion weightlifter would be just the lever his company needed to open the door to the retail trade, and the fact that I'd never sold anything in my life and didn't even have a driving licence didn't deter him. The only vehicle the company possessed was an old Bedford Dormobile, which Lud used for ferrying his wife and four children around, and this was commandeered as both my delivery and sales wagon. My brief was to go out and sell to the retail trade, sports shops and the major department stores throughout the UK and also in the rest of Europe.

I had learned to drive whilst living in Bristol, but during my driving test I was following a lorry up Blackboy Hill when it broke down. The examiner said that I should have anticipated that it might break down and failed me for driving too close. With that, I threw caution to the wind, tore up the 'L' plates and continued to drive as though I was fully qualified. So when Lud produced the Dormobile I didn't tell him that I wasn't qualified and promptly accepted the position, at the same time applying for the earliest driving test I could get, which I subsequently passed.

I had no idea how to approach store buyers, especially when trying to get into the big stores like Harrods and Lillywhites. Each Sunday I used to load the van with about a ton of assorted weights, barbells, supplements and magazines, ready for my rounds for the ensuing week. Then it was off into the Greater London area armed with an A to Z map book and a copy of the *Yellow Pages* in order to locate all the sports stores. The one thing I had going for me was my physical presence. My arrival at a shop, armed with the magazines and samples, caused quite a stir and very few owners refused to see me. I could also talk - not just the general sales patter but about weight training and physical culture and, of course, about my own career, so most of my visits were as much social as sales.

When I started my new venture, very few shops were interested in selling weight training equipment, as the items were bulky, very heavy to move around the store and difficult to display. Also, at that time body-building and weightlifting were very much minority sports. In addition, a major rival company was offering to send equipment, weighing anything from 40lb to 300lb, direct to the customer via a carrier, thus negating the need for retail outlets to stock it. If someone went into a sports store wanting a barbell set, the sales assistant could show the customer an illustrated catalogue from which to choose and then the set would be ordered and delivered direct. Also, firms that had tried selling to the stores used to charge hefty carriage rates, which the customers objected to paying. In the end, however, there is no substitute for seeing exactly what you want 'in the flesh', paying for it and taking it home there and then. Mail order often meant a wait of two weeks for delivery, especially with heavy items, via a disgruntled carrier complaining like mad about the weight.

One of the innovations that I introduced was a stand that could display two barbells and four dumb-bells in an upright position, requiring a base area of just two square feet. This addressed the existing display and space issues and stores could also buy direct from me, thus avoiding all the carriage costs. Added to this, I was able to offer the shop or store inclusion in a stockists list in the magazine. So not only did I sell the gear,

I also delivered it, set it up on the stand where required, and gave demonstrations and talks at the store on how to lift or train properly. Besides doing all that, I had to do all my own driving, navigating my way around the country using street maps and A to Zs, and I was expected to contribute to the magazine by doing reports on weightlifting and bodybuilding events up and down the country.

Lud had received the okay from BAWLA for me to be employed by Weider without any infringement of my amateur status, but little did I know when I joined the company that practically everything I did was going to be scrutinised by the petty-minded officials who made up the BAWLA central council committee. My first brush with officialdom came when I reported on the British Weightlifting Championships in which I competed. This was deemed a breach of my amateur status and I was summoned to appear before the council. What rules or by-laws of the association I'd infringed I do not know, as I wasn't being paid for writing and I didn't receive any expenses for attending. One of the leading members of the central council had been in the employ of the Weider brothers for years, earning sizeable amounts of money from them, but nobody every queried that. Anyway, at the end of the meeting I was ticked off for being a bad boy, instructed that my name wasn't to appear on any more articles and told that my offence this time would be overlooked. I still continued to write reports on events and matches and, as Weider had a whole host of famous American bodybuilders under contract, I just drew a name out of the hat each time I wrote an article. It was quite funny to see some very minor club match reported on by one of the famous physique stars, even though they'd not been in the country let alone attending a minor club match.

The trouble with working with Lud was that he thought he owned me and that he could call on me at his whim to do all sorts of work away from the firm, usually in his home or, worse still, in his garden. It was quite usual to get invited to his home, a new house in Kenley, for lunch or dinner and be asked to arrive three or four hours early. On arrival Lud would have a long list of jobs around the house and garden that he needed doing and for three or four hours I would hump rocks, concrete and rubbish that had been left by the building contractor. Dinner never appeared before all the work had been completed, by which time I was fit to drop and Lud's four children were screaming with hunger. Very quickly I learned my lesson and managed to wangle my way out of his meal invitations.

Harrods and Lillywhites became my major clients and I had a

wonderful association with the two buyers, Alf Cole at Harrods and Mr Grace at Lillywhites. I'll always remember the first appointment with Mr Cole. Harrods in the early 1960s was completely different to the way it is today; it was more like visiting a museum than going to a store. The atmosphere was hallowed. All the buyers wore frock coats and pinstripe trousers and each department seemed to have acres of space. There was a beautiful banking/exhibition hall on the ground floor and the food halls were fantastic. Literally nothing was too much trouble. The boast was that Harrods could supply anything: everything from Christening wear to funeral arrangements could be provided, the pet department could locate an elephant if asked, and even a battleship was not out of the question.

Into this wonderful institution strolled yours truly, fresh from the country and brand new to selling. Alf Cole, or Mr Cole as I always called him (all throughout our 20-year association and friendship), was a short, portly man with an air of authority and a very dry sense of humour. I was ushered into his office by his secretary, Miss Brazier, and I then started to deliver my sales pitch. All went well until I got to the bit about the price of the equipment and uttered, "The suggested retail price is …". He cut into my spiel and retorted, "Don't ever try to tell me what I should sell your equipment for. Harrods is the retailer and I will decide how much the equipment will retail for. I'm certain you do not want me to tell you the price at which I will purchase." He then proceeded to give me a very interesting lecture on the way Harrods worked and what would be required of me and the Weider company if I were to be entrusted with an order. Mr Cole was also very interested in the magazine and the articles I'd fronted, and the offer of a listing as a stockist sealed the deal and secured my first order.

At this juncture, 1963, the Harrods sports department was on the second floor at the Hans Crescent end of the store and, although it was labelled 'sports' it actually only specialised in two things: golf (a section run by golf pro Tom Bovingdon) and cycling. Some of the more exotic sports, such as archery, squash and tennis, were catered for, but for years there were no football boots, swimwear, sports clothing or trainers, which are now standard and major selling items in any sports store. This was changed later when the sports department expanded to take over the whole of the fourth floor and Harrods' Olympic Way was born.

Chapter Sixteen
Going It Alone: from Stifled
Amateur to Enterprising Pro

Life proceeded with the Weider organisation, with me travelling all over the country opening up new accounts wherever I went. However, I never cracked the European market, as I was far too busy dealing with the UK customers and dear Lud wouldn't hire any more staff to make inroads into other markets. I think he only ever saw the trade sales as a minor adjunct to the quite considerable mail order and direct mail sales that they were achieving through Ed Casson's admirable work with the magazines, but the company at least had the prestige of being a Harrods and Lillywhites supplier. Lud was very proud of his collection of celebrity friends and customers, so being a supplier to the store where royalty shopped was very important to him.

I was obviously still training hard and was chasing all over London to different weightlifting gyms in order to train with some of our very best lifters and receive coaching from our best coaches, including John Lear at Boreham Wood; Al Murray, the national coach at the St Brides Institute in Blackfriars; George Manners, the British Light Heavyweight Champion at Balham; Danny Donovan and Sylvanus Blackman in Putney; and Ernie Peppiatt at Kentish Town. I even went as far as Derby to train with our then World Mid Heavyweight Champion, Louis Martin, and his coach Bill Miller.

Lud was still trying to ingratiate himself with BAWLA and had actually bought one of the prestigious Russian Olympic barbells, a most beautiful set, and presented it to the association - but not before he had removed all references to its Russian manufacture and had painted the word 'Weider' in giant letters on every plate in the set. As a result, every time it was used for a championship or an international, any photos that appeared in the magazine or the press prominently featured the Weider name, which obviously was quite a good advertising coup. It was one of Lud's ambitions that Weider (or, in particular, the British Weider company) should have its own Olympic set, not only for the all-important internationals and championships but also to sell to all the weightlifting clubs throughout the country.

At the time, no Olympic sets were being made in the UK and the two best sets on the market were the Russian one and a Swedish one made by the Eleiko Company. Of the two, most lifters preferred using the Eleiko set, as there seemed to be much more 'life' to the bar, whereas the Russian set was 'dead' in comparison. Other sets were manufactured by the York Barbell Company (Pennsylvania, USA), Weider Canada and the Schnell Company in Germany (another great set). Many years later, the Chinese and Koreans each developed a set, too.

In one of the rare attempts that Lud made to help me with my training, he decided that I could convert an unused room at the garage premises from which the company operated into a training room, had a lifting platform made (which he also hired out to clubs or contest promoters) and got Ben Weider in Canada to send over one of the Canadian sets. I began to think I was in clover! My wife Norma became my coach and I used to teach her all the things she had to look out for whilst I was lifting. She would sit beside the platform, watch every lift I made, and then give me an expert critique on how the lift had gone.

The Canadian set looked quite nice, although the bar was a dull metallic colour - nothing like the bright steel used in most of the other sets. Most Olympic sets are made to the highest possible standards, with 90-ton high-tensile steel bars that, during a championship, would take a tremendous bashing, as most lifters at this time just dropped the weight once they'd got the referee's signal that the lift had been completed. This is now outlawed by the International Federation, which controls all weightlifting, as at any major championship it was quite common for 10-30 bars, each costing £200-£300, to be damaged irreparably. The rule now states that the lifter has to control the bar when it's being lowered to the floor after the lift. Lifters still drop the bar from the overhead position, but they keep their hands on it until it bounces on the lifting platform.

The Canadian bar was fine when lower poundages were being lifted, but as soon as heavy weights were used - as in the squat, when the bar is taken over the back of the neck - the damned thing would bend, as it was made from very poor quality, low-tensile steel. Although that might be okay for a home training set used by a novice, it was totally useless as a piece of competition equipment. At one competition where it was used, the lifter who was squatting with 600lb had to be rescued when the bar bent from the centre into a huge bow! That was the end of the Weider bar and also the end of my training at the Weider company.

The 1964 Tokyo Olympics were on the horizon, so I was back to training around the London gyms. 1964 also saw the opening of the new National Sports Centre at Crystal Palace, and I had the honour of being one of the weightlifters selected to put on an exhibition for HRH Prince Philip, who was there for the opening ceremony. At the beginning of the Olympic year I was contacted by the general secretary of BAWLA, Wally Holland, who told me that Olympic selection would be based on performances over the year rather than just on champion status. "Don't rest on your laurels," was his advice. "Get out there and compete in local club matches, county championships, the English native championships, internationals, and finally the British championships. Set up a qualifying total. Entering more competitions will give more chances of achieving the total, which will be three parts of the way towards selection for the Olympics." And this is exactly what I did. I won the English Native Championship, the British Championship and various internationals and managed to exceed the qualifying total.

On the opening day of the National Sports Centre, I and three other British champions from the London area were lifting in a squash court and the Duke of Edinburgh watched us train for a while. We then all traipsed into the large indoor arena and sat on the floor while the Duke delivered his address and declared the place well and truly open.

The Director of the Centre was Emlyn Jones, and before we all split up to go our separate ways I made an appointment to go and see him to discuss the possibility of myself and the other British champions using the centre and its vast array of training equipment for our build-up to the Olympics. When we eventually met up he thanked me for the exhibition work we'd done for the Duke, but then turned me down flat when I raised the possibility of our training there. "The National Sports Centre is established for the use of clubs, not for private individuals, and even though you and your colleagues might be the British champions you still can't train here." I was flabbergasted. Here was this wonderful new facility with all the Olympic weightlifting equipment anyone could wish for, and yet we were not allowed to use it!

I let Mr Jones know what I thought of the centre's ridiculous policy and got up to walk out in a huff. Just as I got to the door of his office, however, he added that the only way I could train there was if I was a member of a club and said, "Why don't you form one yourself? That would solve the problem!" I stopped in my tracks, thought the suggestion over very briefly and decided that if this was the only way to enable me to train there, then a club I would have to form.

Emlyn put me in touch with the Central Council of Physical Recreation, who vetted my instructor's qualification, and I was immediately given the go-ahead to form my very own club. I contacted lots of bodybuilding and weightlifting pals and got publicity in the local press, and by the time the club was opened we had a nucleus of 30 members. I ran the club from 1964 to 1970 and training under its auspices became one of the most popular activities at the centre.

Training went really well during the Olympic year. I had qualified and I was quietly confident about making my very first Olympics - the pinnacle of every athlete's dreams. However, it was not to be. The team was announced and I was not in it. The weightlifting association fobbed me off with the excuse that they didn't have sufficient funds to send a complete team and that the heavyweight division was so far in advance of the totals that I was doing that I stood the least chance of getting anywhere. In fact Louis Martin, our World Heavyweight Champion, who was vying for gold, was the only member of the team who stood any chance whatsoever, and the famous message from Baron De Coubertin, about the honour of competing, not winning, being the essential part, seemed to be forgotten completely.

That, to all intents and purposes, ended my competitive weightlifting career. All interest in competing had gone. I'd been the British champion for three years and, if I carried on competing, the only thing to look forward to was the Empire Games, which were due to be held in Jamaica in 1966. So, after a lot of thought, I decided that there was no point in staying amateur any longer. Instead, I would declare myself professional and see if I could make a career based on my business acumen, my physique and my strength. I duly informed BAWLA's central council of my intention and told them that I would no longer be available for selection. To my surprise I was asked to go for a meeting with Wally Holland.

"Do you realise," he said, "that you could become one of the strongest men in the world?"

"Tell me how," I replied.

"Well, you're 6ft 7in [over 2 metres], you weigh approx. 20 stone [130kg] and you have the frame to be able to get up to 30 stone in bodyweight [420lbs/190kg). At that bodyweight you could be lifting prodigious weights."

My immediate reaction was to point out that it had taken me 14 years to increase my bodyweight from 11 to 20 stone (70kg to 130kg), so how the hell did he think I was going to add on another 10 stone (65kg) of muscular bodyweight? His response was that I would have to go on anabolic steroids and all sorts of other drugs, but he assured me that I could do it.

Drugs in those days were only just beginning to become widespread amongst the world's athletes and they seemed to be the province of the heavy athletes - weightlifters, wrestlers, shot-putters, discus and javelin throwers - and, of course, the bodybuilders. But already there was evidence within the sporting world of the side effects of such drugs and the untold damage that they could have on one's health.

I didn't really have to think about Wally's proposal - I simply didn't want anything to do with drugs. Although I would've loved to have become Mr Universe or achieved the title of World or Olympic Weightlifting Champion, I was not going to resort to drugs or abuse my health in order to get there. So, as planned, I severed my connection with BAWLA and declared myself a pro, and then I started to think about my future.

Lud was always on my back about my training. The crunch came when he called me into his office and told me that I was spending far too much time (my own time, not his, I might add) training.

"Where were you at 5 p.m. tonight?" he asked me one evening, when I was still in the office at 7 p.m.

"At 5 p.m. I was just finishing my last call before making my way back home so that I could go training," I replied.

"You should have been selling right up until the time the shops close at 6 p.m.," Lud responded.

"That just shows how much you know about the selling business," I retorted. "No buyer wants to see a rep when he's just about to close up his store!"

Lud then proceeded to tell me that he'd been thinking things over and I had to make a choice - my training or my job. I didn't even have to mull over that one and handed in my notice immediately - probably telling him in no uncertain terms where he could shove his job!

So I ventured off into the land of self-employment, establishing myself under the trading name of Dave Prowse Enterprises. I began looking for sports agencies that I could continue to rep for around the stores. Whilst working at Weiders we'd had a visit one day from Bill Ludgrove, a famous swimming coach, whose daughter Linda was one of the most successful swimmers in the UK. Bill was looking for Weider to sponsor Linda (not much chance of that with penny-pinching Lud), but I managed to have a chat with them both and offered them some advice for swimmers in terms of progressive resistance training and ploughing hundreds of lengths of the pool.

As a result of that meeting, I was invited to Linda's training pool at the deluxe Dolphin Square complex, where Bill was the superintendent. Speedo was the new in-thing from Australia and a must-have for both male and female swimmers, and the swimwear was only available at that time through swimming clubs. Bill introduced me to the British Speedo importer and I managed to persuade him to let me have the London and Home Counties trade sales rights. It eventually went on to become the most popular and biggest-selling swimwear in the world, and I was proud to have been the person responsible for introducing it to the sports trade. I also took on a range of sports trophies, but this didn't meet with much success.

Then, out of the blue, Lud called me and offered me work as a freelance agent for Weider. I would be doing exactly the same as before and he would supply the van and the equipment, but I would no longer have a wage. I would work solely on a commissions basis, as I did with the other goods I was selling.

So now I had two key products to offer the sports shops and department stores: the Weider range of weights, supplements and magazines and the Speedo swimwear. However, this led to problems, as I was using Lud's van for all my selling. Even though the swimwear was accommodated in one small case, dear Lud asked me to make a payment towards the van expenses - all for the privilege of carrying an extra suitcase! This caused me additional annoyance, and it all came to a head when the lease for the premises in the centre of Croydon expired and Weider moved out. Lud found the cheapest place possible: a deserted warehouse, without a showroom, on a small industrial complex at the rear of a cinema in Purley, south Croydon.

Weider didn't last long after the move and eventually closed down. Lud sold his house in Kenley and he and his family went back to the USA. I never heard anything of him after that.

Although my freelance enterprise was well on its way, I still felt that I needed something else. Then I had one of those flashes of inspiration that only strike occasionally in one's life.

Chapter Seventeen
The Country Goes Bullworker Mad

In 1963 BAWLA decided they would hold their own Mr Universe contest and the Weider company, under Lud's direction, decided to become the sponsor of the event. To say that this was the biggest mistake in BAWLA's history would be the understatement of the millennium, let alone of 1963, but before I reveal all the disastrous twists and turns during and in the run up to the event, let me reiterate the political shenanigans that were going on at the time.

Firstly, bodybuilders and weightlifters have never really got on together; they tolerate each other. They train in the same gyms and use the same equipment, but the 'pure' weightlifter, who trains primarily for strength, tends to look down on the bodybuilder, who is training simply to develop large muscles, with no focus on strength and fitness but rather purely for cosmetic reasons. Added to this, weightlifters and bodybuilders each had their own association and their own magazine. The bodybuilders were catered for by the likes of Weider's *Muscle Builder* and the English bible, *Health & Strength*, and the weightlifters were catered for by the weightlifting historian and photographer George Kirkley and his excellent little journal, *The Strength Athlete*.

Internationally, weightlifting was controlled by an association called the FIHC (Fédération Internationale Haltérophile et Culturiste), to which every country's individual association was affiliated. The FIHC works closely with the IOC (International Olympic Committee), which decrees that a country can only be represented by one association. The trouble with the various weightlifting associations is that they've always had a very small number of members, and bodybuilding, being a much more popular sport, attracted members to their associations by the thousands. This anomaly had always been a sore point with (in this country) BAWLA and they were always looking for ways and means to attract the bodybuilders into the fold.

Slight in-roads were made when they introduced strength set and power lifting (bodybuilders were able to compete on their favourite strength lifts), but these were thwarted when the popular bodybuilding magazine Health & Strength, already the official journal of NABBA (National Amateur Bodybuilders Association), decided to form its own power lifting association, SAWL (Society of Amateur Weightlifters). This action really got up BAWLA's nose, so in a further endeavour to attract bodybuilders they announced that they would hold the only officially recognised Mr Universe contest (sanctioned by the FIHC to give it some sort of credence), which would be held at the Fairfield Halls in Croydon. NABBA, under Oscar Heidenstam, must've been laughing their socks off, as not only had they been running the accepted Mr Universe contest in London since 1948 but also BAWLA had chosen exactly the same day on which to showcase their attempt to usurp the title.

The NABBA show was held at the London Palladium and the judging at the Royal Hotel in Russell Square. I became lumbered as one of the organisers of the BAWLA event and it upset my association with Oscar and NABBA, with whom I'd had a friendly association for nearly 15 years. Word must've gone round the bodybuilding world that there an 'upstart' Mr Universe contest was being organised, and the rally call for support meant that the NABBA contest attracted a phenomenal number of entrants - one of the strongest showings in its history. The BAWLA show, on the other hand, was scraping the barrel: very few of the competing countries had any bodybuilder membership to speak of and the 'physiques' that did turn up, with a few exceptions, were rubbish and would never have got through a qualifying round of the NABBA show. Added to all of this, the two concurrent events caused confusion among the competitors, with some heading off to the wrong contest. Several times I had the unenviable job of going to the NABBA judging to physically remove entrants from their line-up. Although my intervention was not initially appreciated, when they found themselves among the mediocre BAWLA contestants they realised they stood a much better chance of a medal than at the NABBA event.

The one thing our show did have in its favour was the first ever appearance in the UK of the legendary US muscleman, George Eiferman, one of the great physiques of the world. He had a wonderful personality and a very amusing stage act, part of which consisted of a one-legged squat with a young lady on his shoulders whilst at the same time playing the trumpet! The show didn't have much else to recommend it, unfortunately. The Fairfield Halls were less than half full, whilst the London Palladium was packed to the rafters. Our Mr Universe was a very pleasant Arab gentleman by the name of El Guindi who, although the biggest man in the contest, wouldn't have turned many heads walking on the beach. By comparison, the two NABBA winners (amateur and professional) were Tom Sansone and Joe Abbenda, who in 1963 were the top physiques in the world. Needless to say, BAWLA never again tried to organise another bodybuilding event.

El Guindi received numerous awards and, because of the two Mr Universe contests, attracted quite a lot of media attention. One of the awards presented to him was a new training appliance invented by a German physical culturist from Hanover, Gert F. Kolbel, called the Bullworker. It was the opposite of a pair of chest expanders and was operated via compression in various positions. Herr Kolbel had brought a couple of these Bullworkers over from Germany and had been given permission to present the Bullworker on stage to the Mr Universe winner. As part-organiser of the event, I was presented with the other.

Kolbel was a very big man, roughly about my size, and had obviously been weight training and bodybuilding from a very early age. He'd developed an impressive physique from his years on the weights and was strong. Unfortunately, he liked to prove his strength when shaking hands with anyone, turning the greeting into a physical ordeal that left the recipient nursing crushed fingers or a damaged shoulder. Apart from this one foible, he was a very pleasant businessman and was very successful with his marketing of this new equipment on the continent via direct mail and mail order advertising.

In the ensuing year I played with the Bullworker in my home training routines and also read all the promotional literature that Kolbel had left with me. I considered it to be an excellent home training aid, working as it did on the then new principle of isometric exercising. Isometrics had become all the rage in the training world, and fantastic claims were being made by manufacturers of equipment incorporating this principle.

Basically, it was one up on the old Charles Atlas system of dynamic tension, which had been around since the 1920s, and consisted of pushing together or pulling apart the appliance to its limit and then holding it for a single contraction of only seven seconds. To be perfectly frank, the Bullworker was not really an isometric exerciser. Isometric means 'static contractions', i.e., where there is no muscle movement involved, but with the Bullworker there was a small amount of movement over the muscle range and then a contraction, so the Bullworker exercises were strictly isotonic (involving muscle movement). However, isometrics were the in thing, so the appliance was marketed as incorporating this principle.

Irrespective of how exactly the appliance worked, I still thought it an excellent home trainer and so on turning professional I decided to get in touch with Herr Kolbel to see if I could handle sales of the Bullworker in the UK. In keeping with my usual disastrous sense of timing, Gert responded that he would've loved for me to have the sales agency but that only two weeks earlier he had signed a contract with a mail order company in Paddington, London, namely Honorhouse Products.

If ever there was a prize for the most inaptly named company it was this one, for honour - as I was to discover over the next few years - was definitely not part of its business ethics. Gert gave me the names of the two directors of the company, Peter Goldsmith and Geoffrey Kean, and said that although they had the contract he didn't think either of them knew anything about the home training market or physical culture in general and that a personal visit from me wouldn't go amiss. I eventually went to see them at their premises, an old house in Paddington that had been converted into an office/warehouse, from which the company was selling a whole variety of 'suspect' mail order items. They had recently fallen foul of the Post Office, who had refused to accept mailing responsibility for their biggest-selling product, Nuform Nails, because the package contained highly inflammable items and was considered a major fire risk. So when I arrived on the doorstep it was all doom and gloom.

I met with Geoffrey and Peter, plus the firm's copywriter and would-be author, Drayton Bird. Kolbel had obviously been in touch with this unholy trinity and had told them all about me, so their first question to me was: "Just exactly what does it do?" With the expertise and knowledge I'd gained over the last year of using the product, I was able to wax eloquently on the virtues of the Bullworker and was promptly asked if I would like to become a consultant to the company. I asked for time to consider, but being a sales agent and realising the potential of the product I said that if I were to join the company it would only be on a sales commission basis, i.e., I would receive remuneration for every Bullworker sold.

Within days a contract was in the post, and I must've impressed them as they offered me a contract that gave me two shillings (10p) on the first 5,000 sold, three shillings (15p) on 5,000-10,000, and four shillings (20p) on sales of 10,000+. I don't think they really expected to sell all that many, but the contract only required me to act as a consultant to the company. I considered it a very good deal and I would still be able to continue with all my other sales work. The other stipulation of the contract involved my authorising photos and that full details of my physical culture career could be used in their adverts, plus the use of my photograph for all their promotional material - leaflets, adverts, the brochure and a wall chart. And so began an association with the product that would last over ten years and see the Bullworker being sold in every sports shop and mail order catalogue in the country, ultimately becoming the biggest home exercise training product in the world.

One of my first jobs when I was installed with a secretary in Norfolk Place was to help Drayton with the copy for the adverts that would appear in all the national dailies. The Bullworker was developed utilising the principle of isometric and isotonic contractions and, whilst it did have a small effect on physical development, it was primarily a strength trainer and it was, and still is, almost impossible to sell strength via mail order advertising. If an ad were worded, 'Let me increase your strength by performing these simple exercises', the response would be practically nil, but if worded, 'Put three inches on your chest' or 'Reduce your waistline' or 'Build powerful arms and shoulders' - in effect offering the reader the chance of physical improvement - then the replies would pour in.

Each Bullworker exercise took only seven seconds to perform, so we hit on the idea of advertising a physical improvement course that consisted of only seven exercises, out of a full course total of twenty-four, meaning a total daily training time of just under one minute. In addition, we offered a free assessment service, involving the inclusion of a form in the sales pack so that the customer could list all his measurements, give details of his dietary habits and choose, from a selection of three chest or ribcage shapes, the one that most resembled his own. With this information to hand, I then had the job of assessing the sorts of gains or losses I thought could be achieved if the Bullworker was used regularly and attention was paid to eating habits.

Drayton was a great copywriter and, with a combination of his words and writing skills and my knowledge, photos and the sales gimmick of the free assessment service, the first newspaper adverts appeared and took the mail order business by storm. To give you some idea as to how successful they were, the company sold over 30,000 Bullworkers in its first year of business and they were selling at £13 each, which worked out at nearly £500,000 in sales. The Bullworker completely dominated the company's business and more staff had to be taken on to cope.

The company moved from Norfolk Place into sumptuous offices in Church Street, Paddington, and then to a cinema in Camden Town that had been renovated and turned into office accommodation. I had a full-time secretary, business was booming to such an extent that I'd curtailed most of my other sales work, and we'd taken on an additional business manager, former actor Derek Partridge, specifically to coordinate all the Bullworker activities. Despite all this success and with their continual expansion, Honorhouse never seemed to have any money and getting money from them was worse than getting blood from the proverbial stone. In the very early days of my association, in fact just after the first year when they were riding on the crest of a wave, I decided I would invest my earnings in the purchase of a house (at this time I was still in a furnished flat in Thornton Heath) and eventually found a property that I liked for the then grand sum of £7,350. I needed to put down a deposit of £1,350 and the balance of £6,000 would be on a mortgage, so I approached Messrs Goldsmith and Kean for part of the large amount of commission due to me.

Each fobbed me off, directing me from one to the other, and gave me terrible sob stories as to how unprofitable the business was, but I eventually managed to get £800 to keep me quiet. This I immediately paid to my solicitor, setting the house purchase in motion. Little did I know, however, what a problem I would have getting the rest of my due remuneration out of them. Time and time again over the next few weeks I would ask for the balance of the money I needed, but all I received was excuses. Eventually my solicitor rang to say that if I didn't come up with the £550 required to complete my deposit within the week not only would I lose the house but also I would lose the £800 already deposited.

Completion day arrived and I still hadn't managed to get the cash I needed, so I decided to take the bull by the horns. I walked into Geoffrey Kean's office, sat down opposite him and said quite bluntly, "I'm not moving until I'm paid the £550 I'm owed." Geoffrey flapped like mad, probably thinking I was going to resort to violence, and eventually offered to give me a cheque to cover my requirements. I'd had wind that the company's cheques weren't worth the paper they were printed on, so I flatly refused, stood (or sat) my ground and responded, "I want it in cash." Various unsuccessful attempts were made to get me out of the office and a solution was eventually reached when Geoffrey sent a messenger down to the bank in Oxford Street to get a cheque cashed on my behalf. I remained seated in the office, refusing point blank to move until the money from the bank was handed over to me. I then went directly to my solicitor's office in Mitcham, paying over the cash only a couple of hours before the termination of the completion period.

I know this has nothing to do with the Bullworker period of my life, but only on two other occasions have I found myself in problem situations that have necessitated forcefully demanding my rights. The second time was in a Chinese restaurant in Elstree, whilst I was working on *Star Wars*. Before leaving the studio to go for lunch, I'd changed into casual dress and slipped a £10 note in my pocket. I had a very nice cheap lunch, which cost just over £4, proffered my £10 note to pay, but was given change from a fiver. I pointed out to the waiter that I'd given him a £10 note and that I was owed another £5, to which the waiter swore that I'd only given him a £5 note. I argued the toss for a while, and then he went back to the till only to return to say that it contained no £10 notes. I didn't believe a word of it, as there was no way that at the end of a busy lunch period they hadn't taken a single £10 note in payment, but he still refused to give me my correct change. With that, I got up to leave and then positioned myself in the doorway, telling the waiter that I wouldn't let anyone in until I'd been given my £5 change. I was quite happy to let customers out, but I was determined that no new ones were going to come in! Within minutes I was given my £5 and I was on my way back to the studio, transforming myself from the scourge of a Borehamwood Chinese restaurant to the scourge of the Universe for the afternoon.

The other similar incident happened at a very busy petrol station in Penge in London. I'd filled up my car with petrol and once again I was short-changed, this time by a tenner. It was late in the evening, the cashier was in his kiosk, nicely protected, and he was adamant that he'd given me the right change. He flatly refused to do anything about it and suggested I came back the following morning to see whether his takings tallied with his till roll, and if there was a discrepancy of £10 then I would be refunded. Once again I stood my ground, planting myself firmly in front of the kiosk and saying that nobody was going to make any petrol payments until I'd received my correct change. Very quickly a queue of customers formed behind me and some even started to walk away when they realised what was going on. I wasn't going to budge, however, and if he wanted to get rid of me he was going to have to either call the police or pay up - and pay up he did!

If there's any moral to be learned from these three instances, it's to stand up for your rights and principles. Maybe I have an advantage, as my size can make me seem quite intimidating even though I'm actually one of the most docile people you could wish to meet. Although I've spent years working as a bouncer at dance halls, jazz clubs and bowling alleys, I've never had a fight with anyone in my life.

Anyway, back to Bullworker. It became painfully obvious that the only place Honorhouse was going was down the pan, and the sales rights to the product eventually went to one of the largest direct mail and mail order companies in the UK, Leisure Arts of Wandsworth, who were primarily a mail order book club. The managing director, Lenny Joseph, contacted me and asked me if I would continue my association with the Bullworker, so my assessment service resumed. Not only did I agree to this but also I agreed to introduce the Bullworker to the sports shops, which Leisure Arts saw as a lucrative part of the market. Using all my contacts from my days as a representative for Weider, I started selling to all the major stores, Harrods included, and very soon found myself being asked to give sales demonstrations of Bullworker exercising.

At the same time, my acting career was progressing rapidly and whenever I got a job in films or television I would always take a carload of Bullworkers along with me. As I'd become visually synonymous with the appliance, people were always coming up and asking me if I could get them one (usually at a discounted rate). It got to the stage where I used to make more money selling Bullworkers than I was paid for the film or TV job. As the showbiz career snowballed, I found I had less and less time to do the repping that Leisure Arts wanted me to do, so we came to an agreement and I handed over the trade concession to an established sales agent. The trade concession proved to be a very profitable venture and, with hindsight, I've always considered it one of the major mistakes in my business career to let it go so easily. However, I could see my showbiz career flourishing and the heady rewards of fame and fortune outweighed the financial prospects that I thought Bullworker held.

Chapter Eighteen
Mr Bullworker Finds Pastures New

Eventually my stint with Leisure Arts came to an end altogether, when they decided that the product needed a more 'muscle orientated' image and asked the former Mr Universe, Len Sell, if he would take over my role of endorsing the product. It didn't concern me unduly, as I'd had nearly ten years of association with the appliance and people always referred to me as 'Mr Bullworker'. I was now reaching another crossroads in my career and magazine publishing was beckoning.

I think in those days I saw myself as a bit of an entrepreneur. I started up the Bullworker Club of Great Britain and decided to set up my own mail order business, utilising the names and addresses of the nation's Bullworker owners in order to sell them a variety of products ranging from underwear, cufflinks, vitamin pills, Bullworker carry cases, t-shirts and, in fact, anything I thought these newly found physical culturists would want. As a result of my association with the Weider magazines for a few years, I knew that the best way to reach potential members was via a mail order piece, so I decided to put my own physical culture magazine together, which would not only feature articles on weightlifting, body-building, diet, etc., but would also be the official journal of my very own Bullworker Club of Great Britain.

After a lot of soul searching I came to the conclusion that I was much more interested in running my own journal than I was in furthering the cause of the Bullworker organisation, so I set out to try to produce a magazine in which I could air my gripes and grievances and promote whatever I wanted, but, most importantly, through which I could try to unite the weightlifters and bodybuilders to form a single entity. And thus Power magazine came into being.

In my early bodybuilding days the magazines were proper physical culture journals, covering training, diet, bodybuilding, weight training and weightlifting, hand balancing, strand pulling, amateur wrestling and containing a whole host of features on related sports. *Health & Strength* was the oldest of the magazines produced in this country and it is still going to this day. George Kirkley, the famous weightlifting photographer/journalist, was producing a magazine for weightlifters called *The Strength Athlete*, and Reg Park, frequent winner of the NABBA Mr Universe title, was producing his own journal in Leeds. The American magazines, *Iron Man*, *Strength & Health*, *Muscle Power* and *Mr Universe*, were filtering into the country in very limited supplies. Apart from *Strength Athlete*, which was purely a magazine for competing weightlifters, all the magazines tried to cover as much of the spectrum of physical culture as space amongst the adverts permitted.

My vision was to produce a magazine that would not only appeal to physical culturists in general but also would be bang up-to-date. Even now, all magazines have long lead-up dates; for instance, an interview conducted for a monthly magazine wouldn't be published until at least two months later. What I wanted was to be able to do a report on a major show, such as the Universe contest, and have it published and distributed within two weeks at the most. I had, through my years of competing, built up a nice collection of friends who could either write features, supply or take photographs, or report on contests and, in addition, I could tour the major events myself, and my printers were an amenable bunch who would work all hours of the day or night to give me what I wanted. So, with all this going for me, I ventured into the realm of the magazine proprietor.

My first issue of *Power* was a 24-page publication, featuring on the front cover the then strongest man in the world, champion weightlifter, Paul Anderson. It wasn't an aesthetically pretty cover, showing this 25-stone monster of a man picking up over 700lb, but it certainly was an eye-catcher and simply oozed power. When I look at the magazine now, I realise what an amateurish effort it was, but then I remember that I was a one-man band, doing the design, preparing the ads, taking the photos, attending the competitions, and then eventually mailing out the finished product, so I consider it to be quite a feat. Happily, I didn't have any publishing deadlines and I could produce an issue based on the dates of the major shows. There was nobody to complain about not receiving the magazine, as my intention wasn't for it to go on general sale but rather to send it out as an informative, instructional mail order piece. I recouped the costs of production and mailing via the sales I made from the journal and I didn't have to buy expensive lists of names and addresses as my Bullworker contract guaranteed me these details of every purchaser.

By the time I was ready to produce the second issue I had my own range of bodybuilding supplements and had done endorsement deals with the three top bodybuilders in the country: Paul Nash, Mr Europe and Mr Britain; Paul Wynter, professional Mr Universe; and John Citrone, also a Mr Britain and Mr Universe title winner. The giant Russian heavyweight weightlifter, Leonid Zhabotinsky, had just won the world title and *Power* was the first magazine in the world to feature him on its cover, soon after the event, which was a major coup.

I used the editorials in *Power* to air my own personal views on the way I saw things going in the weightlifting and bodybuilding world. I was quite vociferous and at times downright vitriolic, but my writings had the desired effect and saw people responding to put things right. I had no commercial ties and got on well with the officials and show organisers of the three main associations.

Several issues later I took on the services of an old *Health & Strength* magazine designer, John Mendes, and his input turned what was still an amateur mail order piece into what could now be called a magazine. Now that the format was more professional, I decided it was time to get the magazine onto the news-stands and into the shops, so I approached a firm of distributors with this in mind. Harry Webster, who together with his wife Lilian subsequently became lifelong friends, was my contact at the distributors and he liked my attempts at producing a magazine. However, three provisos had to be met before he would take on the magazine: firstly, the magazine had to increase in size (number of pages); secondly, the distributors would need many more magazines than I had printed previously; and thirdly, the magazines would only be taken on a sale or return basis.

It was decided, therefore, to increase the number of pages from 22, including the covers, to 48 and increase the print run from 5,000 to 20,000, but I had no guarantees as far as sales were concerned. It was also explained that I would not know how well, or badly, the magazine had done until the fourth month, when the returns started coming back and the distributor got paid for the magazines that had actually been sold. To give you an example, I produced 20,000 magazines for each month from January to April, but it wasn't until April that the returns started coming back for the January issue, with the remainder for that issue coming back in May together with the start of the February issue returns, and so it went on.

In my idealistic world I hoped that the magazine would sell well or that the returns would be minimal, but the magazine publishing world turned out to be the most imperfect world I'd ever encountered. Those four months of sweat and trepidation as I waited for news of the magazine sales were just the beginning of the nightmare. The fourth month eventually rolled round and I got the news I was dreading. Harry rang to say that out of the 20,000 magazines I'd produced and printed, their January returns showed that only about 500 had sold, which hardly covered the distribution costs let alone the production outlay.

Although distraught at this news, I thought that the second month's figures would be better. Unfortunately, however, there was hardly any improvement at all, and when the third month's sales figures followed suit I really started to panic. I had now produced in the region of 80,000 magazines but had only sold 2,000, my print bill was astronomic and I wasn't doing the business I'd managed when it was only a mail order piece.

Quite frankly, I just couldn't believe the figures I was receiving, so I let the distributor know, in no uncertain terms, that I wanted proof that the magazine wasn't selling. So if Harry's claim that only 500 of any issue had sold was true, then I wanted him to return the remaining 19,500 to me. I figured I could distribute them around the clubs or at shows all over the country, or, at worst, I could sell them as scrap paper. The policy of the distributor, however, was that if I wanted the unsold magazines I would have to pay for all the individual retailers' packing and transport costs. That, of course, would have involved even more expense and there didn't seem any point in chucking good money away on what was obviously a lost cause. The only another alternative I could see was for the retailers to rip off all the magazine covers and return those as proof of unsold numbers, but even then I would have to pay the retailers' charges for this 'service' and would end up with piles of scrap paper all over the place.

In the space of six months, what had been a nice, little, thriving mail order business had descended into a financial quagmire from which I was unable to extract myself and, unfortunately, I had to go into voluntary liquidation. Only three of my creditors turned up at the winding-up meeting: my printers, who were very understanding; the distributors, who I blamed for the situation; and two executives from my weightlifting equipment suppliers, AEI of Wednesbury in Staffordshire, who told me not to worry about it as they'd had a nice day out!

This was one of the worst periods of my life. I'd lost my pride and joy - my magazine; I'd lost every penny I'd ever earned; and, just when I thought things couldn't get any worse, along came another business opportunity that, rather than improve the situation, caused even more problems.

Basically, I found myself working with two of the biggest bastards one could ever have the misfortune to meet: Knox and Caine. Just writing their names after 25 years of erasing them from my memory makes the hairs on the back of my neck bristle. If you go to the movies regularly or watch police dramas on TV, I'm sure you are aware of the good cop/bad cop scenario. The bad cop uses bully boy tactics to try to extract information and, when this fails, in comes the good cop, who is all sweetness and light and bending over backwards to be understanding, when all the time he is doing his job just like his counterpart and trying to screw you in exactly the same way. John Knox was the bad guy, whilst John Caine played the role of the good guy.

This dubious duo, who had set up business in a small industrial park in Hammersmith, turned out to be nothing more than two very smart asset strippers. They would buy into a company that was going through hard times and give the impression that they were trying to save the business, while at the same time selling off all the company's assets and then liquidating the company, leaving all the creditors with nothing. Their most recent acquisition was the slowly dying Weider company that I'd worked for years earlier, whose major asset was the *Muscle Power* magazine and the small amount of mail order business it brought in.

Neither Knox nor Caine had any knowledge about the world of physical culture or bodybuilding and they were desperately in need of an editor who knew the game. I met up with them at their office and, to be perfectly honest, I was initially quite impressed with this dynamic duo. Both northerners, Knox was full of bluster about what he intended to do for the company and Caine was quiet, affable and just the sort of person one would expect to see handling the financial side, and the three of us got on well together. They explained their predicament with the magazine and then asked me if I would like the position of European editor.

As I said earlier, I was at one of the lowest ebbs of my career at the time, and if they'd offered me the job of toilet cleaner I think I would've accepted. I would be working part time to suit myself and my earnings would be on a commissions basis that depended on the volume of sales the magazine achieved. As an offer of help to them, I offered the balance of the stock I had from my own liquidation. It wasn't a lot, just things like bars, weights and collars, but nevertheless it amounted to several hundred pounds' worth and I needed desperately to realise the return on that investment.

As soon as I had delivered the equipment and had edited the first magazine, things changed rapidly for the worse. Knox complained that I wasn't putting in enough time on the magazine, despite the fact that I did most of my work on it at home, and every time I went into the office he would shout, rant, rave and call me all the expletives his vile mouth could emit. It was even worse if I asked for money or wanted to see the magazine's mail order sales figures. Then John Caine would intervene, take me into his office, apologise profusely for John Knox's behaviour and sweet talk me into continuing my editorial work. He'd have his arm around my shoulder, smiling all the time, and keep telling me what a bastard Knox was to work with and promising to sort everything out for me, but I still didn't get access to the sales figures and I still didn't get paid. My equipment was absorbed into the Weider stock and was eventually sold, but still no money was forthcoming.

Eventually, I decided to have a showdown with the pair. However, I turned up at the Hammersmith trading estate only to find that they had liquidated the company after selling off all the stock and assets, and the pair of them had done a runner. I never saw either of them again, although a few years later Knox made the news when he went to prison for some gigantic business scam.

As for the Weider organisation, after all those years in the doldrums it has gone on to become the biggest company of its kind in the world, controlled by the two Weider brothers, Joe and Ben, who are now both well into their eighties and multimillionaires. They have the best bodybuilding magazines and run the foremost bodybuilding contest, Mr Olympia - a professional contest that at one time only former holders of the Mr Universe crown could enter. All the major physique stars in the world bend over backwards just to be able to turn professional and compete in the professional events organised by their association, the International Federation of Bodybuilders (IFBB). Joe, who once offered me a job in California as West Coast editor, a position I turned down, controls his side of the business from the USA, while Ben runs the Canadian side of the empire. Ben has spent his whole life trying to get bodybuilding 'respectability', with the ultimate goal of getting bodybuilding accepted as an Olympic sport. Joe is an avid antiques collector, while Ben, in addition to all his many honours and achievements, is a renowned authority on Napoleon.

Chapter Nineteen
No Such Animal as a Professional
Weightlifter

With the 1964 Olympic Games now history and my non-participation in them a sorry part of the story, I decided that my whole career needed a rethink - and turning professional seemed to be the answer. Of course, the fact that there was no such animal as a professional weightlifter didn't deter me, so I started listing all the possible avenues I could pursue in order to earn money. I considered my options in terms of giving strength demonstrations at physical culture shows, endorsing products and setting myself up as a freelance sales agent, but the one thing that never crossed my mind was a career in show business - the heady world of films, television, commercials and stage appearances.

In my capacity as a freelance sales agent, I still continued to visit all the trade accounts that I'd built up over the preceding years. My days as a weightlifting equipment salesman ended when I refused to pay any additional petrol money and Lud took back the van, so I concentrated on my other lines - the Bullworker, Speedo swimwear and a range of sports trophies, using my own car to get around.

One of my accounts was the famous Mayfair gymnasium in Paddington Street, which was also the home of the famous stunt agency, Tough Guys, which supplied strongmen, stunt performers, wrestlers, boxers and the like to the film and television industries. The agency was run by two well-known bodybuilders, Wally Schulberg, and my old friend and mentor from my early bodybuilding days, Reub Martin. They never bought anything whatsoever from me, but I used to enjoy going to see them just for the ribald conversation. Reub was one of the greatest personal trainers ever, and quite often there was the opportunity to glimpse some famous American film star working out at his gym or meet personalities like comedian Ted Rogers or the famous dance bandleader Victor Sylvester. The walls of the gym and office were adorned with signed photos of all the famous personalities that Reub had trained, but he was never in awe of any of them as they were all his mates.

Out of the blue one day I got a call from an advertising agency

Me with big Lou

With the Bond girls – Brit
Eklund and Maude Adams

Me with author Terry Pratchett

Edward Woodward about to get a 'working over' from me

Me with my book publisher Chris Cowlin, at my home in December 2010, holding my lifetime achievement award to film

Me with big Lou

With the Bond girls – Brit Eklund and Maude Adams

Me with author Terry Pratchett

With the Star Wars characters at Disney, Paris

Comedy legend Norman Wisdom and myself

With Countdown's Carol Vorderman, at the 'Space Mountain' launch, Disney, Paris

Me with Christopher Lee

With 'Mr Playboy' himself – Hugh Hefner, at a convention in Los Angles.
Unfortunately I wasn't invited to the Playboy Mansion!

Me with Arnold Schwarzneggar

The 30th reunion of the 'Tomorrow People'

Me with Mr Universe (many times), the one and only John Citrone

Me with the glamour queen of
the World Wrestling Federation,
Trish Stratus

Me with Henry Cooper

Left: Being introduced to 'DROID', featured for the first time in the Green Cross Code television commercials

With Peter, Kenny and Eileen (Kenny's late wife)

Me with astronaut Charlie Duke

Me with Jimmy Greaves, one of Britain's greatest footballers

Me with Bruce Boxleitner

A joke photo of Gunnar, me and Kane Hodder, studying the pin
up magazine Scream Queens

Me with Phil Collins, the patron of Comic Heritage

With Andrew Sachs and Liz Fraser, at a comic Heritage function

Working with Debbie Reynolds at the London Palladium

Me with Bond actor Richard Kiel

Above: With Arthur C. Clarke and Patrick Stewart at a London convention

Left: Norma, James, me, Rachel and Steven. This photo was taken when I took my family to see Star Wars after it opened in London, December 1997. There was no premiere and no invitations to the cast, I had to pay for my own tickets! I let the press know that I had to pay to get into see my own film!

Me with Bobby Davro and impressionist John Culshaw

Me with Sir Cliff Richard

Above: Getting the team together for the inception of the ill-fated 'Men Behind the Masks' venture – Jeremy, Peter, Kenny, Warwick, and me with the two organisers

Left: The family – James, Norma, me, Rachel and Steven

My daughter Rachel and granddaughter Hannah with Norma and me at Buckingham Palace when I received my MBE in the Millennium Honours list – June 2000. (Photo: Charles Green)

Edward Woodward about to get a 'working over' from me

Me with my book publisher Chris Cowlin, at my home in December 2010, holding my lifetime achievement award to film

enquiring whether I was available to do a TV commercial for Hotpoint washing machines, and Reub, being the only person I knew in showbiz, was the person I asked to negotiate the contract for me. The commercial was to advertise the effectiveness of a Hotpoint spin dryer and when it went on the box it was a huge success. 'Even Britain's strongest man cannot wring water out of a towel that has been spin-dried by the Hotpoint Spinner', the slogan proclaimed - and I couldn't, honestly! Hotpoint even ran a nationwide campaign, offering a free washing machine to anyone who could get water out of spin-dried towels and, although people came up with all sorts of ingenious ways of folding the towels as tightly as possible, I don't think Hotpoint ever had to part with any machines.

Another nice little job that came up around that time was with pin-up magazine, *Mayfair*. They wanted to do a pseudo 'sexercise' photo shoot, featuring me as the strongman doing his training but lifting a rather delectable nude female model instead of weights. On publication, the feature caused quite a stir in the weightlifting world, not because I was lifting a nude lady but because I had the temerity to wear my official Empire Games weightlifting costume for the shoot, which the BAWLA officials thought was very demeaning.

Once I'd established myself as an 'item' with Tough Guys, quite a few other agents came forward to offer me work: Gaby Howard, who specialised in the supply of stunt performers; AMI; and, for a couple of years, the prestigious London Management agency. Whilst on the latter's books I was under the care of the company's top agent, Michael Sullivan, but very little work seemed to be coming my way. Feeling exasperated by this situation, I rang Michael to find out what was the problem.

"I've been represented by yourself and London Management for a few years now, but I never seem to get any work from your efforts," I said.

"Get you work?" replied Michael. "I'm not here to get you work - you get the work and I'll negotiate the fees!"

"But I thought that it was an agent's job to get work for his client," I replied.

"Oh no, dear boy, I'm just here to make certain that for the jobs you get I can negotiate bigger and better fees!"

And, with that, my association with London Management ended. However, I went on to find the best agent, who saw me through the most rewarding years of my showbiz career - Penny Harrison.

Before Penny and her husband Peter arrived on the scene in the late '60s I'd been quite busy doing TV commercials and TV series - *The Saint*,

Department S, Jason King, The Champions and *The Avengers*, and the one film I had to my credit was *Casino Royale*, when I'd worked with such luminaries as Peter Sellers, Ursula Andress, Orson Welles, Chic Murray, Jonathan Routh, Peter O'Toole, David Niven, Daliah Lavi, Barbara Bouchet, and many more. The film had five different directors, including Bob Parrish and Val Guest, but none of them had a clue as to which direction the film, which turned out to be a James Bond spoof, was going. Even Deborah Kerr could not save it. Still, it was fun to work on, even if it turned out to be one of the most expensive turkeys of all time. Now, over 25 years later, it is amazing how the film has developed an almost cult following of fans who liked it.

Penny came up with a film offer for me, working for American director, David Miller, in a thriller called *Hammerhead*, which starred Vince Edwards (of Dr Ben Casey fame), Diana Dors, Judy Geeson, Beverly Adams and Peter Vaughan and featured a host of British TV regulars such as William Mervyn, Patrick Holt and - one of the worst bits of casting ever - Patrick Cargill, as a secret service agent. My old bodybuilding friend Gerry Crampton was the stunt coordinator and we filmed on location in the Estoril area, just outside Lisbon, Portugal, followed by several more weeks back in London at Elstree Studios. Filming was based at the famous Estoril Sol Hotel, close to Estoril itself but nearer the lovely fishing village of Cascais. Guincho and the most westerly point of Europe were within a couple of miles drive.

Vince was making the crossover from TV to films, although his first film in Hollywood many years earlier was as Mr Universe, in a film of the same name, and at the time he had a really great physique. *Hammerhead* was the first of a three-picture deal for Vince and he was playing a James Bond type character. His second movie was a western, and I don't know if he ever got as far as a third, as the first two were absolute disasters.

Most of the filming for *Hammerhead* took place on a luxury yacht moored within view of the bridge spanning the River Tegus. We were all ferried out to the yacht on a tender, which passed the beautiful monuments to the Portuguese mariners and the world-famous Belem Tower. In the film, Hammerhead, played by Peter Vaughan, was an international pornographer, who used to arrive on the yacht in a sedan chair that was lowered from a helicopter. In reality, the sedan chair was kept in situ on the yacht and the helicopter would fly in from its base in Lisbon, hover over the yacht so that the sedan chair could be attached, and then Peter would get into it and be raised about five metres into the air. Then, on the 'action' command, the chair would be lowered to the deck and Peter would make his big entrance - once I, as his big, heavily scarred bodyguard, had released him from the chair.

Of course, numerous takes had to be done and Peter, the helicopter pilot and I did everything possible to give our director what he wanted. The pilot used to work to signals from the yacht that indicated when to raise or lower the chair and also when to finish and clear off back to base. Unfortunately, on one occasion - the last time that Peter would ever get into the chair - signals between yacht and pilot got mixed up and the pilot was given the all-clear to return to base, not realising that Peter was still inside the sedan chair. Off went the chopper, flying across Lisbon at over 1,000 feet, with a now absolutely petrified Peter dangling from the helicopter in a flimsy sedan chair that was tethered by a totally inadequate length of cable.

Once the helicopter had gone and nobody could find Peter, panic set in as the crew realised he was now suspended over Lisbon. Frantic messages were radioed to the pilot to be careful as he had an uninvited passenger in the form of Peter suspended from his plane, and he was instructed to get back as quickly as possible before Peter died of shock or a heart attack. We waited with baited breath for the chopper's return, and fortunately the door of the sedan chair stayed bolted and the entire contraption was deposited on the deck of the yacht without any mishap.

However, when Peter was released he was fuming, as anybody would be after a near-death experience. I don't know what they did to placate him, but, being the real trouper he is, he got over the experience very quickly and the show went on.

Socially, not a lot was happening on set. Beverly Adams was married to Vidal Sassoon and he used to fly over from London to be with her most weekends. Diana Dors had her latest boyfriend with her, and the rest of us used to eat out regularly with the tourists and locals at a lovely little restaurant called Os Três Porquinhos (The Three Little Pigs). I became quite friendly with the owner of the restaurant and I found out at the end of the movie that he'd been employed to procure young local hookers for dance work on the film.

One other incident that stands out in this 'epic' was a stunt involving Vince Edwards, Judy Geeson and myself. As one of the villains, I'd taken Judy as hostage and was trying to escape from two secret service agents, played by Patrick Holt and Patrick Cargill. Trapped in a courtyard, I was using Judy as a shield to stop the agents shooting me, and in the scene I had to back up to a wall about eight feet in height, on which, unbeknown to me, Vince was standing. When I reach the wall, Vince calls out Judy's name, causing me to spin round. At the same time, Vince hauls Judy out of my arms and up onto the top of the wall and the two agents fire a hail of bullets, reducing me to a crumpled heap on the ground.

We had rehearsed the scene several times, with a mattress placed on the cobbled floor to cushion any falls and prevent any accidents. However, this wasn't good enough for the director, who said my backwards walk over the mattress didn't look right, and so he demanded its removal in order to make the whole stunt look more realistic. We all agreed to give it a go, and everything was going well until we got to the bit where Judy was hauled out of my arms and up onto the wall. Just as I was about to go into my big dying scene, I happened to look up and see Vince and Judy falling off the wall towards me. With virtually no time to think, I managed to catch Judy in my arms, but poor Vince came crashing down on the cobbled floor and broke his ankle. He was rushed off to hospital, where the whole of his lower leg, ankle and foot was put in plaster, making it totally impossible for him to walk for the remainder of the movie. Consequently, in all his scenes Vince had to be seated, with his leg well out of sight, and any walking required had to be done by Gerry, my stuntman friend. I think by the time we got to the end of the film there was more footage of Gerry than there ever was of Vince!

Chapter Twenty
Thomas Inch Unliftable Dumb-bell

In 1969 I had the luck to purchase a very famous piece of weightlifting memorabilia, the Thomas Inch Unliftable Dumb-bell. Thomas Inch was a strongman in the 1920s and used to perform with heavy dumb-bells in a variety show act, which was all the rage at the time. Tom had two dumb-bells, one weighing 130lb and the other 150lb, which he used in his shows. They weren't heavy enough for his challenges and dear old Tom was losing money, so he contacted a foundry and asked them to make him one weighing 170lb. Thus the unliftable dumb-bell was born. However, what made it unliftable was not the weight of it - lots of strongmen around the world could pick up that sort of weight and lift it overhead with ease - but the sheer thickness of its handle. Unless one had really large, strong hands, or a vice-like grip with tremendous thumb strength, it couldn't be lifted off the floor.

Somehow or other the dumb-bell ended up in the possession of an old weightlifting enthusiast named Bert Lightfoot, who lived on a caravan site in Waltham Abbey north of London, and he called me one day to see if I was interested in buying it. He told me that it was stored away in a box in the shed at the bottom of his garden and that now, being an old man, he couldn't do anything with it and wanted it to go to a good home where it would be appreciated. So I drove over to see him and was led to the garden shed for a look. He was very keen for me to take it out of its box and onto his lawn, as he wanted to see if I could lift it. I unlocked the box and there inside, wrapped in hessian, was this enormous dumb-bell, with a handle the thickness of a milk bottle.

I bent over the box and tried to remove the hessian protection, but it was tightly covered. So I caught hold of the handle in order to heave it from the box and onto the floor. I figured it would then be easy to extricate it from its wrappings and roll it out of the shed and onto the lawn. I started to pull at the dumb-bell and, much to my surprise, lifted both the dumb-bell and the box (a total weight of around 200lb), as the weight was firmly wedged into the box by the thick hessian cover. I stood up, with the box and dumb-bell held in my right hand and resting just above my knees, against my thighs. Bert was elated, as the weight had never been lifted off the floor, at least not in his memory. I put it back down in order to unravel it from its hessian jacket, lifted it out and then rolled it onto Bert's lawn. I made a succession of 'pulls' at it and several times managed to get it almost to shoulder height, so I decided that it presented an achievable challenge that I could practise in the convenience of my own training quarters.

I paid Bert £50 for the relic and thus became the proud owner of what is one of the most famous pieces of strength memorabilia. At home I used to play about with it regularly, just picking it up and holding it in order to develop grip strength. I never was able to get it right into my shoulders, even though I could pull it up to shoulder height. I think I was very wary of the possibility of injuring myself should I try to put it overhead. I wasn't confident that I could raise this solid lump to arms' length, as being a very tall lifter my leverages were bad for pushing or pressing type lifts. Tall men are very good at 'pulling' weights but not so good at 'pushing', hence the weights I was able to get up to my shoulders far exceeded anything I could get overhead.

Word soon got around that I had the dumb-bell in my possession, but I was still surprised when I received a phone call from Russ Taylor, the press and publicity director of Cutty Sark Whisky, wanting to know if I'd be interested in going on tour with the dumb-bell, challenging all-comers to lift the beast in order to win the marvellous prize of a gallon of their finest.

A meeting was arranged between Cutty Sark, myself and their photographer, Derek Rowe, who was going to cover the tour, and it was decided that we would take the dumb-bell around all the pubs that were well known for their association with weightlifters, boxers, wrestlers, meat humpers, vegetable market porters, and the like. First Cutty Sark had to be reassured that the promotion was not going to cost them too much in the way of gallon bottles of whisky. I showed them the dumb-bell and told them that I was so confident about the success of this promotion that my challenge would be to lift the dumb-bell with one hand from the floor onto a telephone directory, the height of only two inches. Russ and Derek both made several inglorious attempts to get the beast off the ground and, amazed that something so seemingly simple was in reality so hard to achieve, they were convinced that this promotion was a real goer.

We eventually toured all over the country and the promotion attracted a huge amount of attention. However, the actual challenge set for lifting the dumbbell backfired on us somewhat, as we never lost a gallon of whisky and the lack of any successful attempts meant that the local press had nothing exciting to photograph. The tour was covered throughout by the *Publicans Press* and the *Morning Advertiser*, who went to great lengths to get extraordinary photos, e.g., pictures of ladies lifting it off the floor with two hands or fellows putting a tea towel underneath the handle like a sling and lifting it with their teeth. Such feats resulted in fantastic publicity photos and these valiant attempts were rewarded with a gallon of the hard stuff.

Over the years numerous strongmen, weightlifters, bodybuilders, etc., have visited my gym in order to have a go at lifting this dumb-bell, but I think I can only remember six who were able to do anything with it. I've never seen anybody pull it as high as my best attempt, and even some of the world's strongest have failed even to get it off the floor. Lou Ferrigno, the Incredible Hulk, picked it up quite easily but never managed to get it above waist height. South African power-lifting champion Phil Niemandt, who weighed in at around 22 stone (310lb), couldn't get it off the floor, and many strongmen noted for their grip strength couldn't budge it either.

A very well known Australian grip specialist flew over with his father especially to have a go at lifting the dumb-bell. He turned up at my house whilst I was away, but my wife told him that he was still welcome to try and could find the dumb-bell in the shed at the bottom of the garden. The next thing she saw was the father setting up a video camera while the son, after changing into a weightlifting suit, rolled the dumb-bell out onto the lawn. He applied loads of resin to his hands to make certain that they didn't slip off the dumb-bell handle and then began a series of warm-up exercises. The dad was filming all of this and Norma was watching from a discreet distance, probably from behind the lounge curtain, and having a giggle at their antics. Then came the moment they had anticipated, and - surprise, surprise - he never even got it off the grass. Try as he might - and his many attempts were captured on miles of video film - the Inch dumb-bell still stayed firmly on the ground.

The Oscar Heidenstam Awards are held annually and are attended by bodybuilders from all over the world. Each year I'm asked to bring the Inch dumb-bell along, and it still defies almost everybody just to raise it the two inches onto the phone directory. A couple of Mr Universe stalwarts have actually lifted it about 12 inches off the ground, before it has crashed out of control, but I've never seen anybody duplicate what I was able to do with it. Also, a very famous American strongman, Bill

Kazmaier, lifted a specially made replica of the dumb-bell in the USA. However, considering that Thomas Inch was supposed to have been able to lift it overhead anytime he felt like it, one wonders at the strength that Tom Inch must have possessed.

As a footnote to this story, at the end of 2000 I closed my gym after 30 years of business. I had to get rid of everything that I'd collected over the years - pictures, photos, gym equipment, mirrors, sunbeds, etc., and because of the interest that had been shown in the Thomas Inch dumb-bell it was suggested that I put it up for sale on the Internet, which I did. A major bidding war ensued, with offers coming from interested parties all around the globe. The final winning bid came in from the coach of the Cincinnati Bengals football team in the USA, who wanted it for his own strength memorabilia museum. I was sorry to see it go, but at least I'd had over 20 years of fun owning it and it found a good home.

Chapter Twenty-One
The Hammer Years

The next film I was offered after *Hammerhead* began an association with the Hammer Films company that lasted in various forms for over 20 years, even though Hammer's film production years ceased around 1974.

I'd been an avid Hammer fan since my youth and, thinking back on it now, I can always remember having this strange fascination with Hammer's Frankenstein's monster and a desire to play that role, so much so that in the early part of my showbiz career (1967/68) I took the bull by the horns and went knocking on Hammer's door in Wardour Street.

All I knew about Hammer at the time was that the company was controlled by two directors, James Carreras and Anthony Hinds, they made 'Gothic' horror films on a regular basis and they seemed to have a stable of actors and actresses, such as Peter Cushing, Christopher Lee, Ingrid Pitt and Michael Ripper. The latter, with his trademark bulging eyes and raspy voice, probably appeared in more Hammer films than any other performer, often as a villager or landlord of the village tavern. Make-up for the films was done by Tom Smith and Eddie Knight and the special effects wizard was Les Bowie.

Working on a Hammer movie was rather like a family reunion! The same was true of the *Carry On* movies, which also had a stable of regulars, all of whom worked for next to nothing. I only had the pleasure of appearing in one *Carry On* movie, *Carry On Henry*, but more of that later.

On my arrival at Hammer's office I was greeted by James's son, Michael. At that time Michael was being groomed to take over from his father, who was eventually knighted and became Sir James Carreras. I was met with the question, "Yes, what can I do for you?" He had no idea who I was, as a relative unknown in showbiz circles, and my answer was that I'd like to offer myself to Hammer as a potential monster. Michael pooh-poohed the suggestion immediately and I was shown the door.

Two years later, in 1970, I received a call from Jimmy Sangster, who was working for Hammer under a variety of hats, primarily as a writer but also as an assistant director/producer. At that time Hammer had given him the opportunity of writing, producing and directing his own horror movie. I went to see him at his palatial flat, part of the Carlton Tower Hotel in Sloane Street, Knightsbridge, and after a brief chat I was offered the role of the 'Horror' in his project, *The Horror of Frankenstein*. The two leading ladies had already been cast - Kate O'Mara and Veronica Carlson, but Peter Cushing, the regular Hammer Dr Frankenstein, was going through a terrible time due to the death of his beloved wife and so he was unavailable. As a result, the part was offered to popular TV actor, Ralph Bates.

My agent at the time was Gaby Howard, a lady who specialised in the bit-part/stunt-type actor, and she eventually rang me to say that Hammer were making me an offer of the grand sum of £75 per week. Even though we both agreed that this was a ridiculously bad offer, Gaby pointed out that it would get my foot in the door of the Hammer world and could lead to other opportunities. As there was no more money on offer I reluctantly accepted the *Horror of Frankenstein* role, and it indeed proved to be my entrance into the Hammer stable as well as a positive experience. The cast and crew were friendly, Ralph, Kate, Veronica and Jimmy all treated me with respect and the shoot was a very happy one.

The only other thing of note that I remember from the film was being amorously pursued by Jimmy Sangster's American girlfriend, who at one stage confided in me that Hammer were prepared to pay me three times the money that my agent had accepted for my role. *The Horror of Frankenstein*, although being a fun film to work on, never achieved any critical acclaim. Everyone thought that Ralph was an admirable successor to Peter Cushing, but Jimmy wanted to have fun with the film and introduce some comedy sequences - not a popular move for the goth horror aficionados. As a result, apart from introducing the fledgling Darth Vader to the cinema audience, the film was not regarded very highly in the Hammer annals. It was eventually released as a double bill with a Christopher Lee movie, *The Scars of Dracula*.

Ralph died at a very early age after a battle with cancer, Kate is a very busy working actress/producer living in Taunton, Somerset, and Veronica is now living in Florida. I have met up with Jimmy at horror film conventions; in fact, I asked him to ghostwrite this book, which for some reason he declined.

My second spell with Hammer was in 1972 on a film called *Vampire Circus*, directed by Robert Young, who went on to become one of the UK's top directors but at that time was making his debut. Filming was at

Pinewood Studios and the movie starred Adrienne Corri and Thorley Walters. I had worked with Adrienne in 1971 on Kubrick's A Clockwork Orange, so once again it was like meeting up with old friends. I personally thought that *Vampire Circus* was one of, if not the best of, the Hammer horror movies and a great credit to Robert Young. The only problems it encountered were going over budget and over the allocated shooting schedule time, and when the planned six-week schedule was up, Robert still needed about three more days to complete shooting. However, Hammer, in their wisdom, refused to extend the time and said that the film had to be cobbled together with the footage they already had in the can.

I had quite a major role in the film - that of the mute circus strongman, and my death scene, in which I'm shot with a double-barrelled shotgun, created great interest. The scene was filmed from behind me, so the viewer actually sees my back being blown out. Les Bowie, the special effects man, made a metal sheet mould of my back, coated the inner side with a sheet of protective rubber and welded four old English pennies, each with an explosive charge attached, to the outer metal side. Four condoms filled with theatrical blood ('Kensington Gore') were fixed to the top of the charges and the mould was then glued to my back and covered with a thin layer of baker's dough to mimic skin. The wires to the explosive charges ran under my leather skirt, down my legs and across to a control box located 20 yards away. The camera was positioned behind me and slightly to the side so that the actor who was going to shoot me could be seen pointing his gun at me. Les was positioned at the control box and on the signal to 'fire', the gun went off - firing blanks, of course - and the back explosion unit was set off simultaneously, sending the fake blood and dough flying in all directions. I finished up prostrate on the floor, as dead as a doornail.

The film had other great special effects in it, especially the transitions from actors into animals and back again, but its main claim to fame was its overtly sexual nature. I know that 1972 marked the beginning of out-and-out sex in the movies (Ken Russell's epic, *The Devils*, was being filmed at Pinewood in the next studio to us), but even today, nearly 40 years later, it still seems way ahead of its time.

During the early 1970s I had the pleasure of working on three Hammer horror movies. Hammer, as any fan of classic horror films will confirm, had a style all of its own, which hovered bat-like between costume drama and high camp. I always thought highly of the Hammer genre of movies for giving us stars like Christopher Lee, Peter Cushing and Ralph Bates, in rollicking good tales of evil-doers inflicting their wickedness on beautiful maidens while being pursued by the good guy - who was usually accompanied in the final scenes by a crowd of enraged villagers bearing flaming torches, as I recall. While I was under contract with Hammer I worked with these and other illumini, many of whom went on to become household names in the world of serious acting. Yet, as talented, sexy and entertaining as my co-stars undoubtedly were, none of them impressed me as much as Balls the bat.

I was working on a film called *Vampire Circus*, and one scene called for a juicy close-up of a bat crawling menacingly across the softly heaving bosom of a vampiress as she lay in her coffin, recharging after a hard night on the pull. Bats can fly like stunt pilots when push comes to shove and they'll hang around upside-down all day if need be, but the prospect of getting one to shuffle obediently across the required acreage of warm bosom - well, that was something else again.

These days, of course, out would come the computers and the techno-FX team would produce a virtual bat, capable of doing a riverdance if that's what the director wanted. Back in 1972, however, all we had for this scene was a selection of stuffed bats and assorted lengths of fishing line with which they could be pulled along, producing what turned out to be the world's least convincing bat impression. The fact that all this phoney bat-dragging was never going to provide the film with a single frame of stirring footage seemed lost on the special-effects technicians, who carried on applying bat to bosom in resolute fashion, until the director sussed that they were after some special effects of their own and called a halt.

Out of the blue, somebody on the set claimed he knew of a lady who owned a fruit bat. This bat was apparently real, alive, huge, impeccably mannered and perfect for a bit of bosom-crawling. The production office was scrambled and ordered to secure the fruit bat's services at any price and without delay. Within hours, the set of *Vampire Circus* was graced by one of the most impressive male animals I have ever seen.

Balls was called Balls for two very obvious brown and furry reasons. Between his namesakes, Balls had the most enormous penis, seemingly stuck permanently on its semi-erect setting. Balls' entire genital ensemble was, in short, so ferociously impressive that it deserved to be captured on canvas in a work entitled 'Two Kiwi Fruit and a Cigar'. On a set that had seen acting's great and good dispense their magic on a daily basis, Balls' bathood now rendered every jaw slack and every eye wide. There was even a ripple of applause among the scene-shifters.

When laid upon the now genuinely heaving bosom of the now far from sleeping vampiress, Balls' state of semi-erection gave way to a glorious, flat-out hard-on, which produced a collective intake of breath from everyone privileged to witness it.

According to the actress whose bosom accommodated the rampant Balls, "Its revolting bollocks were red hot and almost vibrating with lust - and did you see the size of its willy?" She flounced off the set the instant that Balls had successfully completed his film debut, wrapping her shroud about her and declaring, "And I don't see how you expect anyone to believe that those creatures can fly while carrying that lot!" One of the watching technicians was forced to agree with her, adding, "If Balls ever flew out of Heathrow, he'd have to declare his tackle as excess baggage!"

So that was Balls the bat. He never did get another role - but he certainly had the biggest parts in *Vampire Circus*!

The following year, 1973, I had the dubious honour of becoming the only actor ever to play the Hammer monster twice, this time opposite Peter Cushing in *Frankenstein and the Monster from Hell*. Peter was back into acting again and, although he looked very gaunt and was smoking like a chimney, was cast once again as Dr Frankenstein, this time the resident doctor in a lunatic asylum.

Although I'd enjoyed working on *The Horror of Frankenstein*, I hadn't enjoyed the long sessions in the make-up chair with Tom, spending up to 2½ hours every morning in order to get the headpiece fitted and glued satisfactorily. For *Monster from Hell* it was decided that the whole of the creature's make-up could be achieved using a body built up on a wet suit and a mask for the face. Eddie Knight was in charge of the make-up, and what looked like a horrendous job was actually completed every morning in about 20 minutes flat. Shane Briant and Madeline Smith were the other main characters in the film and all the filming took place in the asylum. I look back on the movie as one of the best acting jobs of my career.

Peter Cushing was wonderful to work with, both on this film - our first time working together - and later on *Star Wars*, when he played Moff Tarkin to my Darth Vader. I was asked to appear on his *This Is Your Life* tribute, went to chat with him at his home in Whitstable, Kent, and finally went to his funeral service and cremation and his London tribute church service. He was a lovely man and wonderful actor, and he was held in the highest esteem by everybody who knew him. Interviewers always ask actors about their favourite people in the business and the same two names always crop up: Peter Cushing and Roger Moore. I've had the pleasure of working with both of them and I heartily concur.

Terence Fisher, the doyenne of Hammer horror film directors, directed *Monster from Hell* -and what a lovely man he was, too. Unfortunately, he was right at the end of his career when we worked together and was not 100 per cent fit at that time. He was recovering from a motor accident and died not long after the film was completed. He made a wonderful job of the film and I think *Monster from Hell* is a fitting tribute to his work.

One memorable scene from the film stands out: a stunt sequence involving me and Peter Cushing. The monster is on the rampage and has broken into the laboratory and is smashing up the place. Peter hears what is going on and dashes to the laboratory to try to restrain his creature. He jumps up onto a table, grabs a bottle of chloroform, takes off his coat and wraps it around the bottle before smashing it. With the coat now soaked in the chloroform, he takes a flying leap from the table onto the back of the monster and somehow manages to get the coat over the monster's head. The monster goes berserk and does everything possible to shake off the doctor, smashing into walls, doing aeroplane spins, etc., but all to no avail and the chloroform eventually starts to take effect. The monster, still with the doctor lying across its shoulders, slowly sinks unconscious to the floor - end of scene. When we finished and got to our feet the whole of the unit crowded round us and applauded. A job well done.

And that, to all intents and purposes, ended my association with the classic Hammer films. The gothic horror film, as originally conceived, was subsequently deemed to be out of date and, in an endeavour to move with the permissive times, it was decided to introduce blatant sex into the movies and nudity became par for the course. *Lesbian Vampires* was the ultimate in kinkiness and specifically designed to titillate the Hammer aficionado's palate. What Hammer didn't realise was that the horror enthusiast wanted pure horror, not kinky sex and bare bosoms, so the fans deserted the sinking Hammer ship and it submerged completely after a couple of real stinkers. Sadly, it has yet to rise.

For years now, the managing director of Hammer films has been trying to relaunch the genre, but nothing ever seems to come to fruition. Producer, Roy Skeggs, took up the reins of Hammer and with his accountant son has been working to get Hammer up and running again as a film production company. I'd always had a happy association with Roy, so when an associate of mine, who runs a mail order model business, got in touch with me about having models made of the two Frankenstein monsters I played for Hammer, I immediately showed an interest. However, I was only prepared to become involved on the proviso that the rights to sculpt and sell the figures were cleared with Roy, as the owner of Hammer and presumably all of its copyrights. I suggested that my colleague and I should go to see Roy at his office at the old Elstree film studios to put the proposition to him.

My colleague had already jumped the gun, so to speak, by having a model of Christopher Lee as Dracula sculpted by one of the top model makers at Pinewood Studios, and so we turned up, model in hand, to show Roy the high standard of the model sculpting and design.

Roy was very amiable, as usual. He was familiar with my work in the business for over 20 years and he very much liked my colleague's enthusiasm for the project and the fact that he was already running a successful model marketing business. Nevertheless, we were surprised when Roy asked us if we'd like to form a company specifically to handle the licensing of the Hammer name. We would both be shareholder/directors of the new company and Hammer Films, the parent company, would receive an agreed royalty fee or commission on all products sold under the Hammer banner.

We were both overjoyed just to be associated with the Hammer name, which was respected worldwide. I immediately got my accountants to register the company, Hammer House of Horror Marketing Ltd, with a registered office within the precinct of my premises at Marshalsea Road, south-east London. We also received a contract from Hammer Films Ltd, giving our company the full marketing rights. As I was dealing with my old friend Roy, I read through the contract, didn't see anything untoward and never considered having it checked out in respect of any legal implications.

We then set out in earnest to discover exactly what Hammer had to offer from a franchising point of view. Also, I decided that I ought to enlist the help of an established franchising agent to help and advise on a consultancy basis. I found an agency in a small mews office in Marylebone, their main client being Olympic medallist Sally Gunnell. They were about to exhibit at a franchise trade show at the Lancaster Gate Hotel and, although no deal had been signed between us, they asked if they could include the Hammer name in the list of clients they were representing. I agreed, and the Hammer association attracted more business interest than the rest of their representations put together, so on the face of it I now had a franchising agent who was keen to come on board.

Whilst this was happening I started to get the feeling that all was not well with Hammer and Roy Skeggs, so I began delving into what Hammer had in the way of rights to their seemingly vast library of films and TV series. To my dismay, I found that they owned absolutely nothing except the Hammer name. The rights to everything had been sold off following the demise of film production in 1974.

When it came to making the model kits, Roy Skeggs would say that all was well. Then we would get legal letters from the new owners of the actual film and the make-up expert who created the character for the film, both wanting royalties before any permission would be given. Numerous companies were involved in the ownership rights and all wanted their cut. Hammer didn't even have any film stills for us to use - these had to be purchased from the respective new owners. All of this was going to increase the production costs of any venture that our company got involved in. Added to all this, the franchise company went behind our backs. They approached Skeggs and Son directly and, the next thing I knew, Hammer had two franchising agents. When I complained to the Skeggs they calmly pointed out the terms of the agreement: it was not 'sole and exclusive'. As such, they felt within their rights to appoint another franchising agent, who would, of course, be working in opposition to my marketing company.

I had already run up legal fees of many thousands of pounds trying to tie the franchising company into Hammer House of Horror Ltd, all to no avail, so I decided to cut my losses and get out. To make matters even worse, my partner had decided to throw in his lot with the franchising agent, so I resigned as a director and handed the company over to him.

I'm a great believer in honour and, as far as Hammer and my attempts to help get Hammer Films out of the mire they were in were concerned, I'm afraid honour was nowhere to be found. And that unhappy note ends my Hammer saga.

I've worked in three good Hammer movies with luminaries such as Peter Cushing, Ralph Bates, Jimmy Sangster, Terence Fisher, Robert Young, Kate O'Mara, Veronica Carlson, Madeline Smith, Lynne Frederick and a host more, together with make-up artists like Tom Smith and Eddie Night and the great special effects man Les Bowie. I have happy memories of working at Elstree and Pinewood Studios and of publicity shoots for *Monster from Hell* and for the promotion of Hammer's book with Veronica, Madeline and Julie Edge. What a shame it all had to end the way it did.

Chapter Twenty-Two
Getting In on the Act

My first taste of acting had started with an offer of a part in a play from the stunt agency Tough Guys, playing 'Death' in a black comedy called *Don't Let Summer Come*, at the Mermaid Theatre.

This was followed by an audition at the BBC for a Ned Sherrin show. I was asked to turn up dressed in a suit and all I had to do was give a hat to that celebrated doyenne of the musical comedy/theatrical world, Hermione Gingold. When I got to the BBC studio, about 20 other guys, all in dress suits, were sitting around watching the rehearsal of another part of the show. I met up with Ned, who told me to sit down and wait, so I found an empty place from where I could see the stage, located close to the door to the dressing rooms. I hadn't been there long before Hermione sauntered in and sat directly in front of me. She then turned around and asked me if I'd got that day's newspaper. I didn't have a copy and apologised, but I then told her that I would go and search one out for her. A few minutes later I found one that had been discarded by one of the auditionees, so I took it back to her and she thanked me kindly. Within minutes Ned Sherrin called for all the guys in dress suits to make a line so that Miss Gingold could decide whom she wanted to work with. She didn't even bother looking down the line, came straight to me and announced, "I'll have him." It was a tiny part, just handing Hermione a hat while she was singing in her inimitable fashion, but for me it was the start of a showbiz career that at times had me in the depths of despair but for the most part took me to the dizzy heights of Hollywood blockbuster hits and world acclaim for my work.

Over the ensuing years the BBC became a good source of TV work. I appeared in the BBC's *The Wednesday Play*, as a bullying owner of a caravan site in 'Mooney and His Caravans', in which I had the pleasure of working with John Alderton in the early days of his career, and I also had a tiny part in the Jonathan Miller production of *Alice in Wonderland*.

I made several appearances on The Generation Game, with both Bruce Forsyth and Larry Grayson. My appearance with Larry Grayson was as the Green Cross Code Man in a road safety game. In one of the

'Brucie' shows I was playing Tarzan in a sketch involving a real live chimpanzee, and the game contestants had to replicate my part, complete with chimp. The crew decided to play a joke on Bruce and, unknown to him, they'd brought in the famous vaudeville star and comedian Arthur Askey to be substituted for the chimp in the finale to the game. Arthur was kept hidden during the show and it was a real show-stopper when I eventually came on grasping the hand of Arthur imitating the chimp. A great reunion of the two stars ensued, with the studio audience and all the production staff in convulsions of laughter. It's a truly great memory and I was proud to be a part of it.

As mentioned in my diary entries earlier, I had a nice part in *The Rose Medallion*, which ranks alongside *As You Like It* from the BBC's Shakespeare series (more of that later) as two of the best acting roles I've ever done, and this includes the *Star Wars* series. I was being seen as myself, not acting under masks or acres of make-up, and I had plenty of action and dialogue that was NOT going to be overdubbed by anybody!

My part in this three-part thriller, shot in and around the Cheddar Caves, was playing lead actor Donald Sumpter's 'minder', cousin Stanley, who was a bit on the slow side and had a penchant for collecting and hoarding junk (that's me in real life!) Donald played a run-down private detective and the two of us, plus the Mafia, were looking for missing treasure. One of the Mafia was Shane Rimmer, with whom I worked years later on one of the *Star Wars* movies. He likes to remind me of the final fight I had with him in the caves, when I threw him into a freezing lake and drowned him. I don't think he's ever forgiven me for that!

I made appearances on *The Two Ronnies* and also on a *Morecambe and Wise* show, playing Mellors the gardener in a take-off of *Lady Chatterley's Lover*. This was my first experience of working with these showbiz legends. My role was to carry Eric into a room where Ernie and Lady Chatterley were waiting and say something like, "Look what I've just found in the garden." When we first rehearsed the scene I simply put Eric down on the floor and then exited the room, but just before the actual take was due to be shot Eric said that he'd like to do a bit of 'funny business' on the floor and asked if I would be okay with that. Of course, I agreed. The idea was that he would pull me down onto the floor and improvise from there. When the filming of the scene started, Eric pulled me off balance, as planned, but instead of any improvised funny business he just jumped up as quickly as possible and carried on with the scene, leaving me struggling to get back on my feet and feeling like a right prat!

Morecambe and Wise changed allegiance from the BBC to ITV soon after that, and I worked with them once more on a very funny sketch called 'Rent A Giant', in which I was the minder/giant employed by Ernie to stop Eric from bullying him and was the butt of their jokes.

Although I was doing lots of work on TV, I never considered myself to be an actor. I hadn't attended drama school or received any dramatic training and I didn't have a résumé that listed any stage work. I was a 6ft 7in bodybuilder who didn't look like a boxer or all-in wrestler and I seemed to fill a niche in the acting world.

Eventually, I did get the opportunity of real acting, when I was offered a part in Jean Genet's *The Balcony*, which was filmed for the Open University drama course. I was then thrown in at the deep end with a role in Shakespeare's *As You Like It*, playing Charles the Wrestler. I was working with a stellar cast, including James Bolan, Angharad Rees and Helen Mirren, and filming took place at Balmoral Castle. I was also asked to be the stunt arranger for the wrestling scene, which required me to choreograph the bout so that I ended up as a convincing loser. At the time I weighed about 19 stone, in stark contrast to my opponent, Brian Stirner, who weighed only around 10 stone when soaking wet! Another worry for me was learning the lines. I'd been okay with the odd bit of dialogue here and there, but the thought of having to learn and deliver several pages of Shakespearean lines concerned me, especially when I discovered that someone from the Shakespeare Folio Society would be on set to ensure that there was no deviation from the original text. In the end, it was much ado about nothing (forgive the pun), as I managed to cope with the dialogue without any problem. The fight ended remarkably well, too, with Brian sending me crashing through the wooden fencing around the wrestling ring, causing a back injury that prevented the fight from continuing and ensured Brian's victory.

Of all the acting jobs I've had over the years, I always regard *As You Like It*, in particular, as a job well done, and I'm very proud of my contribution.

Chapter Twenty-Three
Windows of Opportunity

I'll punctuate my 'highs' with a particular 'low' in my life, which I hope you never have to deal with. If you do, I hope the resolution I finally found will point you in the right direction in dealing with such situations.

I had been living in my house in Croydon for a couple of years when I decided that it would benefit from some improvements and thought that having aluminium-framed double-glazed windows was the answer.

My wife and I requested brochures from manufacturers far and wide and salesmen seemed to be queuing up at the door to offer quotes for the work. After much investigation, price comparisons and studying various aluminium frame sections we settled for a company from Norwich called Target Windows.

I think the value of the order for replacing the two bay windows at the front and the French doors in the back lounge was around £1,400, which was a lot of money in those days. We had visits from Target's surveyor, who had to make certain that our house would accept their windows, and we also had their man in to measure up everything so that the windows and patio doors could be constructed in Norwich and then sent down to us fully assembled and ready for the fitters to insert in place of the old ones.

I should've had a premonition that all was not going to go well when the fitters tried to fit the front upstairs window and found that their surveyor's measurements hadn't included the small transom windows above the main ones. As a result, the whole unit was useless, being about 18 inches too short.

"Don't worry," the fitters said. "This is Target's mistake. We'll get the whole unit replaced with one of the correct height. In the meantime, we'll get on with taking your lounge French doors out and putting the large patio windows in."

The patio windows were huge, measuring about 8ft x 6ft, and extremely heavy, but the fitters had them in place in no time. And very nice they looked, too.

"We'll have to wait for your new upstairs windows to be made, so tomorrow we'll start on your front downstairs windows," they said, as they departed at the end of their first day's work.

The following day I had to be up and away early as I was filming a TV commercial for Outspan Grapefruit with Ronnie Corbett over at Isleworth Studios in West London, and so unfortunately I was not in the house when Target's fitters started to work on the downstairs front windows.

We had just started filming the commercial when one of the assistants came over to tell me that there was an urgent telephone call for me from my wife. I picked up the phone to hear a distraught Norma, practically in tears, asking me to get home as soon as possible as something had gone drastically wrong with the window fitters. She wasn't able to tell me much, except that the fitters had told her they'd hit a snag and under the terms of the small print in the contract they were entitled to walk off the job. There was no way in which I could leave the filming, but when we finished at 5.30 p.m. I did the hour's journey home at breakneck speed.

When I arrived home I was confronted with the horrendous sight of the front of the house boarded up, and on looking through the front window I noticed that the ceiling was now being supported by acrows. I dashed in to find Norma to uncover the facts and she said that all she knew was that the workmen had told her they'd encountered an unforeseen problem and were leaving the job and that I needed to get in touch with Target the following morning.

At 9 a.m. the next day I was on the phone to Norwich and speaking to Target's technical director.

"What the hell is happening at my house?" I demanded.

"Oh, our fitters came up against a problem installing your windows, and if you read the contract you signed with us they're entitled to walk off the job."

"What do you mean by 'a problem' and when are you going to get them back to complete the job?" I queried.

"Well, the situation is that our fitters got the individual windows out but when they tried to remove the main window frame they encountered an unforeseen problem."

"What do you mean by 'unforeseen'? Your surveyor examined the property and said there would be no problems and that my house would accept your windows. So just what has gone wrong?"

"Well, the fitter started to saw through the main frame, there was a loud CRACK from upstairs and the fitter then discovered that he couldn't get his saw out of the cut he'd made. Unbeknown to him the joist he was cutting through was one of the main supports for your roof and the whole of the front of your house has dropped."

"Well, what's the solution and when are you coming back to complete the job?" I asked again.

"We're not coming back and I suggest you get in touch with your own surveyor to sort out the rebuilding of the front of your house, which of course will be at your own expense."

Naturally enough, by this time I was absolutely livid. I was getting nowhere fast with the director, who just kept quoting 'the small print in the contract'. I slammed down the phone and immediately arranged for an independent surveyor to come in and assess the damage. I also got in touch with a solicitor to look into the problem from a legal standpoint.

Little did I know at that stage that all the wranglings over responsibility for the destruction and rebuilding of my house were going to take over six months to resolve.

My surveyor's conclusions were that my house was in a truly dangerous state and that I should move out and into a hotel. I was also instructed to put up a ' danger' notice in the garden to notify friends and tradesmen that they entered at their own risk, and to start legal proceedings against Target. All my entreaties to Target were met with the reply that the matter was now in the hands of their insurance company and that all further correspondence had to be addressed to them.

At that time I was running my acting business from home and had three small children in tow, so I didn't really want to move away and certainly not for the lengthy period that the negotiations between Target, their insurance company, my solicitor and my surveyor seemed to indicate. Eventually Target put all the blame for the delay on their insurance company. Over the ensuing months I made many phone calls to them, but I never seemed to get any nearer a settlement.

After about six months of continual hedging and toing and froing between the parties, desperation to get the job completed really set in. We were still living in the house and the rooms at the front were out of bounds, as they'd been declared too unsafe to use. The old French doors had been nailed across the front of the house to give us some measure of weatherproofing and the acrow supports were still up in the front lounge and bedroom.

I was perhaps at my lowest point when on a Sunday evening I had a sudden brainwave. I decided to try to get Esther Rantzen to feature my predicament on her TV programme. I knew Esther quite well, having been on her show a couple of times a few years earlier. I'd even escorted her to the opening night of one of my films - *Frankenstein and the Monster from Hell* - and although she'd become a major TV personality she was still very approachable. I wrote off to Esther at the BBC and got a phone call from her suggesting that she should come in to see me at work in Harrods and discuss the situation over lunch.

When Esther saw all the photos of the house and heard my tale of woe she immediately got very excited about featuring the story on her programme, which was one of the most popular on the box at that time and had achieved great success in championing the rights of the small consumer against the big barons of business. It was agreed, however, that I should give Target one last chance to put things right and if that failed then she would be only too pleased to feature the saga in her show, which aired at peak viewing time on a Sunday evening and was watched by millions. And so the next day I put pen to paper and sent off the following letter to Target Windows:

To whom it may concern.
Dave Prowse v. Target Windows Ltd, Job No ......

I am sick and tired of having my house referred to as 'the dump up the road'.
I am sick and tired of having to warn the tradesmen that they come into the garden at their own risk.
I am sick and tired of stopping my children's friends coming into the front garden.
I am sick and tired of the acrows up in the front rooms.
I am sick and tired of the front of the house being boarded up.
I am sick and tired of writing to both you and your insurance company.
In fact I am so fed up with this whole situation that I have approached Esther Rantzen to feature the whole sorry saga on her Sunday night programme - which she is keen to do. I therefore give you notice that if I do not hear from either you or your insurers per return to say that you accept full responsibility for the damage your fitters have caused to my house and agree not only to install the windows as per the original contract but also rebuild the front of my house to my surveyor's instructions I will have no alternative but to pass the story and photographs which I have taken over to the BBC for inclusion in Miss Rantzen's programme.

I await your reply,
Yours faithfully

By return I received a letter from Target saying they had agreed to accept full responsibility and asking if a site meeting could be scheduled at the house. Within three days a meeting was arranged, which was attended by representatives of Target, the insurance company and my surveyors, builders and solicitor, and work was started to install the new windows and rebuild the whole front within the week. I always knew that Esther's programme carried a lot of clout, but I really was amazed how much the threat of national exposure achieved.

As a postscript to the aforementioned story, at the site meeting at the house one of Target's directors pulled me to one side and said, "You were really lucky there. You had two of our best fitters doing your windows."

"What do you mean by lucky?" I asked. "What would've happened if I'd had a couple of your worst fitters?"

"Oh, they would've attacked the job with a sledgehammer instead of a saw, and the whole front of the house would've been down."

Some luck!

Chapter Twenty-Four
Commercial Breaks

During my film and TV career, which has spanned over 30 years, I have appeared in quite a few TV commercials in the guise of a wide range of weird and wonderful characters.

The first commercial I ever did was for Kit-Kat chocolate bars. This was made in 1965, a time when all the major manufacturers (irrespective of what they sold) hit on the American idea of sending people dressed up in outrageous costumes (in reality actors and actresses) round to households trying to find out whether the poor, unsuspecting housewife used and had in her cupboards samples of the products they were promoting. I remember seeing a visit from the Fairy Snow Man in the middle of summer, wanting to know whether the housewife used Fairy Snow in her wash and, if she did and could produce several packets, she qualified for a prize of some sort. It was obviously a good promotional gimmick, because lots of major firms got in on the act.

Rowntrees, whose most famous brand was, and still is, their Kit-Kat chocolate wafer bar, were persuaded by their advertising agency, J. Walter Thompson, that a TV commercial along similar lines would do wonders for the product. So they produced a storyboard in which the central characters would be a housewife and a 'dress-up' character - in this case a huge Viking warrior! I was contracted to play the Viking and that lovely comedy actress, Sheila Steafel, who in later years became one of our foremost lady comediennes, was playing the housewife. So we all duly turned up at a house in Hendon, North London, on a freezing cold January morning.

At the beginning of the scene you see me striding down the road resplendent in my Viking outfit, which included a real bearskin cape and the traditional helmet complete with horns. I ring the doorbell, which Sheila answers dressed in a very dowdy housewife's outfit, complete with slippers, apron and turban. The horned helmet had increased my height to over 7ft, in stark contrast to little Sheila, who must be all of 5ft 1in/2in in her stockinged feet, so the size difference between us was very funny. However, Sheila's character isn't phased by me at all and starts to produce Kit-Kats from all her pockets. She waxes lyrical throughout the commercial about how good the Kit-Kat bar is and all I do is stand in the doorway looking huge and impassive. When she eventually finishes I just lean forward, pick her up under one arm and promptly race up the road with her, at which point it dawns that I've come for her and not the Kit-Kats.

When you appear in a TV commercial your agent tries to negotiate the biggest daily filming fee possible, as performers in most TV commercials earn money each time the advert is repeated. So, having completed a commercial for a major advertiser and the biggest advertising agency in the world, I duly sat back and waited for it to air over and over again. With no signs of it on the box a month later, I phoned the advertising agency to find out when I could expect to see it. As soon as I mentioned that I was the Viking in their Kit-Kat commercial, peals of laughter rang out and I was told it was the funniest commercial they'd ever done. They were apparently just waiting to get approval for the commercial before it went on air.

A few weeks later they rang me full of apologies, saying that objections had been raised by the advertisers who actually sent these dress-up characters around the houses and, as a result, the commercial would never be shown. So it was a case of kiss goodbye to all those lovely repeat fees.

Another commercial I remember well was an advert for Birds Eye Cod Steaks. I played the happy husband whose wife gives him his dinner, consisting of the cod steaks, chips and peas. In food commercials it's not just a question of somebody like a PA or a secretary preparing the meal. It has to be produced by somebody appointed by the Good Housekeeping Institute or a similar august body, so that everything you see in the commercial is legit. The products that viewers see on the screen are supposed to be exactly the same as those that consumers get out of the packet. I think on this particular day the overseers must've been having the day off.

At the start of the action the dinner is prepared off set and it is produced when the director and lighting cameraman are ready. Of course, by the time they've got all the lights right and the actors ready the meal is no longer warm, so you now have a plate of cold cod steaks, cold chips and cold peas, all of which I have to consume with an air of great pleasure. Once cold, the meal no longer looks appetising, so the director instructs that they should be painted with gravy browning. The peas have to be sifted through for rejects, as only whole, concentric peas are allowed on the plate. These don't look very appealing either, and neither do the chips, so it's decided that both should be brushed over with cooking oil. Finally, just before the 'action' call for me to tuck into this lot and look as though I'm relishing every mouthful, the director decides the dinner doesn't look hot. So just before the cameras start rolling he comes over to the table puffing a huge cigar, takes an enormous drag and blows the smoke all over the dish. Then, with the cigar smoke slowly rising, the scene is ready to be shot.

I can assure you that it wasn't the most appetising meal I've ever eaten and I can well remember the shot going to about 16 takes, with me spitting everything out on the word 'cut'. Suffice to say, I've never eaten a cod steak since.

Another famous commercial I did was playing Rodin's 'The Thinker' (nude male statue) for a Cadbury's Dairy Flake ad. When I arrived at the studios there was a big flap going on because they'd decided that my modesty had to be preserved at all costs. As a result, the wardrobe people were instructed to make me a G-string out of a piece of gauze. As the statue was going to be filmed from various different angles and it would be hard to avoid showing any ties around the waist, I was offered something that was rather more G than string: a triangular piece of gauze complete with double-sided sellotape! However, it soon became obvious that the gauze triangle idea wasn't going to work either. By now, everybody was beginning to despair, so I turned to the director (who just happened to be Terry Gilliam of *Monty Python* fame) and said that if nobody had any objections I was prepared to do the job in the nude. As The Thinker is sitting down and kneeling forward, from a camera point of view nothing untoward would be seen. Terry jumped at the idea and I was ushered down to the make-up department, where the make-up lady had the job of giving me a full body make-up - and I do mean full body!

I think Terry was most appreciative of the work we did on this commercial and I subsequently worked for him again on his *Jabberwocky* film.

Of course, there have been lots of other TV commercials: The Green Cross Code, Tonka Toys, Max Factor Lip Gloss (no, I wasn't wearing it!), Sampson Beer, Scotch Beef Chunks (me playing Tarzan), and Outspan Grapefruit (me and Ronnie Corbett trying to sell undersized grapefruit!)

Now rightly regarded as one of the hottest directors in the movie business, Ridley Scott began his career by doing TV commercials, and I worked with him on two of his more lavish commercial productions. And what mini-epics they turned out to be, too!

My first encounter with Ridley Scott came as a result of the US Tonka Toy Corporation's desire to break into the UK toy market. Tonka had chosen to employ Ridley's production company to create the right image for their products in Britain. Between Tonka and Ridley, it was decided to build this image around a character who possessed the main design features of Tonka toys - strength and durability. Thus the human embodiment of Tonka Toys was born: The Mighty Tonka, a rugged blend of strongman and native-American, clad in buckskin trousers, a sleeveless shirt and moccasins.

After storyboarding a couple of commercials, Ridley Scott's company came to the UK on the lookout for an actor who could adequately fill The Mighty Tonka's brief - not to mention his buckskin trousers - and I got a call to come and try out for the role. Ridley Scott was present during my audition and I must've impressed him somehow, because he offered me the job there and then. It was explained that I'd have to get my hair cropped short and that the first commercial would be filmed on Eastbourne beach, in southern England.

On the appointed day I pulled on the buckskins, slipped into my sleeveless shirt and, prising the Mighty Tonka's moccasins over my sandy feet, stood on Eastbourne beach with my semi-shaven head, feeling every chilly sea breeze that gusted along the shoreline. While Ridley's crew rigged for filming, I, the ultimate professional, was psyching myself into the role of The Mighty Tonka, while actually looking like a cross between Tonto and the Terminator. Never mind, I thought, it was a nice day and there were worse things an actor could be doing than earning his living looking strong and durable on an English beach.

Then the props arrived. The prop that immediately grabbed my attention was a colossal packing case. This five-foot cube was to be filled with Tonka toys and placed on my head, after which I was expected to trot smartly down the beach with it and toss it into the air. The required effect was to have a torrent of Tonka toys cascading towards the cameras as the enormous packing case hit the beach and split asunder. Nice script, shame about the actuality.

Although the packing case was made from ultra-light balsa wood, the mound of toys were constructed from Tonka's celebrated blend of pressed steel and solid rubber. It seemed that I was the only one present who realised that once the case was filled it would weigh almost as much as I did. Being a five-foot cube, the problems of balance would also have to be considered, as would the hazards of my running along a pebble-strewn beach with a gigantic, flat-sided box on my head that responded like a fat kite to the constantly gusting wind.

Eager to please, I agreed to give the stunt a go, although I immediately had my doubts when it took six men to hoist the case onto my head. However, there's no time for doubt when your neck is propping up a couple of hundredweight of Tonka toys, so I set off on my first run towards the dump-off point that had been clearly marked in the sand. It was a matter of remaining steady, looking cool as I did so, and then launching the crate as far as I could when I reached the jettison marks. Five times I did that run, and five times those toys erupted from their crate bang on target. Even I was impressed with myself.

Sadly, the tremendous efforts we went to in order to shoot that commercial were largely overshadowed by the slogan that Ridley Scott's team came up with. 'GIVE BOY TONKA TOY!' became the Mighty Tonka's most celebrated feature. I'll concede that the sheer memorability of this witty catchphrase was due in part to the fact that I delivered the line whilst jumping up and down like a loony on top of a Tonka toy. I'm sure my West Country accent, left splendidly intact for the commercial, and the arresting contrast it made with the Mighty Tonka get-up, also played a part in anchoring the one-liner in the minds of the nation.

The second of Ridley's advertising productions took place ten years later, when he asked if I would play the part of Superman in a Max Factor TV commercial. We would be promoting lip gloss, or at least the leading lady would, and the only change to the original Superman concept was that my suit would be a charming blend of turquoise and purple.

Shooting was scheduled to take place at Pinewood Studios and my memories of it are mixed. Working with Ridley Scott was great, of course, but the three days that the leading lady and I spent hanging from wires attached to the studio roof will forever dominate my recall of the Max Factor job. We had our share of technical problems on that shoot, too, with the back projection screens failing repeatedly. I also discovered that it's no easy matter to make an elegant landing when you've been dangling for an hour and the feeling has gone from your legs. Hassles apart, we got the job done, often shooting into the early hours of the morning thanks to Ridley's insistence on perfection.

Once again, it was the verbal rather than the visual impact of that project that became imprinted in the minds of the audience. This time my one and only line was, "Your lips, they're suddenly shining," uttered in wondrous fashion by Superman, who by this point in the commercial had established himself as a superior entity beyond the mortal temptation of chatting up women. Obviously, the message was that Max Factor lip gloss makes even superheroes notice you. What I got out of that line was smart-arses gazing into my eyes and declaring, "Dave - your lips, they're suddenly shining," every time I was recognised in the street!

Working with Ridley Scott was a pleasure and no one was happier than me when he claimed his rightful place among the industry's great directors.

Chapter Twenty-Five
Dave McProwse, Global Highlander

My early career as an athlete was interesting, to say the least. In 1960, after nine years of training and competing in local bodybuilding events, I was invited to enter the Mr Universe contest. In 1961 I became the Western Counties Strength Set Champion, I began to break a whole series of British weightlifting records and I placed third in the British Olympic Weightlifting Championships. The following year I became the British Heavyweight Weightlifting Champion and went on to represent my country at the World Championships and Commonwealth Games. In 1963 and '64 I retained my British Championship. Then I had a monumental row with the British Amateur Weightlifting Association (BAWLA) and turned professional in 1965. Thereafter, I announced myself as 'Britain's Strongest Man' and toured the country doing lifting and strength exhibitions. Yes, looking back at those early years, there wasn't much time to be bored.

I've always been the sort of athlete who thrives on competition and my decision to turn pro effectively ended my competitive career. In those days earning anything from amateur sport was a capital offence, punishable by the death of your sporting career. Even the reclaiming of legitimate expenses was fraught with difficulty, and the idea of receiving a few pennies from a sponsor to pay for vital training equipment was, well, as unforgivable as spying for the Russians.

The unfairness of this situation was obvious to everyone except BAWLA, and the final straw for me was being hauled in for a stern lecture after I'd done a radio interview to promote the sport. From the £25 fee paid to me by the radio station, no less than £23 of it was expenses. That left me with a princely £2 to spend on my training needs. To my utter disgust, I was ordered to pay that £2 to BAWLA - or else. I chose 'or else' and told the pompous BAWLA dinosaurs so. Turning pro was my only way forward.

I didn't regret what I'd done for a second, but I sorely missed the thrill of competition. Offers came in from a boxing manager and the notion of starting a professional wrestling career was also mooted, but neither of these worthy pursuits captivated me. I needed a professional, physical outlet that would stimulate me into hard training and at which I would stand a chance of earning money. No one was more surprised than me when, of all things, that outlet proved to be the Scottish Highland Games.

My friend Dave Webster called me from his home in Glasgow and suggested that I should head for the Highlands. A lifelong physical culturist, Dave was a human encyclopaedia on the subject of the Highland Games, Scottish folklore and international weightlifting in general. He seemed extremely keen on my joining the Highland Games circuit and promised that, should I be any good at it, I would earn myself a handy wage.

There was one, entirely unavoidable delay, however, before I could set off for Scotland and begin my training - I had to be measured for my kilt! Dave hadn't mentioned the kilt-wearing bit to me, despite the fact that it's compulsory for all Highland Games contestants. It turned out that I would need the full Scottish regalia, including a jacket, socks and sporran, to complement my new kilt. My initial wariness of giving my all whilst wrapped in yards of knee-length tartan was somewhat relieved by the assurance that although a kilt was compulsory so was the wearing of something under it. Given the amount of rapid spinning, jumping and general bouncing around that goes on during the Games, a substantial set of undies would serve to restrict the concentration of spectators and competitors alike to the sporting activities!

According to my new-found Scottish friends, the redoubtable Pipe Major Donald McLeod was the main man for kilts and traditional clothing, so I sought him out for a fitting. Donald stood a stately 5ft 4ins in his smartly stockinged feet, and his efforts to measure me for my jacket caused an outbreak of disrespectful giggling among the locals. I, of course, wouldn't stoop to anything so vulgar - although I did have to stoop more than once to save Donald from putting his neck out.

With my dimensions safely gathered, I was faced with an important decision that had to be made before the construction of my Highland attire could get under way. Which tartan would I wear? As a foreigner, I was at liberty to choose whichever pattern took my fancy, and Donald told me that most people went for the red Royal Stewart tartan - and very smart it looked, too. However, I decided I wanted something a little different, and after a long search through the dozens of tartans in Donald's shop I realised that the one I wanted had been staring me in the face for the past two hours. Donald was wearing a beautiful tartan with a light blue background, which he proudly informed me was a McLeod pattern. I plumped for membership of Clan McLeod right there and then, and I went on to wear their colours throughout all the events, fetes and functions I attended all over the world.

Bidding Donald farewell, our next stop was Inchmurrin, on the bonnie, bonnie banks o' Loch Lomond. I had little time to admire the scenery, however, as my trainers Jay Scott and Jock McColl, both big names on the Highland Games circuit, tried to instil in me the basics of caber tossing, hammer throwing and heaving 28-pound and 56-pound weights as far or as high as possible. There was a lot to learn in such a short space of time.

Before my arrival, Jock and Jay had been out to chop down an enormous tree. This huge conifer lay on the ground before me, and even with its branches lopped off I knew that the three of us wouldn't be able to lift the thing, let alone me on my own. To my relief, the monster log was only in its pre-caber phase and was there merely to act as a model upon which my trainers could take me through the rudiments of caber anatomy.

As I found out that day, a caber is no mere log. It can measure anything between 18 and 22ft in length and weigh between 80 and 150lb. However, the most important thing about a caber is its taper. You see, cabers aren't tossed for distance but rather for straightness, so the more pronounced the taper the easier it is to toss one straight. Imagine a clock face, with the would-be caber tosser standing at its centre. For a perfect toss, the narrow end of the caber, which starts off in the hands of the competitor (it's extremely difficult to describe this without referring to the athlete as a 'tosser', you know!), must describe a 180-degree arc, flipping up and over, and landing smack in the 12 o'clock position. If this sounds complicated, you should try actually doing it.

In order to gain sufficient forward momentum with which to flip such a heavy, awkward projectile, the competitor is compelled to run with it. In order to be in a position to run with a caber, you need to place your hands beneath the narrow end or 'lip', hoist it vertically to waist level and stabilise it perfectly before beginning the run. Even though you're assisted by two helpers to get the caber from the ground into its vertical position, from then on in you're on your own, and I found that it took more strength, balance, coordination and sheer skill to reach the pre-run stage than I could possibly have imagined. By the time all the intricacies had been explained to me, I was beginning to think that my Scottish sojourn was just a waste of good tartan!

Once you've mastered the lift and balance phase, you then move on to the tricky bit. Running with a vertical tree trunk can only be a short-term affair and caber tossing is no different. As the athlete hits top speed, the top of the caber is allowed to fall forward until it reaches the point in its travel at which a huge upward heave will impart enough rotation to the mass of the caber to carry it through the 180-degree arc. In practice, the thick end of the caber hits the ground and the thinner end travels up and over, landing directly ahead of the competitor at 12 o'clock high. That's the theory, anyway. Perfect throws are seen with about the same regularity as the Loch Ness Monster, but these wondrous happenings are witnessed by thousands - and some of them are even sober. Throws don't have to be perfect to score, thank goodness. Any spot between 9 o'clock and 3 o'clock gets you points, but anything outside these zones is a no-throw, and there are plenty of those in a Highland Games tournament, I can assure you.

Once the small matter of tossing the perfect caber has been taken care of, the top-flight Highland Gamesman turns his attention to the hurling of heavy weights. My first taste of this came courtesy of a lesson in hammer throwing, Scottish style. Now a Scottish hammer is just that, a hammer, only it has a 16-pound spherical head on the end of a three-foot wooden shaft. There's no comfy hand grip at the end of a flexible wire as in Olympic hammer throwing, oh dear me no, and if I thought that the hammer was a bit extreme, when I saw the footwear required of its throwers I really did begin to wonder what on earth I'd got myself into.

Scottish hammer throwers use the sort of boots that the Marquis de Sade would wear for a bit of weekend peasant-stomping. This ferocious footwear has huge spikes affixed to the soles and these literally nail your feet into pre-dug footholes. With his back to the intended landing zone, the athlete swings the hammer with powerful, circular sweeps of the arms, until the momentum is such that the shoulder joints feel as though they're about to detach themselves from the torso. At this point the hammer is released and flies across whichever region of Scotland you happen to be in. The rotational force of this procedure often lifts the thrower clean out of his spike holes, leaving him facing the direction in which the hammer has just flown - or not flown at all but skidded pathetically across the turf, depending on the expertise of the thrower.

Trust me, Scottish hammer throwing isn't easy, and without spiky boots you're a non-starter. I didn't have any and would have to arrange for them to be made especially for me, as my feet are so large. What with my tartan gear and tailor-made torture boots to pay for, I'd have to develop my Highland Games techniques a bit sharpish in order to recoup my expenses. By the time I moved onto the weight throwing stage, I was having grave doubts.

After my crash courses on caber tossing and hammer throwing, the Highland Games philosophy was beginning to dawn on me: they were designed to be as hard, frustrating and awkward as possible. Throwing the weights isn't something that can be taken lightly either, especially the 'little' 28-pound one. This demands more rapid rotation and shoulder wrenching, and, sadly, I was never any good at it. The technique is basically that of the discus thrower, only instead of launching an aerodynamic disc the Highland Games hardship philosophy insists that contestants hurl a quarter-hundredweight iron block.

The 56-pound vertical toss was more in my line, although, like everything connected to the 'heavy' events in Highland Gaming, it demanded muscle-wrenching, eye-popping, gut-busting input from anyone seeking to master it. The idea is to throw the 56-pound weight as high as possible over a pole-vault bar and, although the technique is fairly basic, timing is crucial. The thrower stands with his back to the bar and begins by swinging the weight, one-handed, back and forth between the knees to gain momentum. At the critical moment, a final mighty heave launches the weight up, back and over the bar to glory. Or, if your release is fractionally askew, the weight can drop perilously close to where you're standing - except, by the time it lands, no thrower with any sense is still standing there.

I was quite good at this event, usually placing in the top three, and I can still hear the commentator telling the crowd that hurling the 56-pound weight to a height of 15 feet was like throwing a small boy over a double-decker bus. How the hell anyone arrived at that analogy I can't imagine, but I was grateful that 'small boy chucking' didn't find its way into the Highland Games curriculum.

I returned to Croydon with instructions from my Scottish trainers to purchase a couple of cabers and get down to some serious, toss ... er ... 'work'. Obviously, I couldn't simply swing by my local branch of 'Cabers R Us' and get what I needed, but a caber isn't so far removed from a telephone pole, so I bought a brace of them from the first telephone exchange I contacted, paying just a few pence for these essential training aids. Next I had to find somewhere from which to begin my assault on the world of caber tossing.

With fortune still on my side, I soon found a nearby sports ground where I could store and practise with my telephone-pole cabers. After promising the groundsman that I'd keep my caber-impact divots well away from his football pitches, I began to put in some serious training. As with so many things, practice makes perfect, and while I was a long way from perfection I was soon becoming quite proficient with a caber. That didn't stop me from coming to an important decision, however. I wasn't happy about touring Scotland on the Highland Games circuit, so I'd decided to direct my efforts towards a single big event, the World Caber Tossing Championship, in Aberdeen. While my change of direction didn't set the pages of the sporting press alight, it was nevertheless a bold decision, as I'd be putting all of my Scotch eggs in one basket.

Two men dominated the Highland Games scene in the late '60s, early '70s: Arthur Rowe, the former European shot-put champion and his arch rival from Aberdeenshire, Bill Anderson. Arthur was, without doubt, one of the greatest athletes I've ever had the pleasure of competing against. His sheer strength was incredible, and this was backed with speed, suppleness and mobility to spare. Bill lacked Arthur's speed but more than made up for that with his tremendous muscle power. In addition to his prowess in the caber, hammer and weight throwing, Bill was a formidable Cumberland wrestler, as I discovered when I took him on in an exhibition match - once.

I'd always considered myself to be pretty good at Cumberland wrestling and at 19 stone with strength to match I actually harboured notions of giving a good account of myself against Bill Anderson. Within seconds, I discovered that Bill was possessed of a vastly different centre of gravity than ordinary humans. When I eventually managed to get my arms around his broad back, preparatory to lifting him and dumping him on the floor (I thought), I just couldn't shift him. Then Bill decided that our bout had gone on quite long enough, shrugged off my attempts to unsettle him, and dumped me on my back before I even had time to blink. I've always been a fierce competitor, but I've never been stupid enough to let my desire blind me. Bill was the master of Cumberland wrestling and I knew better than to waste my time trying to prove otherwise.

It soon became obvious that Bill and Arthur had the whole of the Highland Games circuit sewn up between them. There were so many events going on throughout the summer that they saw no need to compete against each other and thereby reduce their individual takings in prize money. Competing three times a week, winning practically everything they entered and avoiding each other like the plague, Bill and Arthur could make up to £300 a week, which was serious money in the 1960s.

Inevitably, there were times when this combination of irresistible force and immovable object converged at the same venue. The Games at Braemar, which are traditionally attended by the royal family, the Chieftain's Cup at Aboyne and my main focus, the World Caber Tossing Championships at Aberdeen, were premier events that attracted the cream of Scottish Highland Games athletes, but Arthur and Bill confirmed their dominance as usual. I competed twice in the Aberdeen Championships, placing third both times behind Arthur and Bill. I've never liked being beaten, but I made an exception in this case. There's no shame in being bested by a legend, and I had two of them to take on.

My two visits to Aberdeen, in 1969 and 1970, for the World Championships were hard going. The cabers used for this tournament were 20ft long, weighed 130lb and had no discernible taper to them, so getting one to turn right over was incredibly difficult. Most of my efforts either ended with the caber toppling backwards or walloping down at points on the 'clock' that didn't score. I did manage a couple of 9 o'clock tosses, which put me in the frame for a placing. The difficulty of those contests can be illustrated by the fact that, apart from the unstoppable duo of Arthur and Bill, no one could achieve a scoring throw.

With that second tournament at an end, my stop-start career in Highland Games had just hit its 'stop' phase, at which point serendipity changed my life for the next three years. To save anyone looking it up, 'serendipity' is defined as 'chance good fortune', and this dose of it took the form of a phone call from the friend who had started me on the Highland Games high road in the first place, Dave Webster. Dave had long nursed the notion of creating a touring troupe of Highland artistes. Dave's vision had heavy athletes, Scottish dancers, pipers and all manner of performers travelling the world to spread the excitement and interest that such offerings generated so effortlessly in their home country. Lack of sponsorship had so far meant that Dave's dream was just that and no more, until he received a call from United Biscuits.

United Biscuits, by the most fortunate coincidence imaginable, were looking for a team of Highland athletes and performers to tour the world in order to appear at British Export Week exhibitions and promote British products, namely United's McVities brand of foodstuffs. Dave got the sponsorship he needed and I was lucky enough to be asked to join his squad of globe-trotting ambassadors.

We certainly trotted the globe in the three years we were together, taking in Tokyo, Honolulu, Sweden, Denmark and major US cities like San Francisco, New York and San Diego. That tour was tremendous fun for all of us and my kilt and I put in some serious air miles together. The squad consisted of five heavy athletes, including myself, Bill Anderson and Arthur Rowe, plus four Scottish dancers, a piper and a performing strongman called Graham Brown, who had one of the most peculiar acts I've ever seen - and after so many years in show business I've seen my share of strange acts.

Graham used to warm up by having a couple of we heavy athletes swinging sledgehammers at a block of concrete lodged on his chest. This stunt alone didn't carry sufficient potential for serious injury, so Graham upped the ante a little by lying on a bed of nails while we hammered away at him. By now well into his stride, Graham would then eat a couple of wine glasses, followed by a handful of razor blades - more as an interlude than anything else. Next, he'd place his neck in two rope nooses, while teams of men on each end of the ropes contested a tug of war, with Graham's neck muscles the only means of preventing his strangulation or decapitation. Graham wasn't finished yet, however. He still had his glorious finale.

What Graham did to close his act often caused members of the audience to faint or vomit on the spot. That said, when the squad first saw him do it, most of us felt pretty queasy, too. Taking a standard shop-bought, solid iron, six-inch nail, Graham would hammer it up his nose until the shaft of the nail had disappeared and the head of the nail was touching his nostril. I swear that the nails he used were real, as was the hammer he employed to drive them through his sinus, and if banging these nails in was toe-curlingly awful to watch, then pulling them out was positively gruesome.

Graham considered that the insertion of six inches of pointed metal into his nasal tissues necessitated a bit of theatre to make it interesting. So, taking a huge pair of pincers, he'd subject the nail to a pantomime 'pull', accompanied by much grunting, groaning and apparent muscular effort. Those members of his audience who could still bear to watch, or hadn't swooned or buried their faces in their handkerchiefs, were privileged to witness the emergence of the nail. This was followed, with perfect timing, by a great gush of blood that continued to spurt plentifully from his nose as he took his final bows to a stunned silence from his horrified public. Quite how Graham Brown's macabre stage act ever came to represent McVities foods I'll never know, but he went on to become a very popular cabaret act north of the border.

During the tours, whether we were performing or not, Highland dress was compulsory. Eventually, I didn't bother even taking a pair of trousers with me and became perfectly at home in my kilt, no matter what activity I was engaged in. The degree of interest provoked by the wearing of a kilt bordered on the absurd at times. I'll accept that grown men rocking the night away at a San Francisco disco, wearing yards of tartan fashioned into a skirt, is certainly unusual, but surely it didn't warrant the amount of fascination we received? I lost count of the times I watched girls contort themselves or invent excuses to stoop to floor level purely in order to catch a glimpse of whatever it was we had under our kilts. All these ladies needed to do was ask and we'd have told them. Catch us later in the night, when the drinks had been flowing, and we would have probably shown them, too. Either way, it was only a very secure pair of underpants that was on offer, so there wasn't actually much to get excited about.

When the tour hit Tokyo I neared the fulfilment of one of my life ambitions. I'd wanted to visit a Japanese bathhouse ever since I'd seen what James Bond got up to in one during *You Only Live Twice*. Naturally, the fact that I was a happily married man would preclude an exact imitation of the sorts of pleasures Agent 007 experienced there. All the same, I was determined to enjoy the luxury and indulgence of it all and, from the moment I discovered that Tokyo was on our itinerary, the bathhouse visit was a high priority.

Speaking of itineraries, we were handed one as soon as we checked into the hotel in Tokyo and it demonstrates to perfection the Japanese mania for efficiency, as each day was scheduled to the minute. It went as follows:

7.00 a.m.	*You will arise.*
7.30 a.m.	*You will be seated at breakfast.*
7.42 a.m.	*You will have completed breakfast.*
7.47 a.m.	*You will assemble in hotel foyer.*
7.52 a.m.	*Transportation will arrive at hotel.*
7.54 a.m.	*You will have boarded transportation.*
7.55 a.m.	*Transportation will depart from hotel.*
8.03 a.m.	*You will arrive at the Seibu Department Store.*
8.07 a.m.	*You will assemble on the roof garden of the Seibu Department Store.*
8.10 a.m.	*You will receive further instructions.*

The roof garden appearances were strange because we were always surrounded by tiers of huge glass aquariums teeming with multi-coloured koi carp. The cultivation and showing of koi are almost a religion in Japan, and fish deemed perfectly marked can command astronomical prices. Understandably, our rooftop shows were limited to dancing and piping - there was no way anyone was going to allow us to start slinging hammers, weights and cabers around up there. Graham Brown's nose-piercing extravaganza was shelved, too, for some strange reason. I'd been really looking forward to the reaction of the good folks of Tokyo as Graham hauled a nail from his nasal septum. If he'd been asked, I bet Graham would've bowed to the tradition of his hosts and substituted a Samuri sword for the nail, too.

No matter where we were, there was always a manic Japanese chap scuttling around behind us like an overwound clockwork toy, chivvying us along with cries of "Hurry, hurry!" I never heard him say another word in English throughout the entire trip. By the end of our ten-day stint in Tokyo it had become extremely wearing, but as representatives of our gracious sponsors we were, of course, obliged to maintain the highest standard of conduct. Bill Anderson was particularly irritated by Mr Hurry-Hurry, and after being chivvied along once too often he said to me in a growl that could be heard from 30 yards, "I wish that little sod would commit 'hurry-kiri'."

Throughout our ten days in Tokyo we were only allowed one day off. Even then, our day had been mapped out to the minute, with a coach tour taking in the famous Kamakura Buddha, which is one of Japan's national monuments, plus a visit to a sumo wrestling training facility. Call us uncultured, but there's no point in denying that the trip to the sumo gym was the highlight of our free day.

The ruthlessly adept organisers of our day scheduled the sumo gym as our first port of call and, although the wrestling season had just finished, there must've been upwards of a hundred men in training when we turned up. It was fascinating to watch the wrestlers - who trained, slept and lived at the gym - going through their rituals and moves. At the end of our visit their trainer came over to tell us that their champion had issued a challenge to us and asked if we would be prepared to fight him to preserve the honour of Scotland. Inside three seconds, Bill Anderson had been installed as defender of Scotland and stepped forward to do battle, sumo style.

Bill had no idea whatsoever about sumo wrestling, so he decided to do what he knew best and simply locked arms with the Japanese guy and remained immobile. The sumo champion could do nothing with Bill, and Bill wasn't prepared to try anything he wasn't sure of, so there they stayed until it was agreed that the fight would be declared an honourable draw, rendering Scotland's honour intact. I know that, given the training, Bill Anderson could've made a name for himself in sumo. Mind you, I'm sure that many of the wrestlers we saw that day could've had a fair go at Highland Games, too.

Reaching the Kamakura Buddha by coach was a three-hour grind through the pouring rain, made more of a trial by the fact that the spiritual significance of the occasion was rather lost on us. Things didn't improve much when we arrived to find the Buddha's temple heaving with wall-to-wall schoolkids. Once again, the sight of us in our kilts and tartan provoked an unholy interest and at one point there was a queue of schoolkids waiting to have their photos taken with us, all thought of piety thrown aside.

The day before we were due to leave Japan I decided to fulfil my bathhouse-sampling ambition. I ordered a taxi and, after enquiring as to which of the bathhouses was the most reputable, I headed off for my dream date. The Pan Pacific Games were going on at the time and after I'd been given a number and ushered into the bathhouse waiting area I was amazed to find myself surrounded by athletes wearing their national team blazers. I was there for a bath and a bit of pampering, but I know there were more basic reasons behind the presence of most of those surrounding me. I didn't blame them for that, but they were definitely pushing it a bit by appearing in the team strip!

Soon a gaggle of young ladies appeared and beckoned half-a-dozen of us towards an elevator, which whisked us to an assortment of bathrooms throughout the building. Gradually, the girls paired off with the gentlemen they were escorting by calling out their numbers and disappearing into tiny cubicles. It was at this point that it began to dawn on me that James Bond's experience of a Japanese bathhouse and my own were likely to differ by a large margin. I'd like to say that I found it slightly disappointing. To be blunt, however, it was rubbish.

For a start, I didn't have any say in which girl was to bathe me, and the one I got didn't look particularly interested in life itself, let alone in my extreme bathing pleasures. She couldn't, or wouldn't, even speak to me. Instead, she pointed and grimaced her way through a selection of signals that told me where to go and what to do. Very stimulating, I'm sure. Then, the bath itself could scarcely accommodate my feet, so by the wayside went the luxurious, indulgent, relaxing soak I'd been promising myself for so many years. To add insult to disillusionment, the gormless geisha that I'd been lumbered with spent most of her time looking into a mirror and repairing her make-up. Oh well, perhaps she'd leap into action, sprout fingers of steel and give me the massage of a lifetime, for this was the bit of the bathhouse experience I'd been looking forward to most of all. Sadly, she was even less interested in massaging than she was in sparkling conversation.

After a massage that was slightly less invigorating than filling in a tax return, I was treated to my hostess's entire repertoire of English, as she droned out an often-repeated invitation. "Youwannee special treatmen' one-thousan' yen, or youwannee special treatmen' two-thousan' yen?" "No thanks, love," I responded. "You seem incapable of giving me a simple bath, so I doubt if there's anything special you can do for me." She didn't understand what I'd said and I was feeling too annoyed to explain it to her, so she repeated her 'special treatmen'' offer twice more. I shook my head and scowled at her, and the universal language of the totally disinterested imparted more than words could ever do - and thus that particular lifetime ambition came to its sordid end.

Whilst I was getting dressed I wondered what the lusty fellows with the team blazers must've made of it all. How anyone could fancy a 'special treatmen'' session in a dump like that was way beyond my powers of reason. Not only was it a particularly grubby venue, staffed by girls who pampered themselves more than their clients, but also each minuscule cubicle had a door with a window in it through which a little old man would constantly peer to check that the girls were doing their best to hand out the 'special treatmen''. What a turn-off it all was. I'd have preferred to sit through the finale of Graham Brown's nose-nailing act any time.

The first thing I did when I got back to my hotel was to run a proper bath and have a lovely long soak - on my own - and vow never to believe James Bond again.

The following year saw us in San Francisco, where we performed our demonstrations in Golden Gate Park. The entire team had the honour of being presented to Her Royal Highness Princess Alexandra, who, like us, was on tour in the USA, although she wasn't required to hurl cabers, hammers and weights around as far as I could see. HRH was doing her bit to promote Britain, so, although the nature of our duties differed widely, the purpose was identical.

Now for that most rare of events, a Dave Prowse confession. I wanted to stay on for a while in San Francisco, so I pretended to be ill. There, that's got it off my chest after all these years. Faking illness was the only way I could wangle some time to meet up with a weightlifter by the name of Bruce Wilhelm. I'd been corresponding with Bruce for over two years and during that time he'd made repeated requests for me to come over and train him, personally. Bruce and his girlfriend were waiting for me at San Francisco airport, and as soon as my Highland party had flown off home I met my pen pal and we went on a tour of the city.

Bruce lived with his doting parents in a place called San Anselmo, around an hour's drive from San Francisco. As soon as Bruce thought we'd seen enough of the city, he headed for home for our first training session. He was fairly strong but woefully short on technique, so my first task was to teach Bruce the rudiments of lifting theory. With so much information to impart, that initial workout lasted over three hours, but I was still surprised when Bruce announced that he was 'pooped' and would be taking a nap to recover. That left me sitting with his parents at 3 o'clock in the afternoon, chatting and having a late lunch. Six hours later Bruce was still sleeping and I'd long since run out of polite conversation, so I decided to wake him up. It was my first time in America and the last thing I wanted to do was sit in all night exchanging pleasantries with Bruce's parents.

On being woken, Bruce declared himself still 'pooped' and claimed that San Francisco was too far away for us to revisit for a tour of its nightlife, which was what I was hoping to do. After intermittent bouts of pleading, cajoling and the odd threat from me, Bruce reluctantly agreed to a quick spin around San Jose, at the southern end of San Francisco Bay. That sounded fine to me. After all, hadn't Dionne Warwick herself immortalised that very town in song? "If it's good enough for Dionne, it's good enough for me," I said to Bruce as we climbed into his car, en route to what I anticipated would be a night of wild partying, loud music and who knows what else. Bruce just yawned and concentrated on keeping one eye open so he could drive.

Well, Ms Warwick, you are undoubtedly a fine lady and a truly great singer, but you sure ain't no tour guide. San Jose turned out to contain slightly less of interest to an eager Brit on tour than an evening with Bruce's parents. The place was obviously too close to the bright lights of San Francisco to make the building of quality night-time attractions worthwhile. The whole place presented itself to me as somewhere to go to recover from the good time you'd had somewhere else. San Jose was a hangover therapy centre and I was right in the middle of it with the whole night to kill.

Bruce knew of only one possible place of entertainment, the Pink Poodle, a sleazy strip joint where the waitresses double as performers, so we installed ourselves at a table there and ordered a couple of beers. Despite having enjoyed a solid six-hour siesta, my 'pooped' companion seemed unable to stop yawning, and by the time 10 p.m. rolled around Bruce was fast asleep at the table, propped in his chair with a beer in his hand. I was alone, in the Pink Poodle, in San Jose, with nobody to talk to. Great.

Keen to try anything to lift the gloom of my wild night on the town, I smiled at the prettiest waitress I could find and mouthed some sort of compliment to her. To my horror, she marched straight to my table and asked me to repeat what I'd just said. I told her that I'd rather see her with her clothes on than the other girls with theirs off, which was fine, considering I'd had only five seconds to think of it. It worked, too, because she asked me to sit with her at the bar where it would be easier to talk. I obliged - well, it would have been rude not to - and from our conversation I learned that she was a waitress who was funding her college education through stripping. She was a sweet girl and a vastly more interesting companion than Bruce, who was by now reverberating with his own snores, his beer still clutched in his hand. My friend the waitress would chat to me for a while, then go and do her stripping routine, after which she'd rejoin me at the bar. At 2 a.m. Bruce inexplicably stirred into life, staggered sleepily from the table and announced that we had to be going home because he needed to get some sleep!

Years later I met that waitress again, only this time she was in my neck of the woods and visited me at Harrods, where I was working as the store's fitness consultant. She was looking for accommodation and I introduced her to a friend of mine who was able to help her. Sadly, that was the last I saw of her and I never did manage to thank her for rescuing what was promising to prove a painfully boring night in San Jose.

Bruce Wilhelm and I lost touch after my 'illness' cleared up and I returned to the UK, although I watched his progress closely. He eventually became the USA's Super Heavyweight Weightlifting Champion and one of the strongest men in the world. It must've been all that sleep that did it! After San Francisco the Highland Games tour came to an end and our troupe was disbanded. We'd had three years of worldwide enjoyment and I wouldn't have missed it for anything. I've still got my kilt and my sporran is in storage should a revival of the McVities expedition ever be on the cards.

Chapter Twenty-Six
Fifteen Years of Harrods Heaven

My selling days came to a halt when Alf Cole, Sports Buyer for Harrods, asked me if I would like to work there for three days a week (Tuesday, Thursday and Saturday) as the Keep Trim Consultant. I was still working freelance and would earn commission on any keep fit or exercise equipment sold. Best of all, I was given the rank of buyer, which entitled me to generous discounts on goods throughout the store.

As I mentioned earlier, Harrods took pride in their reputation of being the only store in the world where one could purchase anything one desired: the pet department could procure an elephant if required, and luxury cars were exhibited in the banking hall on the ground floor. All the heads of departments wore pinstripe suits and long frock coats, and nothing was too much trouble; service and courtesy were the watchwords, as was customer confidentiality. Many famous personalities from all over the globe came there to shop (or telephoned in orders) and while I was the Keep Trim Consultant there I had the pleasure of dealing with Bing Crosby, Perry Como, Richard Greene, John Wayne, Michael Caine and Roger Moore. I even entertained Christopher Reeve for morning and afternoon tea while training him for his Superman role.

It was an honour and a privilege to be part of such an organisation. I look back on my time at Harrods with great affection and the management were amenable when my showbiz career started to blossom and curtailed my three-day week contract somewhat. So long as I wasn't filming abroad, I always made a point of being in the store on Saturdays, even though I could never guarantee what day of the week I could manage.

Prior to the opening of the Olympic Way on the fourth floor (which I officially opened for Harrods, along with the buyers of the golf, horse and ski departments), the sports department was an understated place situated at the far end of the store on the second floor. It was on a quiet day in the old sports department that I noticed a very large man in a raincoat that practically went down to the floor, rummaging around looking for something he couldn't find. I called the other staff over and said, "Do you see who that is over near the bike department?" They didn't recognise him, so I explained, "That's John Wayne!"

So off I went to see if I could be of any assistance. Knowing a bit about the film business, I was aware that he was in town working on a thriller called *Brannigan*, but the last thing I expected was to meet him in Harrods' sports department.

"Can I help you, Mr Wayne?" I asked.

"Yes, you can. I'm looking for a long rope ladder," he replied.

"I'm sorry, we don't sell rope ladders. Will anything else suffice?"

"Well, how about a long coil of rope?"

"No, sorry, we don't do that either. Maybe Pindisports, a mountaineering shop just up the road, will be able to help you."

"Well, thank you for all your help."

"If you don't mind my asking, I know that you're here filming *Brannigan*, but what on earth do you want a rope ladder for?"

"Well, I came over to do this film and they've put me into the Cumberland Hotel at Marble Arch and I've got a suite on the seventh floor. I look out of the windows and there are f---ing bars outside, I go out into the hallways and there are f---ing bars at all the windows, and I'm f---ing frightened to death that the f---ing place is going to catch on fire and I need my own means of escape!"

And with that, John Wayne wandered off.

On another occasion I noticed a customer looking through the limited amount of archery equipment we had and once again went over to see if I could help. The gentleman had a very distinctive voice and told me he was looking for some bows and arrows to take to Ireland for his grandchildren.

I had very limited knowledge of archery, but I was able to ascertain the sizes of the children and suggested suitable bow sizes, the right length of arrow and the buying of quivers, all of which he listened to with great interest. At the end of my sales pitch he ordered everything that I'd suggested and handed me his Harrods charge card. There, to my dismay, was stamped 'Richard Greene' - so for the last 15 minutes I'd been selling bows and arrows to Robin Hood himself! Not surprisingly I felt slightly embarrassed by this comical situation, but he put me at my ease by saying that I'd been most knowledgeable and helpful.

One of the prominent memories of working for Harrods is of the IRA bombing on the last Saturday before Christmas, 21 December 1974.

During the day I'd been doing my seasonal shopping around the store, purchasing a turkey and some ham from the charcuterie, shellfish from the fish department and various presents for Norma and our three children. The store was packed with shoppers. Over 200,000 people had passed through those famous doors that day and both sales and spirits were high. The Olympic Way wasn't even on the drawing board at that time and I was plying my very successful trade in the old sports department on the second floor, managed by Mr Cole, so I stored my purchases in the buyers office there for safe-keeping before continuing my work. At the opposite end of the second floor was the hardware department, managed by Mr Butler and selling an extensive range of paint and every piece of DIY equipment a handyman could possibly want. Beneath this department, on the first floor, was the fabulous fur department.

Trade continued briskly and it was a perfectly normal pre-Christmas shopping day, until at about 3 p.m. a muffled boom was heard. Within minutes hordes of people could be seen scurrying past the end of the sports department, obviously trying to get out of the store as quickly as possible. However, at that point the staff were totally unaware of what had happened and continued working. I went to check out of the window, assuming that something was taking place out on the main road, and it was then that I noticed smoke billowing out of the front of the hardware department.

Just at that moment, all the alarms sounded and the in-store security staff came racing through to tell everyone to evacuate the building as quickly as possible, closing the steel security doors as they moved through the department. No one needed telling twice. We followed the evacuation procedure and the entire staff congregated in the loading bay in Trevor Square opposite the store. We waited patiently for a couple of hours, alternately gossiping and shivering, somewhat shocked even though we didn't know exactly what had happened. We were eventually told that the situation in the store was very serious and were all advised to make our way home. Everyone was relieved to be on their way, especially once we'd been notified by the security police that an IRA bomb had gone off and that sniffer dogs were now searching the store for further explosive devices.

I was making my way to the car park when it dawned on me that our Christmas dinner and all the presents were still in the sports department. It was too late to buy any replacements, so there was no way I was going home without them. An appeal had been made for as many staff as possible to return the following day to help clear up the damage. I would be there, clearing rubble with the best of them, but I was still determined to save our turkey, no matter what. I approached the main entrance and, although I was well known to them, the security personnel wouldn't allow me to enter the building. I therefore hung around waiting, hoping that the dogs would find nothing and I would eventually be granted access. My patience was rewarded after a couple of hours, when the all-clear was given and a security guard escorted me to the department to retrieve my Christmas treats. Looking back, it amazes me that, having escaped injury in a bomb blast, I was so bothered about the loss of a turkey and some trimmings!

I arrived home at around 9 p.m. to an extremely relieved Norma, who had seen the bombing of Harrods on the TV news. Having heard no word from me, she'd started fearing the worst. Why hadn't I thought to phone her? I'd been too busy worrying about that stupid turkey.

The next morning at eight o'clock, I joined the other volunteers in a mission to salvage what we could from the aftermath of the bomb blast. We knew that the bomb had been a fairly powerful one, but the degree of devastation we saw on that Sunday morning in December chilled us more than any winter cold ever could. The hardware department was very badly damaged, as the bomb had been placed in the middle of the paints area. Paint was splattered everywhere and, in addition, the bomb had set off the sprinkler system, so the department had been flooded by gallons water. To make matters worse, the water had cascaded through to the fur department below and into the window displays, causing thousands of pounds' worth of damage - far greater monetary loss than that caused by the explosion itself.

Only the vigilance and prompt action of Jack Butler, the hardware department buyer, had prevented human casualties. He had spotted the bomb lying on a shelf alongside the paint tins and his quick thinking had allowed the security staff to evacuate the nearby departments very quickly. Looking at the aftermath, it was difficult to believe that so much destruction had been inflicted without loss of life. However, the mood at the store was one of gratitude that everything lost could be replaced.

Harrods was a mess and the grand old lady of Knightsbridge needed our help. How pleasing it was when anyone who was anyone in Harrods turned up to help: sales staff, buyers and directors, all shovelling together in work clothes and wellington boots. I'd heard of and experienced a few 'triumph in the face of adversity' moments in my life, and this was certainly one of them.

The press had descended en masse to report on the carnage, of course, and the photos of Harrods' managing director, Robert Midgely, and our hero, Jack Butler, filled newspaper pages throughout the world. I and good friend Trevor Hart, the assistant sports manager, worked as a team, following the management around and getting into as many press photos as possible. I told Trevor that the press publicity would do his Harrods career the world of good and, sure enough, a few months after 'Shovelling with the Management' made all the major national newspapers Trevor was promoted to sports buyer on Alf Cole's retirement.

And, of course, careful study of most of these photos will reveal a tall, well-built man, shovelling sturdily in the background. Even in those days, I'd never let a photo opportunity pass me by!

Chapter Twenty-Seven
Ghostly Haunts and
Underworld Jaunts

In September 1969 I realised a long-cherished ambition when I opened my own gymnasium in Marshalsea Road, London, SE1. Among other things, I'd been Director of Training at the National Sports Centre at Crystal Palace for the previous five years and I knew the time was right to make the move.

Finding the gym came as a result of a publicity campaign I was involved with on behalf of Cutty Sark Whisky. At the time, I'd just watched a business of mine go into liquidation, I was flat broke, and I was more than happy with my situation at the National Sports Centre, so opening a gymnasium was just about the last thing any normal person would've contemplated. However, fate stepped in at this point, as it so often does.

One evening I was conducting the 'Unliftable' challenge in the famous Thomas à Beckett pub in the Old Kent Road, London, when Derek Rowe, a photographer friend, told me about an old boxing gymnasium that had become vacant in SE1. Derek revealed that this gym was close to London Bridge, a mere stone's throw from the City, on several major bus routes and right outside Borough tube station, so it would have all the commercial potential a gym could ever need. I was already selling myself on the idea by now, so I arranged to go and see it with Derek at the first opportunity.

When we got around to viewing the property, the first thing I discovered was that the landlord was none other than Freddie Foreman, an associate of Ronnie and Reggie, the infamous Kray twins. Freddie was otherwise detained (in Leicester prison, as it turned out) at the time of my inspection, and in his absence the gym had become all but derelict.

In its heyday the gym had been Freddie's private club, with a taxicab office on the ground floor, a very basic boxing gym on the first floor and a drinking club upstairs. Freddie didn't bother too much with details, such as a licence for the premises, and the intercom on the front door would often bark out a warning if a police raid was imminent, at which point the upstairs punters, among whom were several chaps that Scotland Yard dearly wished to interview, would scatter across the rooftops and make good their escape.

Despite the state of the place, its potential was obvious, so I negotiated a deal with Freddie's wife, Maureen, and prepared to begin the huge task of renovation, my dream being to turn this wreck of a building into a luxury health studio. With bank managers and financiers still to convince, not to mention dealing with Norma's reaction to the news of my latest great scheme, there was plenty to contend with. What I didn't know at the time was that I'd have a poltergeist to contend with, too, because the gym came with a sitting tenant - the mischievous ghost of a tramp.

A brief check into the building's history unearthed the fact that at the turn of the century it somehow became a dosshouse for the local tramps, drunks and ne'er-do-wells. So dreadful was the building's reputation that a policeman would only visit it with the protection of other officers. Further research, mainly through talking to the older locals, revealed the murder of an old tramp known as 'Bluff'. Apart from the fact that he'd been killed while dossing in my building, little was known about poor Bluff's demise. However, everyone who was in the know about such stuff told us that Bluff's ghost was alive and well and doing its undead thing in my gym.

Stories rarely become more truthful in the telling and, from the versions I've heard over the years, Bluff was either poisoned, strangled, shot, battered with a brick, clouted with a drainpipe, pushed from the roof, stabbed with his own knife, or basically treated to just about every other form of murder that was fashionable at the time. Whatever the actual facts of the matter, Bluff became a fully paid-up member of the Ghosts Union, which entitled him to spend his whole bloody afterlife haunting my gym.

At first I didn't give a spare thought for Bluff's spiritual shenanigans, as I was much too busy devising a way to get the 'Star Gym' off the ground on zero capital. That process took much longer that I had envisaged, and without the support of the members who joined right at the start I would never have made it. As a token of my gratitude to these fine people, I used to hold two parties every year and invite them all for a celebratory shindig. One party was always held on the weekend closest to my birthday in July, and the other was just prior to Christmas. And it was during the summer of 1971 that Bluff decided to gatecrash my party.

The 1970s were the decade of the disco and my parties at the gym were a true sign of their times. I got somebody in to run the music and lights, and one of the local pubs supplied the booze. We still needed to watch the expenses, so we did the catering ourselves using provisions from the nearest cash-and-carry. Disco meant dancing and that demands floor space, so to create as much room as possible we'd dismantle the barbells, weights and anything else we could reduce in size and stack the components against the walls of the gym. Benches were then placed across the solid stacks of weights so that danced-out guests would have somewhere to sit and recover between boogies. I tell you, those parties were as wild as anything the '70s ever saw.

We'd rave on until two in the morning, with the music belting across a square mile of London and party people thrashing about together on the dance floor until chuck-out time. People came from all over the country to attend the Star Gym parties and the locals were never forgotten either. In fact, everyone from the Borough all the way to the Elephant and Castle got to enjoy the music for free - whether they wanted to or not!

When the party was over, a few helpers would stay behind with me to get the place cleaned up and the gym equipment back in their rightful place. On this particular party night, by the time 3 a.m. came around we'd been clearing up for over an hour and had managed to tidy away all of the equipment from the gymnasium floor. With this major task complete, I called a halt to our endeavours and suggested it would be better if we came back later that morning to finish off. One of the lads who'd been helping us had no transport home and asked if he could sleep on one of the massage tables on the second floor, and I agreed to his request. Before he went upstairs to sleep I had a quick check round to make sure that everything was safely locked away and, satisfied that the place was secure, I left for home.

The lad on the massage table fell asleep almost straight away, but not long afterwards he was awakened by a horrendous cacophony of clanging and banging coming up from the gym below. He immediately went downstairs, unlocked the door of the gym and switched on the lights. There, in the middle of the previously empty floor, was a weightlifting barbell loaded up to 130kg (just over 280lb). His senses dulled by partying and lack of sleep, the lad forget about the noise he'd heard and assumed that the barbell had been left out by mistake during our clear-up. He dismantled the barbell, stacked the weights, relocked the gym door and went back upstairs for a much-needed sleep.

Within minutes the banging and clanging started all over again. This time it was a far more apprehensive young man who crept down the stairs to see what was going on. To his horror, the very same barbell and weights that he'd so recently tidied away were now reassembled and sitting in the middle of the gym floor. Now even he knew there was something seriously wrong and so decided to vote with his feet. He ran out as fast as his legs would carry him, leaving the gym unlocked and the lights blazing. I thought about giving him a hard time over abandoning the place but, under the circumstances, would I have done anything different? Actually, I think I would. I'd have left after the first encounter. No doubt about it.

Bluff decided to pump a little uninvited iron on another occasion, too, and chose a similar technique to his first workout. This time no party had been going on and, rather than a disco-weary young lad as the witness, it was my gymnasium manager who saw the aftermath of Bluff's impromptu exercise session.

One of the manager's duties is to make certain that the gym is clean and tidy, with all the equipment neatly put away at the end of every day. Not only is a tidy gym a safer and more pleasant place in which to work out, it's also the only way to stop the cleaning staff moaning like mad about having to move weights before they can pilot their polishers about the place. This manager, Frank, was a diligent chap and he was most particular about tidying away the gear.

It was a Friday night and, as usual, Frank had the place looking perfect at the close of business. All the weights were on their racks and there wasn't so much as a stray sticking plaster on the gym floor. He'd decided to come back to the gym early on the Saturday morning to catch up on some paperwork, but after unlocking the main door Frank found his route blocked by a barbell loaded to 600lb. To make matters worse, not to mention even more weird, every barbell, dumb-bell, weight disc and fixing collar had been strewn across the floor. Nothing was damaged or stolen, just scattered about the place.

Frank knew that the gym doors were double-locked, that each floor was secured by padlocked doors and that all the windows were bolted. He also knew that there was no logical explanation for what he'd seen. Not in this world, anyway.

As I mentioned earlier, the landlord of my health studio was the infamous, but at that time 'otherwise detained' Freddie Foreman. I have met Freddie on several occasions in between his bouts of living in Spain and doing time and, like many men with unsavoury reputations, he has always been most pleasant. In fact, when I first moved into the premises

Freddie insisted that I send him photos of all the girl models and Penthouse Pets that I used to employ for promotional features at the gym. I never got any of these photos back, so they're probably still adorning the wall of a cell in some prison somewhere in the UK.

I had another brush with the 'underworld' during the time that Freddie was my landlord, when I was approached by the London Film School to see if I would be interested in playing the lead in a documentary they were proposing to film, with a view to winning major distribution on one of the TV network channels. I told them I was interested and would like to read the script, which duly arrived and was entitled 'Mad Axeman Mitchell'. I was slated to play Mitchell.

I already knew a little about 'Big Frank Mitchell' from friends who had met him and weightlifters and bodybuilders who had trained with him while Frank was 'inside'. He was a very big man, very strong, and had an exceptional physique, but he didn't get the nickname 'Mad Axeman' for nothing and as a result everybody lived in fear of him. Frank's uncontrollable (not to mention potentially lethal) outbursts got him moved from prison to prison and he eventually finished up in Dartmoor, where once again he exerted his authority and was virtually allowed to do as he pleased, so long as he refrained from pulling anyone's head off. He is even reputed to have gone out on prison work parties in the mornings - after which the wardens would turn a blind eye as Big Frank wandered off, provided he returned to the work party when it was time to go back to the prison.

I started to read the script, which revealed the story of how the Kray brothers were having trouble controlling their protection interests in the West End and therefore decided to spring Big Frank from Dartmoor to do their minding for them. According to the script, factual or otherwise, springing Frank from Dartmoor wasn't difficult. He simply went out on the normal work party, drifted off in his usual fashion and was picked up at a prearranged rendezvous destination by Kray gang members, who drove him back to London and put him in a safe house somewhere in the East End.

To keep Frank happy, apparently Ronnie and Reggie Kray told him that he was their guest and could have anything he wanted. Having been deprived of female company for some time, Frank's first room service request was for a prostitute, who was duly supplied. Rather than merely avail himself of her professional commodities, Frank promptly fell in love with his hooker and wished to abandon his life of crime in favour of running away forever with his heart's desire. The fine female in the middle of all this was also keen on the whole running away idea, which further complicated the situation, but it didn't take the Kray brothers too long to come up with a permanent solution. Coaxing Big Frank into the back of a van, on the pretext of moving him to another safe house, the Krays employed Freddie Foreman and a couple of their boys to dispose of an extremely volatile, love-struck psychopath. A couple of shots were fired and big, bad Mad Axeman Frank Mitchell was no more. Nobody has heard anything of him since.

In the play, it's rumoured that, even after his death, Big Frank's phenomenal strength was put to good use and that he is currently embedded in a block of concrete, playing a supporting role to a motorway bridge somewhere in the UK. In fact, Freddie Foreman eventually admitted to assisting in the murder of Mitchell and claimed that Big Frank's body was dumped into the sea off Folkestone.

You can imagine my consternation at reading all of this. Here I am, being offered an outstanding role in a film that not only accuses my landlord of taking part in a murder but also implicates two of the most fearsome gangsters of modern times. After considering my artistic options and debating the spiritual merit of the role, I decided that I'd be raving mad to go anywhere near the script and returned it to the Film School with a very polite note of refusal written in a firm, yet discernibly trembling hand.

This was not the first time that the Kray brothers had figured in my life. During Christmas 1965, I was appearing in my very first acting job, *Don't Let Summer Come*, at the Mermaid Theatre. I was only involved in the final scene in the play, so I didn't have to be at the Theatre until around 7.30 p.m. for the first house and then again at 10.30 p.m. for the second house. That gave me a couple of hours free every night when I would either go out to eat, have a drink or even go dancing.

One day I received a phone call from the guy who ran the agency, world-famous physical culturist Reub Martin.

"Are you available to do a little job at a pub in the East End next Wednesday?" Reub asked.

"Well, I've got between 8 p.m. and 10.30 p.m. free every night, but I've got to be back at the Mermaid by 10.30 p.m. at the latest."

"Okay, leave it with me and I'll see if that's all right."

The following day Reub called me to say that my hours were okay and asked if I could go to a pub in the Whitechapel Road to meet two of his friends, Ronnie and Reggie Kray, who would be paying my fee of £25 for the evening. At that time I had no idea who the Kray twins were and the following Wednesday I turned up at the pub as requested. I was immediately met by two very smart, dapper little men who introduced themselves as Ronnie and Reggie, and I was told to enjoy myself for the evening and to drink and eat whatever I wanted.

After they'd moved away I had a look round the pub and discovered that the place was filled with some of the biggest, ugliest men I had ever seen. However, they all seemed to be happy eating and drinking, so I joined in with them. Time just seemed to fly by and at about 10.15 p.m. I found Ronnie Kray and told him apologetically that I had to get back to the theatre or I would miss my entrance, to which he replied that it was a pleasure to have had me as their guest for the evening and he thrust £25 in fivers into my hand. I promptly left the pub and got a taxi back to the theatre, arriving in plenty of time to make my entrance for the final scene of the play.

The following day I phoned Tough Guys to let Reub know how the job had gone and to thank him for what must have been the easiest £25 I'd ever earned. I then asked Reub what it had been all about. He told me who the Kray twins really were and that the job I'd been on had been a 'frightener', as the Krays had been expecting trouble in the shape of a visit from another gang. They'd employed the biggest men they could get their hands on just to sit in the pub looking impressive. We must have made a great impression, because nobody showed up!

Chapter Twenty-Eight
The Legendary Stanley Kubrick

Ever since seeing *Spartacus* I'd always had a great admiration for the work of Stanley Kubrick and made a point of seeing everything that Stanley produced and directed, from *2001: A Space Odyssey* to Dr Strangelove and later films like *Barry Lyndon*, *The Shining* and *Full Metal Jacket*.

You can imagine my excitement, therefore, when one day my agent rang and asked me to call Stanley's office to make an appointment to see him regarding a part in a new film he was shooting in the Elstree area - *A Clockwork Orange*, from the controversial book by Anthony Burgess. I duly called his office and was informed that, as Stanley was already out and about scouting locations and filming, an appointment would be difficult to make. However, I wasn't going to let a chance of working with one of the greats of the cinema industry slip away, so I informed the production office that I would fit in with Stanley's schedule even if it meant being seen at midnight.

I think they must've taken me at my word, because an appointment was made for me to see Stanley at the production suite at 8 o'clock in the evening a few days later, and I was informed that I would be expected to do a reading. So not only was I going to be face-to-face with the notorious Stanley Kubrick, who had the reputation of making actors quake in their shoes, I was also going to have to deliver dialogue, which at that time wasn't exactly my strongest point.

I was really sweating buckets in anticipation of meeting Stanley, but I duly presented myself at the production office at the allotted time and there I sat and waited for the great man to appear. After waiting for about two hours Stanley's brother-in-law, who also happened to be co-producing the film, came to see me. He told me that Stanley had been detained on location and couldn't see me that evening, and asked if I would like to make another appointment. Once again I said that I would try to fit in with Stanley's schedule, so another 8 o'clock appointment was made for later that week. Croydon to Elstree is no easy journey and in heavy traffic can take about two hours either way, but I thought it would be time well spent if it secured me a part in the film.

Two days later I was once again at Elstree, waiting for Stanley to appear. This time it was his production secretary, Margaret, who came to inform me after about half an hour that Stanley was tied up on set and she offered to arrange another appointment at a time convenient to myself. To avoid any further repeats of the tiresome journey, I suggested meeting him on an evening when I knew he wouldn't be filming - 8 p.m. on a Sunday night! You can imagine my surprise when this proposed appointment time was readily accepted. And so it was that on the following Sunday evening Stanley and I eventually met.

Stanley was just as I'd imagined him from the photos I'd seen, except that he looked as though he'd just come in from the fields, and he couldn't have been more friendly and apologetic for missing the two previous appointments. We sat down together and talked about a variety of different subjects, mainly sport and my weightlifting career, before finally doing the reading, which was really nothing more than a couple of lines. There I was, acting for all I was worth, and at the end of it Stanley said he felt I was just reading the lines and when we came to filming I would be expected to put more into the role. So much for my acting ability! However, I had secured the role of Julian and my association with Stanley had begun.

I'd heard that Stanley was a hard taskmaster, and turning up for my first day's work at Harlow Hospital should've given me an inkling of what to expect. I don't know why I was called in for filming at the hospital, as none of my scenes involved Alex (played by Malcolm McDowell) - unless they thought they were going to finish there early and then move on to another location. Stanley obviously had other ideas. The scene in the hospital concerned Alex being interviewed by the lady psychiatrist, following his attempt to commit suicide by jumping out of his bedroom window. When I arrived at the hospital at 11 a.m. they were already on take 38 and they finished the scene in the late afternoon with take 70 something!

Most of my filming took place at a very modern, futuristic, open-plan house in Radlett, with a huge garden in which Stanley had arranged for a marquee to be erected to house the cast and crew when they weren't being used. All meals were served by caterers in the marquee, but we were filming in the middle of winter and, although we had blower heaters, it was freezing cold and both the cast and the crew used to linger in the house as long as possible, until Stanley realised that we were only there in order to keep warm. He would then turf us out to make our way back to the marquee to freeze our balls off!

I struck up an instant rapport with Stanley and it was quite usual for us to sit down and chat about things that had happened, what was going on in the news, any sport that had been on TV the previous night and my bodybuilding, weightlifting and Highland Games career. Because of our 'chats' I didn't get evicted from the house all that often. I also had a couple of major scenes to do in the house, so fortunately I managed to spend quite a lot of time inside for 'legitimate' reasons.

My major scenes were (if you remember) where Alex arrives at the house after being released from prison and rings the doorbell. I have been doing some bodybuilding weight training downstairs and have to chase up three flights of stairs to open the front door, whereupon Alex falls exhausted into my arms. I then have to pick him up and carry him downstairs to where my employer, the writer (played by that great Irish actor Patrick Magee) is waiting. A long dialogue scene ensues, with me holding Alex in my arms throughout, at the end of which I'm told to take him up to the bathroom for a bath, which now means running up three flights of stairs.

We shot the scene all day and by the end of it I was so exhausted from running up those stairs about 20 times that I could hardly raise my arms. Fortunately, I had a couple of days off to recover before I did my next scene, and I duly reported to Stanley to discuss the action.

"This is where I want you to carry Patrick down the stairs in his wheelchair and then when you get to the bottom, lower him to the floor, wheel him into the table and then take your seat at the table whilst the dialogue between Alex and the writer ensues."

I turned to Stanley and said something like, "You've got to be joking."

To which he replied, "Dave, you can do this easily. You're a professional strongman, which is the reason you got the part, so let's give it a try and see how you get on."

"Stanley," I said, "I probably can do the stunt quite easily, but your name isn't 'one take Kubrick' and there's no way I can be doing it all day as with the previous scene."

At the mention of the words "one take Kubrick" the whole of the set went deadly quiet and everybody held their breath whilst they waited for Stanley to give vent to his wrath on this upstart actor. However, after what seemed an interminable wait, Stanley just smiled and said that if I agreed to do it he would shoot it in as few takes as possible, which in the end worked out to be about eight.

At the start of this scene the soundman came up and gave the three of us - Malcolm, Patrick and myself - neck mikes, so that they could record the dialogue around the table. I picked up the wheelchair, put the handles over my shoulders and pulled the chair tight into my chest. Patrick, who must have weighed around the 13 stone (180lb) mark, then clambered up onto some steps and transferred himself into the wheelchair seat. At the shout of "ACTION!" I then started to proceed very slowly down the three flights of stairs, got to the bottom, lowered the chair and Patrick to the floor, pushed him into the table next to Alex (Malcolm) and then went and sat down at the table myself.

At the end of the scene the soundman announced that he was getting strange noises over the mikes and wanted to change them, thinking they were faulty. We went through the scene a second time with new mikes, but the soundman achieved the same poor results and so the mikes were changed again. After another 'faulty' take, I could hide my guilt no longer. I'd been doing everything in my power to disguise my heavy breathing when I sat at the table following my physical exertion, but each take had left me feeling even more exhausted and I could no longer cover up the fact that the funny noises being transmitted were my heart beating nineteen to the dozen and my lungs straining not to burst. My neck mike was duly removed and we shot the scene successfully without the extraneous 'noises off'!

Another piece of action that I hadn't bargained for was when Stanley decided to simulate Alex's attempt at suicide. We were filming in a big, high house (which in actual fact was a golf club) and Alex was supposed to be in the attic room from whence he tried to kill himself by jumping out of the window. Stanley initially decided that he wanted the fall to be filmed as though Alex had a camera strapped to him, but this idea got knocked on the head as it was deemed too dangerous. Stanley then hit on the bright idea of buying an old 16mm newsreel camera, throwing it off the roof and propelling it earthwards. It's all very well thinking up these ideas, but putting them into practice is a different matter entirely. The camera was placed inside a polystyrene box, measuring about 2ft square, as a means of protection. The next thing was to find someone strong and fit enough (and also daft enough) to crawl out on the pitched roof of the building, hurl the boxed camera off the roof in such a way that it rotated backwards, and then quickly assume a prostrate position in order to keep out of shot of both the rotating camera and the camera on the ground. You can guess who was volunteered for the job!

The next thing I knew, I was straddling the ridge miles up in the air with a huge, heavy, polystyrene box containing the camera, followed very closely by the camera operator, who had been required to accompany me specifically to switch on the camera - a job I wasn't allowed to do, as I was not a member of the appropriate union. The camera didn't survive the first take and ended up splattered all over the garden below, and to make matters worse the exposed film was useless!

I really enjoyed my first association with Stanley and my involvement in *A Clockwork Orange* - a film that eventually led to my getting other major film roles. Having worked for Stanley, I became accepted for the first time as 'Dave Prowse the actor' rather than just 'the heavy' or being typecast in muscleman roles. Russ Meyer employed me for *Black Snake* because he'd seen me in *A Clockwork Orange*, and the same applied to George Lucas and the *Star Wars* trilogy. I had a good relationship with the Kubrick production team for many years after my first encounter, and if ever I was in the Elstree area I was always welcome to pop round to the Kubricks' house for a cup of tea or a chat as a friend of the family.

I had two subsequent brushes with Stanley, the first when I was up for a part in *Barry Lyndon*, which I lost to wrestler Pat Roach, and later when Stanley was filming the Vietnam War-based *Full Metal Jacket* in, of all places, a disused East London gasworks.

The start of filming with the six principal actors - all American and including the up-and-coming Matthew Modine - was just four days away when Stanley suddenly realised that they would all be as white as sheets rather than sporting the necessary Vietnamese jungle suntans. Panic obviously set in and I got a phone call from Stanley wanting to know if I had a sunbed at my health studio and whether I could get six actors brown in four days. Fortunately, I'd just bought a really good Hi Speed Turbo Solarium, so I said that if I could have the actors every day for about an hour I would definitely be able to change their colour. It was a holiday weekend, so I opened up my studio for the Friday, Saturday, Sunday and Monday and gave them each two half-hour treatments a day. By the time they turned up for filming on the Tuesday they all looked as if they'd just come back from the south of France.

Stanley then decided that they ought to have a sunbed permanently at the location, so I arranged for the manufacturers to install one in a Portakabin in the production unit at the gasworks. A few weeks later I got a call from Stanley saying that they'd finished the filming and the actors had all gone home, so he wanted to know if I would like to make them an offer for the now redundant solarium. Needless to say, I struck a good deal, and the sunbed gave great service right up to the gym's closure in June 2000.

Chapter Twenty-Nine
The Sour Taste of Superman

Of all the films I've been involved in, I've never tried so hard to get a part as I did for the role of Superman.

I was just finishing work on the Terry Gilliam film *Jabberwocky*, which had been shot on location in South Wales and was being completed at Shepperton Studios, when my dear friend and special effects man, Les Bowie, came up to see me and asked whether I knew that the *Superman* production team had moved into the Studios to do the pre-production work for the film. Through another good friend, Leslie Linder, producer of such films as *10 Rillington Place* (about the notorious Christie Murders and starring Richard Attenborough), I knew that *Superman* was about to go into production, but I'd never met the director, Richard (Dick) Donner, or the producers, Pierre Spengler and Ilya Salkind.

At this stage the role of *Superman* hadn't been cast, although many famous names had been auditioned, and I think there was some concern that no leading man had been found, as all the sets had now been built. So the next time I was down at Shepperton I made a point of going to the Superman production office armed with all my *Star Wars* pictures, plus some photos of me as *Superman*, flying through the air with Lois Lane in my arms, from a Max Factor TV commercial, directed by Ridley Scott.

I gingerly knocked on the door and it was answered by a diminutive fellow who, at all of 5ft 3in, said to my navel, "Yes, can I help you?"

"Yes, please. ... I'd like to speak with Pierre Spengler."

"I'm sorry, Pierre is in Paris. Is there anyone else who can help you?"

"Well, the only other person I know on the production team is Ilya Salkind. Can I see him?"

"I'm Ilya Salkind. What can I do for you?"

"I'd like to try out for the part of Superman," I blurted out, embarrassed at not having recognised him.

"I'm sorry, that's impossible," he replied.

Not to be dismissed so lightly, I went on, "Would you please have a look at my photos? I've played Superman before in a big TV commercial."

He then proceeded to flip through my book, at the end of which he muttered repeatedly, "Impossible," before I was ushered out.

Still not prepared to give up, I went back to see Leslie Linder again and he told me not to worry, as he was making arrangements for me to meet Dick Donner, the director. A couple of days later I got a call from Mr Donner inviting me down to Shepperton to talk about the role of Superman. So on went the navy blue suit and horn-rimmed glasses and I trotted down to Shepperton looking every inch a potential Clark Kent. Dick was very pleasant and looked through my photo book, punctuating his perusal with encouraging words such as "Perfect", "Super" and "Just what we're looking for".

His examination complete, he then said, "You're perfect for the part, but we just can't play you."

"Why not? What's the problem?"

"The problem is that you're not an American and we have to play Superman as an American."

"I still can't see what the problem is," I responded. "They didn't get a Jew in to play Christ."

"I'm sorry, but the American public, who are going to account for 80 per cent of the revenue of the film, just would not accept anything but an American for the role."

So that was that.

Then a week or so later, back at the gym, I got a call from Dick Donner saying, "Can you get to the studios as soon as possible to talk about Superman?"

My immediate reaction was that they'd changed their minds about choosing an American for the role, so I dropped everything and chased down to Shepperton Studios as fast as I could.

"Dave, we've got Superman," said Dick Donner.

"Well, thank you very much," I replied.

"No, not you. We've found an actor in New York to whom we've offered the role - a guy called Christopher Reeve."

"Well, thank you very much for informing me, but what do you want me for?"

"Chris is about 6ft 5ins and weighs only around 175lb, so we'd like him to go to your gym and for you to take him in hand and put some weight on him."

"He's positively skinny," I said. "What do you want him to look like?"

"Just like you," was Donner's reply.

End of conversation! And that, to all intents and purposes, was as far as I got with my Superman dreams. I did, in fact, go to see Mary Selway, the casting director, for the part of one of the three villains in the sequel, but I was too big to play opposite Christopher Reeve.

A few days later Christopher Reeve arrived at the gym, as arranged, and I was very pleasantly surprised to greet a personable, tall, well-spoken and extremely affable young man. My brief was that Chris would be donning his Superman suit in six weeks' time and that he needed to put on as much weight as possible - naturally, and under no circumstances using anabolic steroids - on his chest, back, arms and shoulders before then, but that I mustn't work on his legs, as he used to play a lot of football and they were big enough. I was advised that I could feed him whatever I considered suitable and that the Studios would pay for all the supplements used.

Chris put himself totally in my hands and for the next five weeks we trained very hard together. First of all I got in touch with a protein drink manufacturer called Bristol Myers and explained the situation to them. The next thing I knew, their very good canned protein drink, Nutriment, started arriving at the gym by the caseload. When you're trying to gain muscular weight, increasing your protein intake is very important, so, as well as advising Chris to take three or four cans of Nutriment daily, I asked the Studios to let him have as much steak as he could eat.

I also set up a gym in one of the dressing rooms at the Studios, so that Chris could train there as well as training with me at Grosvenor House. I arranged for three of the regular trainers at the gym to act as our training partners, so there was always somebody there to push him through his workouts. We all used to enjoy our training sessions together and the other guys in the gym used to fall over themselves to be of assistance to us.

Chris's progress was really sensational and he was putting on good, healthy muscle at the rate of about 5-6lb a week. He was enjoying the camaraderie of the gym, too, and his physique was altering and improving with every passing week. He was developing a fine taper from chest to waist, his arms and shoulders were looking really good and muscular, and his fitness and physical presence were improving immensely.

At the same time as I was training Chris I also had another prestigious client - His Royal Highness Prince Khalid bin Sultan bin Abdul Azziz, one of the Crown Princes of Saudi Arabia - and towards the end of

Chris's six-week stint I had to go out to Riyadh and Jeddah. I explained the situation to Chris, got him extra cases of Nutriment and arranged for the training partners to look after him and push him hard whilst I was away.

I returned from Saudi after ten days, arriving at London Heathrow early in the morning, but instead of going home I decided to head for Pinewood Studios, where they had started filming *Superman*. As soon as I got there, people were coming up to me and saying what a wonderful job I'd done with Chris, so I was feeling quite proud of myself when I arrived on the set, which was the Daily Planet newspaper office where Clark Kent worked.

I'd only been on the set for a matter of minutes when Chris made his entrance, dressed in a white towelling bathrobe, and headed straight for me. We were standing in the middle of the office, everything on the set had gone quiet, and to be honest I was waiting for Chris to welcome me back and tell me about his continued progress. You can imagine my surprise when I heard his first words.

"Where the f--k have you been for the last ten days?"

"You know where I've been. I've been to Saudi Arabia."

"You've got no f--king right to go to Saudi Arabia. You should have been at the Grosvenor gym, training me."

"I told you I was going out to train with Prince Khalid and I set everything up for you - diet, protein drinks, training partners - before I left. Why? Is there anything wrong?"

"Anything wrong?!" he stormed. "Of course there is. Since you've been away I've lost both weight and shape."

"That's impossible," I replied. "If you've been working out and eating as you were before I left, you should have continued to gain, not lose."

"Look at me," he ranted. "I've lost weight off my arms and shoulders and I don't have that V-taper that I had before you went away."

And, with that, the dressing gown was thrown off and Chris stood posing in the middle of the set with the entire cast and crew enthralled by the exchange.

"To be honest, I think you look even better than when I went away, not worse. You're definitely thickening up everywhere and you've got a good taper from your shoulders and chest down to your very trim waist. I honestly can't see what you're complaining about. What's your weight now?" I asked.

"I'm up to 15st 2lbs, but I'm not happy with the way I look."

"I can't see what your problem is. You've now put on over 2st on my training programme and you've completely transformed what used to be a skinny physique. What more do you want?" I replied, amazed at Chris's tantrum and attitude.

With that, Chris stormed off to see Dick Donner, and the next thing I knew I was being beckoned over by Dick for a private chat out of earshot of the listening cast and crew.

"Humour him," said Dick. "Agree with everything he says and wants. This Superman thing has gone to his head and he's leading us all a merry dance here on the set. He's really coming the 'big star' bit with us all."

The next moment, Chris was beckoned over to join us and he once again took off the bathrobe and started remonstrating in front of the two of us.

"I think you ought to revamp Chris's exercise programme and give him a lot more chest, arm and shoulder work over the next couple of weeks," said Dick.

"Okay," I agreed. "I'll map out a new programme to cover all the areas Chris thinks he's weak on."

With that, Chris stormed off the set again and I made my way home, feeling thoroughly dejected by Chris's attitude. To cap it all off, three days later the film company terminated my contract for his training.

Although several *Superman* films have now been made, because of the sour taste that the Chris Reeve saga left in my mouth I've never had any inclination to go anywhere near the Studios. There was, however, one exception, and that was when Marlon Brando was over in the UK for the first film.

I have always been a great admirer of Brando's work, so I duly turned up at the Studios at Dick Donner's invite to witness the great actor at work. Unfortunately, Mr Brando was suffering from a very heavy head cold at the time and was in no mood to talk to anybody, avid fan or not. However, I did see him sitting apart from everybody on the set in the robes of Jor-El (Superman's father), with a magnificent head of white hair. The only thing I couldn't understand about the set or scene they were about to film was the presence of cue cards or idiot boards hung up on the walls all round the studio, along with strategically placed autocue machines scrolling the actors' lines. The scene they were shooting was where Superman's father is imparting all his words of wisdom to the baby Superman. Susannah York, who played Superman's mother, stands by the side of Brando, who has the infant in his arms, and they place the baby into the crystal-like cradle just before the destruction of their world.

The time came to start filming and Marlon hadn't learned a single line, so he read his entire dialogue from cue cards and autocue. And to think he earned £180,000 a day for the two weeks he was on the film!

Unfortunately, after my sacking from training Chris for the first *Superman* movie, our paths crossed again only once, when I was on the Variety Club's organising committee for the premiere of *Superman 2*. An enormous amount of work had been put into the organisation of the event to make it as successful as possible for Chris and all the personnel involved. At the premiere reception, when I was hoping we would meet up again, Chris just gave a polite nod from the other side of the room. Although I've always found his behaviour towards me totally alien to the camaraderie we had as training partners at my gym, I've always put it down to the pressures of 'stardom' and always hoped that one day we'd get together and iron out any problems that existed between us.

Tragically, on 27 May 1995, Chris suffered an accident whilst competing on his horse, Buck, in a cross-country riding event in Culpeper, Vermont, USA. His horse started to jump an easy fence but suddenly stopped without warning. Chris was thrown over Buck's head, landing on his own head and breaking his neck at the first and second vertebrae. This type of injury is often referred to as a Hangman's Break and is usually fatal. It was a tribute to Chris's great physical condition that not only did he survive but also, over the ensuing years, he struggled very successfully to stay alive against almost insurmountable odds, with the loving support of his lovely wife Dana and their children, and managed to live an extremely active life until his sudden death from cardiac arrest on 10 October 2004.

Chris became the inspiration and role model for spinal cord injury sufferers throughout the world and lived with the eternal hope and conviction that there would be gold at the end of the rainbow in the form of a breakthrough in the medical treatment of paraplegics, whereby spinal cord injuries could be treated successfully and the sufferers could be restored to a full and active life.

Chapter Thirty
A Date with a Prince

Earlier in this book I mentioned visiting His Royal Highness Prince Khalid bin Sultan bin Abdul Azziz of Saudi Arabia. My association with the Prince began in 1973/74, while I was manager of the Grosvenor House Gymnasium in the world-famous Park Lane Hotel in Mayfair, London.

Just as a bit of background, my involvement with Grosvenor House came about while I was working at Harrods. Bernice Weston, managing director of Weightwatchers, had drafted me in to launch an exercise plan at Grayshot Hall, a prestigious health spa, to run alongside the diet regime. She used the gym (health spa) at Grosvenor House, which comprised an indoor swimming pool, a sauna and a workout area that contained mats and a mechanical horse. It was controlled by Edward Hine, whose main claim to fame was that he had taught the royal children to swim. Edward had a theory that stretching exercises were the most healthful and had written a book that he was trying to get published, called *Stretch Your Way to a Long Life*. Regrettably, Mr Hine went to lunch one day, had a heart attack in the street and died on the spot - so much for a long life! Anyway, this sounded the death knell for the Grosvenor House Spa, as no one wanted to exercise anymore after that, although they continued to swim and use the sauna. Bernice suggested to the hotel management (Trust House Forte) that I would be a good candidate for taking over the running of the health complex and they agreed. When the manager of Trust House Forte took me for a tour around the place I thought it had great potential. The only snag was that Trust House Forte didn't want to spend any money on the spa, so any equipment that I wanted to install would have to be supplied by me. Even so, it still seemed a great opportunity for me, primarily because it would introduce me to a completely different type of clientele. The hotel was one of the top places to stay for visiting celebrities, whom I hoped to coax into training under my guidance. With the installation of a selection of barbells, dumb-bells, benches and squat stands, I was able to encourage the patrons to exercise again. I had three happy years there, with a client list that included royalty, politicians, film stars, film producers, models, fashion designers and major players in the business world.

One active member of the gym was the famous osteopath, Dr Guy Beauchamp, who had a list of clients that read like the index of *Who's Who*. One evening Dr Beauchamp came into the gym and asked me if I would consider attending to the personal fitness needs of his most valued client. Naturally, I asked who the client was, only to be told that his identity was strictly secret and that I would be introduced to him at a later date, with Dr Beauchamp in attendance.

Ten days later, at around 8 p.m., I was doing my usual evening tidy-up of the fitness equipment when an almighty commotion erupted outside the gymnasium door. The noise was heading straight for me in the shape of a berobed throng of bustling Arab men, with Dr Beauchamp at their head. Behind Dr Beauchamp, dressed not in robes but in a sharp blue suit, was a tall, well-built man who resembled Omar Sharif. Dr Beauchamp broke away from the now stationary party, beckoned me towards the blue-suited gentleman, and introduced me to his 'secret' client, HRH Prince Khalid bin Sultan bin Abdul Azziz.

My knowledge of Arabian royal etiquette was hardly up to the job of meeting a prince face-to-face, but before I was forced to choose between bowing low or effecting a discrete curtsy, Prince Khalid himself thrust his hand into mine, shaking it firmly and saying, "Please call me Khalid, I'll call you Dave, and we'll get on just fine."

He then gave me a rundown of his fitness problems, the cause of which was a serious back injury he'd picked up during his officer training at Sandhurst Military Academy. The Prince's medical advisors had forbidden any unsupervised training or vigorous exercise and Khalid had gained quite a bit of weight as a consequence. At the time he was barely 30 years old, but his prolonged inactivity had left him seriously out of condition. He clearly wanted to sort himself out, so after further friendly banter we agreed to schedule a full consultation for the following evening. That would give me just enough time to devise a series of tests and routines in order to assess the Prince's strengths, weaknesses and range of mobility.

The next day Khalid came to the gym as arranged and after his assessment we began a training regime that lasted just over six weeks. During that time the Prince not only strengthened his back but also lost a considerable amount of weight, and at the end of his programme we were training hard together, which was progress indeed. I was rather proud of my efforts on behalf of Prince Khalid and it seemed that he had been reasonably impressed, too, as at the end of our final training session he dropped a bombshell.

"Dave, I'm due to return to Saudi Arabia soon," said Khalid, as he towelled himself down, "and I'd like to take you with me as my personal trainer. How would you feel about living and working in Riyadh and Jeddah?"

At that very moment all I felt was dizzy, and it wasn't due to the intensity of the workout. I also felt extremely honoured that my work had been appreciated by a man who could choose from the world's finest, whether it was in clothes, cars, country houses or physical trainers. I was sorely tempted by Khalid's fantastic offer and I found myself asking him for a little time to think it over and discuss it with my wife. With his customary good grace, the Prince agreed to this and from that moment on I began turning over in my mind the ramifications of upping sticks and shifting to Saudi. By the time I arrived home my brain was nearing the point of spontaneous combustion.

Right into the night Norma and I debated the issue. She was her usual wonderful self about the situation, fully prepared to make sacrifices for the good of our family and hold the fort in England while I went to Saudi in search of our fortune. I knew that the salary offered by Khalid would be extremely generous, and with no income tax to bite lumps out of it we'd be better off than we'd ever been in our lives. On a slightly more selfish tack, I'd be required to travel all over the world as part of the Prince's entourage, staying at the best hotels, enjoying the most sumptuous facilities imaginable and hobnobbing with the cream of international society.

Nevertheless, no matter how we juggled the advantages of what was truly the offer of a lifetime, the thought of living apart from my family hovered over me like a spectre. Sure, there would be letters from home, plus plenty of telephone calls, and I knew that I'd be allowed frequent visits to England, but I hadn't married this lovely woman and started a wonderful family just to let them grow up without me. Besides, even when I pushed the impracticalities of the family to one side for a moment, other considerations simply flooded in to fill the void and haunt me further.

Going to Saudi would mean leaving the Grosvenor House Gym, where I was extremely happy in my work - something that has always mattered a great deal to me. I'd just completed the first *Star Wars* movie and offers of work were coming in from all over the place. Scarcely a day went by without calls from my agent concerning a film or TV offer, on top of which I'd just signed a deal with the Department of Transport for the Green Cross Code road safety campaign. Things were certainly happening for Dave Prowse, and apart from one major gig in the Middle East they were happening within range of my wife and family. That was it, then. I'd have to go back to His Royal Highness Prince Khalid bin Sultan bin Abdul Azziz of Saudi Arabia and say, "Khalid, my friend, I'm afraid it's thanks but no thanks."

Khalid could see my reluctance to refuse his generous offer and I know he understood my reasons for my decision. He still wanted me to be involved with his personal fitness regime, so after he accepted my polite refusal he asked, "Well, Dave, in that case would it be possible for you to pick out someone you regard as suitable to come out to Saudi and work under your guidance?" At the time my brother, Bob, was managing my own gym in London, and I knew that he'd be ideal for what the Prince was proposing. Bob was a skilled fitness instructor and he'd served in Jordan during his National Service days, so he already had a grounding in Arabian culture and customs. Yes, Bob was the man, no doubt about it.

Bob thought so, too, and being a single man at the time he jumped at the chance to fly to Saudi and train Prince Khalid. I'd be lying if I didn't admit to pangs of envy as Bob jetted off to the Royal Palace in Riyadh, en route to collect a fine, untaxed salary and who knows what other benefits, but with all that was going on around me back then I had little time to sit around sulking.

The initial part of my supervision contract involved arranging the supply of not one but two complete gymnasiums and their relevant fitness equipment. One set of gear was destined for Prince Khalid's house in Jeddah and the other for the royal residence in Riyadh. I personally selected, ordered and negotiated the shipping of every item, which included two full-size trampolines and literally tons of health-producing hardware, and I accompanied it all on its flight to Saudi.

Even though I'd turned down the chance to live among princes, at least I could go for a nose around and check that brother Bob was settling in. As it turned out, brother Bob was doing just fine, as I saw for myself when his handshake on my arrival at Jeddah airport revealed a solid gold Cartier wristwatch. Fortunately, I've never been the jealous type and I busied myself in the tedious task of steering mounds of crated fitness gear through Saudi Customs Control.

Bob had already warned me that Saudi Customs were seriously

unimpressed with certain items that we Westerners might consider normal travelling companions. For a start, sneaking a bottle of Scotch into Saudi Arabia was the surest route to grief known to man. The same went for 'gentleman's literature', or any magazines with sex as their main content. In other words, I was entering a booze- and porn-free zone and I'd best be completely free of both when scrutinised. Bob said that even my post of personal fitness consultant to Prince Khalid would cut no ice with Saudi Customs should I decide to become an Arabian bootleg-pornographer. I had enough to think about at that time, without considering making dodgy career moves against a country where they cut off your hands for booze smuggling and Lord alone knows what body part for a pornography conviction.

Bob was right about the efficiency of Saudi Customs, as the officials barely blinked an eye when I announced the name of my employer and why I was visiting the country. Those same officials definitely bent the rules for their Prince's cargo, however, because the entire consignment was whisked through Customs in less time than it takes to reclaim a suitcase at any other airport in the world. A small army of Khalid's aides had been deployed at the airport to take care of the carting and loading all the equipment, so it was a pretty painless exercise for me.

Within an hour of landing on Saudi soil I was standing inside the games room of the Prince's superb house, deciding which end of the swimming pool should accommodate the gymnasium and which would better suit the trampoline. Had I really turned down this (literally) golden opportunity? Would Bob mind if I reinstalled him in my London gym and took his job and new watch? Or would it be best if I just got on with my assigned task over there? That amounted to three yeses and there was no going back on my decision now. I reflected on the fact that I could drown what tiny sorrows I had during the feasting and frolics. Prince Khalid had planned a banquet in my honour that evening,

The banquet was to be held at the house and a small but decidedly glittering gathering of Prince Khalid's friends had been invited. I was staying in a nearby hotel, from which my brother, still sporting his presentation Cartier, collected me in the princely limo. We glided towards the banquet, Bob relating tales of life with the royals and his watch bombarding me with golden pinpoints of light as he turned the steering wheel. The face of that watch resembled the eyes of a portrait. During the banquet it seemed to be looking at me wherever I went, its eyes following me around the room. Or maybe I was just jealous.

I spent the first half an hour at the banquet mingling with the great and the good of Saudi society. I recall that the aviation industry was well represented, interspersed with the Prince's personal Arab friends and business associates. Small talk was flowing and everyone was relaxing into the proceedings when the Prince made his grand entrance.

Dressed in his flowing Arab finery, he looked magnificent as he swept down the stairs towards my small group of banquet goers. It was obvious that Khalid was on his way to meet me and the group fell silent at his approach. He was carrying a small, leather-bound box, which he unceremoniously tossed over to me before shaking my hand warmly and exchanging pleasantries for a minute or so. Formalities over, he shook my hand once more and then sedately drifted off into the smiling throng to meet and greet his other guests.

I unwrapped the present that the Prince had so casually lobbed at me, only to discover that I, too, was now the proud owner of a solid gold Cartier watch. As I fingered the exquisite timepiece, I decided that I'd never, ever, been remotely jealous of Bob's Cartier or whatever his new career might bring him, and that life had never been much better than it was right now.

That night marked the first of many visits to Saudi Arabia, all of them enjoyable in their own way, as I gleaned insights into the extraordinary world of Prince Khalid and his friends. I was fascinated by small details, such as their delight in the card game known as kalooki, where the winner gets to wallop the loser's hand with a thick, knotted rope. I was less than keen to get involved in one of Khalid's kalooki schools, but my brother had done so and confirmed that the impact of the rope knot was like a hammer blow. Of course, when Khalid was on the receiving end, a smart tap was about as violent as it got. When the Prince won the right to dish out the punishment, however, that rope came down like a mallet once more, but it was an unwritten rule that no cry of pain must ever pass the lips of the recipient. I never saw anyone so much as whimper during these bizarre games, although the agony in the participants' eyes screamed louder than any cry of pain ever could. Since witnessing the friendly rope thrashings in Saudi, I've never fancied myself as a card player. Strangely, all other card games seem pretty boring in comparison to Prince Khalid's kalooki wars.

Actually, training the Prince was far from easy to accomplish. Bob and I had numerous hassles getting Khalid into the gym, and once we'd won that battle it was harder still to keep him there for more than 20 minutes. Khalid was a busy man with distractions all around him. The training facilities at his house in Jeddah were lavish enough, but in Riyadh he'd built himself a complete sports hall, where the huge range of fitness gear I'd bought for him didn't even fill a corner. Well within distraction range, the Prince had also installed the trampoline I'd brought over, aided and abetted by a table tennis set-up (full-size, naturally) and whatever that month's latest fun acquisition happened to be. Despite the seemingly endless supply of fitness hardware littering the Prince's gym, there was still plenty of room for an indoor football pitch should he so desire. And whatever the Prince desired, the Prince would have.

I remember his enthusiasm for a specially fitted-out executive jet, which was being prepared for use as Khalid's personal transport. Throughout my visits to Saudi the Prince would show me models of the plane and keep me informed on its progress, and I was really looking forward to the flight he'd promised me on its completion. I enjoyed these deliberations with the Prince, as he enthused mightily over everything, from the jet's range and speed to its upholstery and toilet fittings. Khalid seemed to light up when he spoke of his new toy and it was great to see him break free temporarily from his huge responsibilities and revel in the prospect of this new diversion.

On my next visit, however, the models of the plane were gone, as was all reference to it during conversations with Prince Khalid. I thought this strange, but if the Prince chose not to elaborate on it then I felt it would be improper for me to force the issue. Mind you, as soon as I got brother Bob on his own I demanded to know what had happened to the plane. Bob told me that the jet had been delivered and that, if anything, it was even more luxurious than it looked in model form. Khalid was duly taken for his maiden flight and enjoyed the experience immensely, the highlight of the trip being an air-to-ground conversation between the Prince and his young son. Apparently, having landed, Khalid began to think about his own father and how, despite his being Minister of Defence, he had no personal aircraft to transport him around, so he simply gave his father the brand new jet.

Such generosity was typical of the Prince, and so was a waspish sense of humour, as I found out during my last two excursions to Saudi.

I'd just put in a ten-day stint and, during a reasonable morning's training together, Khalid said, "You're going home in a couple of days, aren't you, Dave?"

"Yes, indeed I am," I responded.

"Have you bought your presents yet?" he enquired.

"No, not yet. I'm going to the gold market this afternoon to buy a couple of chains for my wife and daughter," I replied.

"Have you got enough money?" he asked.

"Er … yes thanks, Khalid. I've saved some, so I'm okay thank you."

"No need to spend your own money, Dave, I'll get my driver to take you to the market. He'll have money and he can haggle for you, too."

I protested politely, but to no avail. I then thanked the Prince and we continued our workout.

Later that afternoon I was called to one side by one of the Prince's aides, who handed me a brown envelope. The aide muttered, "With the compliments of His Majesty," before turning smartly and walking away. Rather than rip open the envelope with unseemly haste, I waited until I was back in the privacy of my hotel room. On eagerly tearing it open, I found a thousand pounds' worth of Arab currency. Remember, this was about 30 years ago, so as you can imagine my wife and daughter were presented with some fine souvenirs from that little trip, courtesy of the incredible generosity of Prince Khalid.

My last trip to Saudi coincided with my 42nd birthday. Now, although I'm not the sort of person to exploit the generosity of friends, Bob maintains that in every verbal exchange, whatever the theme of the conversation, I somehow managed to throw in some reference to my birthday, such as: "Oh, I do hope my return flight's on time, because I'm due to arrive back on my BIRTHDAY and I'd hate to be late, because it's my BIRTHDAY and my wife will have planned a BIRTHDAY party for me, like she always does when it's my BIRTHDAY." As if I'd do that.

Just as I was preparing to leave for the airport, another of Khalid's aides sidled up to me and presented me with a small but impressively hefty package, saying, "Please accept this gift from His Royal Highness Prince Khalid, in recognition of your forthcoming birthday and as a token of his friendship." As the full weight of the box settled in my hand, my eyes must have sparkled a little too much, as I definitely detected a tiny grin on the face of the aide before he dismissed himself.

Surrounded by the Prince's staff, I could hardly run into a handy closet and tear open my present, which was what I really wanted to do. Besides, what if it turned out to be a block of gold, or half-a-dozen Rolexes, or a Fabergé egg? No, the only thing for it was to place my present tenderly in my hand baggage and guard it with my life until I got home. If Customs wanted to examine it, they would have to take it up with the Prince, for I was merely a humble benefactor of his immense generosity.

There then followed the longest flight in aviation history, and several times I thought about slipping into the aircraft loo, opening my birthday present and having a quick gloat. However, I knew that I'd then either have to smuggle the contents through British Customs or declare something that was worth untold thousands and probably be hit for tax. Thus, I spent that long, tedious flight and its concluding terminal nonsense gazing fondly at my perfectly wrapped present, occasionally risking a sneaky hand juggle just to check that it really was as heavy as I'd first thought. It was. Oh, yes, it was.

For once there was a taxi available as I left the terminal building at Heathrow and I decided that, having waited so long to see what riches my great friend the Prince had bestowed upon me, another half-hour wouldn't hurt and I would open the package when I got home. Then Norma could share in the wonder of it all, too, which would make the moment perfect.

With the cabbie paid (and tipped generously, may I add) and my suitcases dumped in our hallway, l gave Norma the briefest of welcoming kisses. Then, delving into the small holdall that had been welded to my hand for most of the day, I produced my present with a flourish. Norma was all for getting a pair of scissors with which to snip the elaborate bindings carefully and release my gift in the delicate manner of its wrapping. Not a chance. I'd been waiting more than long enough, so I dug my thumbs beneath the ribbons, prising them off in a second. The outer covering of the package resisted me for a few frustrating seconds, but then I found a join in the wrapping paper and pulled it apart … to reveal … a ten-pound block … of DATES! Yes, dates. Sticky dates, from sunny Saudi, land of the world's finest dates and home to mischievous monarchs who know when clumsy friends are dropping hints like a blacksmith's anvil. No wonder that aide sniggered when he gave me my present.

Very soon after this (and those dates were delicious, Norma said, although I couldn't fancy them somehow) the Prince, in his role of Air Defence Minister, was asked to attend War College in the USA. Due to the number of classified documents he would be handling, it was deemed necessary to leave his personal trainer in London, so Bob was ensconced in a luxury hotel in Knightsbridge, all expenses paid, while doing absolutely nothing all day. The Prince's advisors then informed Bob that Khalid's US trip was to be an extended one and, regretfully, His Majesty would have to dispense with the services of his personal trainer.

So ended an extremely interesting two-year association with one of the most interesting, fascinating and likeable men I've ever met, His Royal Highness Prince Khalid bin Sultan bin Abdul Azziz of Saudi Arabia, who, among other things, certainly made my 42nd birthday a DATE to remember.

I really enjoyed my years at Grosvenor House, but my association with the gym ended when the hotel management informed me that possible new clients would be taking over the running of the club. Trust House Forte had been very reluctant to invest in any updating of the gym and with a new management team in place they wouldn't have to worry. Time for David to move on!

Chapter Thirty-One
The Inimitable Russ Meyer

These days, so many people are referred to as 'unique' that those truly deserving of this label are somewhat devalued. Russ Meyer is unique in just about every sense of the word and, as far as I'm concerned, there's nothing that could devalue him. As a film-maker, Russ will never be enshrined with the Kubricks, Leans and Fellinis of this business, but there are greater human qualities than the ability to produce classic movies and Russ has more than his share of these. Qualities, that is, not classic movies.

My first meeting with Russ took place in an office block interview suite in Mayfair, and from the outset we enjoyed each other's company. Straight after the introductions, Russ told me that he admired my work with Stanley Kubrick in *A Clockwork Orange* - which is always a good start to any conversation involving an actor - after which we embarked on a long and adoring exploration of Kubrick's work. Half an hour into this, I thought it might be wise to steer the conversation towards the film role for which I was being considered, and I found to my great delight that I wasn't merely a candidate, I was being offered the part. And, from an actor's point of view, that's the perfect end to any conversation.

The film in question was *Black Snake*, a typical Russ Meyer creation, in which he would assume the roles of scriptwriter, producer, director, lighting cameraman, focus puller and wardrobe technician, with a sprinkling of make-up duties during his quieter moments. Like Kubrick, Russ's idol, he was a one-man film unit. Unlike the great Stanley, however, Russ Meyer's film genre was very definitely soft-core pornography. To date, his films had been loosely scripted festivals celebrating the lewd capers of supremely breasted females and square-jawed studs. And the prospect of taking part in a Meyer masterpiece made my jaw develop a state of squareness that was visible from 20 yards.

By the end of this book the reader will realise that my life has been beset by 'why me?' moments. Some of these moments have been truly wondrous, life-enhancing instances of serendipity, and others have been complete bastard turns of fortune's wheel. *Black Snake* was very much in the latter category.

It all looked so promising, too, with the filming taking place in the paradise location of Barbados and the crew installed in Sam Lord's Castle, which was undoubtedly the best hotel on the island at the time. When I discovered that *Black Snake* was based on the uprising of the oppressed slaves of a southern plantation, I immediately imagined all sorts of bare-torsoed rompings among the cotton fields, enlivened by the erotic handling of the occasional bullwhip or plantation owner's daughter. My understandable optimism paled at a stroke, however, when Russ explained my character to me.

I wasn't to play a lusty plantation hand or an overprivileged, oversexed and underworked slave master, as I'd hoped, but something called 'The Duppie'. My gloriously square jaw was becoming rounded by the minute, as Russ put flesh on the bones of my role in *Black Snake*. Not too much flesh, though, for it turned out that The Duppie was a type of swamp-zombie that emerged from the undergrowth to terrify the locals. To deflate my jaw completely, this particular Duppie was also deaf, dumb and castrated. Granted, he was scripted as the ex-lover of the stunning Anouska Hempel, the female lead, but even at that stage I knew that being a swamp-zombie was never going to make me a babe-magnet, even in a Russ Meyer movie.

The next great disappointment was Russ's change of thrust from sex to violence. In a typical display of the negative version of the Prowse 'why me?' syndrome, Russ had decided that Kubrick's *Clockwork Orange* had blazed the way for violence to be the next great cinema seat-filler, and at the time he was absolutely right. Damn his far-seeing eyes.

So, out went the Meyer manual entitled 'One hundred hectares of heaving bosom' and in came 'One-thousand-and-one ways to kill your cast'. Every conceivable means of annihilation was devised and unleashed on the characters of *Black Snake*. Some were simply shot, others were eaten by sharks, the odd one was crucified or hanged, and more still were beheaded, thrashed to death with whips, burned to a crisp or reduced to a writhing pile of bloody bits by a loony with a machete; then we had some traditional poisoning, and I do believe that one of us died in the bath after being bitten near the plughole by a deadly snake. Nobody passed on peacefully in their sleep in *Black Snake*, that's for sure.

My own demise was certainly an admirable one, if I do say so myself, and involved the unlikely combination of a double-barrelled shotgun and two pounds of sausages. Anouska Hempel wielded the shotgun and the make-up department carried out the sausage handling to perfection. As I was blasted in the stomach by the leading lady, I fell to the floor clutching my now open-plan stomach. Russ then cut to an overhead shot of me doing some classic pre-death writhing while clutching a pad in my absent midriff that the make-up department (mainly composed of Russ) had smothered with fake blood. Realistic it wasn't. Then Russ thought of the sausages. A couple of pounds of the island's finest were conjured up in minutes, anointed with fake blood and stuffed between my fingers in preparation for an impressive death scene close-up. On the 'action' call, I writhed as any self-respecting, gut-shot swamp-zombie would, squeezing my sausage intestines like fleshy tubes of pork toothpaste, to the acclaim of all who were privileged to witness this fine and sensitive example of performance art. That scene was surely one of the highlights of *Black Snake*, which conveys the overall quality of the film in a fair and objective manner, I'd say.

The overriding awfulness of *Black Snake* wasn't due to its lack of technical or artistic qualities. Indeed, there were so few of both that to judge this movie on what fleeting frames of adequate footage we ended up with would be pointless. No, what made *Black Snake* such an awful experience was the pure bitchiness of those involved in its making. Russ Meyer and a small selection of those on set were fine folks to work with, but the rest just seemed to want to gripe and whinge about everything.

We very nearly had a flat-out 'tools down and walk off' strike on one notable occasion. What cataclysmic breach of human rights had sparked such a reaction? There was no afternoon tea. That was it. No tea - no film. Yes, it was bloody hot, and sometimes we had to go all day without a swim in the sea or a leisurely quench in the hotel pool while getting plastered on rum punch, and most of the crew decided that such hardship really was too much for film folk to tolerate. I've lost count of the times in my life that I've thanked my lucky stars to be making films for a living rather than digging coal or working in a factory, and many of my fellow crew members on *Black Snake* would have done well to submit themselves to a reality check now and again.

Russ Meyer had a worse time than I did, and by a long way, too. Among the crew were some people that Russ, in his affable way, referred to as 'characters'. From what I saw of them, a more fitting epithet would have been 'arseholes'. It was a full-time job for Russ to keep certain members of our crew sober, drug-free and out of the local whorehouse long enough to put in a decent day's work. One of the 'characters', an actor by the name of Bernard Boston, seemed hell-bent on making Russ Meyer's life as difficult as possible, and nobody was ever sure whether Bernard would show up for his scenes or, if he did appear, whether he would be in any fit state to deliver his lines.

The working relationship between actor and film-maker hit an all-time low after Bernard went on the missing list and Russ was forced to despatch a search party to scour Bridgetown and drag the actor from some working girl's flat. With Russ Meyer handling so many of the jobs on set, there were precious few crew members as it was without having to spare some for a posse to round up strays like Bernard. Russ was furious and rightly so. Yet, instead of Bernard taking his bollocking and making some sort of token apology, he decided that he was the victim of some vile conspiracy and vowed to get his revenge on the evil Russ Meyer. As you can imagine, this did less than wonders for the feel-good factor of working on *Black Snake*. If ever the term 'feel-hideous factor' is accepted into general usage, I assure you that it began in Barbados during my brief swamp-zombie period.

Bernard Boston finally saw his chance to avenge his callous mistreatment at the hands of Russ Meyer and, like so much of the chaos on *Black Snake*, the event was inspired by those mischievous twins that formed so much of our crew's recreational regimen - rum and ganja. Typically, Bernard decided against a full-on assault on Russ and chose instead to visit his wrath upon one of the few cast members whose behaviour was impeccable throughout the entire production - a 10ft long Indian python.

This was no ordinary snake. In fact, to the best of the Bajan government's notice, it was the only authorised snake on the entire island. Russ Meyer had to jump through all sorts of bureaucratic hoops to gain permission to import a python from a specialist in Los Angeles, and so important was our reptilian cast member that it lived in splendid isolation in a luxury snake-condo in Russ's house, tended by its own PA, who fed it live rats and chicks on demand. The snake was required for a key scene, where it finds its way into the leading lady's bathtub. It even had its own rubber stunt double.

One night, with Bernard Boston absolutely blitzed on cane juice and weed and Russ in town on a social call, 'someone' (hell, everyone knew it was Bernard) broke into the Meyer residence and flipped the lid on the python's cage. Its flickering tongue smelling the sweet fragrance of liberty, the huge snake looped its muscular coils in a coordinated bid for freedom and headed towards the West Indian wilds. The resourceful reptile had managed to reach the roadway outside the house, when Russ returned in his car and, mistaking the snake for some sort of hosepipe, drove right over the top of it. This annoyed the snake considerably, although, apart from a couple of tyre-patterned scuff marks, it seemed none the worse for being involved in a road accident. Had Russ realised at the time who had been responsible for risking the life of his valued cast member, I really think there would have been another casualty in Barbados that night.

After two days of recuperative sunbathing under its heat lamps and a live rat and chicken buffet, the snake was ready to take its curtain calls once more, much to the dismay of Anouska Hempel, who was absolutely terrified of it. Russ and Anouska had more than the odd spat on set, and at one point Russ swore that he was going to slip the real snake into Anouska's bath rather than the rubber one, but, ever the gentleman, I don't think he meant it.

While the on-set shenanigans raged around me, I lurched about the island clad mainly in mud and a pair of tattered trousers. My hair was shoulder length and my beard was catching up with it by the day. This was the early '70s, a time when I sported a couple of false front teeth, the real ones having been knocked out by a training weight during an over-pumped bicep curl. To add the finishing touch to my swamp-zombie ensemble, Russ begged me to remove my front teeth, which I did on the grounds that life couldn't get any less glamorous than it was already.

At day's end, with another stack of unforgettable scenes safely in the can, I'd always make my way to a special little beach between the island's main hotels, The Hilton and The Holiday Inn. Here was where the local electricity generation plant had its outfall pipe, and several million gallons of bath-warm seawater would gush like a salty spa, around 25 yards from the beach. Wallowing in this glorious uprush of soothing, healing warmth would cleanse me of mud, sweat and on-set tension in minutes. The pipe outlet was protected by a heavy-gauge wire cage and the locals and I would sit around this, indulging ourselves in a pastime now known as chillin'. I didn't know it was chillin' at the time, of course, but that's definitely what I was doing, because my kids have since confirmed it.

If working on *Black Snake* was a trial, the island of Barbados was anything but, and over the six weeks of filming I really felt at home there. One reason for this was the West Indian passion for bodybuilding, which seemed to rank second only to cricket as the most popular sport on the island. I'd be hard pushed to think of a finer place to train and

Barbados has proved its potential over the years with the emergence of top competitors like Earl Maynard, Roy Callender and Al and Darcy Beckles, among others. We had a fine selection of the big-name Bajan bodybuilders working on *Black Snake* and I was always being asked to pose for photos alongside them, even though the tallest of them scarcely reached my armpit.

It was a bitter-sweet moment when my work on *Black Snake* was completed. I'd miss the idyllic atmosphere of Barbados, the power-plant beach spa and the bodybuilding friends I'd made there. I'd miss, too, the splendid company of Russ Meyer, but I definitely wouldn't miss the endless whining and bleating of certain cast members. As I packed in preparation to leave for the airport, I wondered what the professional moaners I'd been surrounded by for the past month and a half would do on a film set in a less hospitable climate. A few weeks on location in Cumbria's winter wonderland would have most of them committing ritual suicide.

To prove what a thoroughly great employer he was, Russ Meyer insisted on driving me to the airport, and during our journey he told me how much he'd enjoyed working with me. As a small token of my appreciation of Russ's efforts to keep us all happy under the most trying circumstances (sun, booze, golden beaches, luxury hotels and swimming pools, that sort of thing) I'd bought him a bottle of one of the better brands of whisky. Handing this inadequate gift to Russ almost reduced him to tears, and I was genuinely amazed when he told me that, in all the years he'd been making films, nobody had ever given him a thank-you present. Russ Meyer's appreciation of what was merely a gesture of common courtesy on my part endeared him to me even more and our friendship has lasted ever since.

If I'm ever in Los Angeles I'm under strict instructions to call Russ immediately, whereupon he will arrange what he describes as a 'man's night out'. These outings involve whatever Russ thinks is worth seeing, doing, eating or hearing about at the time, and I do my very best to return the compliment when he drops into London. Our association is one of the greatest hits of my career and long may it remain so.

Now, it's perfectly obvious that every single one of my readers is gagging to know the fate of *Black Snake* the movie. Strangely, at the time I couldn't give a stuff what happened to it, but out of consideration for my friend Russ Meyer I did keep an eye on it as it lurched around the cinemas of the world.

The initial release (some would prefer the term 'escape') of the film took place in the USA under its original title. Meyer fans flocked to see it, their expectant little minds tuned to absorb scenes of bawdiness and mammalia to rival Russ's previous productions. What they got instead was the entire death catalogue of the Marquis de Sade and a fully clothed Anouska Hempel's all-but-flat chest. Most of those who'd flocked in flocked off out again and Russ decided to recall *Black Snake* and retitle it, under the mistaken impression that it was the film's name and not its content that was at fault.

Thus, *Sweet Suzie - She Ain't No Lady!* was unleashed on the world stage, to precisely the same reaction from cinema-goers as *Black Snake*. Rethink number two caused the penny to drop. Much as he'd tried to change the formula with this film, Russ was stuck with the fact that his public went to see a Meyer movie for what Meyer movies were all about: boobs, bonking and bugger-all much else. This conclusion was accommodated by reshooting some simulated sex scenes using two, more Meyeristically endowed, models to double for *Black Snake*'s leading ladies.

Armed with a higher raunch factor and retitled *Slaves*, the film once more emerged, and this time made a fortune. Perhaps there really is no accounting for taste, although I think my success in *Star Wars* and even as The Green Cross Code Man may have put the odd bum on the occasional seat, for, as soon as my name became well known, Russ Meyer changed the billing of his film to include the words "starring Dave Prowse". To the unparalleled list of movie jobs Russ can handle, the post of publicist can surely be added. As I said, the man's unique.

A few years after *Black Snake, Slaves* or under whatever banner that movie spluttered to a stop, I had a second opportunity to work with Russ Meyer. In a blaze of publicity, Russ breezed into London brandishing a freshly signed contract for a film entitled *Who Killed Bambi?* This was to be the punk rock equivalent of The Beatles' *Hard Day's Night*, in that it would launch the Sex Pistols into international stardom via the silver screen. At the time, the Sex Pistols were punk's premier attraction and they had achieved bankable notoriety in the UK by swearing on early evening TV and generally acting like prats whenever the cameras were around. Russ Meyer had signed a contract with Malcolm McLaren, the Pistols' manager, and it's fair to say that virtually the entire music industry regarded Malcolm as just about the least talented and trustworthy bloke in the business. Band members Johnny Rotten and Sid Vicious were hardly revered either, but the young people of the world imagined themselves to be going through a phase of anarchy at the time, so McLaren and Meyer saw the main chance and went straight for it.

It's testament to my regard for Russ that the prospect of working with him again countered any fears that I had about associating myself with the Sex Pistols or their extremely flaky manager. Come to think of it, Russ wasn't exactly the darling of the establishment at the time, so I was certainly going out on a limb on this one. Possibly for the best, the limb I went out on wasn't very strong and snapped completely after just one day's filming of *Who Killed Bambi?*

That day's work consisted of me, as a chauffeur to an ageing rock star, driving madly through a woodland setting in an open-topped Rolls Royce with a very dead and extremely bloody deer strapped to the bonnet. The single scene that we got in the can showed me in the Rolls convertible, screeching to a halt outside a beautiful country cottage and dumping the deer carcass on the doorstep. With my dirty work done, I was scripted to hide behind the car to see what happened next - as you would, having just launched a blood-soaked stag at someone's country retreat.

The grisly mechanics of dumping the deer meant that I had to heave its blood-saturated corpse onto my shoulders - and this was a real, freshly shot, undrained deer, if you please - walk up the path to the pretty cottage and hoick the whole dripping mess onto the ground. Then, like a naughty boy, I rang the doorbell and ran away to hide. Highly plausible, I'm sure you'll agree. To maintain this credible theme, the cottage door was then answered by a sickly sweet little girl kitted out in a gingham smock and pigtails, who sees the dead deer and immediately bursts into hysterics, screaming, "Mummy, Mummy, they've killed Bambi!" The scene ends with me and my ageing rock star passenger roaring away in the Rolls, cackling and hooting like the deranged chaps we undoubtedly were.

The next day Malcolm McLaren pulled out of the project and that was the end of *Who Killed Bambi?* It was also the end of any regard that Russ Meyer may have harboured for Malcolm McLaren, and Russ never forgave him for what he did.

My last meet-up with Russ coincided with his work on what he regards as his greatest ever film: *The Breast of Russ Meyer*. This subtly titled movie featured a sojourn through the life and times of the man himself, tracing his war experiences through Europe. At least, that was what the theme was supposed to be. I'm the last person to cast doubt on the authenticity of what Russ portrayed as fact in the film, but there was a preponderance of willing women with impossible chests in the clips I saw. Was it life imitating art? Who knows. Only the unique mind of Russ Meyer.

My lasting vision of Russ is of someone with whom millions of men would trade places. In his line of work it was inevitable that he took some of it home with him, although I can't help but notice that he was reluctant to introduce them to me. I met Russ's 'friends' on rare occasions, though, including the spectacular Miss Nude America, Kitten Natividad. Kitten's figure borders on the unbelievable but, beneath that fantasy form of hers, she's a great girl and was good company during a night out with Russ. There was never a problem attracting the attention of a waiter when Kitten was at your table, that's for certain.

When I had my recent hip replacement operation, Russ sent me a best-wishes message in the form of a photo of himself with yet another stupendous lady, to whom he referred as his fiancée. Her name was as subtle as Russ's films and, like them, and him, what you saw was what you got. I thought maybe, at long last, Russ Meyer had found the girl of his dreams in the exquisitely proportioned and perfectly entitled Miss Melissa Mounds.

Chapter Thirty-Two
Looking Down at the Stars

It has been my pleasure to have met, known and worked with many members of what is now collectively known as the glitterati: stars, celebrities, the show business elite, call them what you will. Here they are as I saw them.

Cary Grant
In 1947 my sister Jeanne, an attractive 16-year-old, was working as a cashier in a butcher's shop in the Henleaze area of Bristol. As well as cashiering she was also required to make the occasional delivery to customers' private houses.

A frequent customer to the shop was an old lady by the name of Mrs Elsie Leach. Jeanne's boss, Mr Shaul, had informed her that she was the mother of one Archie Leach, who had left Bristol and found fame and fortune in Hollywood under the name of Cary Grant. Elsie Leach used to buy odd bits and pieces for herself and get bones and scraps for her spaniel dog.

Jeanne quite often used to go round to Mrs Leach's house and Elsie would take great delight in showing Jeanne all the scrapbooks and framed photos of her world-famous son.

Cary was always asking his mother to go out to Hollywood to visit him, but she never went, due mainly to the fact that she was getting on a bit and didn't want to travel alone. As a result, he would make periodic pilgrimages back home to see her, although he would never stay at the house, preferring the luxury of Bristol's Grand Hotel.

Just prior to one of his visits, Elsie called Jeanne to tell her that her beloved son was coming over and to ask if she would like to come round for afternoon tea. Jeanne wasn't much of a film fan, but she thought that Saturday afternoon tea would be enjoyable and initially accepted the invitation.

However, at that time Jeanne was courting her childhood sweetheart, Roy, and instead of supping tea with a mega Hollywood star she decided it was much more important to go to watch Roy play football.

Cary Grant never knew what he'd missed.

Many years later, about 50 to be precise, she still has no regrets about turning down that date. She eventually married her footballing carpenter boyfriend. After a courtship that lasted the best part of three years, the marriage survived five months.

Daniel Day-Lewis

My acquaintance with Daniel was extremely short and disappointing, not through any fault of Daniel's, or mine for that matter, but the tale's worth telling.

Our association began with a telephone call from Andrew Mitchell, who was the head of the EMI studios at Elstree. Andrew asked me how I'd feel about getting Daniel Day-Lewis into shape for a major forthcoming production of *The Last of the Mohicans* (released in 1992). In fact, Andrew had anticipated my answer and had put my name forward to ZZY Productions in Hollywood and the producer of the film, Shel Schrager.

Shel Schrager rang me and we entered into discussions about Daniel and the physical demands of his role in the film. He was concerned that Daniel's level of fitness wasn't up to the rigours of the script, especially the many action scenes, most of which were scheduled to be filmed on location in the forests of North America. An intensive bodybuilding and toughening-up regime was prescribed for Daniel, and I assured Shel Schrager that, provided his actor followed my training programme, there should be no problem getting him super-fit in time for filming.

Daniel was in Paris for a couple of days, which gave me time to plan out his training schedule in conjunction with a suitable dietary regime, which would allow him to maximise the benefit of his fitness work. I'd followed much the same process in preparing Christopher Reeve for his role of Superman, and I remembered that Christopher's film company's publicity department had regretted not taking any 'before' pictures of him prior to getting him into his 'after' shape.

The next day, with this thought buzzing in my head, I rang ZZY in Hollywood and spoke with one of their assistant producers about getting Daniel photographed right from the start. The chap I spoke to thought it was a great idea and even said that he wished he'd thought of it first. We agreed to clear it with Daniel when he came in to train and then take it from there. The assistant producer thanked me for taking such an interest in the project, and I continued with my plans for the rebuilding of Daniel Day-Lewis.

The following day all hell broke loose! Shel Schrager phoned me from Hollywood, ranting and raving and accusing me of leaking stories to the press. Apparently, a few lines had appeared in the *Daily Mail*'s Showbiz column, announcing that Daniel Day-Lewis had landed the lead in *The Last of the Mohicans* and that he was attending a well-known London gym to prepare him physically for the role.

Shel Schrager had concluded, quite wrongly, that the leak had come from me because the story had appeared in the press the day after I'd been given the job of training Daniel. The main flaw in that theory, apart from the fact that I wasn't guilty of the accusation, was the fact that neither my gym nor I myself got a plug from that column, so where was my motive for leaking the story? As I explained to the now incandescent Shel Schrager, if I was unscrupulous enough to sell out my employers to the national press, the least I would've wanted in return was a bit of free publicity!

This logical revelation cut no ice with Shel Schrager, who continued to rant on regardless, culminating in a mega-decibel declaration that the studio bosses wanted me off the payroll immediately. I wasn't even on the payroll yet, and right now it looked as though I never would be. Shel Schrager eventually calmed down to a mild simmer and, before hanging up, he even promised to approach his bosses and try to get them to reconsider. Inside an hour he was back on the telephone with the final word on the subject. I had been found guilty as charged, no appeals would be heard and I was summarily dismissed from the payroll I'd never been on.

The story doesn't end there, however. I'd been offered the job on the Wednesday and then sacked on the Friday, but Daniel Day-Lewis had been left completely in the dark about it, so he turned up on the following Monday to begin his training programme. All Daniel wanted to do was get in shape for his film role, and when I explained the goings-on in Hollywood he assured me that he'd do everything he could to get me reinstated as his trainer. There then followed an extremely productive and enjoyable workout, during which Daniel showed himself to be an extremely pleasant, friendly and understanding person.

After that single session I knew that Daniel would respond extremely well to the training schedule I'd devised for him. He was athletic, mobile and extremely receptive to the information I gave him about his diet and exercise regime. In short, Daniel was just about the ideal candidate for physical improvement and I would've loved to have continued his training routine as planned. The session finished with the two of us swapping jokes like old friends and Daniel went away determined to sort everything out with Shel Schrager in Hollywood. Sadly, this was not to be, as Daniel explained when he telephoned me the following day to express his regret that the studio bosses would not change their minds. Another trainer had been appointed and, this time, I was off the case for keeps.

Peter Sellers
In 1966 I was under an agent called Gaby Howard. She called me one day to ask if I wanted to make my film debut. This was a stupid question and Gaby knew it. I was champing at the bit to break into movies and on hearing her next words I almost bit the bit in half: "You'll be playing the part of a bear in a production called Casino Royale and you'll be opposite Peter Sellers. Now, that's all I can tell you about the part, so get down to Shepperton Studios - they're expecting you tomorrow."

I was at Shepperton bright and early the next morning, only to find just about every big bloke in the movie-extras business lining up to audition for 'my' role. I was most put out by this and considered taking the easy option of turning on my heels and heading back home. Then I decided to try another approach.

The first assistant on *Casino Royale* was a guy called Dominic Fulford, who went on to become a good friend of mine and have an extremely successful career in the movie business. I'd never met him before that day, but rather than make my way home with my tail between my legs I decided to storm into his office and demand to know why a posse of candidates was waiting to try out for a role that, according to my agent, had already been assigned to me. This bold (some would say arrogant, or even plain crazy) tactic could've backfired spectacularly, and Dominic would've been perfectly within his rights to tell me to sod off home. To his eternal credit, however, he gave me the benefit of the doubt and dismissed the crowd of waiting extras. The role of the bear was mine and I was in the movies.

My next stop was the wardrobe department, where I discovered that I was to play the part of a giant teddy bear by the name of Superpooh. Yes, they had to run that by me a couple of times, too, before I could take it in. Not quite Shakespeare, then. Never mind, David, everyone has to start somewhere.

For those who don't recall the plot, the film was a spoof on the James Bond theme and Peter Sellers was playing one of the many 007s depicted in it. Peter's character turns out to be haunted in his sleep by his teddy bear, except that the bear had transformed from the cuddly little Winnie the Pooh into the monstrous, slobbering Superpooh.

Two costume fittings later, I was ready to endow Superpooh with every ounce of acting talent I possessed. Unfortunately, Peter Sellers was running very late on his filming schedule and still had work to catch up on from the previous week's shooting list. And so it continued. Day after day I would turn up, ready to be a memorably super Superpooh, and every day there would be nothing for me to do because Peter wasn't available. So I would stand around watching scenes being filmed that didn't include me. This continued for a number of days, but there were compensations.

In the meantime, I had become friendly with *Candid Camera*'s Jonathan Routh and the great Scottish comedian, Chic Murray, who greatly lightened the boredom of standing around with nothing to do. Jonathan and Chic were playing a pair of idiotic bad guys, and it was wonderful to see them work at close quarters like this. At least they were working, and so was Peter Sellers, because when Jon and Chic had finished their scenes I went over to watch Peter and the stunning Ursula Andress getting it on for the cameras. I even witnessed the sight of several hundred Scottish pipers advancing through the mist, kilts swirling, bagpipes skirling, and Peter O'Toole doing a cameo part in the middle of it all.

I saw many fascinating things during my days as an observer on *Casino Royale*. The thing I didn't see, however, was any sign of Peter Sellers and I doing a scene together. An entire week of non-activity ticked by until, on the Friday afternoon, I got the call to dive into the Superpooh suit and get ready to act. First, there was a rehearsal to get through. The scene was set in a dungeon, with me as Superpooh inside the dungeon, clawing madly at the bars as I tried to escape and attack Peter. Having started so late in the day, we managed to shoot only a small part of the scene before it was time to wrap it up and send everyone home for the weekend.

We all exchanged the usual pleasantries and "See you on Monday" comments - all except Peter, that is, who was at the end of his contract. Here's where things became seriously complicated. Peter told the film company's accountants that his contract for *Casino Royale* had run into its penalty clause and, from Monday onwards, he was due to be paid a full week's salary for every day he worked. A story went round the set that, when Peter arrived at the studios on the Monday morning, he made a beeline for the cashier's office to make certain that the company had sufficient funds to pay him his new daily rate. On hearing that the company was now liable for vastly inflated wages, the accountants became extremely agitated, and Peter realised that extracting his 700 per cent pay penalty was going to be anything but straightforward.

The next, and last, line that Peter Sellers delivered in *Casino Royale* was: "Thank you very much. You know my terms and, if you want me, I'll be in Switzerland." He then walked off the set, never to return. Sadly, when Peter went, so did my glorious Superpooh scene, together with my precious film debut. I ask you - what's a bear supposed to do?

David Niven

Two weeks after my Superpooh fiasco, the *Casino Royale* production office contacted me. They'd moved their facility from Shepperton to the MGM studios at Elstree, and they had a rather strange question to ask me.

"Dave, was it you we measured for the Frankenstein outfit?" enquired a production assistant. I hadn't the slightest idea what he was talking about and asked him what the problem was. "Well, we have a Frankenstein sequence to film here at MGM and nobody knows who was fitted for the suit and headpiece. I don't suppose there's any chance that you could come up to the studio to see if it fits, is there? If it does, you've got the part playing opposite David Niven and Woody Allen."

Naturally, I wanted to rekindle my movie career, which currently amounted to around 45 seconds' worth of discarded footage. So I headed straight for Elstree to re-enact the defining scene from *Cinderella*, with me as Cinders and a ready-made Frankenstein outfit as the glass slipper. I didn't want to marry the prince, but when the Frankenstein get-up fitted as though it had been made for me I was almost as happy as any panto Cinderella.

It appeared that my glorious film debut wasn't destined to be a portrayal of a ridiculous, slavering teddy bear. Instead, I was to be immortalised on celluloid as Frankenstein's monster, which was a far more dignified prospect, I trust you'll agree.

My scene, and there was only one, wasn't exactly demanding. All I was required to do was walk in monster fashion along a corridor, collide with the end wall, then turn and walk back. At some time within this carefully choreographed routine, David Niven, playing another 007 who is attempting to evade the clutches of the evil Woody Allen, approaches me to ask directions. Being a bit-part monster and unversed in social niceties, I brush David aside and carry on walking. That was it. The whole debut. Well, at least it made it to the screen.

It would be wrong to pretend that I really got to know David Niven during our brief acquaintance on *Casino Royale*, but, like the rest of the cast on that movie, I found him to be a perfect gentleman. He had a warm, friendly manner about him, and absolutely none of the 'big star' mentality that can afflict those in our industry. David Niven had time for stars and stagehands alike and he often killed time between scenes by playing cards with the extras. Much show business gushiness is quite phoney, but I could introduce you to dozens of people who would name Niven as a consummate professional who was adored by all who worked with him.

Charles Bronson

Working on *Casino Royale* was a productive exercise for me. Not only did I break (just about) into movies, I also got to notch up a fair number of star encounters.

Whilst we were shooting *Casino* at MGM, another film was being made in other parts of the studio complex. That film was *The Dirty Dozen*, which went on to become one of the defining productions of its kind, not to mention a box office smash. In terms of impact on the world of entertainment, *Casino Royale* couldn't compete with *The Dirty Dozen*. That film was awash with star names and action heroes, yet we had something very special on our sets that theirs lacked: girls, and loads of them.

The lure of the *Casino* kittens was such that, as soon as the actors on *The Dirty Dozen* had finished filming for the day, they would drift on over to our studio to watch the girls in action and chat them up. I can't say I blamed them - those ladies were stunning. With so many remarkable women around me, you may think it odd that it was the sight of a man that got me most excited during that production. However, this was no ordinary man. This was Charles Bronson.

I spotted Charles standing quietly by himself, watching the filming of a scene. I'd been an admirer of his for years, enjoying the types of films he made and the presence he brought to them. As a bodybuilder, Charles's main attraction for me was his physique. He was always in great shape whenever I saw him on screen, and his roles in *House of Wax* and *Drum Beat* showed off all aspects of Charles Bronson to perfection.

While Charles watched the girls on set, I moved in slightly behind him so as not to impede his view of the action. I couldn't pass up this opportunity of speaking to one of my heroes, so I said quietly, "Excuse me, Mr Bronson, I hope you don't mind my asking, but could you tell me what you do in the way of training to maintain your physique?"

Charles chose not to turn around to see who was asking him about his training. He kept those piercing eyes of his fixed on the scene before him and muttered, "I don't do any training. Never have done. Probably never will." I was taken aback at this and found it hard to accept that such a cultured physique had occurred naturally. No man could be that lucky, not even Charles Bronson.

"Surely, Mr Bronson," I continued, still puzzled by the answer to my first question, "you must've been doing some sort of weight training to get in the fantastic shape you were in for *House of Wax* and when you played Cochise in *Drum Beat*."

"Nope. Never trained. Don't intend startin'," was the deadpan reply, and with that he walked away, having never once turned his head towards me. Who knows why Charles found it necessary to deny the fact that his superb physique was hard-won through hours of dedicated training. That such was the case was perfectly obvious to anyone who'd dedicated as much of their life to physical culture as I had. I know the difference between muscles that are worked on and those that are donated by genetics alone. Mother Nature had, indeed, been kind to Charles Bronson, but Father Training had played his part, too.

Perhaps, if I'd caught Charles at a better moment rather than disturbing his girl-watching reveries, he would've been quite happy to talk training with me. Compared to ogling a bunch of long-legged, bosomy Bond girls I must've run a very poor second indeed!

Clint Walker

Clint Walker was one of the Dirty Dozen, too, and he was a lot bigger than Charles Bronson. His status as a serious weight trainer was well known, so when I finally got to speak to Clint I knew that there was little chance of his clamming up and pretending that his muscles had been left by the tooth fairy.

Although he was far more sociable than Charles Bronson had been - he actually looked at me, for a start - I didn't get much more out of him than I got from Charles. Doggedly, some would say annoyingly, I tried every which way to get Clint to reveal his training regime. Then I lowered my sights a fraction and tried to get him to give me a straight answer to just one of my questions. I failed on all counts, as Clint stonewalled me on the subject of his training.

My friendly interrogations would go along the lines of:

"So, Clint, what sort of weights do you handle in the dead lift these days?"

Clint would then deliver a denial in that soft, bass voice of his. "Well, I don't do dead lifts at all, since I injured my back."

"How about the standing press then?" I'd counter. "How much do you put above your head?"

"I have to be real careful about pressing, due to my injured shoulder."

"How much do you bench press then?"

"Haven't bench pressed for ages. It wouldn't be good for my chest injury."

And so we'd continue. No matter what type of exercise I asked Clint about, he had some reason to avoid it.

Despite his unfortunate inability to exercise, Clint was in prime condition, and that undoubtedly saved his life a few years later when he had a gruesome skiing accident. As a result of a crash on the slopes, Clint fell forward onto his ski pole and it almost went through his chest. Only his muscle mass and tremendous strength prevented the accident from being fatal.

During the side-by-side filming of *Casino Royale* and *The Dirty Dozen* I saw Clint quite frequently and offered him the facility of training with me at the Crystal Palace National Recreation Centre, where I was director of weight training. Clint declined the offer, saying that he didn't like training in public places. Shortly afterwards he began training with a friend of mine, Harry Brooks, who also had a part in *The Dirty Dozen* as a German officer. Harry and Clint trained in Harry's small gymnasium at his flat in Knightsbridge. Some time after both films were finished I met up with Harry and asked him what sort of training methods Clint Walker used. Harry told me that Clint really did avoid lifting heavy weights, preferring to do all of his exercises at double-time with very light weights, backing up his weight training with running, to improve his cardiovascular fitness. So, where Charles Bronson was fibbing, Clint Walker told the truth.

The Beverly Hillbillies

Rarely have I found the entire cast of a top-rated show thoroughly likeable. Usually, someone will be playing the prima donna or one star won't get on with another, but when I worked with the actors from the sitcom *The Beverly Hillbillies* I found myself among the nicest bunch of film folk anyone could wish to meet.

The show was massive in the States and had made a successful transition 'across the pond' to the UK, too, making big stars of Buddy

Ebsen, Irene Ryan, Donna Douglas, Nancy Kulp and Max Baer Jr. Stardom hadn't affected any of them at all and their friendly, down-to-earth way was a pleasure to be around. They were doing some shows in the UK to accommodate a storyline that saw Jed Clampett searching Scotland for his ancestors. Where Jed went, Granny, Ellie-May, Miss Hathaway and Jethro had to follow.

I was playing a Scottish drunk in the episode we all worked on together, and when we weren't filming I'd borrow a couple of the stage weights and improvise a weight training session with them. This attracted the attention of Donna Douglas, who confided in me that her boyfriend back in the States was a dedicated weight trainer. "He's just about as big as you, too," Donna told me. I asked her his name and she said, "Oh, you wouldn't have heard of him, I'm sure." I told her that I knew most of the big US bodybuilders and weight trainers, and that there was a good chance that I'd heard of him. "I doubt that," giggled Donna. "His name is Clint Walker."

Benny Hill

I had the pleasure of working with the late, great Benny Hill on many occasions, but one instance always comes to mind when I'm asked to recall the shows and sketches we did together. I've noticed that this particular sketch, although performed many years ago, still features in film festivals around the world. Benny's fans will know it as the Wishing Well sketch. Benny plays an elderly man who is out walking in the woods with his equally ancient wife, when they come upon a wishing well. Benny's old man throws a coin into the well, and his old wife is magically replaced by a nubile young woman in a well-filled bikini. She takes one look at Benny, throws a coin in the well and he's replaced by a huge, muscly bloke - that was me. Typically, the muscleman turns out to be gay and wishes Benny to replace the gorgeous girl. Rather than be lumbered with an enormous gay companion, Benny hastily casts his final coin, gets his old wife back and they walk off into the sunset arm-in-arm. Marvellous stuff, and Benny Hill at his best.

Like so many great funny men, Benny was extremely serious about his work. He was one of the most meticulous performers I've ever met and nothing was too much trouble if it meant getting that extra laugh from the audience.

Frankie Howerd

Frankie was a unique character, a hugely talented comic and a friend of mine for many years. Our first meeting took place on the set of *Up Pompeii*, when he was filming the big screen version of his hit TV series. For those who don't remember it, it was a bawdy romp through the days of the Roman Empire and starred Frankie as a slave called Lurcio.

I'd been called to Elstree Studios to meet Bob Kellett, the film's director, who'd told my agent that there was a small role in *Up Pompeii* that was perfect for me. Like the accommodating chap I am, I got myself along to Elstree and sat patiently in the outer office, waiting for someone to call me for my interview. After three hours of waiting I wasn't feeling quite so accommodating, and things became a tad fraught when a studio aide casually informed me that he didn't know why I was still hanging around, because all the parts had gone. Now, I've never been one to take a brush-off lightly, and I snarled at the aide, "I've wasted two hours driving all the way down here at your company's request, I've got a paralysed backside from sitting on your rotten plastic chair for half a day, and now you tell me that I'm to run off home without even being seen? You've got a bloody nerve!" Normally, barking at the staff is not the way to get on in the film world, but this time it had a positive effect. Before I'd time to make my angry but dignified exit I was called into the production office.

I was then offered the job of stunt double in a wrestling scene. However, despite my eagerness for a job, I declined this on the grounds that I had long since decided that stunt work was not going to be my thing. This makes me appear ungracious and choosy, I know, although that wasn't the case at all. Being large, fit and muscular, I could've had plenty of minor stunt roles; indeed I was offered them without asking. To me, however, stunting was a separate profession and I wanted to be an actor. It looked as though my chances of appearing in *Up Pompeii* were at an end when the aide inflicted with my outburst informed me with a smug expression, "We're sorry, but the stunt double's job is all that's left." I held his gaze just long enough to make him feel uncomfortable and, in childish fashion, to claim the 'last hit'. I was turning to leave for the second time when the producer entered the office and told me that there was, after all, one final part yet to be cast. And what a part it was, too: the lover of Madeline Smith, who was certainly one of the loveliest, sexiest and most desirable women around at that time. Considering the general tone and direction of *Up Pompeii*, I knew that Madeline's lover would not spend his time engaging her in philosophical debate. Did I want that role? Let's put it this way: I would've paid them to do it!

Then, as the prospect of working closely with Madeline Smith filtered through my expression, the aide saw his chance of winning our petty little war once and for all. "Just one thing, Mr Prowse. You only get the part of Madeline's lover if you agree to do the stunt double's job, too." Now, I've always been a man of strong principles, but I've never allowed them to turn me into an idiot, so I signed for *Up Pompeii* with more haste than dignity. And that's how I came to be working alongside the great Frankie Howerd.

As you can imagine, rehearsals with Madeline were more than bearable. She was clad in an unfairly revealing gown for filming, but even in civvies that girl looked sensational. I swear that, when Madeline drifted into the studio, so many men immediately turned to get a better look that the sound of neck joints cracking echoed across the set like gunfire. Being a professional, I'd never allow anything to affect my work or my appreciation of a fellow actor, but it has to be said that Madeline was staggeringly sexy and I was unprofessionally sad when rehearsals were over and it was time to shoot our big scene.

The script had Frankie Howerd as Lurcio running into a Turkish baths to evade a gang of Roman villains who were set on killing him. Madeline and I were also in the Turkish baths, groping and fondling each other amid the steam. Frankie trips over our writhing bodies and I rise from the steam to shout, "Oi! Watch what you're doing!" Frankie replies, "Oooooooh, I'd rather watch what *you're* doing." As you can see, *Up Pompeii* didn't draw its direction from Wilde or Coward, but it was great fun to watch and also to work on.

Clad only in towels, Madeline and I perfected our 'dress' rehearsals in a frustratingly short time, while Frankie had his line perfected from the first run-through. The director decided that we were ready to go for a take. With the cameras rolling, the scene was point-perfect until Frankie was due to respond to my "Oi! Watch what you're doing!" line. Instead of delivering the scripted dialogue to me, Frankie replied, "Oh, hello David. Wife and kids okay, are they?" Frankie thought that I was getting into character a little too deeply and this was his way of slapping me down in front of Madeline and looking after my wife's best interests at the same time. Thinking about that incident, I never did get around to thanking Frankie for his care and concern. Ungrateful creature that I am, I merely wished to strangle him at the time.

After *Up Pompeii* was finished, Bob Kellett and I bumped into each other at Elstree and he asked me if I was available for Frankie's next epic, *Up the Chastity Belt*. Bob offered me the part of Sir Grumble de Grunt, one of the film's main characters. I'd enjoyed my work on *Up*

Pompeii so much that I said yes on the spot. Bob climbed into his car and drove away. Seconds later, I saw his car reversing towards me. He poked his head out of the window and said, "Your role requires you to ride a horse. You do ride, don't you, Dave?" The first rule of showbiz is: 'Never admit you can't do something'. So, running on autopilot, I affected my most confident manner and replied, "Horse riding? Me? Of course I can ride a horse, mate, I'm a natural." Maintaining my self-assured grin, I tapped the roof of Bob's car in a final gesture of conviction and continued grinning inanely until Bob and his car were out of sight.

Then I felt sick.

I'd never been much of a horse rider. In fact, I'd never been anything of a horse rider, ever. You see, when you're 6ft 7in tall, you weigh 20 stones and you can tip over a family car if the need arises, you rarely come into close contact with anything bigger and stronger than you are. Horses are both. Plus, they've got teeth like bolt cutters, steel toecaps at every corner and the ability to use both to attack anything they don't like. Horses don't have an on/off switch either; they get in bad moods and they can run at 40mph. Why anyone would voluntarily attach themselves to one of these lethal creatures had always been a mystery to me, and I fully intended it to remain so, until *Up the Chastity Belt* came along and spoilt my resolution.

My natural optimism translated the horse riding requirement in the film into nothing more than a short in-saddle walk, or a gentle canter at worst. So when the production office contacted me to discuss my jousting scenes, I swear that the room began to spin. There was nothing else for it. I had to learn to ride a hideous horse, I had to learn to ride it well and, more importantly, I had to do both bloody quickly. Taking my courage in both hands, I signed on for a crash course in equestrianism.

As is often the case, confronting fears diminishes them considerably, and I soon discovered that not every horse had been placed on earth specifically to kill people. I even began to enjoy my daily lessons and looked forward to the supervised hacks into the Surrey surrounds, my pleasure increasing by the day as I became a tolerably proficient horseman. By the time filming was due to begin, I was Dave Prowse, weightlifter, muscleman, actor and horse rider. I was ready to mount up for the silver screen.

Then the production office called again and told me they'd decided that a stunt double would do my jousting scenes, so I wouldn't be required to ride a horse, just sit on one occasionally. It was at that moment that my new-found affinity with the horse became complete, because I really knew what it felt like to want to kick someone.

Of the hundreds of stars I've met, known and worked with over the years, Frankie Howerd was one of the few I always kept in touch with. I regarded Frankie as a true friend, right up to his death in 1992. When he was honoured by the Variety Club, I was honoured, too - because Frankie asked me to sit at the top table with him.

He was a fantastic bloke and is sadly missed.

Bill Cosby

I was in New York to address a sci-fi convention and I decided that I couldn't leave the Big Apple without visiting its most famous sandwich bar, The Stage Deli. On Sunday morning, I went into The Stage for breakfast and, true to its name, the place was lined with photos of the hordes of famous folk who'd eaten there. In addition to the photographs on the walls, the Deli's menu read like a showbiz *Who's Who* - a roll-call of famous personalities with either a burger or a sandwich named in their honour.

When I made my Stage debut, Bill Cosby was enjoying breakfast in the company of boxing personality Jim Jacobs, and although I'd never met Bill before he recognised me and kindly asked me to sit at his table. I soon discovered that Bill was a huge *Star Wars* fan and, like any other follower of that massive trilogy, he wanted to know all about what went on during filming, plus the whole range of questions that countless fans have asked me over the years. Bill was extremely easy company and his enthusiasm made answering his questions a pleasure. That breakfast was one of the most memorable meals I've ever eaten and, just before we finished, the owner of the Deli looked set to immortalise the occasion for all time by offering to include a Darth Vader sandwich in his glittering menu. Wow - I'd really made it into the big-time!

When the owner asked me to name my favourite sandwich, I didn't have to think twice and reeled off the ingredients without hesitation.

"I love fresh, crusty bread, butter, Cheddar cheese - so tangy and mature that it almost burns your mouth, some sweet beetroot in light vinegar and a few rings of mild onion."

The owner of The Stage paused, his pencil hovering above his notebook ready to continue with my list of ingredients. After several seconds, he looked at me quizzically and said, "What? That's it? No meats, no relishes, no peanut butter, jams, jellies or pickle?" He was aghast at my lack of exotic sandwich filling choices.

"Not for me. I prefer just cheese, beetroot and onion."

The owner considered my dream sandwich for a further second before snapping shut his notebook and poking his pencil behind his ear in a gesture of finality.

"I'm sorry, sir," he said, "there's no way I could put something like that on my menu. Nobody in this country would ever go for it. Sorry."

And that's why neither Dave Prowse nor Darth Vader ever made it in the world of the New York delicatessen.

Alan Yentob

I was doing *The Horror of Frankenstein*, my very first job for Hammer Films, when a message was circulated around the studio that a BBC film unit would be arriving to record a documentary. Unsurprisingly, the subject of the documentary was horror films and, more specifically, various people's attitudes towards them. Being decidedly unfamous at the time, my name was not on the list of those scheduled for interviews by the BBC crew, so I took little notice of them as they drifted between my co-stars, gathering celebrity insights along the way.

Ralph Bates was playing Frankenstein, so he was immediately snapped up by the BBC interviewer, who turned out to be an enthusiastic young chap by the name of Alan Yentob. Kate O'Mara was next on the televised interrogation list, followed by Veronica Carlson and the multi-talented Jimmy Sangster, who was the writer, producer and director of *The Horror of Frankenstein*. With all of the big names processed, the BBC documentary crew was about to pack up for the day when, for reasons known only to himself, Alan Yentob dragged them all over to interview me.

As Alan and I chatted casually, I found him to be an easy person to talk to, and very early into the interview he began to stray from the main theme of horror and ask me questions about my career, how I'd broken into acting and my life history in general. Alan then declared that he'd found our chat extremely interesting and that he wished to make a programme about me. From being unworthy of an interview for a documentary, I was suddenly the subject of one. Such is the world of entertainment.

The idea of a whole programme dedicated to me set my ego racing and I knew that the TV exposure would do me no harm at all, so I agreed to Alan's request without hesitation. Within days, my house was under siege from cameramen, sound technicians, lighting specialists and a whole unidentifiable mob of TV people, who just seemed to wander about clutching clipboards and getting in the way. Glamorous it was not.

I would advise anyone who is approached by a film crew, with a view to using their home as a set, to turn down the offer immediately unless a very hefty fee is involved. Within that fee must be provision to clear up more mess than you ever thought your house could accommodate and sufficient funds to pay for a crack squad of cleaners capable of reclaiming your home from the tip that the film crew leaves behind. Trust me, a horde of drunken Vikings couldn't inflict the amount of disruption on one's home that a film unit can.

My family and I were filmed doing every family activity possible. I swear that the crew would've followed us into the bathroom if we'd allowed it, and this was way before the fly-on-the-wall documentaries became the reveal-all monsters they are today. I was filmed in bed and being woken by my boys, who were toddlers at the time. Then the cameras were pointed at the incredibly interesting process of me and my family eating breakfast, before more fascinating footage was captured as I drove to work in my car. More film was used on my caber-tossing training at the local sports ground, before the crew tracked me through my personal training routine at the gym. Apart from the training stuff, I couldn't help thinking that most of what Alan Yentob's crew had shot was, well, dull.

When the programme was aired on BBC2, however, I had to applaud Alan's efforts wholeheartedly. Whether it was his idea or not I don't know, but someone had the ingenuity to cut the shots of my normal family life together with sequences from *The Horror of Frankenstein*, and the stark contrast of the two was truly captivating. I wasn't overimpressed with the tile of the programme, mind you. *Profile of a Monster* wasn't too bad, but its subtitle of *Your Sexy Neighbourhood Fiend* was less than flattering, I thought.

Alan Yentob, as well as being extremely pleasant to work with, was obviously destined for greater things, and he proved this by eventually becoming Controller of BBC2 and BBC1, followed in succession by his appointment as BBC Television's overall Director of Programmes, Director of Drama, Entertainment and Children's and Creative Director, as well as fronting BBC programmes as a presenter. That's all very well of course, but my wife still hasn't forgiven his film unit for trashing our house.

Muhammad Ali

Ali really was The Greatest, and I seriously doubt if the sporting world will ever see his like again. I count myself privileged to have seen, albeit only on television, Ali in his boxing prime, and now that those days are long past I only wish I'd made more of my first opportunity to meet the man in person.

I was working as the fitness consultant to Harrods at the time and I was in the store when the buzz went around that Ali and his entourage were in the gentlemen's clothing department, with the man himself trying on shirts. As if by magic, Harrods simply emptied, with staff and customers alike pouring into the gentlemen's clothing department on the ground floor to catch a glimpse of a living legend. In minutes, the ground floor was a seething mass of admirers and it was clear that Ali loved every second of it. The Harrods bosses soon realised that each of those seconds that ticked by were costing the store money, as virtually everyone was gawking at Mohammed Ali rather than buying. Eventually, on the pretext of customer safety, Ali and his entourage were escorted from the building. How I wish I'd had the nerve to speak to him then.

I did get the chance of meeting Ali many years later, when he was visiting the famous Thomas à Beckett Pub and boxing gym in the Old Kent Road. The years between this meeting and the Harrods encounter had cost Mohammed Ali dear in terms of his health. Rumours abounded that he'd been damaged by the number of head punches he'd taken, especially during the latter part of his boxing career. However, in 1984 he was officially diagnosed with a form of Parkinson's Disease, suscepti-bility to which is vastly increased by head trauma. The man I met at the Thomas à Beckett was but a shadow of the mercury-limbed ring warrior I'd admired for so long. His speech was slurred and his actions slow and jerky. Yet, if a touchy subject was broached or a joke made, Ali would suddenly revert to his bombastic best, spouting tirades and quips just like he did in the days when he ruled the world of professional boxing.

I was thrilled to meet The Greatest, but it is my permanent regret that I didn't get to meet him when he was in his prime. Rather than escorting him from Harrods all those years ago, we should've locked the doors and invited him to hold court for a while. I, for one, would certainly have paid to see that.

Remar Sutton
I know that the name Remar Sutton won't be instantly recognised, despite his status as one of the most popular authors in the USA and his impressive record as a campaigner for consumer rights. I have included him in my all-star memories for one very basic reason. Sure, to his millions of readers and supporters he is a star in his own right, but to me

he merits inclusion because, in the words of a certain Mr Vader, Remar Sutton is "impressive, very impressive". Here's how he impressed me.

Remar first contacted me because he had decided to write a layman's guide to fitness. This book would explain to Mr, Ms and Mrs America everything they needed to know about exercise, diet, and weight loss and gain, and it would do so in a language that real people could understand. Remar is big on real people, as those who know his work will confirm.

Being a realist, Remar decided at the outset to play the guinea pig in terms of the advice and methods outlined in his book. He consulted the world's top fitness authorities with a view to developing nothing short of a total body-transformation regime and gave himself a year to effect the massive change he'd prescribed. His 1987 book, *Body Worry*, chronicles the events as they happened.

Remar telephoned me to ask if I would be his personal trainer and I agreed, 'sight unseen'. If I'd had the chance to see Remar first, I wouldn't have taken him on, as at the time he was embarking on his quest for transformation he was a wreck.

I found out just what I'd taken on when Remar flew from his home in Georgia to meet me at my gym in London. He was 45 years old, 6ft 2in tall, sported a 34in chest and 43in waist, had arms like drinking straws and was a heavy smoker. To complete the cycle of anti-fitness, Remar's diet would have given a rubbish bin ulcers, and the effort of climbing a flight of stairs caused him to collapse in a gasping heap. He was, in short, hardly the ideal candidate for a successful fitness demonstration. Or perhaps he was ideal. Only the next 12 months would tell.

To my intense embarrassment, I actually allowed my jaw to drop in dismay when I looked at Remar for the first time. I'd been thinking 'physical' for so many years that the sight of my latest project standing before me, his round shoulders heaving with the effort of scaling a few stairs and all of his wide bits where his narrow bits should be, overrode my basic manners. I'm afraid I gawped at Remar, unable to disguise my thoughts of 'What the hell have I agreed to, here?'

Remar was unfazed by my rudeness and explained the concept of his book to me. As he put it, he was "striving for hunkdom" via the advice of the best fitness guys in the business. He was determined to put himself through what was obviously an entirely alien ordeal, and as he expounded on what he hoped to achieve I found myself warming to him by the minute. There would be artistic licence for him; he'd be doing everything his physical training gurus had planned for him. He'd eat only what he was supposed to eat, he'd give up smoking, and by transforming his life he'd do the same to his body. By the time that first meeting had ended, I knew that Remar Sutton would accomplish everything he'd set out to do.

The whole venture was being funded by the *Washington Post* newspaper, and Remar's progress (or lack of it) would be charted in his regular column in the paper, culminating in the release of the book of his hunkdom regime around 18 months later.

Remar's first step towards the body beautiful was a large one. He immediately relocated to the Bahamas, accompanied by a personal trainer who was working under my direction, and he enrolled into the best gym on the island. The transformation of Remar Sutton had begun.

To say that the venture was a success would rob Remar of his rightful degree of credit. No mere 'success' was this; it was a triumph of good living over former bad habits. Remar's remarkable metamorphosis actually reversed his chest and waist measurements, placing the 43in and 34in dimensions where nature intended. The near-dormant muscles in his arms, shoulders, thighs, calves and back were awoken from their slumbers and responded admirably to the alarm call. Remar Sutton had achieved hunkdom, and he'd achieved it in a single year. The *Washington Post* broadcast his success to the American public and the book that began it all became a best-seller.

For me, the best news of all is that Remar has maintained his healthy living regime and remains in great shape, still enjoying his tennis, swimming and cycling workouts enormously. He tells me that having a healthy body has also improved the fitness of his mind, and I think he's proved this by branching out into fiction and writing another best-seller, this time a murder story.

Remar Sutton is endowed with seemingly limitless energy and drive and his many successes have given him an enviable lifestyle. Yet, like all 'real' people, Remar has never allowed anything to separate him from what really matters in this world. He's a truly genuine person, and he showed his friendship towards me when he flew from the USA to visit me in hospital after my hip operation. He then wrote the story of that visit in the *Washington Post* to let the Darth Vader fans in America know how I was getting along.

Terry Gilliam

Early in my acting career, as previously mentioned, I played - if 'played' is the right word for remaining motionless - the part of Rodin's celebrated statue, 'The Thinker', in an advertisement directed by Terry Gilliam of *Monty Python* fame. Later, in 1977, he contacted me again, this time with a view to my playing a part in a film he was directing, called *Jabberwocky*.

"I'd like you to consider the part of the Red Knight, Dave," said Terry, in the Anglo-American accent of a Stateside lad who'd worked for years in the company of English artistes.

"What does the Red Knight have to do, then?" I asked.

"Oh, he's the King's champion and he has to go and kill the dragon that's terrorizing everybody. We're filming down in Carmarthen Castle. It's in Wales."

"Yes, I know it's in Wales, Terry."

"Well, we'd love to have you with us. So, what do you say, Dave?"

"Count me in, Terry. I'd love to do it."

Terry was back on the phone a few days later with a request.

"Dave, you know you're playing the Red Knight, who goes off to fight the dragon?"

"Yes, Terry."

"Well, on his way to fight the dragon, he meets the Black Knight and gets killed, so it's the Black Knight who gets to fight the dragon."

"Oh, that's a shame."

"Well, not really, because I'd like you to play the Black Knight as well. Any chance of you doing that?"

"If you can work it, Terry, I can play it. No problem."

Two days later Terry was on the phone again.

"Dave?"

"Yes, Terry."

"You know how you're playing the Red Knight, who goes off to fight the dragon but gets killed by the Black Knight, who you also play and who ends up going off to fight the dragon?"

"Er ... yes, Terry."

"Well ... Dave ... mate ... We ... um ... wondered ..."

"Yes, Terry," I said, by now pretty sure what he was about to ask.

"Well ... we wondered if you'd play the dragon as well."

I must've been as mad as Terry in those days, because I agreed to the dragon's job as well. In the event, I didn't play this role, however. The dragon was such a peculiarly constructed beast that a tall and extremely skinny ballet dancer had to be drafted in to operate it. Even then, the poor man had to sit back-to-front inside the dragon because that was the only way he could flap the beast's wings to a remotely convincing degree.

When filming began I discovered that *Jabberwocky* was blessed with a cast of wonderful people, including the great Max Wall, Michael Palin, Simon Williams, Warren Mitchell and Gordon Kaye. *Jabberwocky* was filmed before Gordon's tremendous success in the comedy series *'Allo, 'Allo!*, and he was playing, of all things, a nun. Simon Williams was already a big star, thanks to his acclaimed portrayal of the son in the drama series *Upstairs, Downstairs*, and he was much admired by the ladies for his dashing good looks and Errol Flynn screen persona, which included a decidedly Flynn-esque moustache.

Simon was playing the part of the handsome prince, who single-handedly storms the castle to rescue his princess. In the rescue scene Michael Palin's character blunders mistakenly into the princess's bedchamber and the princess, who is attended by her nuns, including Gordon Kaye, mistakes Michael for the prince. Then, a grappling iron thrown by the real prince hooks into the battlements as Simon makes his daring bid to save his love. Unfortunately, just as the prince's hands and helmet appear over the battlements, the stonework crumbles and he falls to his death. Simon's face was never shown on screen, and that was after Terry had made him shave off that trademark moustache especially for the part.

For me, the most memorable part of *Jabberwocky* was the scene where I was battered, bruised and then very nearly killed. Yes, that's definitely the one I'll take to the grave with me.

We were shooting on the edge of a water-filled quarry and I was playing the Black Knight. The scene required me to be on horseback, fully armoured and flailing away at the scrawny dragon with, well, a flail (a spiked ball on a chain attached to a wooden handle). And that unwieldy contraption all but cost me my life.

In the script, what later became the 'scene of near-death' seemed perfectly straightforward. I would guide my willing steed towards the camera, make a couple of swings with my flail, overreach on the final swing and fall from my horse onto a comfy pile of mattresses. Easy. Well, not easy at all, as it happened.

Constricted by a full suit of metal armour (Terry had no hesitation in swapping my comfort and safety for realism), my vision restricted severely by the visor on my helmet, and mounted on an animal that was justifiably spooked by the clanking, slashing, ill-balanced burden on its back, I should've known that disaster was not just likely, but pretty much inevitable.

Filming got under way bright and early that morning, and it was still under way when late afternoon rolled around. By this time I'd fallen from that horse more than 20 times and had the bruises to prove it. Terry still wasn't satisfied. Now, I'm a bit of a trouper where this sort of thing is called for, and many's the time that I've risked my personal safety to get a shot exactly as my director wants it, but even I was getting thoroughly irritated by the proceedings by now.

Although I hadn't uttered a word of complaint, Terry sensed that I was nearing the end of my tether and, after the crew had hoisted me back into the saddle yet again, he sidled up to me and asked if I'd have one more go at the scene, with the promise that this really would be my last take, no matter what happened. Oh, how right he almost was.

The mental state of my horse had deteriorated alarmingly by this point. It had begun the day as merely skittish, progressed to seriously jumpy at around the fifteenth take, and now, as we prepared for take twenty-something, it was totally freaked out. I wasn't far behind it either and was becoming increasingly worried by the difficulty I was having dislodging my metal-plated feet from the stirrups each time I fell from the saddle. "One more take," was my only source of consolation as I lined up my horse for our last hurrah.

"Action!" was called, and during the next frantic minute the horse and I certainly gave Terry Gilliam plenty of it. As I stood in the stirrups to begin swinging my flail, the horse decided that enough was enough and it was time to vote with its feet. It bolted like a thoroughbred from the stalls, catapulting me over its hindquarters and onto the ground. My fears about the stirrups were realised at the worst possible moment, as my feet became stuck fast and I was dragged at high speed towards the flooded quarry.

Despite towing my 20st, plus 50lb of armour, that horse hit full gallop with terrifying ease and looked set to run straight into the watery depths of the quarry. If it did, I was dead, simple as that. There was no way I could do anything except sink like a brick - the armour would see to that. Then providence stepped in to save me. The saddle girth snapped and I skidded to a grateful halt just yards from the quarry edge, while the horse ploughed on. Battered, bruised, breathless and bloody frightened, I was alive, and right then that was all I was interested in.

The horrified crew raced over to pick me up, check that I wasn't seriously injured and remove the armour. Terry, on the other hand, sauntered over in his own good time and, instead of enquiring after my health or apologising for what had happened, he congratulated me warmly on my great performance in the scene and told me that my crash-and-drag stunt was definitely the one he'd use in the film. And he did. In fact, he used the entire sequence - which included a fleeting glimpse of a Hertz Rent-a-Van that was picked up by the camera as my near-death experience was filmed from start to finish.

There aren't that many medieval epics that feature Hertz Rent-a-Vans, but then, there's only one Terry Gilliam. And on that day in Carmarthen, one Terry Gilliam was just about all my body could stand.

David Jason

David is currently one of the biggest stars on British television. His talent spans the diverse worlds of comedy and drama with equal success. He's earned every plaudit he gets and few have worked harder over the years than him. To see the accomplished performer that entertains millions as Del-Boy Trotter in *Only Fools and Horses*, or hauls in the ratings as the captivating Inspector Frost, it's hard for me to believe that this is the same, terribly insecure young actor I first met on the set of the BBC's own police series, *Softly, Softly*.

The director of *Softly, Softly* was a Welsh man by the name of Malcolm Taylor, now a well-known TV director. Malcolm had a high regard for Welsh actors and populated *Softly, Softly* with a veritable gang of them, including David Jason. The episode I worked on was distinctly unmemorable, apart from my being rebuked by the producer because my West Country accent wasn't strong enough. Bloody cheek.

A few years later David Jason's star potential was spotted and to launch him into the big time a film script was commissioned especially for him. *Albert's Follies* was designed to be the vehicle that transported David Jason to stardom.

Ray Selfe was the director on *Albert's Follies* and he called me in to discuss playing a role that was little more than an extra's job. Circumstances dictate that sometimes actors can't be choosers and I turned up at the film company's production office in Wardour Street to see Ray. Just in case, I took along my portfolio and a list of credits and reviews from the various jobs I'd done. Ray studied this and, after consulting with his producer, he decided to offer me one of the main roles in the film, that of a crook. I'd even have a bit of love interest, in the glorious shape of Sue Bond. I distinctly remember kissing the cover of my portfolio as I left Wardour Street that day.

Filming took place at Twickenham Studios. The fact that *Albert's Follies* will never rate a slot, even on late night TV during a particularly slow Christmas schedule and not even if it coincided with David Jason

Appreciation Week, should tell you what an unmitigated disaster this movie was. In the unlikely event that David has need of a CV, I'll guarantee that *Albert's Follies* won't be on it. But for his talent and resilience, that film could have done for David Jason what Watergate did for Nixon.

I do remember two incidents from the making of *Albert's Follies*, though. First, I almost had my kneecap torn off performing a stunt that I shouldn't have been doing; and second, I did my first, and only, bedroom scene. Looking back, I have to say that nearly losing my kneecap was only marginally more uncomfortable than doing the bedroom scene.

Ray Selfe, in his direction to Sue Bond and myself, said that he wanted us to be "romping around in bed together". To enhance the moment - and, God only knows, that film needed some serious enhancing - Ray had decided to film our big love scene in a suite at the Westminster Hotel, near Victoria, rather than on set at Twickenham Studios. The unit had been cut to just Ray and the cameraman, leaving Sue and I to romp ourselves into a frenzy, uninhibited by prying film folk. With the camera in position and the protagonists beneath the sheets, I was all set for my first taste of on-film erotica.

Sue was set, too - set like concrete, and every bit as cold. She spent the entire day frightened to death that any part of me was going to touch any part of her. Erotic? It was about as erotic as unblocking a drain, only less inviting. At the start of filming, Ray was expecting full-on, simulated sex. By the time we'd wasted his time, his direction and several hundred feet of film stock, he would've settled for a simulated snog. I'd given up altogether. There was a World Cup football match on the TV later that night, so while Ray explained the finer points of fake sex to Sue I thought that I might as well just lie back and think of England.

All credit goes to David Jason that not even *Albert's Follies* could hold back what has become a magnificent career in entertainment. We meet occasionally at showbiz functions and it's great to see how the man has developed in line with that career. We never speak of 'that' film anymore, and I wouldn't be surprised if David has secretly bought up every reel of the original footage and burned the whole rotten lot.

Samantha Fox

A few years back I was approached by the organisers of a major body-building competition, who wanted me to make a personal appearance and present the awards. I declined, mainly because I'm not particularly impressed with the direction that modern bodybuilding contests are taking. However, the organisers then told me that, should I accept their invitation, I would be working with Samantha Fox. Within three seconds I'd convinced myself that perhaps I was being unfair to modern body-building and that I'd give it one last chance to change my mind.

Sam Fox has been one of my dream girls for many years and I'd kept a keen eye on her 'progress' throughout her pin-up years and beyond. It wasn't just her outstanding figure and pretty face that captivated me, either. Whenever I saw her being interviewed, Sam always came across as being 100 per cent natural. Female attraction is, thank goodness, largely indefinable, but whatever it is, Sam Fox has loads of it. So I wasn't about to turn down the chance of meeting her, even if I had to endure several hours of the vulgar circus that bodybuilding has sadly become.

I'd been attending bodybuilding contests for the best part of 40 years. Well, they were the best part until the advent of anabolic steroids and the presence of screaming, air-horn wielding audiences turned them into the opposite of what they're supposed to represent. Physical culture should be about the promotion of health and fitness and the tremendous benefits these bring to the human body. Steroids may allow the development of muscle mass, but they're anything but healthy. Among their many side effects, steroids promote not only muscle development but also aggressive tendencies, and perhaps this explains the overwhelm-ing air of aggression that afflicts both participants and audiences at these shows.

Voting seems largely dictated by the reaction of the crowd, who, with klaxons, air horns and screeching voices at full throttle, seem able to blast their favourite to victory by virtue of decibel count alone. Perhaps I'm old-fashioned, but I preferred the days when physical culture really did have some culture about it. Anyway, what did I care? I had Sam Fox to meet.

Sam looked splendid, as always, as we doled out the awards that night, and the presentations went off without a hitch. I'm afraid that the show itself was horrendous, with most of the audience members seemingly there purely to out-scream their rivals. By the time the last award had been handed over and the last exaggerated smile had faded from our faces, Sam and I were in dire need of a few minutes' relaxation in the venue's green room, if only to bring our hearing back to normal. Although we'd been working together all night, Sam and I had yet to be introduced or even swap a line or two of conversation, so I was looking forward immensely to our meeting properly. If anything, Sam looked even more gorgeous up close than she did during the many sneaky peeks I'd had of her as she presented her share of the awards that night. I was smiling my Mr Suave smile as we were formerly introduced, but before I could captivate Sam with a complimentary one-liner she said, "Of course, you know we've met before, Dave." I politely assured her that she must be mistaken, because out of all the many beautiful ladies I'd met in my time I would surely have remembered her. She smiled indulgently at me before replying. "Oh, I promise we have met, Dave. You see, I was at junior school when you came to give a Green Cross Code talk."

Yeah, thanks Sam. You made a happy man feel very old.

Sir Harry Secombe

One of the most popular, and certainly the most innovative, comedy shows of the 1950s was *The Goon Show*. Written and performed by Harry Secombe, Spike Milligan, Michael Bentine and Peter Sellers, *The Goon Show* changed the face of British comedy for ever and is generally acknowledged to have been the prime influence behind the creation of *Monty Python's Flying Circus*, among other classics. Our own Prince Charles is a huge fan of The Goons, too, and he does a fair imitation of most of the characters, I'm told.

One of the most celebrated bodybuilders of the time was the well-known bandleader and radio personality Ray Ellington. Ray was also a great comedian and singer, although he wasn't related in any way to the legendary Duke of the same name. Ray's passion for bodybuilding was a public one and, although he was never in contest-winning shape, he was a big, well-built man who loved to work out, and he'd been featured in the *Health & Strength* magazine.

I met Ray when his group, The Ray Ellington Quartet, landed a job at the Mecca ballroom where I worked in my younger years. The Glen employed a ten-piece band and the Tommy Allen Trio at that time and we had to find cover for their holidays. And one particular year we struck lucky when the famous Ray Ellington Quartet stepped in. Whilst touring the country playing Mecca venues, Ray's quartet were called to provide the musical interludes on *The Goon Show*. Typically, Ray and his musicians were incorporated into the comedy sketches, too, and the Ellington Quartet became friends with the frenetic foursome that comprised The Goons.

When Ray's Mecca contract brought him to The Glen in Bristol, it was inevitable that our shared interest in training would throw us together.

Having such a lot in common, we hit it off right from the start, and I ended up taking a selection of my weights, barbells and dumb-bells to The Glen so that we could train together around the side of the ballroom. Soon, we became the best of friends and we trained together throughout Ray's stint at Bristol.

One day Ray told me that Harry Secombe, who was appearing at the Bristol Hippodrome, wasn't feeling too good and was confined to his bed at the Royal Hotel. He said that he was going to visit Harry to help cheer him up and he asked me if I'd like to go with him. This was my first brush with celebrity and I jumped at the chance.

Ray and I piled into his brand new, top-of-the-range, black and white Ford Zodiac and raced off to the Grand Hotel, and I really thought: this is the life! On the way, Ray revealed to me the exact nature of Harry's affliction: the arch Goon was suffering from an acute attack of piles. This was my first demonstration of the fact that, no matter how big the star, life has a way of reminding us just how mortal we all are. In this case, Harry's reminder had been a haemorrhoid, or, to be medically correct, a bloody great bunch of them.

When Ray and I were ushered into Harry's room, he was lying on top of the bed in his pyjamas, looking as comfortable as anyone could in his condition. While his manager pottered about, we presented Harry with a bottle of something spiritual and uplifting - brandy, I think it was. I then spent the next hour laughing as I'd never done before, as Ray and Harry swapped gags and quickfire banter in a way that no stage routine could ever have matched. Harry laughed as loud and as long as I did, and I was genuinely worried about the effect of our visit on his piles, because by the time we had to go I know that I ached all over. Just before he waved us farewell from his supposed bed of pain, Harry kindly invited me not only to see his show at the Hippodrome but also to be his guest at a recording of *The Goon Show* at the BBC theatre in Piccadilly, and I meant it when I said that I'd love to take him up on his offer the next time I was in London.

My chance to do just that came up two months later, when the Mr Universe contest was held in London. I wasn't anywhere near good enough to compete, but I still like to make a pilgrimage there every year, just to see what I should be aspiring to. I may have worked for a company that called itself Mecca, but I knew where my own Mecca was, and this event was it. With all of this devotion flying around, how odd it is that 50 years on I can't remember a single detail about the Mr Universe contest I attended on that Saturday in London, yet I can recite virtually every line of *The Goon Show* recording I watched the following day. Perhaps that day was when I first heard the siren of showbiz humming a few bars of her song? Or perhaps I'm just forgetful? Who knows?

At the recording I had a seat in the middle of the front row, and when they'd finished they all came down to the auditorium to meet me. The Goons all went out of their way to make me feel welcome, and once Peter Sellers discovered my interest in bodybuilding he immediately launched into an impromptu posing routine, supported by a commentary from his fellow Goons. I was surrounded that day by a human wall of comic genius and I laughed so much that the act of drawing breath became a real worry at one point. It was an encounter I'll cherish as long as I live, now made all the more precious since the passing of Ray, Peter, Spike, Harry and Michael.

I used to meet up with Sir Harry - oh yes, he became a knight - quite regularly, due to our mutual connection with the charity Comic Heritage, which raises funds to care for variety performers who need financial help. The charity also remembers those who graced the world of comedy and are no longer with us, by putting up plaques in their memory. Sir Harry passed away in 2001.

Bob Monkhouse

Between *Star Wars* and *Empire Strikes Back* I continued looking after the Grosvenor House Health Club and one of my celebrity clients was the head casting director for ATV - Alec Fine. One day he told me that ATV had taken over the franchise for a popular American TV show called *Hollywood Squares*, which they were going to anglicise and air on TV for an initial run of 39 shows. He had the idea of making a big presentation of the £1,000 top prize in hard cash and asked me if I would like the part of the guard who brings on the money at the end of the show.

"There's not much money - just £50 a show, but we'll film four shows over two days," he said. "On top of this you'll meet nine different celebrities at each show, i.e., 36 over the two days, and you'll be invited to have dinner with everybody each evening. Add to this the fact that Bob Monkhouse is going to be the compère and he's really dead keen on your joining the show."

Although the money was poor, it really was an offer I couldn't turn down and so a few weeks later I turned up at the ATV Studios just across the road from where I'd filmed *Star Wars*. I'd become quite excited about the part, as it had been explained to me that they would be adding lots of variation, so that one show I might come on as a security guard, the next as a pirate with a chest full of booty, another as a gangster with his ill-gotten gains, and so on.

I went into the studio and almost the first person to welcome me was Bob Monkhouse himself, dripping compliments and insincerity. "Dave, we're all so thrilled to have you working with us," he oozed. "We have tremendous plans for the show and you're to be a major part of it."

For the first show I was dressed in a navy blue suit, looking for all the world like a security guard, and the studio security guard handed me the briefcase containing the £1,000 cash just before I had to go on and do my little bit. My big moment arrived, I walked on, opened up the briefcase and the £1,000 of pound notes were revealed to the nervous contestant. On the first show the contestant didn't answer the questions correctly, so I promptly had to close the case and walk off - end of show. Everybody was ecstatic with the first attempt and we all went off to the studio restaurant to have a wonderful cold buffet together with the nine celebrities from that episode and the nine coming in for the evening show. The scene would repeat itself the following day.

Before we could get to the second show the casting director pulled me aside and said that Bob had decided he only wanted the briefcase full of money and my hands to be seen in the £1,000 question slot. So, thanks to Mr Monkhouse and despite the smarmy build-up, for the next 38 shows that was all you ever saw of Dave Prowse. It was strange, too, that although I did 39 shows and went to 19 such dinners Bob hardly ever spoke to me again.

Whilst I enjoyed the shows, the highlights of the two days were the dinners, where I mingled with all the famous and not so famous. I had a wonderful meeting with Vincent Price at one dinner and he paid me the compliment of saying that he'd seen all my movies and was looking forward to doing a horror movie with me. Christopher Lee was a regular guest on the show, too, as were Patrick Mower and Helen Mirren. Over those 39 shows, lots of celebrities used to come into the game every couple of weeks and I must've met and dined with 300 famous people whilst I did my stint as the man with the money.

Michael Jackson at Famous Monsters

Some years ago I was appearing at a Famous Monsters convention in Los Angeles, where the guests included Boris Karloff's daughter, Sarah, Lon Chaney Jnr's son, Bela Lugosi's son, Forrest J. Ackerman, Al Lewis, Tom Savini and Batman himself, Adam West. It was a great convention and I had the pleasure of re-enacting a Batman script as a radio play in front of a huge audience. It was the first time they'd heard Darth Vader speak at anything and I got a rousing reception for every line of dialogue I uttered.

Hordes of people turned up to the convention dressed as their favourite horror characters and I'd been asked if I would be one of the judges for a masquerade contest to be held later in the evening. The contestants really took the contest seriously and spent the whole evening prior to the event parading around in character. One of those acting his heart out was someone dressed up as Nosferatu from the legendary horror film of the same name. He looked great, with a long brown overcoat, hat, ghastly white face and chalk-white hands, which he held at the sides of his suitably contorted face most of the evening. He was among the fantastic line-up in the contest and, after much deliberation from the judging panel, he came fourth out of the six placings.

The contest over, all the competitors dispersed, and Nosferatu in particular was conspicuous by his absence. Later that evening Ray Ferry, the convention organiser, was chatting to me and told me that Nosferatu was none other than Michael Jackson. By all accounts, he'd phoned Ray and asked if he could take part in the masquerade, but only on the condition that Ray promised not to make his identity known. He wished to participate incognito and depart at the end of the contest without anybody knowing that he'd been there.

Fantasticon at the Raddison
One of the most interesting conventions, aptly titled Fantasticon, was held at Heathrow, London. Initially, the guest list included Jon Pertwee of *Dr Who* and *Worzel Gummidge* fame, William Campbell from *Star Trek* who had come over from the States and myself. However, during the course of the weekend the lady who coorganised the event received two memorable phone calls that would turn a fairly ordinary convention into an outstanding one.

The first call was from author Arthur C. Clarke, space visionary and author of *2001: A Space Odyssey*. He was making a visit to London from Sri Lanka, where he was residing, and was at Stanley Kubrick's house when he called. He had somehow heard about the convention and wanted to know if it would be all right for him to attend purely and simply as a patron. To say that the organiser was flabbergasted would be an understatement and, of course, Arthur was duly invited. The second phone call was from Patrick Stewart, Captain Picard of *Star Trek* fame, who was also in London, saying that he would like to arrive at the convention unannounced and just attend it as a sci-fi fan.

In the event, Arthur and Patrick agreed to go on stage and give talks, and both of them brought the house down. I had one of the best seats in the house, in the front row, from which I managed to take some great photos and also 'heckle' both speakers. Patrick sat with me during Arthur's talk and I had the welcome task of helping Arthur around the convention and up to the bar when he'd finished.

A couple of years before this meeting with Arthur, while I was attending yet another convention in the States, I happened to come across a booth that was promoting a company called Southern Cross Entertainments. On their stand they were advertising a proposed dive for missing treasure out in Sri Lanka. One of the items being used to promote the dive was a solid block of silver ingots, which I picked up gingerly and put down even more gingerly when I was told it was worth over half a million dollars. Southern Cross were thrilled with my, or at least Darth Vader's, interest and asked if I would care to join the dive. It turned out that Arthur had discovered the whereabouts of a sunken galleon with treasure aboard and wanted to lead an expedition to retrieve it. Unfortunately, nothing ever happened about the dive, as the political problems in Sri Lanka made it impossible to organise. In addition, of course, Arthur was getting older and more infirm.

At the time of this convention I'd never met Arthur before even though he knew of my proposed involvement in the dive. When the time for questions and answers came I stood up and asked, "Can you tell us what is happening about the Southern Cross dive in Sri Lanka?"

Arthur's reply was that the dive was still going ahead and that they were thrilled that Dave Prowse would be taking part. The whole audience erupted into laughter, realising that Arthur hadn't actually recognised me. It didn't take him long to work out that Dave Prowse and the questioner were indeed one and the same, and after his talk I met up with him and Patrick. We were joined by Bill Campbell and Jon Pertwee and had a great time.

Hart to Hart

Fans of *Hart to Hart* might be interested to know that I've met both stars of the show - Robert Wagner and Stefanie Powers. I was at Pinewood Studios in the office of a well-known film producer, chatting away, when who should walk in but Roger Moore. I'd worked with Roger years previously on an episode of *The Saint* and had also had lunch with him whilst doing *The Horror of Frankenstein*. The three of us hadn't been in conversation long when Robert Wagner walked in and I had the pleasure of being introduced. A brief conversation followed with my producer friend, after which both Roger and Robert Wagner left the office. A few minutes later there was a knock at the door. Robert Wagner had returned. He came straight over to me and said, "Dave, I'm sorry, I left without saying goodbye to you." We shook hands and he departed for the second time. I was amazed that he'd been so thoughtful and courteous. After all, I wasn't anybody in particular, just the producer's friend. However, it's a gesture I've never forgotten.

Stefanie Powers came over to the UK in 1991 to appear in a stage musical called *Matador*, starring opposite well-known singer/actor John Barrowman, who went on to make successful appearances in *Miss Saigon*, *Guys and Dolls* and *Beauty and the Beast*. John was an avid trainer and came to my gym to work under my tutelage. As soon as he was contracted for *Matador* he asked if Stefanie could come in and work with us, resulting in the three of us training together throughout the run of the musical (which wasn't very long as it wasn't very good). A beautiful lady and very easy to get along with, it was a pleasure to have Stefanie working out at my gym.

American Football with the LA Rams

I'm quite a fan of American Football and some years ago, whilst I was personal trainer to the famous racehorse owner, Charles St George, I received an invitation from the owners of the LA Rams, Carol and Gloria Rosenbloom, to go to see the team play from the comfort of owners' private box at the LA Stadium. Charles and Carol were great gambling buddies and the private box list read like a Hollywood *Who's Who*. I sat between Ricardo Montalbám and Rod Steiger's wife, and sitting directly behind me was Candice Bergen. Also present were minor celebrities like US jockeys and TV stars from the US soaps. Of course, our view of the game was unparalleled, but I had terrible problems following the ball. In the end I thought it best to keep watching one of the numerous TV monitors in the box, which showed every play over and over again in slow motion. This solution, coupled with Ricardo's helpful advice on the rules of the game, made for a very pleasant day out.

Chapter Thirty-Three
When I Was Green

With over 25 years in show business behind me, I've had the privilege of working with some of the most talented, charming, charismatic, famous and downright gorgeous people imaginable. It may therefore come as a surprise when I declare that the best gig I've ever had was my 14-year long portrayal of the Green Cross Code Man.

It's true. That job remains the spiritual pinnacle of my show business career, and I know that, whatever the future holds for me, nothing will do more for me as a person than playing the Green Cross Code Man did. *Star Wars* gave, and continues to give, so much to be grateful for and so many of my memories and experiences throughout my working life are truly priceless, yet the Green Cross Code Man gave me something that no other job ever could. It allowed me to help save thousands of lives.

This is no exaggeration. I know, as do all those who were involved with the Green Cross Code campaign, that there are thousands of people alive today who would not be here if the Green Cross Code Man hadn't worked his magic. The Green Cross Code Man didn't invent a new vaccine or a solution to Third World hunger, and he didn't bring peace to war-torn nations, but in simply teaching children to cross the road safely he did make a huge difference. With over 40,000 children then being involved in traffic accidents annually on the roads of the UK alone, the intervention of the Green Cross Code Man was as necessary as any medical breakthrough.

I became the Green Cross Code Man back in 1976, the same year that my involvement in *Star Wars* began. The Green Cross Code, an updated version of the old kerb safety drill, had been introduced in 1971, when the Department of Transport decided to do something positive about the appalling road accident figures involving children. The old kerb safety drill required us to 'look right, look left, look right again' to check that it was safe to cross the road. As a system it was fine, but it had been around so long that its message was failing to reach the children of the 1970s. The country needed a new, more comprehensive, road safety code that the children could easily learn and put into practice.

When the Green Cross Code was formulated and introduced to the children of the UK, its effect was immediate and very encouraging. Every child in Great Britain was expected to learn and use the new code, and it was indoctrinated into parents, teachers, the police and young people's organisations throughout the country. Through road safety projects, backed by high-profile TV campaigns featuring popular sports and music personalities, the Green Cross Code began to make a real difference to the accident statistics and fewer children were being hurt and killed on British roads. This happy state of affairs continued until 1975, when a 'blip' in the figures showed a rise again in the accident rate. So much had been achieved by the Green Cross Code campaign that, quite rightly, the government deemed it imperative that no more ground should be lost. The cause of the blip had to be established immediately and a new strategy formulated just as quickly.

Quite how the Department of Transport's researchers arrived at their diagnosis I can't imagine, but they concluded that the messages given out by the various Green Cross Code advocates were becoming confused. By using so many different representatives, the campaign had clouded the issue and the children needed a clearer definition of what the Green Cross Code really meant. Thus, the Department of Transport made a decision. The Code would have one main message, given by one main messenger. This was the 1970s, the era that gave us *Superman* and *Star Wars*, so, not unnaturally, it was decided that the Green Cross Code messenger would take the form of a superhero.

The high-powered advertising agency, Ogilvy, Benson & Mather, was commissioned to come up with the character of the Green Cross Code Man, and by a stroke of good fortune my agent's husband was one of this agency's creative directors. Within days of the decision to cast a superhero in the role of the Green Cross Code Man, I was asked to meet the agency's photographers for an on-location photo shoot. 'On location' turned out to be the streets of Clapham, which at the time were nicely chilled by the worst that an English January could throw at them.

My provisional superhero costume wasn't likely to set the universe buzzing with intergalactic admiration, either. I was wearing a pair of cream-coloured flannel trousers, white canvas sneakers and a black sweater covered by a white singlet with a large green cross stuck on the front of it. I didn't look like a superhero at all. I looked more like a cross between a 1940s tennis professional and an orderly from the psychiatric wing of a trendy hospital.

My main props for that photo shoot were a couple of children hired by

Ogilvy, Benson & Mather from a model agency. Time and time again the local traffic would be held up to enable photos to be taken of me guiding these children across the road. Whether it was my glorious superhero costume, general interest in the safety campaign or anger at the cause of so much traffic congestion, I really can't say, but that shoot certainly attracted attention. Some of the locals thought that I was the first of a new breed of lollipop lady, and I had mums with prams and grannies with ancient little dogs on leads coming up to thank me for the great job I was doing!

Anyway, the mass of photos taken that day were thoroughly approved of by all that saw them and the concept of the superhero Green Cross Code Man was given the official go-ahead. Personally, I couldn't wait for the campaign to begin, and when my agent called I immediately asked her when I would be starting work as the Green Cross Code Man. "When you've passed the audition, Dave," came the reply, which I have to say made me less than pleased. I told my agent that, while I appreciated that her husband's agency had come up with the original concept, it was the pictures of me that had sold the idea.

Like any good agent, mine had her contacts, and after she'd called in a favour or two she phoned me back with the good news. The Green Cross Code Man job was mine, although I'd still need to attend the audition just to make everything look fair and above board with the officials from the Department of Transport. No problem, I thought. I can do auditions, especially when they're nicely loaded in my favour.

At the audition, about 20 big blokes turned up and all were interviewed by a selection panel of executives from the advertising agency and the Department of Transport. I was the final candidate to be interviewed and, after a protracted chat about the sort of work I'd done previously, we concentrated on talking about my own children and my attitude towards them in terms of road safety. The selection panel were obviously tremendously impressed with my answers, because I was given the job there and then.

The next hurdle I had to cross was working out how I was going to fit in the filming of the Green Cross Code commercials with the *Star Wars* project. I'd already started work on the film and my contract ran for the next five months, so if the Green Cross Code people needed me during that time George Lucas would have to be feeling flexible. If George said no, then there was nothing that I or anyone else could do about it. Sure enough, right in the middle of my *Star Wars* obligations, the agency wanted to shoot three TV commercials. Now what? Bravely, I passed this

particular buck straight to my agent and wished her luck in her negotiations with George. Either her powers of persuasion were at their peak
or George was in a generous mood that day, because the next thing I
knew was that George had agreed to my having the time off. The Green
Cross Code Man had been given his final green light.

Like the original photo shoot, the TV commercials themselves would
be filmed on location. Unlike my first portrayal of the Green Cross Code
Man, however, I wouldn't be dressed as Fred Perry meets One Flew Over
the Cuckoo's Nest. My tasteful green costume was pure superhero, with
a fetching pair of green tights below my body-hugging, long-sleeved
tunic. Accessories included a fine pair of shoulder extensions, green and
white gauntlets and compulsory superhero knee boots. My chest was
emblazoned with a huge green cross, and various smaller green crosses
re-emphasised the theme throughout the ensemble. All in all, the Green
Cross Code Man looked the part.

South London was chosen as the backdrop for the first three
commercials and all were considered extremely successful when aired
nationwide. As with everything that meets with success in the UK, the
Green Cross Code advertisements immediately attracted their share of
detractors and imitators. This is a fact of public life in Great Britain and
it is as tedious as it is predictable. First our media built an icon, and then
they set about demolishing it. We tend to resent success over here,
almost as though such a thing is un-British and slightly vulgar. I think
the Americans have got it about right. They prefer to celebrate success
and feel no overwhelming desire to drag their heroes through the dirt.

To be fair to the UK media of the day, the Green Cross Code Man was
given a decent shake, all things considered. In fact, it was a televised
series of indecent shakes that brought about the first negative publicity,
and for once I was totally blameless.

Thanks to a comprehensive TV advertising campaign, the popularity
and recognition of the Green Cross Code Man were both huge and
instant. He was a symbol of trust and dependability right from the first
broadcast. These two qualities are great sales points, of course, and it
didn't take long for the marketing men to cash in on them on the back
of our successful campaign.

First in the queue of rip-off merchants were Williams Furniture Stores,
who found themselves a Green Cross Code Man lookalike and featured
him in their TV commercials, prancing around among sofas and
sideboards. The imitation of my costume was good, but only on the
outside. What the impostor forgot was the essential 'control' mechanism

that allows large men to wear tights in such a way that the public isn't constantly reminded just how large and manly they really are. I am, of course, talking about a jockstrap. Thus, with no restraint save for the flimsy mesh crotch of his green tights to ... er .... soften the contours of what lay beneath, it was entirely possible to tell that the Williams Furniture Stores superhero was very probably Jewish. As he cavorted from dining set to dressing table, the main content of his tights responded to his movements like a conductor's baton, only bigger and more bendy. After a time lapse composed mainly of shock and disbelief, the telephone lines went into meltdown, with waves of protesting viewers launching accusations of lewd and obscene conduct at the advertisement. Apparently, amid the storm of protest there were small rafts of grateful ladies, who rang to express their gratitude and to enquire when the Williams guy was scheduled to show off his soft furnishings again. It takes all sorts, I guess.

Whilst the unrestrained impostor was jiggling his way to notoriety, another imitation Green Cross Code Man was launching himself on an unsuspecting public. I later discovered that he was one of my fellow auditionees for the role of the Green Cross Code Man. He had set himself up as 'Mr Safety', complete with costume, and was going around to schools and giving road safety talks. Not content with aping the success of our campaign, the bogus Mr Safety made it his business to declare the Green Cross Code Man positively lethal, and ranted on about how the commercials should be banned from the TV. Basically, Mr Safety was a deluded loser who had spite where his talent should have been, but his ravings about the commercials did make us examine them in minute detail. This, in turn, led to a change in our presentation, so at least he achieved something in his life.

The original commercials showed me magically appearing out of thin air to offer road safety guidance at the kerbside or to prevent an accident. Some children, however, rather than seeing these interventions for what they were, i.e. a very basic camera trick, really did expect me to zap out of nowhere to save the day and therefore saw no point in bothering with road safety. The credibility of the Green Cross Code Man had worked a little too well it seemed.

When it came to filming the second set of commercials, instead of ending them with the original mantra, 'Every time you cross the road - always use the Green Cross Code', we changed it to a new one, 'Always use the Green Cross Code - because I won't be there when YOU cross the road', thus switching the responsibility for accident prevention from me to the children and making the kids think for themselves. It was a simple and wonderfully effective change that made a great campaign almost perfect. Complete perfection wasn't quite on the cards yet, however, as it was decided to overdub my voice with that of an American. This was the first time my voice had been dubbed, but it certainly wouldn't prove to be the last!

The decision to dub my voice was due to my Bristol accent, which I prefer to call my warm and educated West Country burr. It has a distinctive, friendly little inflection, which I've always had and I've no intention of getting rid of it. Being an actor, it wouldn't be at all difficult for me to sentence my accent to death-by-elocution, but, unlike some in my trade, I'll never forget where I came from. Sadly, the officials from the Department of Transport decided that kids with strong accents of their own, from places such as the North East, Scotland and Birmingham, wouldn't be able to understand what I was saying, so they replaced my voice with what they referred to as a Mid-Atlantic accent.

Had the Department of Transport's fears about my vocal delivery held true, the planned nationwide tour of schools in the UK would have been quite a problem. I had visions of a voice-over specialist standing next to me during my safety talks and repeating everything I said to the kids in fake-American. As it turned out, I inflicted my own dear version of the English language on children from Carlisle to Plymouth, and not one of them said, "Sorry, Mister, I can't understand your stupid accent." Well, not to my face, anyway.

When that first tour came to an end the press officer from the Department of Transport reported that my message was coming over loud and clear in all parts of the country. Happily, whenever the Green Cross Code Man spoke, whether on TV or live, his body and voice from that time on were one and the same. He never forgot to wear his jockstrap either, I might add.

The response and effect of the Green Cross Code campaign seemed to grow by the day. My road safety superhero was now part of the consciousness of a nation and his creators were keen to keep it that way. I was immediately asked to sign up for another two tours of duty, only these were monsters, with the Department of Transport asking me to set aside no less than eight months out of the coming year to do them. Again, I faced a dilemma. With *Star Wars* ready to astound the world and the Green Cross Code campaign projecting me from every TV in Britain, I was about to hit the peak of my exposure as an actor. I knew that the offers would come in, and I also knew that if I was teaching kids to cross the road from one end of the country to another I'd have to turn those offers down. Yet the chance to do something as worthwhile and rewarding as helping children to avoid injury and death wasn't something I could turn down either. There was no choice to make really, so I put my own 'cross' on the Green Man's tour contract.

Nobody could have foreseen that the life of the Green Cross Code Man would stretch to 14 years, but stretch it did, and throughout those years the child casualty rates fell encouragingly. In addition to our extensive coverage of England, the road safety tours were extended to Wales and Northern Ireland, and on one memorable trip we travelled to Germany for a mini-tour of the British military bases over there. This became a regular feature and the last tour I did there was to Berlin, shortly before the demolition of its notorious wall united the people of East and West once more. That trip was eerie, steeped as it was in the repressive history of that divisive monument. As an athlete myself, my head swam with emotion as I stood inside the Berlin Stadium. This was the venue of the 1936 Olympics, where Hitler so disgraced himself with his Nazi ideals of an Aryan super-race by refusing to acknowledge the sporting supremacy of a black athlete by the name of Jesse Owens. Jesse ran a series of superb races all of his own, winning five gold medals for the USA. Hitler wouldn't shake the hand of Jesse Owens, but Jesse shook Hitler's entire world during those games, and I could still feel the vibrations as I stood there in awed silence, over 40 years later.

Right from the start of the Green Cross Code campaign I was determined to be much more than the big guy in the superhero suit. The job was always more than just another gig, and it became ever more important to me as the campaign progressed. I saw the success of what we were doing and I knew it saved lives, so whenever I had a spare hour or two between tours I would try to invent new ways of spreading the Green Cross gospel.

One idea I had was to make a record that kids could enjoy and learn something from and that could possibly raise funds for a children's charity I had in mind. By a huge coincidence, I was approached by a lady who announced herself as "Mrs Geraldo, widow of the Geraldo, the bandleader". She told me that she had a Green Cross Code song that she would like me to sing, with a view to making a record. After a brief chat about the proposed recording project, Mrs G delivered a demo tape, to which my own voice and those of a choir of children would be added if negotiations worked out to the satisfaction of all concerned.

I listened to the demo with interest and I quite liked it. Then, seeking the ultimate opinion, I played it to my wife, followed by my agent and a select group of listeners whom I knew I could trust to give me an honest opinion. Their opinions were favourable, so I contacted Mrs Geraldo to confirm my interest. She was delighted at the news and promised to come back to me with a contract proposal, which would obviously include the financial arrangements regarding any revenue generated by the record.

The prime purpose of making a record was always to spread and strengthen the road safety message to the children. Of secondary importance, but still a serious consideration, was making money for the charity, and if things went according to plan there was no reason why both of these goals couldn't be accomplished. Whilst waiting for Mrs Geraldo to return with her offer, I consulted some friends in the recording business to find out about the sort of profits-percentage deal I should be negotiating. My sources agreed that the going rate for the major artist on a recording was 10 per cent. That sounded fair to me, so I made it the basic bargaining point from which to sort out an arrangement with Mrs G.

The good Mrs Geraldo obviously hadn't consulted the same music business moguls that I'd used, because when she came back with her offer it amounted to one-eighth of one per cent! Someone had made a serious error in their calculations and, had I consulted just one of my recording industry contacts, I could have believed that the fault was mine. However, the chances of all five of my experts being wrong and Mrs G being fair and correct were about as slim as her chances of getting me to exploit the Green Cross Code campaign merely to line her pockets. Had Mrs G been a man, my rejection of her offer would have been slightly more 'robust', shall we say. As it was, I refrained from telling her to get stuffed, or worse, but I made it clear to the good lady that I was looking for a figure close to 10 per cent and that if her figures weren't revised radically there would be no deal and no record.

A few days later another call came in from the redoubtable Mrs G. Before revealing the extent of her financial rethink she told me that the studio, backing group and children's choir had all been booked for the following week, when she expected the recording to take place. Well, that was just fine, wasn't it? So, my rejection of her derisory offer in my firm but gentlemanly way had been taken as a definite yes and she'd steamed ahead and booked the recording studio. Perhaps I should have forgotten what my mother taught me about not using bad language in front of ladies, especially ladies who are plainly bonkers.

Eventually, Mrs Geraldo unveiled her new and improved offer, which had soared to the dizzy heights of one quarter of one per cent. It was now plain that Mrs G and I were not about to become a musical item, so I told her firmly that there was no deal or any chance of one in the future. Instead of accepting my refusal, she completely ignored what I'd said and told me that she expected to see me at the recording studio the next week. Flogging dead horses isn't my favourite pastime, so I left her to her delusion and put down the phone.

Days went by and nothing more was heard from Mrs G, until the date of the non-agreed recording session arrived. That morning I received a telephone call from an extremely irate Mrs Geraldo, who was demanding to know why I wasn't at the studio, where the choir and backing group were waiting to support me in my new recording venture. By now, I'd had more than enough of this weird woman's bizarre behaviour, but for one last time I held my temper and said, "Look, Mrs Geraldo, as I've already said as plainly as I can, your offer was nowhere near reasonable and I can't accept it. You wouldn't listen to me and went ahead and arranged the recording session anyway. It's not my fault, it's yours. Now go away and leave me alone." And, yes, I really did say "go away" rather than the phrase that first formed in my mouth.

Still as potty as ever, Mrs Geraldo screamed down the phone at me, hollering about how generous her offer had been, how greedy I was, and how she didn't need me anyway because she was going to make a much better record without me. I had no intention of replying to yet more of her nonsensical ravings, but before I could slam down the phone Mrs G got her slam in first. From what I heard, the unique Mrs Geraldo went ahead with her recording, sans Green Cross Code Man, although the eventual result never made it past the studio bin.

I eventually got around to making a record for the campaign, which featured me talking my way through a slightly shortened version of the Green Cross Code and then joining the children's choir to sing the jolly chorus of "Stop, look, listen and think", which eventually became the title of the song. It turned out to be a lot of fun to do and was a very successful vehicle for the campaign. One thing I did ensure was that the charity stood to collect 10 per cent of the profits.

When I took home the record I told my daughter that it was called 'Stop, Look, Listen and Stink'. With the uncluttered logic of a child, she told me that calling a song 'Stop, Look, Listen and Stink' was really stupid and that I was stupid to have come up with such a stupid name. "Not at all," I told her. "All we want you kids to do is to find a safe place to cross, then stop at the edge of the kerb, look all around and listen for traffic, then stand there and stink for a while. It's easy. Anyone can stink." She wasn't the least bit impressed and told me that I was 'really very stupid' to think that children would even sing the 'stupid' song, let alone stand by a 'stupid' road trying to make themselves stink. I had the giggles by now, and this just annoyed my daughter even more, with her now assuming the role of disapproving adult while I played the 'stupid' kid. Being with kids is great. Being a kid yourself is better still. That's why I still try to do it whenever I can get away with it.

My daughter may not have been keen on the swapping of 'think' with 'stink', but it made me laugh, so I included it in the finale of the very next road safety lecture I did. The kids loved it, especially when I played them the record and absolutely forbade them to say 'stink' when they sang along with the chorus. Of course, every little voice in the school, plus most of the teachers, I noticed, sang 'stink' as loudly as they could, and my Green Cross Code show ended with everyone laughing their heads off. The staying power of that 'stupid' little play on words was demonstrated years later, when I was presenting a Green Cross Code show at a British army school in Aldershot. Out of costume, I'd just arrived at the school and was making my way towards the school, when I passed two boys chatting. The eldest boy recognised me and began to tell his friend about my road safety show, and I heard the older lad say, "And then we get to sing that song, 'Stop, Look, Listen and Stink'!" I asked the boy how he knew what my show was all about, and he told me that he'd seen me do one when his dad was stationed in Germany, three years earlier.

It's been over 20 years since I hung up my road safety superhero costume, yet I still get regular requests to pull on my boots and get involved in all manner of Green Cross Code Man-type projects. More recently, I was asked by the EDF energy company if they could use a short clip from one of the Green Cross Code commercials to evoke 'nostalgia of the seventies'. Their ad featured quite a few clips from popular commercials of the time and mine was the first one - if you blinked, you missed it!

If sponsorship for a new Green Cross Code campaign could be arranged, I'd love to give it another go, albeit in a different role than last time around. One thing I'd really like to do is to take the Green Cross Code idea and turn it into a global phenomenon. I've already taken the programme to the USA as part of a tour on behalf of the National Organisation on Disability, and the Green Cross Code translated perfectly.

The American tour came about at the request of Eunice Kennedy, who is now Arnold Schwarzenegger's mother-in-law, of course. Eunice asked me to become involved in the Special Olympics movement, which led to my meeting with the National Organisation on Disability and eventually taking on the job of Master of Ceremonies at the annual general conference on Employment of the Handicapped, held in Washington DC. By the time I'd finished that tour, I hadn't a clue what charity I was supposed to be working for, but the important thing was that the children of the USA readily accepted the message of road safety carried by the Green Cross Code Man.

Once I knew that the Code was universal, I pushed like crazy to take it right around the globe. My plans for world domination fell slightly short, but not before I'd given talks to over 2,000 schools in 700 cities throughout the UK, Germany, the USA, Australia, Barbados and even the Cayman Islands. Over half a million kids heard my message and all but a handful of them were a pleasure to teach.

I did have the odd unruly brat to contend with, of course, and I couldn't conclude this chapter without recalling one or two of the less inspiring venues into which I carried the flag of road safety. To my intense embarrassment, after 14 years of touring, covering hundreds of thousands of miles, possibly the worst place I ever appeared in was my home town of Bristol, during a two-school visit that I'd been looking forward to doing for a long time. To bring things even closer to home, one of the schools in question was on the housing estate where I used to live and would have been my very own place of education had I not won a scholarship to Bristol Grammar School.

The details of that horrendous day are a combined blur of unbelievably disobedient children, apathetic teachers who'd lost the plot completely and an all-pervading feeling of frustration at my complete failure to pass on the vital message of road safety. At several points in that awful day I was more concerned for my own safety than anything else, as I struggled to establish any sort of order among a seething, itching, squabbling mass of juvenile delinquency. I swear that the combined resources of a three-ring circus would have found it impossible to entertain those children, yet there I stood alone, with 400 howling pupils and 45 of the most tortuous minutes ever endured by man in which to captivate and educate the horde.

By the time it was all over I was a spent and empty superhero, who felt anything but super. To add to the confusion and disbelief of that day, when I made it to the teachers' common room for a much-needed drink I was inundated with congratulations for the content of my show and for my incredible ability to keep the kids under control. These days, I'd have prescribed myself a hefty course of counselling to stave off post-traumatic stress after that. The fact that the teachers thought I'd kept the little monsters on their best behaviour confirmed for definite that they'd lost the plot; in fact, it's a wonder they could still function at all.

In defence of my beloved Bristol, I have to state that this wasn't the only place in which I found schools that appeared to specialise in producing children from hell. The town and its wayward school shall remain nameless, but it was a long way from Bristol and here the horrible children within it were mainly from well-off families. Once again, the teachers seemed powerless to stem the tide of indiscipline as their charges ran riot from first to last.

At one point, a little boy ran out from the audience and clamped himself to my leg like a monkey on a stick. This child clung on regardless and no amount of requests, orders, threats or attempts at dislodging was going to shift him. Whenever I managed to peel one bit of him off me, some other part would wrap itself around me even tighter. Incredibly, the entire school staff sat watching this, utterly unmoved, save for an occasional snigger as I staggered around the school hall trying to pretend that there wasn't a strange child attached to my leg. This ludicrous situation continued right up to the end of the show, at which point the school headmaster finally decided that it might be wise to unclamp the child from my leg and send him on his way.

Those tiny black spots could never taint the fantastic years I spent teaching children to be safe on the roads, however. And if you think I may have attached a little too much importance to my time as the Green Cross Code Man, consider the following statistics. When we began the campaign, over 40,000 British children were being injured or killed on the roads. By the time the campaign was over, that figure had been reduced by an average of 50 per cent per annum. That's 20,000 fewer accidents a year, over the course of 14 years, making a total of 280,000 fewer children involved in road traffic accidents in the UK alone. To save one life is a marvellous thing. To save thousands of lives produces a feeling like nothing else on earth. I say again, my role as the Green Cross Code Man was the best gig I ever had - and now I hope you can see why.

At the end of 1999 the Green Cross Code campaign received its three highest accolades. First, the TV ads were voted into the top 100 most memorable TV moments from the '70s, '80s and '90s in a poll conducted by Britain's *Sunday Observer* newspaper (we came in at number 63!) Second, BBC TV's Christmas Eve *Dale Winton Show* ran one of my Green Cross Code ads and it was voted number 10 in the Top 10 list of most memorable TV highlights of the '70s. Both these results were amazing, as public service commercials had never figured in the popularity polls before. Finally, I personally received the best possible accolade when I was awarded an MBE in the Queen's New Year's Honours List in 2000 for my services to road safety and charity.

So popular was the campaign that in February 2000 I was asked to get the Green Cross suit out of mothballs and front a campaign aimed at both motorists and children, sponsored by Vauxhall cars. The campaign was designed to make drivers more aware of the hazards of night driving and offered free lessons to drivers through the Institute of Advanced Motorists and also targeted the kids by offering them free reflective armbands and stickers so that they would be easily picked out by car headlights.

The campaign started off with a national photocall at Britain's most famous zebra crossing - the one outside the Abbey Road recording studios immortalised on the cover of The Beatles' *Abbey Road* LP. Following a press launch in London I then toured Great Britain, drumming up publicity and awareness for the campaign and doing press, radio and TV interviews in Bristol, Cardiff, Belfast, Glasgow, Newcastle and Ipswich. In each city I visited local schools and had the pleasure of showing them selections of the original Green Cross Code TV commercials. Further visits were arranged to Birmingham and Manchester.

I must say that I had certain qualms about putting on the Green Cross Code suit again after a ten-year lay-off. I couldn't make up my mind whether it was right for me, at 64 years of age, to be acting up like Superman again - albeit for such a worthy cause. Would the press want to take the mickey? Would the kids react in a positive way to the icon that their parents had grown up with? I needn't have worried. The press, radio and TV people turned up in their droves, all dying to see Darth Vader/Green Cross Code Man after his ten-year absence. The kids in the schools loved the visits and Vauxhall got the most wonderful send-off to their awareness campaign.

I've always said that saving children's lives is one of the most rewarding jobs I've ever had, and if I thought I could still be saving lives in another ten years' time, I'd be only too pleased to get the old Green Cross Code suit out once again.

Chapter Thirty-Four
A Gay Failure

When you're in the movie business you realise that most of your memorable experiences begin with a call from an agent. Here is one such incident that probably says something quite profound about me. I haven't a clue what it is, but I bet there's a swarm of amateur psychologists out there who would tell me.

I remember a period in 1973 when I was going through a particularly lean patch in my acting career. The only action my office telephone saw was me ringing out, mainly to check that my agent hadn't died. There was no film or TV work on offer and the only endorsements I had to my name were on my driving licence. Times were tough for the big guy from Bristol.

It is during such episodes of one's life that introspection takes hold. All actors are, to some extent, self-obsessed. They have to be to thrust themselves forward in the belief that the rest of the world will consider them worth paying to see. Public acclaim, the approval of one's fellow professionals and the odd positive remark from critics all serve to build self-esteem as sure as lifting weights builds muscles. Then a lack of work forces a break in this emotional weight training and that superbly honed body of self-regard begins to go flabby.

I began a dedicated fault-finding mission by staring into my office mirror. Why wasn't I getting offers? What's wrong with me these days? Is that a squint I see developing? Why hasn't Norma cleaned this mirror lately? Then I started to question my nose. Had it moved? Perhaps if it had been broken once or twice I'd look more rugged and I'd be first pick for the hard-man roles that my agent used to get me auditions for, in the days when I had no need to check that she was alive.

I'd had just about as much of this navel-gazing nonsense as I could take, when my contemplation was disturbed by the sweetest sound on this earth. The office telephone was ringing. It was my agent, alive and well, and functioning as an agent should. Sainted woman that she was - and obviously I'd never doubted her for a single second - she'd got me an audition for a West End play entitled *Boys in the Band*. Although I'd already decided that this glorious production was bound to rival *The Mousetrap* in terms of audience appeal and longevity, I hadn't a clue what the play was about, save for the fact that I would be required to read for a character called 'Cowboy'.

"A cowboy's good. I can do a cowboy." I repeated this mini-mantra all the way to my audition in the Charing Cross Road. There the assistant producer, a dauntingly camp young fellow who seemed to be playing a supporting role to the largest, droopiest moustache a human lip could accommodate, met me at the theatre. After an uncomfortable, damp handshake, he said, "So, Dave, you're up for our dear Cowboy are you?" I nodded, smiling cheerily through an inkling that life was about to throw me another of its little curves. "Well, that's lovely," continued the assistant producer. "Are you familiar with the storyline of the play at all?" I told him I wasn't.

He went on to explain that my involvement centred on a party that takes place in the play, where my character is hired as a sort of Cowboy-a-gram, as an amusement for the leading man. Now, I'm not normally stupid or even slightly slow on the uptake, but the penny that should surely have dropped at this point hadn't. The fact that it didn't was, I'm certain, due to the lack of pennies dropping into my bank account at the time and the optimistic desperation I was cultivating. Thus, I heard myself say to the ragingly camp assistant producer, "Well, I just hope he likes me." I was given the assistant's hand-dampened copy of the script and waved away to a quiet corner to read the scene in which my debut was to be made, provided I passed the audition, of course.

Two lines into the scene I discovered that *Boys in the Band* was a gay play. In fact, publicly and privately, the entire cast was gay and the part I was going for was not the sort of rootin', tootin' cowboy I'd envisaged. Oh, yes, Cowboy was scripted up to do some serious rootin', and he'd have no end of tootin' opportunities, too, from what I was reading - mainly because dear Cowboy was the lead actor's lover for the night. Great. There I was, starving for work, yet I was just about to turn down a perfectly valid role simply because I couldn't face a bit of simulated gay sex with a fellow actor. Come on, Prowse, call yourself a professional?

What I really called myself was 'scared as all hell', but to my immense credit I waved to the assistant producer to let him know I was ready to audition. He waved back and smiled. This did not help me at all. Still, I refused to give in to my ridiculous, unprofessional fears, so I walked over to him and announced my readiness to try out for 'Cowboy'.

"Ready to give your all, then, love?" said the camp assistant. His pantomime gay affectation made the word 'all' sound like 'hole', and I felt quite dizzy for the five seconds it took for my mind to replay and decipher what he'd said. "Yuh," I grunted, in my most manly voice, hoping that I would convey in that one syllable a deep regard for my wife, family, contact sports and all things heterosexual. "Good," said the gay PA. "He's ready and waiting for you."

In the play my grand entrance takes place when the party is in full swing and the leading man hears a knock at the door. Opening the door reveals me, as Cowboy, standing oiled and willing, clad in nothing more than a pair of micro-briefs and a ten-gallon Stetson. My first action is to step boldly into the party, gather the leading man in my arms and give him a massive snog, full on the lips. Simple. No problem at all. Just a matter of knocking, stepping and snogging. I could do that, and it had to be better than starving.

By the time the camp assistant had set up the first run-through, I'd convinced myself that this was a unique opportunity to increase my acting repertoire. Imagine the work I'd get when I became known for my ability to play gay roles as well as straight ones. Afraid? Not me. I was so very grateful for this wonderful chance to stretch myself, so to speak.

"Action!" barked the camp assistant. Rattity-tat! went the knocker. Everything was going so well. The leading man swung wide the door, I stepped forward, gathered him in my arms and, as he pouted in antici-pation, I lowered my lips to his, pausing scarcely an inch away from mouth-to-mouth contact. Then I paused a bit more. Then more pausing still, as seconds ticked by in trembling slow motion, until the actor in my embrace groaned, "Well, are you gonna kiss me or what?"

Sadly, it could only be 'or what'. I unfurled my arms and released my leading man, this gesture of defeat enacted to a disapproving chorus of gay tongue clicking and silently shaken heads. I'd failed to be the least bit gay. I was a gay failure. Sheepishly, I apologised for wasting everyone's time and told the leading man that it was nothing personal and that I simply wasn't ready for that sort of a challenge just yet. Then, avoiding another damp handshake from the assistant producer, I strode to the foyer, flung open the theatre door and immersed myself in the blessed sunshine and traffic fumes of the Charing Cross Road.

Chapter Thirty-Five
Meeting the World's Greatest
Bodybuilders

Due to my history of bodybuilding, weightlifting, weight training and Scottish Highland Games, I'm always being asked about any associations I've had over the years with the more famous personalities in the sports world.

Steve Reeves

My all-time bodybuilding idol was Mr America 1947, Mr World 1948 and Mr Universe 1950, the one and only Steve Reeves, who eventually went on to have a very lucrative film career in the old Italian *Hercules* movies.

I never had the opportunity of meeting Steve whilst I was actively competing and it was only a few years ago that an opportunity arose for us to meet up. I'd been to a celebrity autograph-signing convention in Los Angeles, which featured a lot of lesser-known or half-forgotten film 'stars', ex-Playboy bunnies of yesteryear and current 'Scream Queens'. To be honest, that sort of convention wasn't really my cup of tea. At the end of the show the organiser approached me, told me he'd appreciated my input and asked me if I'd like to go to his next show. I wasn't very excited about doing another show of this type and I didn't particularly fancy a weekend in New Jersey either, so I politely refused his offer. "Great pity," he said. "I wanted you to top the bill with Steve Reeves as your co-signer."

Just the mention of that magic name changed my mind immediately, and I couldn't get to the paradise location of New Jersey quick enough.

Steve had been to England the previous year to receive an honorary award for his services to the bodybuilding world, but unfortunately I'd been on tour and hadn't managed to link up with him. However, I'd been in touch with the organiser of the presentation to get his observations as to what Steve was like, and I was told that he was very pleasant but very quiet and he didn't seem to want to talk very much. I figured that now he'd reached his seventies he'd probably had enough of talking to idolising fans and maybe yearned for the quiet life.

So it was with some trepidation that I went to New Jersey to meet up with my idol after 40-plus years of hero worship. I first saw Steve in the hotel restaurant. He was with his wife and obviously didn't recognise me, so I didn't want to pester him over dinner. So there he was, sitting just a few tables away from me, and, after all those years of buying his photos and reading all the bodybuilding magazines in which he appeared and wrote, all I could do was sit and look.

The following day we were seated at our respective tables, only about 10 yards apart, both dealing with long lines of autograph hunters, and every so often we would look at each other and smile or grimace at the length of the queues. When things eventually died down, I went over to introduce myself. Standing in front of his table, we shook hands and he was kind enough to give me a selection of his photos, all of which he autographed and personalised for me. His wife joined in the conversation, and I couldn't help thinking how different he was to the description I'd been given. I then moved to Steve's side of the table and sat next to him. All of a sudden he seemed to go strangely quiet. I would ask a question or make some sort of statement and either it would pass without comment or his wife would give an answer. Then it suddenly dawned on me that Steve had a hearing problem and, unless I was standing in front of him so that he could lipread, he couldn't hear what I was saying. He was very complimentary about one of my physique photos from the Hammer Horror film *Vampire Circus* and also the monster photos from *The Horror of Frankenstein*. I went back to his table several times over that weekend, but I always made certain that we were facing each other. By the end of the convention we'd become the best of friends. Before going our separate ways we exchanged addresses, and I came away with an autographed copy of his new bodybuilding book, suitably inscribed of course. I still consider him the greatest physique that the bodybuilding world has ever seen.

Arnold Schwarzenegger
Lots of people ask me about my association with Arnold Schwarzenegger, whom I first met when he came to London from Munich as a 19-year-old to enter the National Amateur Bodybuilding Association's (NABBA) Mr Universe contest. Although he had a great physique, especially for his age, he failed to win the title, coming second to Chet Yorton. Back then, I thought him an arrogant young man - a first impression that was soon to change. The following year he came over again and won the contest, the first of many wins he had over the

ensuing years.

At the time, as a consequence of achieving the title of British Heavyweight Weightlifting Champion I was getting lots of requests to give exhibitions at physical culture shows up and down the country. Quite often I would find myself on the same bill as Arnold, who would be giving an exhibition of training and posing. Over the years we got to know each other really well and I'm pleased to say that the association has continued right up to the present time. I'm also proud to say that I was one of the judges at the last Mr Universe contest he won.

Lou Ferrigno

Lou Ferrigno is another bodybuilder I met in his very early days, when he came to London to enter the Mr Universe contest. Many years later that friendship was rekindled, culminating in his coming to England in 1998, together with his wife Carla and son Brent, to spend three weeks with me at my home in Croydon. We started meeting up at US conventions, and the two of us together attracted hordes of camera-toting fans.

I organised my own convention in the UK in September 1998 and invited Lou to be my major guest. I then organised a three-week tour of the UK, in which we both did seminars and signings in gymnasiums, health clubs and sci-fi sales. During that time, Lou introduced me to the delights of air rifle target shooting, a sport that has now become a major hobby for me and my two sons, Steve and James.

Tom Platz

Tom was famous as having the biggest thighs of any competing bodybuilder, and he had the rest of the physique to match. He came over to the UK to promote sales of his bodybuilding book and his public relations company asked me if I would look after him at my gym whilst he was in London and also if I could organise a seminar for him at the lecture hall of the London School of Economics. He was the world's most popular bodybuilder, so on the night of the seminar the hall was jam-packed. Just before 7.30 p.m., when Tom was due to start the seminar, I got a phone call from the PR people to say that he'd been delayed at the BBC, where he'd been doing a TV interview, and that he wouldn't be arriving until 8.30 p.m. So they asked me if I could entertain the audience for an hour.

Addressing an audience has never worried me, but the thought of having to do an hour of ad-libbing off the top of my head was a bit

301

daunting. As it happened, the crowd understood the situation and the following hour was one of the best I've ever spent in front of an audience. I chatted about anything and everything, including body-building, weightlifting, caber tossing, training famous people; in fact, anything I thought they might find interesting. I was enjoying myself with the audience so much that I was quite disappointed when Tom eventually arrived and I had to come off. Tom went on to a tremendous reception and did a seminar second to none. His posing brought the house down. As good as he was, however, at the end of the evening I was inundated with requests to do more seminars, as I was told that the hour spent listening to me was much more interesting that Tom's seminar.

Frank Zane
Frank Zane, another top bodybuilder, trained with me at my gym for a short while, which was an interesting experience. Frank had one of the world's great 'classical' physiques: good muscle size, perfect proportions and a beautiful poser. He's one of the most knowledgeable of bodybuild-ing writers, has numerous books to his credit and still manages to maintain a great physique, health and fitness the older he gets.

Lee Haney
Lee Haney has won the world's number one physique contest, the Mr Olympia title, more times than any other bodybuilding champion. He lives in Atlanta, Georgia, and a personal friend there - the former Secretary of State for Georgia, Max Cleland - introduced me to him.

I have digressed a bit, but Max arranged for us to meet Lee at a very nice restaurant in Atlanta, and for me it really was a pleasure to meet this icon of the bodybuilding world that had been undefeated in the major bodybuilding competitions for seven years. Lee is a very interesting man, who is deeply religious and says he puts complete trust in the Lord for everything. He has a wonderful gym at the police headquarters in Atlanta and has purchased (with a lot of help from the Lord) an old mansion, set in umpteen acres of land, that he is turning into a home for underprivileged kids. Listening to him tell the story of how he found the property and how, with the Lord's help, he overcame all the financial, political and social problems of setting it up is enough to turn any non-believer into a devout Christian. I pay visits to Lee's gym whenever I'm in the Atlanta area and the photos that Lee gave me used to grace the walls of my gym in London.

John Carroll Grimek

Although Steve Reeves was my idol in the physique world, there is one man who stood head and shoulders above everybody - the legendary John Carroll Grimek, who died in November 1998.

I didn't get to know John until well after his physique career had finished. John was the US Mid Heavy Weightlifting Champion and represented the USA at the infamous Berlin Olympics in 1936. He was the only person ever to win the Mr America title twice. (The judges thought he was so good that he could win it however often he decided to enter, so after he won it two years on the trot they brought in a rule that no competitor could win the title more than once.) He won Mr USA, Mr World and eventually the NABBA 1948 Mr Universe contest held in London in connection with the 1948 Olympics. John then retired from bodybuilding and weightlifting and started working for Bob Hoffman, the millionaire American publisher of *Strength & Health* and owner of the famous York Barbell Company. John was associated with the company for many years until his retirement and will always be remembered for his editorship of the York magazine, *Muscular Development*.

The first time I saw John he was outside a hotel in London surrounded by a whole host of bodybuilding fans. John was never a show-off, but he reluctantly obliged when somebody asked if he would roll up his trouser leg, revealing an enormous calf muscle that left all the onlookers in awe. I met up with John years later, when he was in his sixties. He came to London to receive an honorary award for his services to bodybuilding and, much to my surprise, he seemed to know as much about me as I knew about him. At that time he was having arthritic hip problems, but he was really worried about invasive medical intervention. He knew that I'd had operations on both my hips and was really inquisitive about the whole process: how long I took to recover, how long I was in the hospital, whether I was free of pain, whether my walking had improved, etc. My answers were all very positive about the operation, procedures and recovery and they seemed to put his mind at rest.

We kept in touch with each other and it pleased me no end when he decided at the age of 86 to go ahead and have the hip operation. I told him that if our Queen Mum could have hers done at 96 he had nothing to worry about. I tried to get him seen by my surgeon in Atlanta, Thomas Moore, but he said he'd have it done in his hometown of York, Pennsylvania. Unfortunately, his operation didn't go quite as well as my own and he experienced quite a lot of pain with it. Then, to make matters worse, he fell over and cracked the other hip joint, necessitating further hip surgery.

He was well on the way to recovery and was getting around really well when he developed fluid around the heart, suffered a massive heart attack and died on 20 November 1998. Angela, John's loving wife, came to see me when I was in York just after John's passing and gave me three great photos of him at his very best. John's son, daughter and grandchild all came to see me and it was wonderful to hear from them the esteem in which John held me. When somebody like John passes on, you always have regrets of some sort. I'm thankful that I had his friendship for 20 years, but oh how I wish I'd known him personally for a lot longer.

Chapter Thirty-Six
A Force for Good

In 1986 I suffered a bad injury to my hip whilst training at my gym in London. I was doing an exercise called the leg press, where you lie on a padded base inside two upright tubes and push a sliding platform loaded with weights with your feet. It really is the reverse of squatting or deep knee bends and it's a great leg strengthener and developer, as it doesn't put any strain on the lower back or make your gluteal muscles (your backside) any larger. I had quite a lot of weight on the machine (around 400lb) and was exercising merrily away when all of a sudden my right hip gave way and the weight came crashing down, pinning me to the machine base. I was rescued by my training partners, but on trying to stand up I found that I couldn't put any pressure on the hip or my right leg without experiencing the most excruciating pain. I eventually had to leave the gym hopping and supported on the shoulders of my mates.

I've had loads of minor injuries in my time and, as usual, I thought that with a little rest, a bit of massage and some heat-inducing ointment all would be well.

However, in this particular instance, there was an added complication in that within a couple of days I was contracted to do a tour of Nebraska, Iowa and North and South Dakota on behalf of The Centering Corporation, which is a bereavement counselling organisation run by two personal friends, Drs Marv and Joy Johnson.

When the time came to fly out of London, I was still in a lot of pain and was having great difficulty walking. However, I thought about all the work that Marv and Joy had put into organising the tour and couldn't bring myself to opt out at this late stage. So, against everybody's advice, I embarked on the tour. On arrival at Omaha airport I was in so much pain that I had to be taken off the plane in a wheelchair, so an urgent appointment was made for me to see a chiropractor. This treatment didn't help at all, despite repeated visits, and for the next three weeks I literally hobbled through my tour of the four states, doing radio, press lunches and dinners. The Governor of Nebraska, Kay Orr, officially welcomed me to the state at one lunch and at another I officially became a 'Big Red' when I was presented with my Nebraska Reds blazer.

We were nearing the end of the tour and were making our way back to Omaha (driving) when it was suggested that, as my hip was still giving me a lot of pain when trying to walk, I should go to see one of Nebraska's leading orthopaedic surgeons. This I did. At long last the hip was X-rayed and the surgeon pronounced that I had the start of an arthritic hip. I was about 50 at the time and, I thought, far too young to have arthritis, so on my return to the UK I started to read up on self-help for arthritics. As a result, with a lot of attention to diet (including liberal doses of fish oils) and sensible remedial exercising (no leg pressing!), I managed to get my hip functioning and pain free within about 18 months.

In 1989 I was in the gym one spring evening and started thinking about leg pressing again, as my hip by now seemed to be working perfectly. I started very gingerly, with relatively light weights, but soon got carried away with how good it felt and started, foolishly, to pile on the weights. You can guess what happened next. I was straining hard with a fairly heavy weight and, once again, I found myself trapped in the machine, unable to get the weight up no matter how hard I tried. I was eventually rescued again and, as before, I found I couldn't put my foot down on the floor without experiencing excruciating pain in my hip. My first thoughts were that I'd cured it once so I'd do it again, but this time all my efforts over the next couple of months were to no avail and I eventually found myself reduced to hobbling around with a walking stick.

It was during this period that I was invited to appear on the *This Is Your Life* tribute to Peter Cushing. Peter, who was quite frail towards the end of his life, came on the programme leaning heavily on a walking stick, and when I was introduced to him and the audience at the TV studio I was also sporting a walking stick. Peter roared with laughter and shouted, "SNAP!"

The weeks passed and I eventually decided to make an appointment with my family doctor, who sent me to see a rheumatologist who, in turn, arranged for me to see an orthopaedic surgeon. The latter took one look at the X-rays and told me that I now had a fully developed arthritic hip and the only remedy would be a replacement hip operation.

I enquired as to when I could have the procedure and was told that it would depend on whether I intended having it done privately or on the National Health (state funded health cover paid for through weekly/monthly salary deductions). Although I'd paid into the National Health scheme for the previous 40 years, I was told that I would have to wait for about two years if I went down that route, whereas if I paid for it privately I could have the operation immediately. This annoyed me intensely and is the reason why an increasing number of people in the UK are opting for private health care plans and companies specialising in this type of insurance are mushrooming. As I was, in theory, a staunch supporter of the National Health system, I said that I would opt for the National Health operation and so hobbled away to await the call, hoping against hope that I wasn't going to be incapacitated for the next two years.

Some weeks later I was reading a newspaper and came across an article entitled 'Major Breakthrough in Arthritis Research', which referred to work being carried out at the Royal National Hospital for Rheumatic Diseases in Bath, Somerset, not far from Bristol where I was born and brought up. I decided to telephone the hospital to find out if any of the research would be of benefit to me and spoke to the head of research, Professor Peter Maddison. As luck would have it, Peter turned out to be a big *Star Wars* fan. He recognised my name immediately and promptly invited me to visit the hospital, both to see the research labs and to meet the kids in the wards who were suffering from juvenile arthritis.

After an extensive tour of the hospital, lots of autograph signing for the kids and a working lunch, Peter asked me if there was any chance of my working on behalf of the hospital's charity, which was trying to raise millions for further research and new research laboratories, to which I readily agreed. The hospital put out a press release to say that I was now associated with them as one of their major fundraisers. The story was eventually picked up by a PR company specialising in medical and phar- maceutical publicity, who contacted me and asked if they could come on board and help, free of charge, in any way possible. After a succession of meetings between myself, the PR company and the hospital it was agreed that I would set up a charity under the auspices of the hospital charity and that we would all work together to get the right sort of media access, the all-important publicity and the even more important funds.

We formed the charity and called it Dave Prowse's Force Against Arthritis. I continually pushed the PR people for an official date when the charity would be launched to the media at a big press conference in London.

Finally a date was agreed and the chosen venue was the prestigious Queen Elizabeth Halls right opposite Westminster Abbey and the

Houses of Parliament. I arranged for various 'celebrity' friends to come and support me on the day and the reception really got the Force Against Arthritis off to a flying start. The hospital was excited about the publicity we'd attracted, the press coverage was fantastic and Shire Hall, the PR company, had lots of follow-up ideas. One of the things they'd arranged was charity sponsorship by the world's largest producer of cod liver oil, Seven Seas, as cod liver oil was the only non-medical remedy for arthritis that was endorsed by the Bath Institute.

However, within days our bubble of euphoria was set to burst when, out of the blue, we became the victim of a scathing attack by one of the other arthritis associations in Great Britain - Arthritis Care. Their director, Jean Gaffin, who had in the past been very supportive of what I'd been doing for the arthritis cause (I'd even helped them launch their Arthritis Care weeks on several occasions), suddenly launched a vitriolic attack on me, the charity, the hospital and Seven Seas. All this came about because Shire Hall, without knowing any better, had arranged the launch of Force Against Arthritis during what was designated as Arthritis Care Week, and for some reason she thought we were trying to muscle in on her territory.

The major focus of Jean Gaffin's attack was the sponsorship by Seven Seas Cod Liver Oil, which she thought was positively criminal. What she failed to mention was that Arthritis Care had commercial sponsors, too, one of which - New Zealand Green Lipped Mussel - was scoffed at by the Bath Institute Research Department as having no scientific foundation whatsoever. Her attack sounded the death knell in terms of my association with the Bath Institute, Seven Seas and Shire Hall, all of whom were frightened to death of adverse publicity. I was politely informed that due to the bad press they could no longer afford to be associated with 'The Force'.

So, there I was, left with an organisation that had no public relations, no sponsor and no major cause to work for, all because of a simple mistake on the part of the PR agency.

I obviously wanted to continue my work for arthritis research. The more you discover about the disease, the more widespread you find it is. For instance, in the UK alone:

* 15,000 children suffer from juvenile arthritis.
* 80 million working days a year are lost because of rheumatic or arthritic conditions.
* One in four people who visit the doctor have rheumatic or arthritic

complaints.
* Only one in four doctors have any exposure to rheumatism or arthritis in their training.
* 98 per cent of the population will suffer from rheumatism or arthritis before they die.

The facts are horrifying, aren't they?

Within days of the whole project blowing up and everybody bowing out I received a phone call from the Director of Orthopaedics at the Institute of Orthopaedics at Oswestry, a major hospital on the England/North Wales border. He said that he'd heard about the problems I'd been having with Arthritis Care and asked if I would like to become associated with their appeal. They were trying to raise £2.75 million for the establishment of a new Arthritis Research Centre. As a result of this approach, Force Against Arthritis started working under the auspices of the charity appeal of the Institute.

As for my own condition, I soldiered on though 1989, chasing all round the UK and touring the USA to give road safety talks at schools and attending sci fi and horror conventions. Walking was very painful all through the year, but I was determined to fulfil my commitments.

I was still attracting a lot of publicity and getting good press about my Green Cross Code work, and as a result of one article in particular, which told the world about my hip problem, I received a phone call from a very well known orthopaedic surgeon in the UK - Mr Khalid Drabu. He said he'd been reading all about my arthritis problems, was a big *Star Wars* fan and wanted to know if he could do my hip replacement operation for me straight away. It was August and I was due to embark on my biggest Green Cross Code tour ever on 11 September, so he said he would wait until that was over and do the operation for me in the middle of December.

During the three months of the tour he got hold of all my X-rays and after studying them he decided that he shouldn't proceed with an operation until I'd had extensive tests to determine the state of my joints and the level of bone deterioration. It was arranged for me to go into Guy's Hospital in London, two weeks before Christmas, where just about every test imaginable was carried out, including a brain scan to see if I was suffering from agromelia (giantism!)

At Guy's I met up with two surgeons, John Spencer and Richard Munn, both of whom advised against a hip replacement operation until the results of the tests came through. Even after three weeks of extensive tests they were still not convinced that my hip joint would accept the new hip prosthesis, so it was decided to 'exhibit' me at a symposium of surgeons that was being held at the hospital. Over 50 surgeons from all over the UK listened to my case history, studied my scans and X-rays, and poked and prodded me around - at the end of which it was generally agreed that the hip replacement operation was a going concern but that, because of my relatively young age, a screw-in rather than a cement replacement should be carried out.

Within three weeks I was in hospital at Guy's and the replacement hip operation was carried out by Richard Munn, ably assisted by John Spencer. All went well with the recovery until the day before I was due to be released, when I was asked by the Professor of Neurology if I would go before a doctors' panel to be studied. I was taken by wheelchair to the study room and sat on a high gurney trolley. All through the study my hip felt peculiar and I was pleased when it was all over and was able to be wheeled back to the ward and put back into bed.

I hadn't been in bed for more than a few minutes when I suddenly felt my hip go 'POP' and the whole joint dislocated. There wasn't much pain when it came out, but there was a major panic on the ward and Mr Munn was called in to decide what to do. However, before he could do anything I had to be taken to the X-ray department to find out exactly what it now looked like, and that was when the pain really started in earnest. All the lifting in and out of bed and on and off trolleys caused absolute agony.

When I got back to the ward Richard Munn said they were going to relocate the hip there and then, while I lay in the bed. He gave me an injection, which must've put me out straight away. The next thing I remembered was coming out of the anaesthetic to find my right foot in plaster and tied to the end of the bed, with a big triangular pad between my legs to keep them apart. "Well that's you for the next three weeks," said Richard. "That'll give the internal scar tissue time to heal."

And so began one of the most boring three weeks I can remember. Imagine, if you can, being on your back, unable to twist or turn, unable to get out of bed even to go to the toilet, in fact unable to do anything but lie there for a whole three weeks. I eventually got up again 21 days later, only to be told that I had to spend the next three months on crutches. When I came out of hospital I was dying to get back to working at the gym, not necessarily to train but mainly to get my hands on the helm of business again. I'd been asked not to drive and I'll always remember going home and going out to sit in the car. I'd only been away from it for about six weeks, but I must say that I felt very uncomfortable and completely lacking in confidence - driving myself was completely out of the question. I then got my wife to drive me to the gym and once there I discovered that during my absence from the previous September, when I'd gone off on the Green Cross Code tour, until now - the beginning of April, the gym had found itself in a terrible financial plight. My only alternative to closing the gym was to run it on my own, thus drastically reducing the overheads.

My gym was in a very old building in South East London and the business operated on five floors with no elevators. I retained the cleaner, but the manager and the instructors all had to go, and for the next three months I had to run the place on my own, opening at 10 a.m. and closing at 10 p.m., five days a week plus a Sunday morning session. The gym had a press-button door-entry system and phones on each floor, so I placed an exercycle right next to the phone and the door buzzer, cycled merrily away all day and controlled everything from that position. I literally cycled dozens of miles every day on the bike, and of course my hip and leg got stronger and stronger as a result. I could manage without my crutches within a few weeks and was soon driving competently, so the only question mark hanging over me was the state of my left ankle, which was appearing to get more and more disjointed as the weeks went by.

The arthritis saga continued.

Some months later I was doing some floor exercises at the gym when the phone rang. I sprang up off the floor to answer it and suddenly there was a 'CRACK' from my ankle. I subsequently discovered at Guy's hospital that I had sustained a hairline fracture of the fibula (calf bone). An elasticated bandage was applied by the Guy's staff, which I kept on for about a week, and that was all the treatment I received. From the time that the bandage was removed I've never been able to walk properly on that ankle.

I eventually decided to go back to see John Spencer at Guy's about my condition. I told him that I was very concerned about my ankle and the fact that I couldn't walk properly anymore. He told me in a very matter of fact way that I basically had four options open to me:

1) I could carry on as I was, have nothing done and hope that ankle surgery techniques improved over the next few years, at which point a replacement ankle joint might be a possibility.
2) I could wear a support calliper.

3) I could have the ankle joint fused, which would give me a stiff ankle.

Or ...

"What's the fourth?" I asked.

"Well," he said, "we could do a below the knee amputation and give you a false leg and foot. This way you would be walking around on your false leg within about four to six weeks. You'd be a lot more mobile than you are now."

It didn't take me long to work through the options and plump for the calliper. Whilst you've got your leg and foot there's always the possibility of a cure. If you've lost those limbs you're never going to grow new ones.

Once the replacement of my right hip had been carried out and my left ankle had been restrained in the all too familiar grip of a calliper, I thought my medical future was assured. The following eight years of my life were just waiting to prove me wrong.

Things began well, with my right hip now pain free and functioning normally. The calliper on my ankle was a mechanical attempt to keep the ankle joint correctly aligned and, although the site of the break was a bit unsightly, I was managing to get around well enough. I had a barely discernible limp, which I could disguise completely when necessary, and my trouser leg covered the calliper's unsightly steelwork, which anchored the structure into my shoe heel. I was a walking marvel of medico-mechanical engineering.

Then, with no prior warning, a call came through from the giant Hasbro toy corporation, who had the *Star Wars* merchandise contract. They wanted to know if I was available to reprise the Darth Vader role for a new computer video game called *Rebel Assault 2*. I told the Hasbro people that I'd love to play Vader again and a most encouraging contract was negotiated.

This was all too good to be true, of course. Before the ink was dry on the contract, Hasbro got in touch to say that the Lucasfilm people had heard I was walking with a limp and had insisted that I take a screen test. Thus, I was faced with the absurd proposition of taking a screen test to decide if I was suitable to recreate a role that I'd created in the first place. I said that I had no problems with the test and so Hasbro came to my gymnasium to film me. I thought that I'd put everyone's mind at rest - including my own - as I walked, strode and stomped around in true Darth Vader fashion, my calliper lending its support with total invisibility.

Hasbro were happy with the test, but then the filmed footage was sent off to Lucasfilm in San Rafael, California, where they promptly rejected it, saying I was limping too badly. Hasbro called again, telling me, "We definitely want you to do the Darth Vader role, so will you please take another screen test but this time, please, please don't limp." Once again, the film unit turned up at the gym and again I strutted my Vader stuff all over the place to the complete satisfaction of all present. Fortunately, this time I'd also satisfied Lucasfilm and I clinched the part.

Filming took place in a studio in North West London and the set was a recreation of the corridor on the Death Star, as seen in *Star Wars*. Determined to capture the essential magic of *Star Wars*, the film company had lured lighting cameraman, Gil Taylor, out of his retirement on the Isle of Wight to light the set exactly as he'd done in the original movie. They'd also arranged to have the Darth Vader suit sent over with a dresser from Lucasfilm, and supplied me with a voice tape of James Earl Jones doing all the dialogue, which I subsequently had to learn and then act in time with it. The schedule was very tight - we only had the Monday, Tuesday and Wednesday to shoot the entire 50 minutes of film, as I was under contract to fly out to the USA on the Thursday. We worked each day from early in the morning till way past midnight, but in the end we achieved everything that Hasbro desired, so I headed off to America on the Thursday exhausted but satisfied that I'd done a good job.

Everybody on set was very excited about working with me and I had many photos taken with the various Hasbro executives who came in to watch the shoot. The fellow who accompanied the suit over from San Rafael also had a brief to take still photos of the shoot, and Hasbro employed their own photographer to take photos, too. What amazed me at the time was the difference in attitude between this shoot and shooting *Star Wars*. Whereas in 1976 no one was allowed to take any photos of me getting into or out of the suit, this time the photographers seemed to have a completely free hand, with no restrictions whatsoever. I was very pleased some months after the shoot when the official *Star Wars* magazine, *Star Wars Insider*, published the first ever authorised photo of me actually holding the mask and helmet under my arm, so that the whole world could at last see the real Darth Vader unmasked.

Although the calliper was supposed to keep my ankle straight, it was obvious every time I took the contraption off that my ankle was getting increasingly disjointed and very soon I would have to consider some form of surgical intervention. Years previously, when touring Scotland with the Green Cross Code campaign, I'd met a wonderful American family from Atlanta while visiting Culloden, the site of the last battle between the Scots and the English. Butch Schmitt was touring with his lovely wife Yvonne and their three kids as a graduation present for their daughter Evie. Butch turned out to be one of the foremost paediatric surgeons in the USA and over the ensuing years we became great friends. Somehow he heard about my ankle problems and the possibility of an amputation and he invited me over to Atlanta to meet up with his orthopaedic surgeon friends to see if anything could be done about saving my ankle and foot. Knowing American medicine, the first thing I queried was the cost, but I was told not to worry about it at that stage.

So off I went to Atlanta to see Butch, who took one look at the disjointed ankle and promptly called in his colleague, Thomas Moore, an ankle specialist at the Emory Clinic - Atlanta's best. Tom examined my ankle and said there would be no problem saving the joint and foot, but it would mean an ankle fusion. I readily agreed to this procedure, which would be carried out the following Tuesday, and I was told that all surgeons' and hospital fees would be waived, i.e., it would all be done for free. It was a tremendous feat of engineering to break the ankle joint and rebuild it with all sorts of pins and bone grafts. Within five days I was released from hospital in a walking plaster, and off I went to Los Angeles to do a weekend convention, which amazed everybody.

The plaster was eventually removed and replaced with a new one whilst I was in LA, something that Dr Moore had arranged with an associate from his medical school days, who just happened to be one of the world's foremost authorities on osteoporosis. He gave me a beautiful, new, black plaster - something I'd never seen before - and said that the only remuneration he required was an autographed photo for the consultancy wall.

The next thing on the arthritis calendar was that I soon started getting trouble with my left hip. Walking with a fused ankle had probably put undue pressure on the hip and that, too, was now turning arthritic and walking was becoming more and more painful. Once again I contacted Dr Moore in Atlanta and an appointment was arranged approximately a week before the world famous Dragoncon in Atlanta - the world's largest fan run charity convention, which regularly attracts over 20,000 fans over the 4 July weekend.

At the appointment I underwent some X-rays, which confirmed the worst - the hip was arthritic. Dr Moore once again offered me an immediate operation, all 'on the house'. I went into hospital on the Monday, had the replacement surgery on the Tuesday, was up sitting on the edge of the bed on Wednesday, was in a walking frame on Thursday, was walking on crutches on Friday and was released on Saturday. I went straight to work that weekend, doing autograph signings in toy stores and bookshops around Atlanta. I knew I had to take things easy, but I couldn't see any problem just sitting around signing autographs. What I hadn't taken into consideration, however, was the getting in and out of cars and the walking to and from stores, all of which, with hindsight, was foolish considering I'd had a major hip operation only five days earlier.

All went well the following week. I took things fairly easily (for me!) as Dragoncon opened on the Thursday. Both Dr Moore and Butch Schmitt came in with their families to see me signing and to make sure I wasn't doing anything stupid. They went away not wholly convinced.

On the Saturday night we all got invited to the convention banquet at which the world famous sci-fi author Clive Barker would be giving a talk. It was a buffet meal and during the main course Clive started to address the throng. At that point I decided to go and get my dessert, so that I could then sit and listen to Clive speaking, and on my return to the table, as I went to sit down, my hip popped out of joint.

To say that the pain was excruciating would be an understatement - I was in agony. The metal prosthesis had come out of its housing cup in the pelvic joint and had gone up into the muscle of my backside. Everybody in the banqueting room heard me scream out when it happened and numerous people came rushing to my aid. Film director Fred Olen Ray was supporting me in the chair, as I had to lie back and try to keep my body rigid in order to relieve the pain. Gunnar Hansen (Leatherface in *Texas Chainsaw Massacre*) was at my feet, trying to hold my leg still, whilst others were chasing around phoning 911 for the emergency services.

By dialling 911 you get the lot, so the Fire Department, Police and Ambulance Service all arrived on the scene. I was eventually lifted onto a stretcher and carried away in an ambulance, back to the Emory Clinic to have the hip relocated. Although it was all very traumatic at the time, I look back at it with a certain amount of humour. Even with all this turmoil going on, not once did Clive Barker stop during his talk. I've often wondered what he was thinking. The hip joint was relocated under anaesthetic and a couple of hours later I was walking out of the hospital and back to my hotel. The emergency treatment was not 'on the house' and the total cost of the relocation was $1700 - which, fortunately, was covered by my medical insurance.

A week later, this time in Chicago, I was having dinner in a Chinese restaurant, and on trying to extricate myself from the booth in which I was sitting I dislocated my hip once again. All the emergency services turned up, as before, and I was rushed into hospital for yet another relocation procedure. Again, as soon as it was back in place and the effect of the anaesthetic had worn off, I walked out of the hospital.

The last time my hip went was about ten days later, while I was still in Chicago. I was sitting on the edge of the hotel bed and wasn't doing anything untoward, just wiggling my foot in order to ease it into my shoe without bending fully, when out it popped again! This time it wasn't anywhere near as painful, but one of my legs was now three inches shorter than the other. I called the front desk to see if they could send anybody up to help me. The reception manager duly arrived and I explained to him that I had a hip dislocation. Stupidly, I thought that if I could get him to pull my leg out we might be able to pop it back without all the rigmarole of going back into hospital. He refused point blank even to touch me and phoned for an ambulance straight away. So I had to go into hospital for yet another relocation job.

I came home from America walking comfortably on the hip that had been giving me all the trouble. However, within a week of being home, I suffered yet another dislocation, once again while trying to put on my shoes. The ambulance service arrived and had terrible problems getting me down the stairs from my bedroom on a stretcher, but they eventually got me into Mayday Hospital in Croydon and the hip was relocated by one of my consultant surgeons, Mr Fadhil Kashif. X-rays of both hip joints were taken and I think they came to the conclusion that I was getting the hip dislocations because of the angle and the shallowness of the hip cup joint. They didn't want to do anything about it, however, since it would right itself eventually and dislocations would then became a thing of the past. Mr Kashif did have some bad news: the hip replacement done ten years earlier was now getting loose and, in his view, it would have to be replaced very soon.

So it was that in August 1998 I went into Mayday Hospital to have a replacement replacement (!) of my right hip. It was explained to me that this would be a major operation, as getting the old prosthesis out would be a difficult procedure. However, my consultant, Mr Miller, was confident that with the help of Mr Kashif and an American consultant, who was coming over from Florida to be in on the operation, all would be well.

The operation did turn out to be a major one. The femur had to be split and extensive bone grafts were made to the hip, but fortunately the whole process was pain free and I was looked after admirably during my five- day stay in the Mayday University Hospital.

When I actually got on my feet, however, I was in for a bit of a shock. My right leg, housing the new prosthesis, was about 2½ inches longer than the left! Mr Miller said that this was intentional and that he expected it to settle to an acceptable length - something that has never happened. In an effort to walk properly I've had to undertake a series of experiments in order to get the left shoe built up, so that I don't walk with a 'John Wayne' rolling gait!

More trouble was to follow when I went to Austria (Graz) to be the guest of honour at the World Power Lifting Championships, where I was to be made 'A Legend of Weightlifting' by the World Power Lifting Association. I was there with my friends from the South African team and I met up with their chiropractor and their masseur, both of whom remarked how badly I was walking and asked if they could take a look at me. I submitted willingly to their probing and was eventually told that the muscles of my hip had been cut about and that I needed stretching and mobility exercises. I was shown one that involved lying on my back with one knee up and then pulling the leg across to stretch the hip muscles. I forgot completely that the worst possible thing one can do with artificial hips is to do anything that involves crossing the legs.

The following morning I woke up very early and was lying in bed trying to decide whether it was time to get up, when I decided to try the exercise suggested by my South African friends. Lying flat on my back, I caught hold of my knee, pulled it gently across and promptly pulled my hip completely out of joint. Once again, panic stations. I was raced off to hospital for a relocation job yet again. I fully expected to walk out of the hospital, as before, only to awake to find my leg encased in plaster, with a two-foot rod running through it to stop me twisting and turning. Worse still, they wanted me to have at least a week in Graz and I was booked to fly home that very day. Hasty calls to my medical insurers got a nurse flown out to Graz and eight seats taken out of a British Airways flight back to London, whereupon I was whisked back into Mayday Hospital for a relocation job. I don't know whether I feared the wrath of my wife Norma or the wrath of Mr Miller most. Both thought I'd been stupid to do what I'd done, which was true. The hospital wouldn't release me until I'd had a hip and thigh brace made, which ensured that I was never going to twist and turn again during my recovery period.

Obviously the arthritis problem is not going to go away; in fact as I get older it is probably only going to get worse. Through it all, however, I've tried not to let it stop me from doing anything. I travel all over the world and train at least three to four times a week, working around my obvious arthritis problems, and people all over the world contribute to the arthritis charity by purchasing autographs and signed *Star Wars* memorabilia.

Although the arthritis charity is closest to my heart, because I'm an actual sufferer, I'm now involved in quite a few other charities, such as Action Research, The Multiple Sclerosis Association, Comic Heritage and various cancer charities, and not a day goes by without getting letters asking for autographed photos for school fêtes, local charities, etc. For years I donated to everything, whereas now I'm a bit more selective. Although I still donate a lot to the charities I support, I am helped by the money that comes in from charging all the fans who write in for freebie photos and autographs.

I'm hanging in there, living life to the full, holding the arthritis at bay and hoping that in some small way my experiences and story can provide inspiration to fellow sufferers worldwide.

The arthritis and my hip and ankle problems have all brought me tremendous publicity. When my hip dislocated in hospital it made the centre spread of the biggest daily newspaper in Great Britain - they even published pictures of the X-rays of the dislocated hip joint! Every time an article appears about me in the press it seems to inspire people to write to me, either about similar problems they've had or, more often than not, to offer help, prayers and advice. My arthritis seems to have moved people worldwide and the prayers that have issued forth from friends and fans alike have touched both my wife and myself deeply.

Chapter Thirty-Seven
Car Crazy

I have always been a huge car enthusiast, and one of my Grosvenor House clients shared my enthusiasm. Hilary Floyd, one of London's foremost fashion designers, had a passion for classic Jensen cars and I persuaded her to sell me her old CV8. It had been stored in a garage in the country and its condition had started to deteriorate. The engine and bodywork were still good, but the paintwork and interior upholstery needed a lot of attention.

I set to work restoring it to its former glory, changing the colour from brown to a beautiful black cherry and having it re-upholstered at the same time. Then, before I'd even driven the revamped car, I received a substantial offer for it that was too good to refuse, so off it went to a new owner.

Hilary went off to America to pursue her career, but a few years later I received a phone call from her to say that she was back in the country and enquiring whether I would be interested in buying her other Jensen, which was stored in a garage in North London. I went to view the car, bought it and then arranged for a garage in Southwark that specialised in resprays to change the colour from gold to metallic maroon.

I picked up the car after an evening session at my gym in Marshalsea Road. It looked magnificent. I proudly started the journey home, but it wasn't long before the water temperature rose rapidly and steam started pouring out of the bonnet. Not being mechanically minded, I hadn't a clue how to sort out the problem, other than to refill the radiator with water. After about the sixth refill I decided to call the RAC, only to discover that I'd lost the bottom radiator hose and, as it was a classic Jensen, it couldn't be repaired there and then. So I had to suffer the indignity of being hoisted up onto a trailer and delivered home.

News spread about my latest classic purchase, however, and I soon received another offer I couldn't refuse, from a dentist. Years later, when I was signing autographs at a *Star Wars* show, a gentleman came up to my table and showed me a photo of the car, which he'd subsequently purchased from the dentist. As with all real car enthusiasts, he wanted to know as much as possible about the car, so I was able to fill him in on its history.

Another car enthusiast and spasmodic member of my gym was Geoffrey Robinson, Labour MP for Coventry NW from 1992 to 2005. I'd seen him around the pool and sauna, but he never seemed to come in to train, so he was something of a nameless member to me to begin with.

However, I got a surprise one morning, when I arrived to find him exercising away merrily. So we quickly got into conversation about what sort of training programme he should be following, although I still didn't know who he was. The conversation then got around to one of my favourite subjects - cars, and he asked me what sort of car I drove. At the time I'd just returned from Germany after an autograph signing session with Caroline Munro for Jens Reinheimer, a good friend and Hammer Horror fan. Jens' mother had kindly loaned us her car, a Mercedes 300 SEL left-hand drive. I'd found it to be the nicest, most comfortable car I'd ever driven, so I'd asked if I could buy it from her, to which she agreed. When I proudly told him that this was the car I was driving, he said, "Why on earth do you want to drive a German car? Why don't you drive an English one?" I made some lame excuse and told him that I'd really fancied the new British-made Jaguar XJ12 but it was way out of my price range (around £15-20,000 at that time).

Nothing further was said and once training was over we went our separate ways. A couple of days later, as I walked through the hotel car park, I spotted the car of my dreams: an olive green XJ12 with a dark green leatherette roof. When I'd stopped drooling I made my way to the gym and found Geoffrey training hard.

"I've just seen my dream car in the car park," I enthused, "the XJ12 two-door coupe."

"It's mine," Geoffrey responded.

"How did you come by one of those," I asked.

"I just happen to be the managing director of Jaguar," he revealed. "My name is Geoffrey Robinson. Would you like me to get one for you?"

"You've got to be joking!" I laughed. "There's no way I could afford it."

"Leave it with me," said Geoffrey. "I'll see what I can do for you."

I thought that would be the last I heard about it. However, true to his word, Geoffrey called to say that there was a demo model going through the racing department at the factory and I could have it for £2,000 if I wanted to go over and collect it. I couldn't get to Coventry fast enough!

I was met at the station by Geoffrey and the Jaguar sales manager and as we walked to the station car park I was looking everywhere for my XJ12. We stopped by a fantastic looking red sports car, which had the makers' name covered with sticky film. It was Jaguar's new and still very secret sports car, the XJS, and to my delight I was invited to drive it back to the factory. I moved off very carefully and felt exhilarated by the power of the car. I was even more excited when they invited me to drive it back to Jaguar's premises on the motorway, so that I could experience the extent of the car's power. At one stage of the journey the speedometer rose to 145mph, but they both thought the car seemed sluggish! Perhaps having three large men in the car had something to do with it. Finally, we arrived at the factory and I paid for my beautiful XJ12. Driving back to London in it was like floating on air.

I kept my XJ12 for quite a few years and resigned my Mercedes to life in a garage, as left-hand drive cars are difficult to sell. Then a car dealer friend, whom I trained with at Grosvenor House, told me he had a potential buyer for the Jag in Australia, so I decided to let it go and brought my Merc back out of retirement. I loved the Merc, but it was a very thirsty beast. So, as an economy measure, I decided to convert it to LPG, giving me the option of running it either on gas or petrol. The only problem was, at that time, very few garages sold LPG.

The Merc served me well for several years, until one day, whilst driving through Beckenham, I noticed flames licking out from under the bonnet. It was about 11.30 a.m. and I was in the middle of the road, approaching a busy roundabout at the time, but my only thought was to get out of the car as quickly as possible, so I abandoned it. I had visions of the fire spreading to the huge gas tank in the boot. Somebody called the fire brigade, who arrived within minutes and doused the blaze, but I'm afraid that was the end of my car and it had to be sold for scrap.

Another friend and car enthusiast, whom I met through my association with Harrods and Grosvenor House, was Lou Reizner. I didn't realise when I first met him that he was the manager of rock group, The Who. He and his wife had a very nice flat in Knightsbridge, at the entrance to Hyde Park, where I visited from time to time.

Lou owned a Rolls Royce and a Citroën Maserati, a prestige two-door coupe sports car with a unique air suspension system that kicked into action on ignition - a great experience, like floating on air.

I hadn't known the Reizners very long (but long enough to be regarded as a good friend) when Lou's wife rang to tell me the tragic news that Lou had died (June 1977). Lou had told her of my interest in the Citroën, so she said that it was mine if I wanted to buy it. It was a much sought-after model, so I jumped at the chance to become its proud owner. I kept it for quite a number of years and it created a lot of interest when I used it for the early Green Cross Code tours. Schoolchildren would gather round the car to watch it rise and fall as the air suspension went on and off. Unfortunately, the car came to a sad end when some idiot crashed into me and, being uneconomical to repair, it had to be written off.

Well, that's a little bit about my car craze, so I'll now tell you about one of the craziest car experiences of my life!

Chapter Thirty-Eight
The 1992 Euro Rally:
25 September-3 October

I was approached by Judy Birchley of the Stars Organisation for Spastics (SOS) to see if I would be interested in going on the forthcoming Euro Rally, both as a driver and as a representative of the charity, and I readily agreed. The rally would involve visiting every EEC capital city over the course of a week, starting in Paris and finishing in London. The only provisos I stipulated were that my car would have to be big enough to take my 6ft 6in frame comfortably and that, because of the calliper I wear on my left leg, the car would need to be automatic. I was asked if I knew a motoring personality who might be interested in starting the rally, and I arranged for John Surtees, the former World Motorcycling and Formula One Champion to do the honours from the Euro Disney complex in Paris. As it happened, John had to back out at the last moment, which in a way was a relief, as he would have been competing with the Donald Duck and Goofy characters supplied by Euro Disney to see the cars off.

A few days before the start of the rally I received a phone call from Richard Patching of Trident Television, whose TV unit would be following our car's progress for a TV documentary on the event. He told me that the car being supplied for our use was a manual souped-up version of the VW Golf and that even he, at 6ft 2in, had trouble getting in and out of it, so he couldn't see how I would be able to cope with spending six hair-raising days cooped up in it. Also, being a manual car, the most I would be able to do would be to act as a part-navigator. In view of this new set of circumstances, I was told that my decision regarding participation could be held off until I saw the car at Volkswagen's test track on the coming Friday. I was also offered the alternative of travelling on the team bus, which was going to follow the cars but unfortunately would be missing out Lisbon, Madrid, Athens, Copenhagen and Dublin.

It didn't take me long to decide that I still wanted to be part of the Euro Rally, whether my role would be driving or navigating or just taking personal photos as part of the back-up team travelling in the crew bus. My participation would obviously help the SOS, both with their fundraising and their publicity, and I would be involved with a jaunt around Europe, the like of which I would never get the opportunity to do again.

Finally, the first day of my Euro Rally venture dawned - and what a day it turned out to be!

Day 1 - Friday 25 September

I was picked up from home at 7 a.m. by our team back-up bus driver, Ian Gorrie, to make the journey to the Novotel, Heathrow, picking up Tina Murray (PA to the Producer, Richard Patching) from Claygate en route. Traffic on the M25 and into London was horrendous, so we arrived at the hotel at least an hour behind schedule, only to discover that our presenter/driver, Bob Hall (a well-known television presenter from the Midlands), had hurt his back and was unable to make the drive. Therefore, there was a possibility that I might be required to present the programme. We picked up a further two drivers, Paul O'Malley and Jane Holland, and then started out for the VW test track at Milton Keynes. Even the mid-morning traffic was bad, but we eventually arrived at the VW factory, where we picked up the car and had some lunch. It was painfully obvious that the car would be too small for me to drive, irrespective of whether it was manual or automatic, so I resigned myself to making the trip in the crew bus, a seven-seater Leyland Daf, which was diesel-powered, capable of cruising at 90mph, and had a revolutionary air-suspension system that enabled better road holding and a very comfortable ride.

The whole of the afternoon was spent at the test track, where they filmed the handing over of the car to our drivers (VW were having an open day for the press so they could test drive the complete VW range). By now, news had come through that a second driver for the van had been located, who would need picking up from Welling en route to Calais, and that a third driver, Huw Higginson (a star of TV series *The Bill*), would be flying out to Paris and would meet up with us on the Saturday.

We left the test track around 6 p.m. and the drive back down from Milton Keynes to Welling was even worse than the drive up in the morning. We stopped off at the Novotel, Heathrow, and then took the M25 and M2 down to Welling, which took ages at that time of the evening. We picked up our van co-driver, Graham Eaglestone, and then made our way to Dover, hoping to catch the 9.30 a.m. ferry, but we arrived a few minutes too late and had to hang around for the 11.30 a.m. crossing. We eventually arrived in Calais at about 2 a.m. UK time (3 a.m. French time) and made our 275km drive down to Euro Disney, on the outskirts of Paris, arriving at 6 a.m. local time. Although I'd managed to get some sleep on the way down, it was then straight to bed for three hours prior to the start of filming around Euro Disney at 9.30 a.m.

Day 2 - Saturday 26 September

I was up at 9 a.m. and was whisked off to the Euro Disney park to do the filming. It was quite a good day, but it involved a lot of walking around and my ankle was starting to feel worse for wear. Richard asked if he could do a filmed interview with me about the work of the SOS, which we did on top of a Mississippi paddle steamer as we were sailing around.

I met up with three London taxi drivers, who were doing the rally in a black cab, and they stayed with us for most of the day. I also went into the Star Wars Simulator, which was really good - everything from hyperspace to flying through meteorite storms. I think the experience was as good as the one at Huntsville Space Laboratory in Alabama that I'd been to a few years earlier. As it was a weekend there were lots of people in the park, but when you consider that at that time it had up to 18,000 employees and entry tickets cost £27 per person, they needed to attract good crowds.

I got separated from the team and made my way back to the hotel on the tour bus. I had the French-American version of spaghetti Bolognese for dinner, which wasn't too appetising, and then finished off the day with a nice relaxing bath - the lull before the storm, as the rally was due to begin in earnest at 7.30 the next morning.

Day 3 - Sunday 27 September

I was up earlier than necessary, at 5.30 a.m., as I hadn't been informed that the French clocks had gone back, so I was at the rally start point by 6.30 a.m. Over 40 cars were taking part in the rally and they all got away between 7.30 a.m. and 9 a.m.

The competitors needed to locate checkpoints (usually at the Novotel hotels) in the following European capitals (though not necessarily in this order): Paris, Lisbon, Madrid, Rome, Athens, Luxembourg, Bonn, Copenhagen, Amsterdam, Brussels, Dublin and London. This journey of over 6,500 miles had to be completed in just one week in order to be back in London on Sunday 4 October for the official 'drive past' (driving past the Bank of England at 1 p.m.). Every country's speed limits and road safety laws had to be adhered to (tachographs were fitted to each vehicle to check).

We left Euro Disney just after 9 a.m. for the drive down south, Bordeaux being our first planned stop. We weren't going to either Lisbon or Madrid, but we were hoping to film the cars passing us as we drove through southern France into Italy. We started off by doing road tracking and passing shots of various competitors, following our own car for a while, and we arrived in Bordeaux at around 3.15 p.m., having come across only one other competitor en route.

Strange noises were coming from the van's transmission every time we throttled back, but the decision was made to continue the journey southwards to San Sebastian. However, all of a sudden the van's rear suspension went, which was obviously the cause of the noise (with the gradual lowering of the vehicle, everything was going out of alignment). We pulled off the autoroute into a service station and made frantic phone calls to both Leyland Daf and DKW in the UK to try to get somebody out to repair the faulty suspension.

We found a hotel in a place called Belin, booked in for the night and then waited for a mechanic to appear. As there was no sign of anybody coming to our rescue, at 7 p.m. we decided to order dinner. A message then came through that no French mechanic would be available until 8 a.m. the following morning. Fortunately, however, we were well ahead of the rally, which had to go to Lisbon and Madrid, so a relaxing evening was had by all. One of the drivers told the hotel owner that Darth Vader was staying at his hotel, which caused great excitement, and I ended up signing many autographs for the staff and patrons.

Day 4 - Monday 28 September
I didn't have a very good night. The evening meal played havoc with my stomach and I brought the lot back up in the early hours of the morning. There was also a lot of noise coming from downstairs - it seemed there was a party going on till well past 2 a.m. When I arose for breakfast at 7.30 a.m., all was gloom and despondency.

The mechanic didn't show up until after 10 a.m. and came in the shape of a young lad who didn't seem to have a clue what he was doing. He was quickly followed by another breakdown vehicle, which eventually took the van away to Bordeaux. All sorts of contingency plans were discussed, including giving me the option of going home by plane, so the whole morning consisted of Richard and Tina making frantic phone calls just in case the van was unusable.

We learned that all the teams were running behind schedule due to the bad weather and there were concerns that our team might miss the Athens leg, as it was touch and go whether they would make the Brindisi ferry in time for the crossing. Missing Athens (or any other stage of the rally) would mean automatic disqualification.

Fortunately, news came just before midday that the van could be repaired and we would soon be back on our way. So we then had the job of reloading the van to resume our journey across southern France into Italy and down to Rome. We left the hotel around 4 p.m., heading for Toulouse. There had been terrible floods in the south-east of France due to heavy rain and we expected more trouble in this respect as we made our way to Rome.

The van was repaired by a French garage in Marseille but continued to break down on the rest of our journey. Eventually a Daf engineer was flown out to deal with the problem, but by then it was far too late.

Richard decided that he, Tina, Gary Hawkey (cameraman) and John Biddlecombe (sound engineer) should catch a plane to Bari to get them to Brindisi and eventually to Athens and back, in order to capture as much film footage as possible. To add to our woes, just before leaving we received news that our Spanish unit had had all their equipment and tapes stolen!

We arrived at Toulouse, dull and overcast but at least not raining, at 6.45 p.m. and headed straight for the airport so that Richard could change some money. However, he spent so many panic-filled minutes trying to locate where he'd stashed his passport and travellers' cheques that by the time he'd found them in the side pocket of his holdall the Bureau de Change had closed!

We had to decide where best to place ourselves to film the passing cars, so we continued on to Perignon to wait for the competitors coming through from Spain. News had come through that only 11 cars had passed through the Madrid checkpoint, our car being one of them. We waited nearly four hours, two more than planned, and in all that time we only saw two cars.

Day 5 - Tuesday 29 September
At 5 a.m. we passed through Marseille, but it was still dark so I didn't see a lot of it. I had managed to sleep a little in the van, but the sleeping position played havoc with my back and backside. As we headed towards St Tropez I saw a nice sunrise and the weather looked promising. We hit

Cannes at around 7.45 a.m. and Nice at 8.15 a.m. We then stopped at a service station just outside Monte Carlo, as the van had started to play up again, with a recurrence of the suspension and transmission problems. However, we were on our way again by 9.15 a.m. and crossed into Italy a few minutes later.

Richard, Tina, Gary and John had decided to get a plane to Bari and then hire a car to get them into Brindisi and Athens, while I and two production assistants would make our way to the checkpoint hotel in Rome. That way, Richard would know where to find us and hopefully we would be able to get the van sorted out there. We discovered that the parts needed to repair the van had been sent out to us and were in Rome, but unfortunately the customs workers were on strike and we couldn't get the parts through. Therefore, we decided that we would stay overnight in Rome and then drive up to Zurich the following day, where we could get the van either repaired or replaced by the Leyland Daf people, who were bringing over another van just in case. So Richard and the others arranged to fly back into Zurich to meet up with us, so we could continue on together from there.

Unfortunately, we got stuck in a bad traffic jam just outside Florence, so it was a good job that the others had flown on ahead; otherwise, they wouldn't have made their connections. We finally arrived in Rome, but finding the hotel was a different matter. We must have driven around for the best part of an hour in an attempt to locate it, so in the end we stopped a taxi, which of course took us there within a matter of minutes!

We checked into the hotel, The Pullman Boston, and met up with a team of deaf people who had missed out Athens and had therefore been disqualified from the rally. We were allocated a two-bedroom suite, so a third bed had to be installed, and we joined the deaf group for an authentic Italian spaghetti Bolognese at a local café just across the road from the hotel.

After dinner we returned to the hotel for a few drinks and met up with a party of Americans from the Boston area. Prices in the hotel bar were horrendous - £50 for a round of five drinks, and one of them was a shandy! The hotel management explained away the extortionate charges by stating that it was a Piano Bar and we were paying for the entertainment. The deaf group responded that they couldn't hear the pianist anyway, but we only received a slight reduction on the bill. The evening finished at around 1 a.m.

Day 6 - Wednesday 30 September

I was up at 7 a.m. for a bath and hair wash followed by a really good breakfast, and then I waited for Richard to phone with the ongoing arrangements. I would've liked to do some sightseeing in Rome - the Coliseum and the Vatican - but, as I suspected, there was no time to do so as we had to be on our way to Switzerland.

Day 7 - Thursday 1 October

I woke at 6 a.m., but as it was already daylight I had missed my opportunity to take pictures of the sun rising over Lake Como. We had parked the van at one end of the lake, but the views weren't brilliant.

We crossed into Switzerland, arriving at Zurich airport at 12.10 p.m. I was unable to take any photos on the way, as Ian didn't want to jeopardise our making the midday deadline by making any unnecessary stops. We did make a brief pit stop at a motorway service station, but as it was full of lorries and surrounded by overhead cables no photo opportunities presented themselves there.

At the airport we were met by two mechanics, who had flown out from the UK. They immediately started work on the van, replacing faulty suspension units and even repairing our windscreen washers to boot! On a test drive the van behaved impeccably, so we bade our farewells to the mechanics, who were heading back to the UK as their van had been booked by another party on the Saturday. The original plan, however, was that they would stay with us and, if we considered their van fast enough, drive the crew on the last legs of the tour and follow the competitors while we returned to the UK in our van.

Things went from bad to worse. First, Ian broke a tooth and was in a lot of pain, and then I realised that I'd mislaid my camera containing all the photos taken so far - either I'd left it at Zurich airport or it was on the mechanics' van and on its way back to London. To make matters worse, while Graham and I were having a bite to eat Ian turned up and announced, almost in tears, that the suspension on the van was down again; air way hissing out and he couldn't repair it. There then followed a series of frantic phone calls to and from the UK and to various service garages in the Zurich area to try to find a Leyland Daf agent that could help us out, but by 6.10 that evening we'd still had no joy. Richard and the team were due in half an hour and were expecting us to have a fully working, reliable van so that we could hotfoot it up to Luxembourg, about a six-hour drive away.

The party from Athens arrived at Zurich as planned, but it was almost two hours before they emerged from the airport. Ian met them and gave them the bad news about the van, so they immediately hired a car in which to complete the tour. Richard said that if anyone wanted to go home a flight could be arranged, but I decided to stick with the van, which was now going directly to Calais.

The Daf mechanic eventually arrived (in a nice Jag), but he was unable to repair the van at the airport car park, so we said farewell to the rest of the team in their hire care and followed the mechanic to his own garage, which seemed miles away. By 9.40 p.m. the van was over the pit, jacked up and wheels off, with an estimate of two hours to complete the job. Richard had told me he wanted to see me back in London for some more filming, but I was at a loss as to why seeing as he'd wanted me for bugger all during the tour.

There seemed to be an issue of money between Richard and Ian, with Richard claiming that he'd given Ian sufficient funds to pay our expenses for the entire tour and Ian saying that although he had given him some money he'd taken it back minutes later. Richard told me that I shouldn't have to pay for the hotel in Rome or for any food on our travels - it really made me wonder what was going on.

We received news of our team, which wasn't good. Although they had arrived in Athens okay, they were unable to find the checkpoint and had therefore been disqualified. Ironically, they discovered too late that they'd within 200 yards of it! Even so, the decision was taken to continue with the route just for sheer pleasure.

Breakdowns permitting, we were due to leave Calais that night, so we were hoping to catch up with the others sometime the following evening. It turned out than the van's problems were due to a faulty plastic valve, which the mechanic replaced with a metal one, so at around 10 p.m. we were on our way. We stopped off at the last service station before reaching German soil, so I spent all my remaining Swiss francs on chocolate. On crossing the border into Germany, we parked up in the first service station lay-by we came across, where we spent another cold, uncomfortable and miserable night in the van.

Day 8 - Friday 2 October
I couldn't sleep at all and we were up and on our way by 7 a.m. The drive back across Germany and France was pretty uneventful and we arrived in Calais at 4.30 p.m. We were due to meet up with Richard and the gang that night, so that we could get the midnight ferry back to Dover. Since we had plenty of time to spare, we decided to go and have

a look around the big hypermarket. Graham bought loads of cheap plonk to take home, while Ian and I bought a few oddments for our evening meal, which we ate in the van. Unfortunately, it made me feel quite ill again. By 11 p.m. we still hadn't seen a single team come through.

Day 9 - Saturday 3 October

The teams started to drive through at around midnight, but we only saw about eight in total. Richard and the completely exhausted camera crew (Gary apparently hadn't slept for four days) didn't arrive until about 1.30 a.m., so we missed the midnight ferry. Rather than take the next ferry, we decided to wait for our team to arrive so that we could travel across with them. Unfortunately, they were running behind schedule and weren't due for about five hours, so we faced another horrendous night in the van, this time with seven tired bodies vying for space. To make matters worse, it rained all night!

Our team eventually arrived at 6.30 a.m., having encountered quite a few traffic problems en route. Now they faced the problem of getting to the final checkpoint in Dublin and then back to London in time for the Sunday lunchtime drive past. Although it would cause further delays, they had no alternative but to make the ferry crossing from Calais to the UK. On top of that, Huw, one of the drivers, had to attend an important wedding on the Sunday, so he would have to fly back from Dublin anyway. Despite all this, although understandably tired the driving team looked remarkably good and reported that the VW had performed fantastically well, with top speeds of over 140mph.

Richard again announced that if anyone wanted to get home early they could go ahead of the crew bus. At that point it dawned on me that I was actually the only expendable member of the group, so these offers must have been directed at me. However, I decided to see it through to the end, as we had already gone through so much together.

I eventually arrived back home at around 10.30 p.m., took a hot shower and then went straight to bed, relieved that it was all over except for the final drive past in London the following day.

Day 10 - Sunday 4 October

I went into the City to watch the teams - numbering 20 including our car and that of the deaf team - drive past the Bank of England, although I hadn't been invited officially by either the event organisers or Trident Television. I saw them filming there, but felt I was being excluded and ignored, particularly as the competitors were being taken to a gala reception at the Mansion House, so I returned home.

Sadly, I never did find out who won the Euro Rally. Neither did I ever receive any thanks for my participation from either Trident or the organisers. There was a final get-together for all those connected with the rally at Heathrow's Novotel on Saturday 17 October, but again I wasn't invited!

Chapter Thirty-Nine
Infections, Dislocations,
Aberrations and Battle Stations

In February 2001 my body and immune system seemed as if it had gone haywire. I awoke on the morning of 16 February to find my left arm completely paralysed. I felt fine in myself and was looking forward to flying out to Germany later that day to do a sci-fi conference for my old friend Jens Reinheimer. The first thought that sprang to mind was that I'd slept in an awkward position and possibly trapped a nerve, so I hoped that it would right itself and I would regain full use of my arm as the day progressed. However, come the time that I was due to leave, the feeling had still not returned. As I otherwise felt okay, I decided to continue with the trip, not wishing to let Jens or the fans down and expecting that the paralysis would soon disappear.

I arrived in Germany and was met by Jens, who drove me straight to my hotel. I went straight to bed.

You can imagine my consternation when I woke up on the Saturday morning to find that I had now lost the use of both my arms. After struggling for what seemed like hours to get out of bed, I gave up and waited for Jens to come and collect me at the prearranged time. When he arrived he was able to help me get dressed. The strange thing was, even though neither of my arms was functioning I still felt well in myself, with no pains to speak of. However, I was becoming increasingly concerned about how I would manage to sign autographs at the convention the following day in my current state.

The whole of Saturday was spent visiting Jens' friends. During lunch I noticed that everything tasted salty, which I thought was a little odd, and shortly after finishing the meal I vomited. But then, joy of joys, the feeling started slowly returning to my right arm, which was the one I would need for signing autographs. By the end of the evening that arm was back to normal, but I still had no feeling in the left one.

Sunday arrived and I still felt fine, which was fortunate as I had a busy day ahead signing autographs. Signing photographs did prove somewhat problematic, however, as it needed two hands - one to sign and the other to steady the photograph. I managed by lifting my left arm onto the photo to clamp it down and then lowering it back into my lap afterwards!

By Sunday evening I had started getting some pain in my lower back and hip to add to the continuing paralysis of my left arm, and to be perfectly honest I was glad when the time arrived for Jens to take me to the airport on the Monday morning so that I could get myself back home.

I arrived home around lunchtime on the Monday, by which time I was beginning to feel a little worse for wear. I told my wife, Norma, that I would go straight to bed, as I thought I was coming down with the flu. Fortunately, Norma had the foresight to phone the doctor and explain my symptoms to him. Within an hour the doctor was by my bedside, by which time I was sweating like mad and experiencing uncontrollable fits of the rigours, and the pain in my hip and back was really severe. The doctor immediately arranged for me to be admitted to hospital.

I was in Mayday Hospital from 16 February to 6 March, during which time I had blood and plasma transfusions, intravenous antibiotics six times a day, and I was placed on a morphine drip. The rigours had stopped, but I was hallucinating. It sounds strange now, as I look back on this terrible period, but I kept seeing the faces of famous people in a bowl of Sweet Williams at the end of my bed! Beethoven was a regular visitor, only to be replaced by Darth Maul when he disappeared! Norma thought I'd really gone round the bend!

During my three-week hospital stay I had an endoscopy to assess the negative effects of non-steroidal anti-inflammatory drugs on my system, as I had been taking Volterol for many years for the relief of arthritis pain. When doctors prescribe these drugs they don't tell you that taking them over a long period of time can have a seriously damaging effect on your insides, potentially leading to untreatable conditions such as an ulcerated stomach and intestine. Then you end up being prescribed even more drugs to combat the effects of the first drugs! I also had an MRI scan to examine my heart and a flush-out of the shoulder joint, which brought all the feeling back. When I went into hospital I weighed nearly 250lbs and I came out weighing 220lbs!

Although I had long ago resigned myself to periodic bouts of hospitalisation, the one thing I couldn't stomach was hospital food. I just couldn't cope with the blandness and what seemed like the smell of boiled cabbage, which accompanied every meal. The addition of salt and pepper helped slightly, but if there's one area of the NHS that needs a revamp it's definitely the catering! My son sent me a get well card - even the recycled cardboard from which it was made seemed a tastier option! In desperation I even tried the ethnic choices, but these seemed even less palatable.

Once back at home, within 10 days of my wife's cooking and nurturing my weight was back up to 230lb and gaining. When I visited my GP to let him know that I was now well on the road to recovery he admitted what a close call I'd had that night when he visited me at home. I had already lapsed into a delirious state and, had the septicaemia that was attacking my body penetrated my brain, I would have died!

That year illness continued to plague me. I ended up back in hospital on 14 April for another four days due to hip and back pain. An endoscopy confirmed that my oesophagus and gullet had been irreparably damaged by the non-steroidal anti-inflammatory drugs I'd been taking for my arthritis. I was then referred to the Royal Marsden Hospital for a white blood cell scan, which was carried out on 23 April.

While at the Royal Marsden I was asked if I'd like to go and meet the kids in the cancer wards. It was a heart-rending experience meeting these boys and girls, aged from youngsters to teenagers, together with their parents, all trying to cope with this life-threatening disease. I spent the whole day chatting with them and signing autographs and photos. They really seemed to appreciate a visit from Darth Vader!

The back and hip pains returned with a vengeance at the beginning of May, so it was back to the Mayday Hospital for another month. This was probably one of my worst hospital stays, as the scan result had revealed that my problems were being caused by an abscess at the base of my spine, affecting the bottom two lumbar vertebrae and discs, so I was put back on the intravenous antibiotics and had to remain permanently on my back, which I hated. Once again my weight plummeted, this time down to 216lbs.

At the end of June, although I'd only been home for about a month, I started going back to the gym. I wanted to try to get myself in shape and also do some remedial exercises for my back and hip. I'd been to see a private physiotherapist, who told me that my back was in such a bad state that I would never be able to touch my toes again. However, I was determined to prove him wrong! I went from two crutches to one, then to using a walking stick, and finally was even able to walk around the house without any aids at all. And I even managed to touch my toes!

For my birthday on 1 July my wife and son, Steve, took me out for the day to Leigh-on-Sea in Essex. I'm a big fan of Rick Stein's cookery books and in one of them he mentions that this is where the best cockles in the country can be found. So off we went in my car, which at the time was a big left-hand-drive two-door Mercedes 500 coupe. We spent a nice couple of hours walking around the resort and sampling the seafood, before making for home late afternoon. As we were nearing Croydon, while in a queue at some traffic lights a car suddenly hit the rear of the Merc, shunting us forwards about four feet and into the back of the car in front of us. The driver admitted full responsibility and no one was hurt, but although the damage to the other two cars was minimal my Merc was effectively written off - the estimated cost of repairs, at £6,000, was more than the car was worth!

I don't know whether it was the result of the impact or not, but following the accident I started to get more hip and back problems. Worse still, I found that I was once again unable to walk without the use of a stick or crutch, and eventually I had to be readmitted to hospital for another week. I persuaded the doctors to grant me an early discharge, as I was on oral antibiotics that could be just as easily taken at home rather than occupying valuable space at the hospital.

The next year, 2002, began well and I was fit and able to attend conventions both at home in the UK and in the USA. My surgeon, Mr Miller, had told me that he planned to carry out another hip operation early that year, but that it would be a fairly minor procedure that wouldn't put me out of action for long. The intention was to take out a portion of the hip prosthesis on the right side to shorten that leg, as my left leg was about two inches shorter than the right following a series of hip replacement procedures and an ankle fusion. So an appointment for the operation was made for the end of January.

However, about three weeks before my operation was due I received a call from the hospital to notify me that Mr Miller had changed his mind and was now going to do a total hip replacement. By this time my diary was getting full and all sorts of contracts for shows had been arranged that I couldn't get out of. I explained my predicament to Mr Miller, who obligingly said that I should honour my work commitments and that he would reschedule my operation for later that year (September).

So from February through to the beginning of September I travelled all over the world attending sci-fi conventions. During this time I was pain free and able to walk with the aid of a single crutch.

Little did I realise that my hip operation on 26 September would herald another year of hip problems.

I was advised that the hospital had obtained a special prosthesis from

Germany that would be positioned at a slightly different angle and effectively reduce the length of my leg - enough for me to be able to walk a bit better. And, to all intents and purposes, my operation was successful. However, on being transferred from the operating table to the gurney my hip dislocated and I ended up straight back in theatre! Two days later, while I was asleep, it dislocated again, and then for a third time when I was trying to get back into bed after a trip to the toilet! Each dislocation necessitated a visit to theatre to have it rectified under general anaesthetic. Eventually, however, it seemed to settle down, and I was discharged home on 16 October with a hip and back brace.

I was obviously very wary of the problematic hip joint, but I wasn't offered any help by the hospital in terms of physiotherapy and rehabilitation and so I started doing some light training at a local gym together with my wife. All seemed to be going well until 12 January 2003. I'd just settled into my armchair for a nice afternoon watching rugby on TV, after returning from the gym, when the hip dislocated again. So it was back to the hospital in an ambulance for another relocation job!

A similar thing happened again at the end of May, while sitting in a garden chair at my daughter's house at Cambridge. This time I had a change of scenery, as I was taken to Addenbrooke's Hospital, and at the same time I also managed to entertain my grandkids, Hannah and Josh, as to their great amusement I was hallucinating on the gas and air given to me in the ambulance!

Finally, in July, while on a sci-fi tour of Hungary, the hip dislocated again at a roadside restaurant near Lake Balaton. I was raced to hospital by ambulance and had my hip relocated by the most efficient hospital team I have ever encountered. I dislocated my hip at midday, reached the hospital by 1 p.m., was x-rayed immediately, was in theatre by 2.15 p.m. and had the hip sorted by 2.30 p.m. Then it was back to the recovery room, where I was looked after by two lovely trainee doctors, and at 5 p.m. I was given the okay to leave.

Normally with a hip dislocation you go into hospital as an emergency, get the operation done as soon as possible - usually the same day, and then stay overnight. However, when it's happened in America I've sometimes been rushed into hospital, had the manipulation done immediately, and literally just got off the operating table and walked straight out of the hospital!

I had another dislocation in Austria after which the surgeon gave me some x-rays and explained that I would require some reconstructive surgery on my hip at some stage. Apparently, the persistent dislocation problems were due to the fact that the head of the prosthesis inserted in my operation of 26 September 2002 was too small for the cup joint. So, armed with my x-rays, I intended to confront Mr Miller - only to find that he'd retired!

I decided to seek a private appointment at the London Hip Clinic, with surgeon Miss Susan Muirhead-Allwood, who was renowned for repairing 'bodged' operations. On checking my x-rays and after taking certain measurements she determined that the 28mm prosthesis head was "slopping around" in a cup joint measuring 45mm! Although she confirmed that she could carry out an operation to make the hip more stable, she could give no guarantee that I would be able to walk any better afterwards. So I decided against the suggested operation and soldiered on for the next two years, appearing at sci-fi shows all over the world supported by a single crutch. I was fortunate to get wheelchair assistance from all the airlines and I was well looked after by the convention organisers at every venue.

On 10 May 2004 I went to see my GP about a couple of cysts that I'd had on my back for years, one on my shoulder and one right between my shoulder blades, which had never previously given me any cause for concern. They were what I call 'blind cysts', meaning that however I contorted myself I just couldn't reach them (not that I wanted to anyway!) For some reason, however, towards the end of April the cyst in the middle of my back suddenly started to enlarge, and by the second week of May it had grown from the size of a large pimple to that of a currant bun! It looked horrendous, as it was filled with blood and pus, and it hurt like crazy every time I leant back. My GP, Norman Rodriguez, was so amazed when he saw it that he asked his colleagues within the practice to take a look at it. He decided not to lance it there and then but to arrange a further appointment a couple of days later. By that time it looked even gorier than ever, so it was lanced and I was put on a course of antibiotics. Within a week there was no trace of it whatsoever!

I thought that this was the end of it, but after a few days I developed another abscess, this time right in the middle of an old operation scar on my outer right thigh. I went back to my GP and had this one lanced, too, which appeared to sort out the problem. I'd been having my wound dressed by the nurses at the GP practice and thought that everything was okay, but my wife commented that she'd noticed some blood on my bedclothes, so we thought we'd better check how it was healing. We removed the dressing, took one look at the wound and made an urgent appointment to see the GP. Within hours I was back at the surgery and my GP phoned Mayday to arrange for my immediate admission.

Within two hours of being admitted I underwent an operation, this time carried out by Mr Kashif, one of the orthopaedic specialists, to clean out the abscess. This was followed by a week on intravenous antibiotics, which seemed to settle the infection. I was discharged on 13 July, on strict instructions that the wound must be dressed every other day either by the district nurse, at the hospital or by the nurse at the GP's surgery.

All seemed to be progressing well. At what turned out to be my last outpatient appointment with Mr Howell, Mr Miller's successor, I was told that the wound was healing nicely. He decided to probe the wound a little deeper, just to make sure that there was no further infection lurking underneath the scar, and much to my delight he confirmed that all was okay and he probably wouldn't need to see me again.

However, on 12 August Norma once again remarked that the bedclothes were bloodstained. It was obvious that the wound had erupted again, so it was back to the doctor's surgery followed by immediate referral to Mayday's A&E department. By 1 p.m. that day I was back on Ashburton ward, much to the surprise of the nursing staff, who thought they'd seen the last of me. Over the next seven days I underwent five 'flushing out' operations, each one carried out with a spinal tap injection, which anaesthetised the whole of my lower body but meant that I was awake throughout the procedure and could talk to the theatre staff. It was a very interesting experience being able to see what was going on in the operating theatre while feeling sensations of pushing, probing or leg manipulation but without any pain. At one point I looked up to see that on of the doctors had my iodine-coated leg raised up and resting on his shoulder and yet I didn't feel a thing! One of the joys of a spinal tap is that there are none of the queasy feelings associated with coming round from a general anaesthetic; I was fully awake and able to enjoy the peace of the recovery room.

After the five 'flushing out' operations I was told that the hospital was bringing in a special type of vacuum pump (a US-developed device that was revolutionising the process of open wound healing). The pump itself cost over £10,000, and it was on hire to the hospital at a cost of £40 a day!

The abscess in the operation scar on the side of my thigh continued to erupt and subside for nearly four years. The swelling took around seven to ten days to develop into an egg-sized lump, which would then burst or need lancing, followed by a period of healing, including daily dressings carried out by my wife, of around two weeks. It would then remain dormant for a couple of weeks before the whole cycle started again. I underwent a couple of debridements, necessitating admission to hospital to have the wound cleaned out surgically. Each time I hoped that it would put an end to the problem for good, but sadly it wasn't to be. The infection was set deep within the metalwork of the hip joint. Pathology was apparently unable to grow anything from the wound samples and my consultant surgeon, Mr Howell, was becoming increasingly despondent. As a last resort it was determined that I should have a complete two-stage hip-revision operation, involving the removal of all the old metalwork, a few weeks on intravenous antibiotics, followed by the insertion of a completely new hip joint.

As there appeared to be no other solution, arrangements were made for me to be admitted to Mayday Hospital on 24 November 2009 for the removal of the metalwork. I then spent two months with no hip joint (in bed at home) on intravenous antibiotics administered through a Picc line. The Picc line proved problematic, as it kept getting blocked, which meant calling an ambulance to have it unblocked at the hospital. It even happened on Christmas Day and I missed my Christmas dinner!

Once my surgeon was convinced that the infection had disappeared, I was admitted to a different hospital, at Epsom, on Thursday 11 February 2010 to have the new hip inserted and I was told that the operation had gone well. After five days recuperating in hospital I had improved sufficiently to be allowed home. However, the trip home in a small ambulance car was uncomfortable, and on arrival home I found I couldn't put any weight on my leg due to excruciating pain in my hip joint. I think somehow the cup joint had become loose and was out of position. Trying to get around, even on crutches, was really painful. A visit from the physiotherapist confirmed that all was not well and I shouldn't be experiencing that level of pain. I found the physiotherapy exercises prescribed too difficult and so hydrotherapy was suggested. I began a course of that on 22 April and all seemed to be going well.

However, on 19 May I noticed that the abscess on my leg was returning. Here we go again! Within a couple of days it burst, so I was back to daily dressings, visits to the wound care centre and check-ups with my consultant. By this time he admitted that he really didn't know what else to do and asked if I would like to consult another specialist. This wasn't the response I was hoping for. I had put my trust in my consultant, Mr Howell, and the last thing I wanted to hear was that he was giving up on me and wished to pass me on to someone else.

Fortunately, that same week I saw an article in a daily newspaper listing the top ten hip surgeons in the country, two of whom worked from St George's Hospital in Tooting. I showed the article to Mr Howell and it turned out that he knew the two specialists, Philip Mitchell and Simon Bridle, personally and would arrange for me to see them.

Within a couple of weeks I had seen both surgeons. X-rays were taken, together with a biopsy, to find out exactly what was causing the infection. The biopsy report confirmed a staphylococcal infection and, on meeting the surgeons again, I was told that an examination of the X-rays indicated that a lot of complicated surgery was on the cards for me.

Although I know that the forthcoming operation is major and might possibly need to be repeated later in life, I really am looking forward to having it done and getting my life back to normal after so long.

Throughout the four years of persistently recurring abscesses I never stopped working. I continued to travel all over the world, representing the charities I support, making personal appearances and attending sci-fi and horror conventions. I just had to take bags of dressings with me in order to deal with the eruptions as and when they occurred. Fortunately, they didn't cause any pain or discomfort, though my activities were sometimes severely restricted. For example, I wouldn't be able take advantage of hotel swimming pools, Jacuzzis and saunas. However, I was able to make full use of the gymnasium facilities and was proud of the workouts I managed to do at the young age of 72!

For years I have struggled around the world in wheelchairs and on crutches to fulfil my work commitments. Not being able to walk properly has had a detrimental affect on my acting career. As you can imagine, there aren't many parts for the wheelchair bound or crutch reliant!

I had the operation on the 13th of May - replacement of hip, femur and knee. The hospital states it was the largest prosthesis it had put in and and the operation took over 7 hours. I am recovering nicely and have gone from walking with a frame, then 2 crutches, and now one. The surgeons are pleased with my progress after such a major procedure. I am looking forward to acting both in films and on TV, touring the world, appearing at comic and sci-fi conventions and meeting friends and fans worldwide.

Beating Prostate Cancer

My brother, Bob, who is three years younger than me, had just moved into a new flat when he began to have problems with his bladder. He went to see his GP, who sorted out the problem but also said that it was very unusual, as such problems are much more common in women. As there was a chance that Bob's problem might be connected to his prostate gland, it was arranged to him to have a PSA (prostate-specific antigen) test. Although the results were within acceptable limits, the GP referred him to a specialist. A rectal examination was carried out and a three-month course of radiotherapy was recommended. At the end of the treatment he was given the all clear and he's had no further problems, although he has regular check-ups to monitor the situation.

Towards the end of his treatment, Bob approached me with the idea of raising funds for the Prostate Cancer Charity. We mulled over various ways of doing this and wondered whether we could work around one of Bob's passions in life - golf. As he's a member of Hawkhurst Golf Club in Kent, I suggested that with the club's permission we could organise a golf tournament and all the proceeds raised could go to the charity. I told him that I would arrange for special Star Wars/Darth Vader trophies to be made and that we could call it the 'Dave Prowse/Darth Vader Challenge Trophy'.

We got the go-ahead from the club and so we both started drumming up local publicity and invited other golf clubs in the area to enter teams or individuals. A date was arranged and I went through my collection of Darth Vader models to find the best three that could be mounted onto imposing trophies. Also, I got in touch with the various garrisons from the Star Wars 501 Squadron (of which I'm the commander-in-chief worldwide) to see if we could get uniformed stormtroopers to come and help us, not only with publicity but also to help with the stewarding of the event, car park management, posing for photos and having fun with the kids that were expected, as it was being promoted as a family day.

On the day the weather wasn't kind to us, with intermittent showers throughout the afternoon. However, this didn't deter the competing golfers or the families that had turned up. The golfers and families alike had a great day. Following the competition everyone congregated in the clubhouse to enjoy the club's hospitality and present the awards to the winners. The day culminated with the presentation of a cheque to the lady representative of the Prostate Cancer Charity. Bob and I were thanked for our fundraising efforts and the lady turned to me and said, "Have you ever been tested for prostate cancer?" I responded, "No, I am perfectly okay down there. No problems going to the toilet and at 74 I still manage an occasional erection." "Well, all men over 50 ought to have a PSA. It's very easy - just a straightforward blood test," was her reply.

I didn't give this any more thought, until I had to see my GP a few weeks later about something completely unrelated. While I was there I asked the doctor for a pathology form for a PSA test, which could be carried out at the hospital opposite the surgery. I underwent a rectal examination before I left, just to make sure that there was no abnormality, and although my prostate was slightly enlarged my doctor said that there was nothing to worry about.

However, within a week of having the PSA blood test I received a call from the hospital, telling me that I needed to have a biopsy. I became a little concerned. I attended the hospital a couple of days later and saw a pleasant, older Indian doctor. I knew I was in a potentially serious situation, but I couldn't help seeing the funny side. All I could think of was that this doctor, highly qualified and experienced, spent most of his working week sticking his fingers and the biopsy gun up men's backsides! To add to my amusement, the department employed an attractive nurse to sit by your head and engage you in conversation to distract you from what was going on at the other end!

When the biopsy sample was taken I felt 12 small 'thuds', but it wasn't the least bit worrying or uncomfortable. The results showed that, of the 12 samples taken, 10 were suspicious. In other words, they confirmed that I did indeed have prostate cancer, but on the good side it had been caught early.

I then had to make a decision regarding treatment. I chose to proceed with radiotherapy, which would be administered by the country's foremost cancer hospital, The Royal Marsden Hospital in Sutton, Surrey. The radiotherapy involved treatments five days a week over a period of eight weeks and, despite the circumstances, it turned out to be one of the nicest hospital experiences I'd ever had. My daily appointments were at 10 a.m., lasted 10 to 15 minutes, and transport was laid on both there and back. I could be homeward bound in anything from 15 minutes to two hours, depending on how busy the hospital and ambulance service were on any particular day. Either way, I found waiting in the reception area a cathartic experience, as I was recognised by people. Mothers would bring their ill children to me for autographs and other patients would sit and chat. The drivers were friendly and you couldn't wish to meet two nicer ladies than the dispatchers there. My treatments went very well and I suffered no after effects whatsoever.

To be honest, I became quite emotional after my last treatment when I had to say goodbye to all the staff that had been so kind to me over the previous few weeks. However, I have kept in touch with them and give my support to the Royal Marsden Charity, returning to give a talk and deliver some Star Wars toys to the kids there.

I am still monitored by the Royal Marsden Hospital and the news continues to be good.

Chapter Forty
On a Final Note ...

For as long as I can remember I've always had a passionate interest in music. Even as a schoolboy I was an avid record buyer, but my choice of music was never pop. I loved jazz, classics and opera. The first record I ever bought as Mel Tormé's 'Mountain Greenery', closely followed by big band jazz favourites such as Stan Kenton's 'Peanut Vendor' and 'Intermission Riff', which I used to listen to in awe and wonder, marvelling at the stratospheric trumpet player Maynard Ferguson. With the dream of emulating him, I bought myself a trumpet on hire purchase, but I fell behind with my payments and my mother sent it back to the shop.

As I mentioned previously, I actually got to meet Mel Tormé in person in San Francisco while attending *Star Wars* shows in the USA. On another, more recent visit to the USA, I was invited to dinner at a very swish restaurant/nightclub owned by Herb Alpert of Tijuana Brass fame. Dinner was great, but the highlight of the evening came when the bass player of the jazz group came to the table. Not only was he a great Star Wars fan, he was also none other than Stan Kenton's bass player all those years ago. Needless to say, I got some great photos of us all together.

Going way back to when I was 13 years of age, I was recruited into the Bristol Grammar School's choir and my favourite solo piece was 'Where'er You Walk' from Handel's oratorio *Semele*. I was also invited to sing in the school's Madrigal Society, but my singing pursuits were short-lived due to my subsequent 'TB knee' problems and long hospitalisation.

However, I have always loved to sing, and many years later, while lecturing on a Saga cruise about *Star Wars* and my life in showbiz, I became friendly with the entertainers on the ship, particularly Richard Beavis, who was the male lead vocalist and sang all the well-known standards and ballads. At the end of the cruise I confided in Richard that I would've loved to be a singer like him. I told him that I used to sing in the school choir 50 years ago and he suggested that I should find a singing teacher, so that my singing ability could be assessed.

As luck would have it, at that time I had a publicity agent who was an operatic soprano, and a good one too. She suggested that I went to see her teacher, the acclaimed Scottish tenor James Anderson. James specialised in training singers for operas and stage musicals and had a client list as long as my arm. He fitted me in for a trial session and we ran through the scales to assess my range and capabilities. At the end of the session he told me that I was a bass baritone and should've become an opera singer, which I took as a great compliment. My lessons began on a weekly basis, with lots of scales to develop my range, and James suggested various show songs that he felt would suit my voice. 'Ol' Man River' from the musical *Show Boat* was one of my first serious efforts at ballad singing, followed by 'Soliloquy' from *Carousel* and 'I Won't Send Roses' from *Mack & Mabel*.

A few years ago I was trolling through the conventions listings, looking for *Star Wars* shows, when I came across a convention called 'Starstruck in Vegas', where fans could meet the stars of film and television and collect autographs. The headliners were two of my favourite singers: Howard Keel, world famous for his Hollywood musicals; and Shirley Jones, famous for her role as Julie Jordan in my favourite musical of all time, *Carousel*, in which she starred opposite another great singer, Gordon MacRae. I phoned the organisers in Vegas immediately and asked if they would like to have Darth Vader at their convention. They were quite excited at the idea, but they had to turn me down as they'd run out of money and couldn't afford my airfare. Desperate to be there, I said that I would pay my own airfare provided they took care of the hotel costs for the weekend and gave me a dealer's table so that I could sell my photos. This arrangement was acceptable, so I was Vegas bound to meet and work with two of my screen idols.

When I arrived in Vegas I discovered that Shirley Jones had cancelled due to health problems, which was a huge disappointment. I'd met Shirley just after the filming of *Star Wars* and had been invited to her house in Los Angeles to meet her son, pop star David Cassidy. However, I was in for an even greater surprise when I was told that Shirley had been replaced by another great star, Kathryn Grayson, the soprano in the Mario Lanza movies!

The organisers had put the three of us together, with Kathryn at one end, Howard in the middle and me at the other end. Howard and I could talk easily, but to talk to Kathryn, which I did frequently, I had to walk to her table. I was keen to find out as much as I could about her singing partnership with one of the world's greatest voices, Mario Lanza.

As an aside, Mario was also a keen weight trainer and, because of his prodigious eating and drinking habits, he had to train hard in order to keep in shape for his movie work. One of his personal trainers was famous American bodybuilder George E. Eiferman, with whom I did a tour of the UK just prior to my wedding in 1963.

Howard and his wife Judy were a lovely couple and we seemed to have lots to chat about. Howard was a major charity fundraiser and hosted an International Golf Tournament in the UK every year.

During a lull in the autograph signings Howard asked me what I was doing these days, to which I replied that I was having singing lessons. So he wanted to know what songs I was working on.

"'Soliloquy' from *Carousel*," I replied.

"That's a great piece. I recorded that some years back," he said.

He then began singing the first verse: 'I wonder what he'll think of me / I guess he'll call me the old man ...'. The song continues with the singer anticipating fatherhood, with a son or possibly a daughter. It's a lovely piece to sing and comprises about 13 pages of music. I joined in with the singing and everybody at the convention crowded around us, giving us a huge ovation at the end.

Flushed with success, I asked Howard if he'd ever come across Robert Preston, as I'd also worked on 'I Won't Send Roses' from *Mack & Mabel*.

"Bob?" Howard replied. "He's a great friend."

And, with that, we both launched into the song, and again received a rapturous reception.

When the crowds had dispersed a guy approached me and introduced himself as LaToya Jackson's ex-husband. He said he had his own recording studio in LA and wanted to offer us a recording contract should we be interested in singing together! Howard was 84 at the time, so I couldn't see much chance of that. In addition, he'd just been diagnosed with colon cancer and within six months of that convention he died (November 2004).

I look back on that afternoon singing with Howard as one of the highlights of my life, and he and his wife Judy were two of the nicest people I've ever met.

I'm pleased to tell you that I'm still persevering with the singing lessons and I'm working with a jazz pianist in San Francisco, who is arranging music and putting down tracks of songs that I'd like to record.

Watch this space!

www.apexpublishing.co.uk